The Bill of Lading

The carriage of goods by sea starts off with a contract of carriage, an essentially simple and straightforward contract between two parties, the shipper and the carrier. Very often, however, a bill of lading is issued and a third party appears on the scene: the holder of the bill of lading. The holder was not involved in the making of the contract of carriage, but does have rights, and possibly obligations, against the carrier at destination. The question then is how the third-party holder of the bill acquires those rights and obligations.

Analysing the different theories that have been proposed to explain the position of the third-party holder, this book makes a distinction between contractual theories and non-contractual theories to explain the holder's position. Contractual theories build on the initial contract of carriage and apply contract law mechanisms while non-contractual theories construe the position of the third-party holder independently.

Following the analysis and appraisal of the different theories, this book makes the case that the position of the third-party holder of the bill of lading is not obvious or self-evident; and submits that a statutory approach to the position of the holder of the bill of lading has advantages and would be preferable.

Frank Stevens is Assistant Professor in the Law School at Erasmus University Rotterdam, the Netherlands. He is also admitted to the Antwerp Bar.

The Bill of Lading
Holder Rights and Liabilities

Frank Stevens

LONDON AND NEW YORK

First published 2018
by Routledge
2 Park Square, Milton Park, Abingdon, Oxon OX14 4RN

and by Routledge
711 Third Avenue, New York, NY 10017

Routledge is an imprint of the Taylor & Francis Group, an informa business

© 2018 Frank Stevens

The right of Frank Stevens to be identified as author of this work has been asserted by him in accordance with sections 77 and 78 of the Copyright, Designs and Patents Act 1988.

All rights reserved. No part of this book may be reprinted or reproduced or utilised in any form or by any electronic, mechanical, or other means, now known or hereafter invented, including photocopying and recording, or in any information storage or retrieval system, without permission in writing from the publishers.

Trademark notice: Product or corporate names may be trademarks or registered trademarks, and are used only for identification and explanation without intent to infringe.

British Library Cataloguing-in-Publication Data
A catalogue record for this book is available from the British Library

Library of Congress Cataloging-in-Publication Data
Names: Stevens, Frank (Lawyer)
Title: The bill of lading : holder rights and liabilities / Frank Stevens.
Description: Abingdon, Oxon ; New York, NY : Routledge, 2018. | Based on author's thesis (doctoral – Universiteit Gent, 2017). | Includes bibliographical references and index.
Identifiers: LCCN 2017040328 | ISBN 9780815380061 (hbk)
Subjects: LCSH: Bills of lading.
Classification: LCC K1178 .S74 2018 | DDC 346.02/5—dc23
LC record available at https://lccn.loc.gov/2017040328

ISBN: 978-0-8153-8006-1 (hbk)
ISBN: 978-1-351-21422-3 (ebk)

Typeset in Galliard
by Apex CoVantage, LLC

Contents

Table of cases   ix
Table of statutes and conventions   xx

1   **Introduction**   1

2   **The functions of the bill of lading**   5
    2.1 Introduction 5
    2.2 Terminology 7
    2.3 Receipt for the cargo 8
    2.4 Evidence of the contract of carriage 14
    2.5 Document of title 19
    2.6 Conclusions 28

3   **Contractual theories**   30
    3.1 The first group: the holder steps into the shoes of the shipper 30
        3.1.1 Enforcement of a debtor's claim 31
            3.1.1.1 The concept 31
            3.1.1.2 The holder of the B/L as the enforcer of his debtor's claim 32
            3.1.1.3 When does the relationship come into being? 32
            3.1.1.4 Intermediate holders 33
            3.1.1.5 The non-contracting shipper 33
            3.1.1.6 Appraisal 33
        3.1.2 Agency 34
            3.1.2.1 The concept 34
            3.1.2.2 The consignee as the agent of the shipper 37
            3.1.2.3 The shipper as the agent of the consignee 39
            3.1.2.4 When does the relationship come into being? 48

    3.1.2.5 *Intermediate holders* 49
    3.1.2.6 *Appraisal* 50
  3.1.3 *Assignment of rights* 54
    3.1.3.1 *The concept* 54
    3.1.3.2 *The bill of lading holder as the assignee of the shipper* 57
    3.1.3.3 *When does the relationship come into being?* 59
    3.1.3.4 *Intermediate holders* 60
    3.1.3.5 *The non-contracting shipper* 60
    3.1.3.6 *Appraisal* 61
  3.1.4 *Novation* 65
    3.1.4.1 *The concept* 65
    3.1.4.2 *The transfer of a bill of lading seen as novation* 66
    3.1.4.3 *When does the relationship come into being?* 67
    3.1.4.4 *Intermediate holders* 67
    3.1.4.5 *The non-contracting shipper* 67
    3.1.4.6 *Appraisal* 68
3.2 *The second group: the holder has a position of his own* 68
  3.2.1 *Third-party beneficiary clause* 71
    3.2.1.1 *The concept* 71
    3.2.1.2 *The bill of lading holder as a third-party beneficiary* 74
    3.2.1.3 *When does the relationship come into being?* 78
    3.2.1.4 *Intermediate holders* 83
    3.2.1.5 *The non-contracting shipper* 85
    3.2.1.6 *Appraisal* 86
  3.2.2 *Multi-party contracts – accession* 97
    3.2.2.1 *The concept* 97
    3.2.2.2 *The bill of lading as a multi-party contract* 99
    3.2.2.3 *When does the relationship come into being?* 112
    3.2.2.4 *Intermediate holders* 116
    3.2.2.5 *The non-contracting shipper* 117
    3.2.2.6 *Appraisal* 119
  3.2.3 *A direct contractual relationship between the carrier and the holder* 128
    3.2.3.1 *The bill of lading as an offer to contract* 128
    3.2.3.2 *Implied,* Brandt v Liverpool *type contracts* 129
    3.2.3.3 *A* sui generis *contractual relationship* 134
    3.2.3.4 *Appraisal* 134
3.3 *Contractual theories: conclusions* 136

4 Non-contractual theories   151
  4.1 The holder as the owner of the goods 151
    4.1.1 The concept 151
    4.1.2 When does the relationship come into being? 152
    4.1.3 Intermediate holders 152
    4.1.4 The non-contracting shipper 152
    4.1.5 Appraisal 153
  4.2 The bill of lading as a quasi-contract 153
    4.2.1 The concept 153
    4.2.2 The bill of lading creating a quasi-contractual relationship 154
    4.2.3 Appraisal 155
  4.3 The position of the holder as a statutory position 155
    4.3.1 Explicit position: the UK Bills of Lading Act 1855 and COGSA 1992 155
      4.3.1.1 The Acts 155
      4.3.1.2 When does the relationship come into being? 161
      4.3.1.3 Intermediate holders 165
      4.3.1.4 The non-contracting shipper 170
      4.3.1.5 Appraisal 171
    4.3.3 Implicit position 175
      4.3.3.1 Belgium: Art. 91 of the Maritime Act 175
      4.3.3.2 Germany – The Netherlands 176
      4.3.3.3 The position of the holder as an 'institution' 177
      4.3.3.4 When does the relationship come into being? 178
      4.3.3.5 Intermediate holders 178
      4.3.3.6 The non-contracting shipper 179
      4.3.3.7 Appraisal 179
  4.4 The bill of lading as a negotiable instrument 179
    4.4.1 The concept 179
    4.4.2 The bill of lading as a negotiable instrument 184
    4.4.3 When does the relationship come into being? 194
    4.4.4 Intermediate holders 194
    4.4.5 The non-contracting shipper 195
    4.4.6 Appraisal 196
  4.5 The bill of lading as a voluntary engagement 199
    4.5.1 The concept 199
    4.5.2 The bill of lading as a voluntary engagement 200
    4.5.3 When does the relationship come into being? 201
    4.5.4 Intermediate holders 201

        4.5.5 The non-contracting shipper 201
        4.5.6 Appraisal 201
   4.6 Conclusions 202

5 Bill of lading clauses   208
   5.1 Contractual – the holder steps into the shoes of the shipper 209
   5.2 Contractual – the holder has a right of his own 210
   5.3 Non-contractual 212

Bibliography   216
Index   226

Cases

Belgium

Cass. 23 January 2017, Case C.16.0247.N, *T.B.H.* 2017/6, 600. fn. 138 p. 193
Cass. 12 September 2013, Case C.13.0089.N, *Pas.* 2013, 1642;
 R.A.B.G. 2014, 597. fn. 336 p. 109
Cass. 7 January 2011, Case C.09.611.N, *R.A.B.G.* 2012/12, 836,
 R.H.A. 2010, 238. fn. 335 p. 109
Cass. 7 January 2011, Case C.09.0275.N, *R.H.A.* 2010, 230. fn. 7 p. 210
Cass. 18 September 1987, *Arr.Cass.* 1987–88, 82, *E.T.L.* 1987,
 529, *Pas.* 1988, I, 75, *R.H.A.* 1987, 175, *R.W.* 1987–88, 714,
 R.D.C. 1988, 376 (*ms. Regina*). fn. 132 p. 62, fn. 167 p. 70
CA Antwerp, 4th Division, 18 January 2016, *not reported*,
 Case N° 2013/AR/3097. fn. 168 p. 70, fn. 331 p. 108
CA Antwerp 7 January 2013, *unreported*, Case N° 2011/
 AR/1401. fn. 331 p. 108
CA Antwerp 5 October 2009 (interim) and 9 May 2011 (final),
 Case No. 2008/AR/1841, *T.B.H.* 2011, 731 (case analysis)
 (*ms. Moa*). fn. 9 p. 3, fn. 149 p. 198
CA Antwerp 30 November 2009, *R.H.A.* 2010, 54. fn. 19 p. 215
CA Antwerp 5 October 2009, *T.B.H.* 2010, 93 (ms. *Pietersgracht*). fn. 228 p. 87
CA Antwerp 3 December 2007, *R.H.A.* 2009, 361 (*ms. Star
 Ikebana*). fn. 171 p. 206
CA Antwerp 6 November 2006, *unreported*, Case N° 2005/
 AR/1955. fn. 332 p. 108, fn. 384 p. 120
CA Antwerp 13 February 2006, *R.H.A.* 2007, 162
 (*ms. Ocean Island/ms. Sri Arika*). fn. 168 p. 70, fn. 331 p. 108
CA Ghent 28 November 1996, *R.W.* 1996–97, 1441. fn. 185 p. 75, fn. 332 p. 108
CA Antwerp 10 October 1990, *R.H.A.* 1993, 115. fn. 80 p. 175
CA Antwerp, 16 September 1987, *E.T.L.* 1987, 695. fn. 81 p. 176
CA Antwerp 16 April 1986, *R.H.A.* 1986, 133. fn. 81 p. 176
CA Antwerp, 9 April 1986, *E.T.L.* 1986, 397. fn. 81 p. 176
CA Antwerp, 26 February 1986, *E.T.L.* 1986, 216. fn. 81 p. 176
Comm. C. Antwerp 6 March 2013, *E.T.L.* 2013, 418
 (*ms. Atlantic Trader*). fn. 325 p. 107

x *Cases*

Comm. C. Antwerp 19 June 2007, *unreported*, Case N° A/05/
2148 and A/05/4054. fn. 325 p. 107
Comm. C. Antwerp 18 December 2003, *R.H.A.* 2005, 67. fn. 384 p. 120
Comm. C. Antwerp 18 June 2002, *R.H.A.* 2003, 156 (*ms. MSC
Dymphna*). fn. 137 p. 63, fn. 325 p. 107
Comm. C. Antwerp 9 February 2000, *Transportrechtspr. BVZ*
n° 587a. fn. 327 p. 107, fn. 328 p. 107, fn. 329 p. 108
Comm. C. Antwerp 20 February 1995 *R.H.A.* 1995, 165
(*ms. Nordfels*). fn. 325 p. 107, fn. 327 p. 107, fn. 328 p. 107
Comm. Court Gent, 26 April 1994, *T.G.R.* 1998, 223. fn. 24 p. 37
Comm. Court Antwerp 1 June 1992, *R.H.A.* 1995, 48
(*ms. Nordic Stream*). fn. 132 p. 62, fn. 325 p. 107, fn. 326 p. 107
Comm. C. Antwerp, 9 October 1941, *J.P.A.* 1941, 337. fn. 184 p. 75

European Court of Justice

ECJ 13 July 2017, Case C-368/16, *Assens Havn v v Navigators
Management (UK) Ltd.* fn. 17 p. 214, fn. 18 p. 214
ECJ 20 April 2016, Case C-366/13, *Profi t Investment Sim
SpA v v Stefano Ossi et al.* fn. 4 p. 31, fn. 164 p. 70, fn. 3 p. 209,
fn. 6 p. 210, fn. 14 p. 213, fn. 15 p. 213
ECJ 14 March 2013, Case C-419/11, *C´eská spor˘itelna v
Gerald Feichter.* fn. 471 p. 147
ECJ 7 February 2013, Case C-543/10, *Refcomp SpA v
Axa Corporate Solutions Assurance SA.* fn. 3 p. 31, fn. 4 p. 31,
fn. 163 p. 70, fn. 14 p. 213
ECJ 20 January 2005, Case C-27/02, *Petra Engler v
Janus Versand.* fn. 471 p. 147
ECJ 5 February 2004, Case C-265/02, *Frahuil v Assitalia.* fn. 471 p. 147
ECJ 17 September 2002, Case C-334/00, *Fonderie Offi cine
Meccaniche Tacconi SpA v Heinrich Wagner Sinto
Maschinenfabrik.* fn. 471 p. 147
ECJ 9 November 2000, Case C-387/98, *Coreck Maritime v
Handelsveem.* fn. 1 p. 30, fn. 3 p. 208, fn. 6 p. 210, fn. 14 p. 213
ECJ 27 October 1998, Case C-51/97, *Réunion Européenne v
Spliethoff's Bevrachtingskantoor.* fn. 471 p. 147
ECJ 3 July 1997, Case C-269/95, *Benincasa.* fn. 3 p. 208, fn. 14 p. 213,
fn. 15 p. 213
ECJ 20 February 1997, Case C-106/95, *MSG.* fn. 3 p. 208, fn. 14 p. 213,
fn. 15 p. 213
ECJ 17 June 1992, Case C-26/91, *Jakob Handte & Co. v
Traitements Mécano-chimiques des Surfaces.* fn. 471 p. 147
ECJ 11 July 1985, Case 221/84, *Berghoefer.* fn. 3 p. 208, fn. 14 p. 213
ECJ 19 June 1984, Case 71/83, *Partenreederei ms. Tilly Russ
and Ernest Russ v NV Haven- & Vervoerbedrijf Nova and
NV Goeminne Hout.* fn. 1 p. 30, fn. 131 p. 62, fn. 384 p. 120,
fn. 3 p. 208, fn. 5 p. 209, fn. 14 p. 213
ECJ 14 December 1976, Case 25/76, *Segoura.* fn. 3 p. 208, fn. 14 p. 213
ECJ 14 December 1976, Case 24/76, *Estasis Salotti.* fn. 3 p. 208, fn. 14 p. 213

France

Cass. 7 July 2009 (B 08–17.375), *E.T.L.* 2009, 641. fn. 155 p. 68
Cass. com., 4 March 2003, *D.M.F.* 2003, 556, *J.C.P.* G
2004 II, 10071 (*Navire Houston Express*). fn. 132 p. 62, fn. 169 p. 70
Cass. com. 16 January 1996, *D.M.F.* 1996, 627
(*Navire Monte Cervantes*). fn. 305 p. 103, fn. 306 p. 103
Cass. com. 19 December 1995, *D.M.F.* 1996, 389
(*Navire Ramona*). fn. 370 p. 116, fn. 388 p. 121
Cass. com. 29 November 1994, *D.M.F.* 1995, 209
(*Navires Harmony et Nagasaki*). fn. 299 p. 102, fn. 359 p. 113
Cass. com. 29 November 1994, *D.M.F.* 1995, 219
(*Navire Stolt Osprey*). fn. 299 p. 102, fn. 301 p. 102, fn. 359 p. 113
Cass. 22 December 1989, *Bull.* 1989 A.P. N° 4 p. 9,
D.M.F. 1990, 29 (*Navire Mercandia Transporter II*). fn. 137 p. 192
Cass. fr. 8 December 1987, *Bull. civ.* I, n° 343. fn. 247 p. 92
Cass. civ. 25 November 1986, *Rev. crit. DIP* 1987, 396. fn. 395 p. 124
Cass. 21 November 1978, *Recueil Dalloz Sirey* 1980, 309. fn. 181 p. 73
Cass. (fr.) 20 May 1912, *R.I.D.M.* XXVIII, 326. fn. 184 p. 75
Cass. (ch. des requêtes) 19 October 1891, *R.I.D.M.* Vol. VII
(1891–1892), 385. fn. 297 p. 101
Cass. 13 January 1862, *Pas. fr.* 1862, I, 136, *Sirey* 1862, I, 207. fn. 98 p. 26
Cass. 17 August 1859, *D.* 1859, I, 347. fn. 88 p. 24
Cass. 1 March 1843, *S.* 1843, 1.188. fn. 28 p. 38
CA Aix-en-Provence 9 November 2011, n° 10/22956
(*Navire Elbfeeder*). fn. 305 p. 103
CA Pau 18 May 2011, n° 10/05093 (*Navire Sava Ocean*). fn. 295 p. 101
CA Paris 22 October 2003, *D.M.F.* 2004, 601 (*Navire Theophano*). fn. 229 p. 87
CA Caen 20 March 1997, *D.M.F.* 1997, 714 (*Navire
Westfi eld*). fn. 307 p. 103, fn. 382 p. 119
CA Aix-en-Provence 28 October 1993, *D.M.F.* 1994,
764 (*Navire Chang-Ping*). fn. 2 p. 30
CA Montpellier 1 December 1987, *D.M.F.* 1988, 250
(*Navire Mercandia Transport II*). fn. 137 p. 192
CA Rouen, 1 December 1977, *D.M.F.* 590. fn. 410 p. 128
CA Aix-en-Provence 28 April 1976, *D.M.F.* 1977, 27
(*Navire Talita*). fn. 300 p. 102
CA Alger, 7 February 1891, *RIDM* Vol. VII (1891–92) 23. fn. 73 p. 47
Trib. civ. Tunis, 14 November 1889, *RIDM* Vol. V (1889–90) 698. fn. 73 p. 47

Germany

BGH 9 December 1991, Case II ZR 53/91, *TransportR* 1992,
106 (*The Aquila*). fn. 58 p. 19
BGH 25 September 1986 (Case N° II ZR 26/86),
N.J.W. 1987, 588. fn. 188 p. 76, fn. 240 p. 91
BGH 23 November 1978, *BGHZ* 73, 4, *NJW* 1979, 1102
(Case II ZR 27/77). fn. 338 p. 109
BGH 27 October 1960 (Case N° II ZR 127/59), NJW 1961, 665. fn. 188 p. 76

xii *Cases*

BGH 10 October 1957, *BGHZ* 25, 300, *NJW* 1957, 1917
(Case II ZR 278/56).   fn. 338 p. 109, fn. 28 p. 161,
   fn. 82 p. 176, fn. 125 p. 187
Hans. OLG Bremen 25 April 2014, *TranspR* 2015, 452.   fn. 156 p. 200
OLG Rostock 27 November 1996, Case 6 U 113/96,
TranspR 1997, 113.   fn. 11 p. 4, fn. 379 p. 119,
   fn. 435 p. 134, fn. 436 p. 134
OLG Düsseldorf 26 October 1995, Case N° 18 U 46/95,
NJW-RR 1996, 1380, *TranspR* 1996, 165.   fn. 379 p. 119, fn. 435 p. 134
OLG München 3 November 1988, Case 24 U 814/87,
NJW-RR 1989, 803.   fn. 377 p. 118, fn. 378 p. 118, fn. 435 p. 134
OLG Bremen 2 November 1978, Case 2 U 55/78,
VersR 1979, 667.   fn. 377 p. 118
LG Bremen 10 October 2007, Case 11 O 381/05,
BeckRS 2010, 25028.   fn. 379 p. 119, fn. 435 p. 134

Netherlands

HR 26 maart 2004, Case N° C02/266HR, (*Anthea Yachting/
ABN Amro Bank*).   n° 51 p. 183
HR 4 April 2003, *RvdW* 2003, 71, *S&S* 2003, 122, *NJ* 2003,
592 (*Damco Maritime International/Meister Werkzeuge
Werkzeugfabrik*).   fn. 83 p. 177
HR 29 November 2002, *N.J.* 2003, 374, RvdW 2002, 197,
S&S 2003, 62 (*ms Ladoga 15*).   fn. 189 p. 76, fn. 213 p. 82,
   fn. 364 p. 115, fn. 173 p. 207
HR 19 April 2002, *RvdW* 2002, 73, *S&S* 2002, 126,
NJ 2002, 456 (*Zürich/Lebosch*).   fn. 234 p. 89, fn. 29 p. 161,
   fn. 100 p. 182, fn. 162 p. 203
HR 22 September 2000, *N.J.* 2001, 44, *S&S* 2001,
37 (*ms Eendracht*).   fn. 189 p. 76, fn. 211 p. 81,
   fn. 362 p. 115, fn. 172 p. 206, fn. 173 p. 207
HR 26 November 1993, RvdW 1993, 237, *S&S* 1994, 25,
NJ 1995, 446 (*Condorcamp/ Bosman*).   fn. 324 p. 106, fn. 145 p. 197,
   fn. 148 p. 197
HR 17 September 1993, *NJ* 1994, 173 (*Gerritse/HAS*).   fn. 162 p. 203
HR 23 June 1989, *S&S* 1989, 120 (*ms Padus*).   fn. 457 p. 141
HR 15 February 1980, *S&S* 1980, 63 (*ms. Agatha*).   fn. 220 p. 84, fn. 130 p. 190
HR 15 April 1977, *N.J.* 1978, 163 (*Staalcom '66 BV/
Neher Nederland BV*).   fn. 314 p. 104, fn. 393 p. 123, fn. 398 p. 124
HR 21 January 1966, *N.J.* 1966, 183 (*Booy/Wisman*).   fn. 314 p. 104
HR 13 February 1924, *N.J.* 1924, 711 (*Gouda/Ontvanger der
Registratie*).   fn. 201 p. 79
HR (Dutch Supreme Court) 18 January 1856, *W.* 1856, N° 1717.   fn. 113 p. 185
HR 26 November 1841, *Weekblad van het Regt* N° 249
(6 January 1842) (*De Goede Hoop*).   fn. 42 p. 15, fn. 70 p. 47
CA The Hague 28 July 2009, *S&S* 2010, n° 109, (ms. *MSC Claudia/
Kapitan Kudlay*).   fn. 216 p. 83

CA The Hague 26 June 2008, *S&S* 2008, 115
(*ms. OPDR Lisboa*). fn. 181 p. 73, fn. 189 p. 76,
 fn. 205 p. 80, fn. 311 p. 104
CA The Hague, 27 June 1975, *S&S* 1976, n° 3 (ms. *Velswijk*). fn. 205 p. 80
CA The Hague 28 November 1817, reprinted in F. Frets,
De kracht van een cognossement, en het regt van den houder,
Rotterdam, F. W. Krieger, 1818, at pp. 77–96. fn. 93 p. 25
Court of Rotterdam, 24 June 2015 (ECLI:NL:RBROT:
2015:5032). fn. 312 p. 104
Court Rotterdam 10 October 2012, *S&S* 2013, 38
(*ms MSC Daniela*). fn. 189 p. 76, fn. 312 p. 104
Court of Rotterdam 4 April 2007, *S&S* 2008, 126
(*ms Svanetiya*). fn. 324 p. 106, fn. 358 p. 113
Court Rotterdam 19 April 2006, S&S 2008, n° 33
(*ms. OPDR Lisboa*). fn. 2 p. 30
Court of Rotterdam 3 November 2004, *S&S* 2005,
n° 86 (*MSC/Wilmink Air & Ocean*). fn. 215 p. 83, fn. 366 p. 115
Court of Rotterdam 20 February 1985, *S&S* 1985,
91 (*The Gosforth*). fn. 21 p. 157
Court of Rotterdam 6 January 1984, *S&S* 1984, 58, (*ms. François*). fn. 324 p. 106
Court of Rotterdam 12 May 1980, *S&S* 1981, n° 6
(ms. *Nedlloyd Kyoto*). fn. 205 p. 80, fn. 324 p. 106
Court of Rotterdam 27 June 1977, *S&S* 1977, n° 97
(ms. *Sennar*). fn. 205 p. 80, fn. 324 p. 106
Court of Rotterdam 19 June 1973, *S&S* 1973, 73
(ms. *John Schehr*). fn. 205 p. 80, fn. 324 p. 106
Rb. Amsterdam, 20 November 1840, *Weekblad van
het Regt* N° 144 (4 January 1841). fn. 14 p. 4, fn. 69 p. 46

UK

Aegean Sea Traders Corp. v Repsol Petroleo SA & Anor (The Aegean Sea) [1998]
CLCCLC 1090, [1998] 2 Lloyd's Rep 39 (Queen's Bench Division (Admiralty
Court), 7 April 1998). n° 24 p. 162, n° 25 p. 164, n° 29 p. 169
The Albazero, see *Owners of Cargo Laden on Board the Albacruz v Owners of the
Albazero*.
Alexander M'Gonnell v Craig & Rose (1879) 6 R. 1269 (Court
of Session, 1st Division, 15 July 1879). fn. 50 p. 166
Allen v Coltart & Co. 11 QBD 782 (Queen's Bench Division,
12 June 1883). fn. 412 p. 129, fn. 414 p. 130
The Aramis, [1989] 1 Lloyd's Rep 213 (Court of Appeal,
17 November 1988). n° 141 p. 132
SS Ardennes (Cargo Owners) v SS Ardennes (Owners) [1951]
1 KB 55, [1950] 2 All ER 517; (1950) 84 Ll. L.
Rep. 340 (King's Bench Division, 5 July 1950). fn. 39 p. 14, n° 15 p. 17
The Athanasia Comninos and Georges Chr. Lemos, [1990] 1 Lloyd's
RepLloyd's Rep 277 (Queen's Bench Division, Commercial
Court, 21 December 1979). fn. 44 p. 41, fn. 374 p. 117

The Berge Sisar, see *Borealis AB v Stargas Ltd. and others and Bergesen D.Y. A/S*
Borealis AB v Stargas Ltd. and others and Bergesen D.Y. A/S
  (The Berge Sisar) [2001] UKHL 17, [2001] 2 All ER 193
  (House of Lords, 22 March 2001). n° 23 p. 162, n° 24 p. 163,
        n° 25 p. 164, n° 29 p. 169,
        fn. 46 p. 41, fn. 415 p. 130, fn. 32 p. 162
Brandt v Liverpool, Brazil and River Plate Steam Navigation Co. Ltd.
  [1924] 1 K.B. 575 (Court of Appeal, 19 November 1923). n° 140 p. 131,
        n° 158 p. 142, fn. 121 p. 59,
        fn. 412 p. 129, fn. 413 p. 130,
        fn. 414 p. 130
Brown, McFarlane & Co. v Shaw, Lovell and Sons (1921) 7 Ll.L.
  Rep. 36. fn. 41 p. 40
The Captain Gregos, No. 2, see *Compania Portorafti Commerciale v Ultramar Panama Inc.*
Carlberg v Wemyss Coal Co. Ltd 1915 S.C. 616 (Court of Session,
  Inner House, First Division, 11 March 1915). fn. 455 p. 140
Chappel v Comfort, 10 CB(NS) 802, 142 ER 669 (Court of
  Common Pleas, 29 May 1861). fn. 414 p. 130, fn. 417 p. 131
Cho Yang Shipping Co. Ltd v Coral (U.K.) Ltd [1997] 2 Lloyd's
  Rep 641 (Court of Appeal, 14–15 April & 15 May 1997). n° 144 p. 133,
        fn. 11 p. 4, fn. 50 p. 17
Clarke v Earl of Dunraven (The Satanita) [1897] A.C. 59
  (House of Lords, 19 November 1896). fn. 284 p. 98
Cock v Taylor 2 Camp. 587, 170 ER 1261 (Nisi Prius, 26 February 1811),
  13 East 399, 104 ER 424 (King's Bench, 2 May 1811). n° 109 p. 112,
        fn. 414 p. 130, fn. 418 p. 131
Cork Distilleries v Gt. S. & W. Ry. of Ireland (1874) LR 7 HL 269. n° 23 p. 40
Compania Portorafti Commerciale v Ultramar Panama Inc.
  (The Captain Gregos, No. 2) [1990] 2 Lloyd's Rep 395 (Court
  of Appeal, 21–25 March 1990). n° 141 p. 132
Dawes v Peck (1799) 8 T.R. 330, 101 ER 1417. n° 23 p. 39
The Delfini, see *Enichem Anic SpA v Ampelos Shipping Co Ltd.*
Dobbin v Thornton 6 Esp. 16, 170 ER 816 (Nisi Prius,
  3 March 1806). fn. 418 p. 131
The Dunelmia, see *The President of India v Metcalfe Shipping Co Ltd.*
East West Corporation v DKBS AF 1912 A/S [2003] EWCA Civ 83,
  [2003] Q.B. 1509, [2003] 3 WLRWLR 916 (Court of Appeal,
  12 February 2003). fn. 69 p. 171
E. Clement Horst Company v Biddell Brothers [1912] A.C. 18
  (House of Lords, 3 November 1911). fn. 84 p. 24
*Effort Shipping Co. Ltd. v Linden Management S.A. (The Giannis
  N.K.)* [1998] A.C. 605, [1998] 2 WLRWLR 206, [1998]
  CLC 374 (House of Lords, 22 January 1998). fn. 52 p. 166, fn. 69 p. 171
The Elli 2, see *Ilyssia Compania Naviera S.A. v Ahmed Abdul-Qawi Bamaodah.*
Enichem Anic SpA v Ampelos Shipping Co Ltd (The Delfini) [1990]
  1 Lloyd's Rep 252 (Court of Appeal, 28 July 1989). fn. 72 p. 22
The Eurymedon, see *New Zealand Shipping Co Ltd v AM Satterthwaite & Co Ltd.*
Evans v Martell (1697) 1 Ld. Raym. 272, 12 Mod. 156, 3 Salk. 290. n° 23 p. 39

Evergreen Marine Corporation v Aldgate Warehouse (Wholesale) Ltd
[2003] EWHC 667, 2003 WL 1610235 (Queen's Bench
Division (Commercial Court), 28 March 2003).   n° 33 p. 52, fn. 81 p. 50
Fortis Bank S.A./N.V., Stemcor UK Ltd v Indian Overseas Bank
[2011] EWHC 538 (Comm); 2011 WL 806786 (Queen's Bench
Division (Commercial Court), 17 March 2011).   n° 23 p. 42
Fox v Nott (1861) 158 ER 260, 6 Hurl.&N. 630 (Court of
Exchequer, 25 April 1861).   fn. 52 p. 166
*General Accident Fire and Life Assurance Corporation and others v Peter
William Tanter and others (The Zephyr)* [1984] 1 Lloyd's Rep 58
(Queen's Bench Division (Commercial Court), 12 July 1983).   n° 102 p. 98
*General Accident Fire and Life Assurance Corporation and others v Peter
William Tanter and others (The Zephyr)* [1985] 2 Lloyd's Rep 529
(Court of Appeal, 20–23 May 1985).   fn. 283 p. 98
Geofi zika DD v MMB International Limited (The Green Island)
[2010] EWCA Civ 459, 2010 WL 1608507 (Court of Appeal,
28 April 2010).   fn. 52 p. 17
The Giannis N.K., see *Effort Shipping Co. Ltd. v Linden Management S.A.*
Giles v Thompson (1993) WL 963259, 143 N.L.J. 284 (Court of
Appeal, 11 January 1993).   fn. 138 p. 63
Glyn Mills Currie & Co. v The East and West India Dock Company
(1882) 7 App. Cas. 591 (House of Lords, 1 August 1882).   fn. 46 p. 16,
fn. 124 p. 59, fn. 418 p. 131, fn. 461 p. 143
The Green Island, see *Geofi zika DD v MMB International Limited.*
Gt. E. Ry. v Nix (1895) 39 Sol. J. 709.   fn. 41 p. 40
The Gudermes, see *Mitsui & Co Ltd. v Novorossiysk Shipping Co.*
The Helene Br. & L. 415, 167 ER 426 (High Court of Admiralty,
3 March 1865).   n° 67 p. 69, fn. 16 p. 157
Heskell v Continental Express Ltd., [1950] 1 All. ER 1033 (King's
Bench Division, 03 April 1950).   fn. 102 p. 27
*Hispanica de Petroleos S.A. and Compania Iberica Refi nadera S.A. v
Vencedora Oceanica Navegacion S.A. (The Kapetan Markos N.L.
(No. 2))* [1987] 2 Lloyd's Rep 321 (Court of Appeal, 28–30
April and 1 and 5 May 1987).   fn. 44 p. 41, fn. 384 p. 120,
fn. 410 p. 128, fn. 473 p. 147
Homburg Houtimport BV v Agrosin Private Ltd (The Starsin)
[2003] UKHL 12, [2004] 1 A.C. 715 (House of Lords,
13 March 2003).   fn. 16 p. 157, fn. 25 p. 160, fn. 163 p. 203
Houlder Brothers & Co., Limited v Commissioner of Public Works
1908 A.C. 276 (Privy Council, 2 April 1908).   fn. 41 p. 40
Howard v Shepherd 9 C.B. 297, 137 ER 907 (Court of Common
Pleas, 16 February 1850).   n° 46 p. 58
The Houda, see *Kuwait Petroleum Corp v I&D Oil Carriers Ltd.*
*Ilyssia Compania Naviera S.A. v Ahmed Abdul-Qawi Bamaodah
(The Elli 2)* [1985] 1 Lloyd's Rep 107 (Court of Appeal,
22–24 October 1984).   fn. 422 p. 131
*Jennifer Simpson (as assignee of Alan Catchpole) v Norfolk &
Norwich University Hospital NHS Trust* [2011] EWCA
Civ 1149, WL 4706949 (Court of Appeal, 12 October 2011).   fn. 138 p. 63

xvi   Cases

Jesson v Solly 4 Taunt. 52, 128 ER 247 (29 June 1811). fn. 418 p. 131
J. Evans & Son (Portsmouth) Ltd. v Andrea Merzario Ltd. [1976]
   2 All ER 930, [1976] 2 Lloyd's Rep 165, [1976] 1 WLR 1078
   (Court of Appeal, 13 November 1975). fn. 52 p. 17
John Wallis v Gt. N. Ry. of Ireland (1903) 12 Ry. & Can. Tr. Cas. 38. fn. 41 p. 40
The Kapetan Markos N.L. (No. 2), see *Hispanica de Petroleos S.A. and Compania Iberica Refinadera S.A. v Vencedora Oceanica Navegacion S.A.*
Kuwait Petroleum Corp v I&D Oil Carriers Ltd (The Houda)
   [1994] CLC 1037, [1994] 2 Lloyd's Rep 541 (Court of
   Appeal, 21 July 1994). fn. 60 p. 19, fn. 71 p. 21, fn. 452 p. 140
Leduc v Ward 20 QBD 475 (Court of Appeal, 13 February
   1888). n° 67 p. 69, fn. 16 p. 157, fn. 68 p. 171
Lickbarrow v Mason (1794) 5 TR 683. n° 19 p. 21, n° 21 p. 24, n° 23 p. 26
*London Steamship Owners' Mutual Insurance Association Ltd v
   Spain & Anor (The Prestige)*, [2015] EWCA Civ 333, [2015] 1
   CLC 596 (Court of Appeal, 1 April 2015). fn. 477 p. 148
Merchant Banking Company v Phoenix Bessemer Steel Company
   [1877] 5 Ch D 205 (Chancery Division, 8 February 1877). fn. 95 p. 26
Meyerstein v Barber (1869–70) LR 4 HL 317 (House of lords,
   22 February 1870). fn. 98 p. 26
Michael Toth v Emirates [2011] EWPCC 18, 2011 WL 900254
   (Patents County Court, 13 June 2011). fn. 286 p. 99
Mitsui & Co Ltd. v Novorossiysk Shipping Co (The Gudermes) [1993]
   1 Lloyd's Rep 311 (Court of Appeal, 16–27 November 1992). n° 141 p. 132
Monarch Steamship Co., Ltd v Karlshamns Oljefabriker (A/B) [1949]
   A.C. 196 (House of Lords, 9 December 1948). fn. 75 p. 173
*Motis Exports Ltd v Dampskibsselskabet AF 1912, Aktieselskab &
   Anor* [2000] CLC 515 (Court of Appeal (Civil Division),
   21 December 1999). fn. 455 p. 140
*New Zealand Shipping Co Ltd v AM Satterthwaite & Co Ltd
   (The Eurymedon)* [1975] A.C. 154, [1974] 2 WLR 865, [1974]
   1 All ER 1015, [1974] 1 Lloyd's Rep 534 (Privy Council
   (New Zealand), 25 February 1974). fn. 282 p. 98, fn. 424 p. 132
*Owners of Cargo Laden on Board the Albacruz v Owners of the Albazero
   (The Albazero)* [1976] 3 WLR 419, [1977] A.C. 774 (House of
   Lords, 28 July 1976). fn. 34 p. 39
Peter Cremer v General Carriers S.A. [1974] 1 WLR 341, [1973]
   2 Lloyd's Rep 366 (Queen's Bench Division, 5 July 1973). fn. 424 p. 132
The President of India v Metcalfe Shipping Co Ltd. (The Dunelmia)
   [1969] 3 WLR 1120, [1970] 1 Q.B. 289 (Court of Appeal,
   8 October 1969) n° 23 p. 41, fn. 458 p. 142
The Prestige, see *London Steamship Owners' Mutual Insurance Association Ltd v
   Spain & Anor.*
Primetrade AG v Ythan Ltd. (The Ythan), 2005 EWHC 2399 (Comm),
   [2005] 2 CLC 911 (Queen's Bench Division (Commercial Court),
   1 November 2005). fn. 32 p. 162, n° 24 p. 163, n° 25 p. 165, fn. 73 p. 172
Pyrene Co. LD. v Scindia Navigation Co. LD. [1954]
   2 WLR 1005, [1954] 2 Q.B. 402 (Queen's Bench Division,
   14 April 1954). n° 21 p. 39, fn. 92 p. 53, n° 144 p. 132

Cases xvii

The Roseline [1987] 1 Lloyd's Rep 18 (Federal Court of Canada, 23 March 1984). fn. 375 p. 118
Sanders Brothers v Maclean & Co. [1883] 11 QBD 327 (Court of Appeal, 28 April 1883). fn. 72 p. 22, fn. 84 p. 24
Sanders v Vanzeller 4 QBR 260, 114 ER 897 (Exchequer Chamber, 2 February 1843). n° 46 p. 58
The Satanita, see *Clarke v Earl of Dunraven*
Scarf v Jardine 7 App.Cas. 345 (House of Lords, 13 June 1882). fn. 145 p. 66, fn. 149 p. 67
Seakom Limited, Seakom International Limited v Knowledgepool Group Limited [2013] EWHC 4007 (High Court of Justice Chancery Division, 18 December 2013). fn. 147 p. 65
Sewell v Burdick (The Zoe) 10 App.Cas. 74 (House of Lords, 5 December 1884). fn. 53 p. 18, n° 18 p. 157, n° 26 p. 167
Smurthwaite v Wilkins 142 ER 1026, (1862) 11 CB(ns) 842 (Court of Common Pleas, 11 February 1862). n° 26 p. 167, n° 29 p. 169
Snee v Prescott (1745) 1 Atk. 239. n° 23 p. 39
The Starsin, see *Homburg Houtimport BV v Agrosin Private Ltd.*
Stindt v Roberts 5 Dowl. & L. 460, 79 R.R. 869 (Queen's Bench, 1848). fn. 412 p. 129, fn. 416 p. 130, fn. 418 p. 131
Sze Hai Tong Bank v Rambler Cycle Co [1959] A.C. 576, [1959] 3 WLR 214, [1959] 3 All ER 182, [1959] 2 Lloyd's Rep 114 (Privy Council (Singapore), 22 June 1959). fn. 452 p. 140
Tate & Lyle Ltd v Hain Steamship Co Ltd [1936] 2 All ER 597, (1936) 55 Ll. L. Rep. 159 (House of Lords, 11 June 1936). fn. 15 p. 156
Texas Instruments Ltd. v Europe Cargo Ltd., The Financial Times, July 6, 1990. *Sub nom. Texas Instruments v Nason (Europe)* [1991] 1 Lloyd's Rep 146. n° 23 p. 41
TICC Ltd. v COSCO (UK) Ltd [2001] EWCA Civ 1862; [2002] CLC 346 (Court of Appeal, 5 December 2001). n° 23 p. 42
Thompson v Dominy 153 ER 532, 14 M7W 403 (Court of Exchequer, 20 June 1845). n° 46 p. 58
Wegener v Smith 15 C.B. 285, 139 ER 432 (6 November 1854). fn. 418 p. 131
Young v Moeller 5 El. & Bl. 755, 119 ER 662 (Exchequer Chamber, 29 November 1855). fn. 412 p. 129, fn. 415 p. 130, fn. 417 p. 131, fn. 418 p. 131
The Ythan, see *Primetrade AG v Ythan Ltd.*
The Zephyr, see *General Accident Fire and Life Assurance Corporation and others v Peter William Tanter and others.*
The Zoe, see *Sewell v Burdick.*

USA

All Pacific Trading, Inc. v M/V Hanjin Yosu 7 F.3d 1427 (9th Circuit, 22 October 1993). fn. 343 p. 110, fn. 344 p. 111, fn. 345 p. 111
APL Co. Pte. Ltd. v Kemira Water Solutions, Inc. 890 F.Supp.2d 360 (S.D.N.Y., August 22, 2012). n° 24 p. 46, fn. 343 p. 110, fn. 344 p. 111
A/S Dampskibsselskabet Torm v Beaumont Oil Ltd. 927 F.2d 713, 1991 A.M.C. 1573 (2nd Circuit, 11 March 1991). fn. 349 p. 111

Ataei v M/V/ Barber Tonsberg 639 F.Supp. 993 (S.D. New York,
   2 July 1986). n° 107 p. 112
Blanchard v Page 8 Gray 281, 74 Mass. 281, 1857 WL 5865
   (Supreme Court of Massachusetts, March Term, 1857). n° 24 p. 44
Blum v the Caddo 1 Woods 64, 3 F.Cas. 753 (Circuit Court
   D. Louisiana, 1870). fn. 51 p. 43
*The Burlington Northern and Santa Fe Railway Co. v Interdom
   Partners Ltd.* 2004 WL 734081 (N.D.Tex. March 26, 2004). n° 24 p. 45
The Carso 43 F.2d 736, 1930 A.M.C. 1743 (S.D. New York,
   July 17, 1930). fn. 34 p. 13
Excel Shipping Corp. v Seatrain International S.A. 584 F.Supp. 734
   (E.D. New York, 13 April 1984). fn. 449 p. 138
F.D. Import & Export Corp. v M/V Reefer Sun 248 F.Supp.2d 240
   (S.D. New York, 4 December 2002). fn. 344 p. 111, fn. 346 p. 112,
   fn. 347 p. 112
Green v Clark 13 Barb. 57 (Supreme Court, New York, April 5, 1852). n° 24 p. 43
Griffith v Ingledew 1821 WL 1807, 9 Am.Dec. 444, 6 Serg. &
   Rawle 429 (Supreme Court of Pennsylvania, April, 1821). n° 24 p. 44,
   n° 74 p. 78
Higgins v Anglo-Algerian S.S. Co. Limited 248 F. 386 (Court of
   Appeals 2nd Circ., 13 February 1918). n° 51 p. 62, fn. 446 p. 137,
   fn. 454 p. 140
In re M/V Rickmers Genoa Litigation 622 F.Supp.2d 56, 2009
   A.M.C. 609 (S.D. New York, 31 March 2009). n° 24 p. 46, fn. 196 p. 78
Ivaran Lines v Sutex Paper & Cellulose Corp. 1987 A.M.C. 690
   (S.D. Florida, 12 February 1985). n° 108 p. 111
Kanematsu Corp. v M/V Gretchen W 897 F.Supp. 1314
   (D. Oregon, September 15, 1995). fn. 61 p. 45, fn. 344 p. 111
Kawasaki Kisen Kaisha Ltd. v Plano Moulding Co. 2012
   A.M.C. 2611 (7th Circuit, 29 August 2012). fn. 343 p. 110
Kirno Hill Corp. v Holt 618 F.2d 982 (C.A.N.Y., March 31, 1980). fn. 59 p. 45
Korea Express Usa, Inc. v K.K.D. Imports, Inc. 2002 A.M.C. 2446
   (D. New Jersey, 28 August 2002). fn. 350 p. 112
Kukje Hwajae Insurance Co Ltd v M/V Hyundai Liberty 408 F.3d
   1250 (9th Circuit, 26 May 2005). fn. 344 p. 111
Louisville & N.R. Co. v Central Iron & Coal Co. 44 S.Ct. 441
   (US Supreme Court, 5 May 1924). n° 108 p. 111
Madison, I. & P.R. Co. v Whitesel 11 Ind. 55, 1858 WL 4096
   (Supreme Court of Indiana, November 22, 1858). fn. 51 p. 43
Menzo W. Finn v Western Railroad Corp. 112 Mass. 524, 1873
   WL 9026 (Supreme Court of Massachusetts, September
   Term, 1873). n° 24 p. 44, fn. 79 p. 48, fn. 84 p. 51
Metallia USA Inc. v M/V Buyalyk 1999 WL 717642
   (E.D. Louisiana, 13 September 1999). fn. 344 p. 111
Mitsui & Co (USA) Inc. v M/V Mira 111 F.3d 33 (5th Circuit,
   28 April 1997). fn. 344 p. 111
Naviera Neptuno S.A. v All Intern. Freight Forwarders, Inc.
   709 F.2d 663 (C.A.Fla., July 11, 1983). fn. 59 p. 45

Nebraska Wine & Spirits, Inc. v Burlington Northern Railroad Co. 1992 WL
  328938 (W.D.Missouri, September 29, 1992). n° 24 p. 45
Norfolk Southern Railway Co. v Kirby 543 U.S. 14 (Supreme Court, 9
  November 2004). n° 24 p. 46
Pollard v Reardon 65 F. 848 (1st Circuit, 18 January 1895). fn. 101 p. 182
Polo Ralph Lauren L.P. v Tropical Shipping & Construction Co. Ltd.
  215 F.3d 1217 (11th Circuit, 21 June 2000). fn. 195 p. 78
Smith v Lewis 3 B.Mon. 229, 42 Ky. 229, 1842 WL 3315 (Court of
  Appeals of Kentucky, October 25, 1842). fn. 51 p. 43
States Marine International v Seattle-First National Bank 524
  F.2d 245 (9th Circuit, 16 October 1975). n° 108 p. 111
Steamship Co. v Joliffe 69 U.S. 450, 1864 WL 6611, 17 L.Ed. 805,
  2 Wall. 450 (U.S. Supreme Court, 1 December 1864). fn. 10 p. 154
Steel Warehouse Co. v Abalone Shipping Ltd. 141 F.3d 234
  (5th Circuit, 21 May 1998). fn. 347 p. 111
Taisheng International Ltd. v Eagle Maritime Services, Inc.
  2006 WL 846380 (S.D.Tex. March 30, 2006). n° 24 p. 45, fn. 345 p. 111
United States Of America vs. Ashcraft-Wilkinson Company,
  1927 A.M.C. 872 (N.D. Georgia, April 28, 1927). fn. 398 p. 124
United States v M/V Santa Clara I 887 F.Supp. 825, 41 ERC 1101,
  1996 A.M.C. 910, 64 USLW 2016, 26 Envtl. L. Rep. 20,624
  (D.South Carolina, May 8, 1995). n° 24 p. 45
West India Industries, Inc. v Vance & Sons AMC-Jeep 671 F.2d 1384
  (C.A.Tex., April 09, 1982). fn. 59 p. 45

Statutes and conventions

Bills of Exchange Act, UK (1882): n° 51 p. 183
Bills of Lading Act, UK (1855): n° 46 p. 59, n° 61 p. 66, n° 109 p. 112, n° 141 p. 131, para. 4.3.1., n° 84 p. 204
Carriage of Goods by Sea Act (COGSA), UK (1992): n° 46 p. 59, n° 61 p. 66, n° 141 p. 131, fn. 452 p. 140, para. 4.3.1., n° 66 p. 196

Civil Code, Belgian

– Art. 1271: fn. 150 p. 66

Civil Code, Dutch

– Art. 3:33: n° 114 p. 114
– Art. 3:37.(3): n° 114 p. 114
– Art. 6:251.(1): n° 105 p. 103
– Art. 6:254.(1): n° 72 p. 73, fn. 269 p. 95, fn. 309 p. 103
– Art. 8:375: n° 69 p. 197
– Art. 8:415.(1): fn. 170 p. 70, n° 105 p. 106, fn. 399 p. 125
– Art. 8:417: fn. 62 p. 20, n° 22 p. 26
– Art. 8:440: fn. 357 p. 113
– Art. 8:441.(2): fn. 104 p. 28, n° 68 p. 70, n° 105 p. 106, n° 130 p. 125, n° 155 p. 139
– Art. 8:481.(1): n° 115 p. 114
– Art. 8:488: fn. 77 p. 174

Civil Code (BGB), Germany

– § 311.(1): fn. 155 p. 199

Code Napoleon (1804)

– Art. 1119: n° 71 p. 72
– Art. 1121: n° 71 p. 72

Commercial Code, Dutch (1927)

– Art. 506.1: n° 2 p. 5
– Art. 517a: n° 21 p. 25

Commercial Code (HGB), Germany

– § 363.(2): n° 54 p. 185, fn. 142 p. 195
– § 365.(1): n° 54 p. 185

Statutes and conventions   xxi

- § 486.(1): fn. 32 p. 12
- § 488.(3): fn. 224 p. 85, fn. 166 p. 205
- § 494: n° 65 p. 195
- § 513.(1): n° 145 p. 133, n° 37 p. 176, fn. 166 p. 205
- § 513.(2): fn. 6 p. 7
- § 520.(1): fn. 372 p. 116, fn. 146 p. 197
- § 522.(1): n° 68 p. 70, n° 130 p. 125
- § 524: fn. 62 p. 20

Contracts (Rights of Third Parties) Act, UK (1999): n° 71 p. 72, fn. 178 p. 72, fn. 179 p. 73, n° 74 p. 77

Hague Rules

- Art. 3.4: n° 11 p. 13

Hague-Visby Rules

- Art. 1.a: fn. 447 p. 138
- Art. 1.b: n° 146 p. 134, n° 154 p. 138
- Art. 3.4: fn. 121 p. 187
- Art. 3.6: fn. 463 p. 144
- Art. 7: n° 36 p. 176

Hamburg Rules

- Art. 1.6: n° 154 p. 139
- Art. 1.7: n° 2 p. 6

Harter Act, USA: n° 14 p. 16, n° 86 p. 205, n° 14 p. 214

Law of Property Act, UK (1925)

- Sect. 136: n° 43 p. 56

Maritime Act, Belgium

- Art. 59: n° 10 p. 12
- Art. 89: n° 106 p. 107
- Art. 91: para. 4.3.3.1, fn. 7 p. 210

Maritime Code, Norwegian

- Sect. 251: fn. 6 p. 7
- Sect. 259: fn. 32 p. 12
- Sect. 267: fn. 77 p. 174
- Sect. 292: n° 2 p. 6
- Sect. 310: n° 130 p. 126
- Sect. 325: n° 68 p. 71

Maritime Navigation Act 14/2014, Spain

- Art. 203: fn. 1 p. 1
- Art. 251: fn. 62 p. 20, n° 22 p. 26, n° 68 p. 71, n° 130 p. 126
- Art. 276.(2): n° 69 p. 197

Property, Law of – Act, UK (1925)

- Sect. 136: n° 43 p. 56

Restatement (Third) of Agency

– § 1.02: n° 18 p. 37

Rotterdam Rules

– Art. 1.1: n° 155 p. 139
– Art. 1.8: fn. 4 p. 1
– Art. 1.9: fn. 10 p. 3
– Art. 1.14: n° 2 p. 6, n° 154 p. 139
– Art. 1.15: n° 2 p. 6
– Art. 4.1: fn. 168 p. 205
– Art. 50: fn. 357 p. 113
– Art. 51: fn. 357 p. 113
– Art. 57: fn. 76 p. 174
– Art. 58: fn. 60 p. 169, fn. 65 p. 169

Sale of Goods Act, UK

– Sect. 16: fn. 19 p. 157
– Sect. 20: fn. 19 p. 157
– Sect. 32: n° 35 p. 52

Transport Code, France

– Art. L. 5422–3: n° 10 p. 12

Visby Protocol: n° 11 p. 13, n° 51 p. 62, n° 85 p. 205

1 Introduction

1 The existence of a bill of lading presupposes the existence of a contract of carriage.[1,2] This contract of carriage may be an explicit, written[3] contract such as a charter party, or an implicit, verbal one, the existence of which is proven indirectly by the later issuance of the bill of lading.

2 In essence, a contract of carriage is a simple, two-party contract between a shipper and a carrier for the transport of certain goods from a place of departure to a place of destination.[4] Sometimes, the constellation stays as simple as that, and no third parties are or become involved. This is the case when the shipper is also the consignee of the carried goods. This can happen, for instance, when

---

1 On terminology: the term 'contract of carriage' is the most general term, referring to any contract that deals with the carriage of goods or passengers. 'Contract of affreightment' largely covers the same scope, but is generally not used to refer to the carriage of passengers. Charter parties, on the other hand, are contracts for the use of (a part of) a vessel. In some legal systems, charter parties on the one hand and contracts of carriage on the other hand are strictly distinguished and deemed to be mutually exclusive. It is clear, however, that at least a voyage charter party is very similar to a contract of carriage. In common law countries, (voyage) charter parties and bills of lading are usually seen as two subtypes of the more general category of the contract of carriage. In the Netherlands, Article 8:370.(1) of the Civil Code explicitly provides for the possibility that a contract of carriage may take the form of a voyage or a time charter party. The Spanish Act 14/2014 on Maritime Navigation provides in Article 203 that 'charter party' is another name for 'contract of carriage' (*"Por el contrato de transporte marítimo de mercancías, también denominado fletamento . . ."* – The contract for carriage of goods by sea, also called charter party . . .).

2 This principle is generally accepted. See, for example, R. Aikens, R. Lord and M. Bools, *Bills of Lading*, London, Informa, 2006, n° 7.6 at p. 125; P. Seck, *Reisbevrachting en cognossementsvervoer*, Zutphen, Uitgeverij Paris, 2011, at p. 129.

3 'Written' is taken to include modern forms of writing such as emails. Bookings these days are quite often made by email.

4 The shipper (*chargeur, Absender, afzender*), in the legal sense of the term, is the party that enters into the contract of carriage with the carrier.
   See A. Kpoahoun Amoussou, *Les clauses attributives de compétence dans le transport maritime de marchandises*, Presses Universitaires d'Aix-Marseille, 2002, n° 433 at p. 276; M. Spanjaart, *Vorderingsrechten uit cognossement*, Zutphen, Uitgeverij Paris, 2012, at p. 31.
   Article 1.(8) of the Rotterdam Rules explicitly confirms this definition.
   The shipper in this sense is not necessarily the party that is identified in the box marked 'shipper' on the bill of lading.

a manufacturer ships semi-finished products from one of its locations to another for further processing.[5]

3 In most cases, however, the consignee is not the same person as the shipper. The contract of carriage is still made between the shipper and the carrier, but there is, right from the very start, the presence of a third party looming in the background. In the port of destination, the consignee, holder of the bill of lading, will be able to claim delivery of the cargo from the carrier. Conversely, the consignee may be bound to pay freight or other costs to the carrier. So, even though the consignee did not negotiate or enter into the initial contract of carriage, there clearly is a relation between the consignee and the carrier, with rights and obligations on both sides. The question then, of course, is what is the nature of this relationship? How and when does it come into being?[6] These questions are the main focus of the present research.

4 The question what the exact nature is of the relationship between the carrier and the holder is not always explicitly raised, let alone answered. Sometimes, the relationship is readily assumed to be of a certain nature, without much analysis or reasoning. Standard or preconceived ideas, however, may turn out to be incorrect upon closer inspection. The relevance of the research lies firstly in recalling to the attention the fact that the nature and characteristics of the relationship between the carrier and the holder of the bill of lading is indeed a question which merits to be raised explicitly and the answer to which is not obvious or self-evident. The relevance of the research further lies in the attempt that is made to find a solid and convincing answer to the questions indicated above, which is relevant both on a theoretical and on a practical level. The theoretical importance of these questions hardly needs explaining. A coherent legal system requires a theoretical basis for every legal concept that is part of that system.[7] The importance is, however, more than merely theoretical, of interest to academics only.[8] Even today, the relation between the carrier and the bill of lading holder has not been entirely charted. To what extent, for example, is a third party holder bound by statements or agreements in the initial contract of carriage, that are not included or referred to in the bill of lading? Does a third-party holder become liable for events that predate his holdership, such as demurrage in the loadport? The theory that explains how and why the relation between the carrier and the holder comes into being will also

---

5   Compare H. Tiberg, "Legal qualities of transport documents", 23 *Tul. Mar. L. J.* 1998, at p. 3.
6   R. De Wit, *Multimodal Transport: Carrier Liability and Documentation*, London, LLP, 1995, n° 5.1 at p. 243; G. Ripert, *Droit Maritime*, Tôme II, Paris, Editions Rousseau et Cie., 1952 (4th Ed.), n° 1579 at p. 489; J.-P. Tosi, "L'adhésion du destinataire au contrat de transport", in X., *Mélanges Christian Mouly*, Paris, Litec, 1998, at p. 175.
7   P. Seck, *Reisbevrachting en cognossementsvervoer*, Zutphen, Uitgeverij Paris, 2011, at p. 162.
8   During the parliamentary debates on the new Dutch Civil Code, it was explicitly pointed out that the question of whether or not a third-party holder of the bill of lading becomes a party to the contract of carriage has immediate practical relevance, as the answer to this question may have an influence on the validity of jurisdiction clauses. See M. Claringbould, *Parlementaire Geschiedenis Boek 8: Verkeersmiddelen en Vervoer*, Deventer, Kluwer, 1992, at p. 474.

provide the answer, or at least the building blocks to construe the answer, to new problems in this respect.

5 That theory will also need to bring clarity in more complex situations than the one sketched above, where the bill of lading is directly transferred from the shipper to the consignee. In certain trades, it is customary for the bill of lading to be negotiated several times before ending up in the hands of the party that will present it in the port of destination. What is the legal position of those intermediate holders, who, for a certain period of time, hold the bill of lading but do not present it to the carrier to obtain delivery? Do they have rights against the carrier, and perhaps even more importantly, does the carrier have rights against such intermediate holders? Is it possible, for instance, for the carrier to collect the freight or other costs from an intermediate holder if the ultimate holder is unable to pay?

That this is not unimportant is illustrated by the case of *The Moa*.[9] Because of engine problems, the vessel had dropped anchor in dedicated anchoring grounds in the river Scheldt. When the tide turned, however, the anchor dragged and the vessel went partially aground, requiring tug assistance to be refloated again. Part of the salvage award was initially paid by the cargo interests. The cargo interests however claimed that the engine problems and the subsequent stranding were caused by unseaworthiness of the vessel, and therefore sued the carrier to recover their payment to the salvors. The Antwerp Court of Appeal held that such a claim is a claim under the bill of lading, and can only be brought by the party that held the bill of lading *at the time of the salvage operations*, which is not necessarily the party that ultimately presented the bill of lading at destination.

6 The theory will also have to explain the position of the 'non-contracting shipper', i.e. the party that delivers the goods to the carrier but has not itself made the contract of carriage with the carrier. This is, for instance, the case in an FOB sale, where the buyer must arrange for the carriage of the goods that he bought. The shipper in such case will deliver the goods to the carrier, and may receive the original bills of lading from the carrier, but was not the contract partner of the carrier.[10] There are also non-contracting shippers in case of subcarriage, where A enters into a contract of carriage with B, which then, as principal, enters into a second contract of carriage with C. The bill of lading is issued by C

---

9 CA Antwerp 5 October 2009 (interim) and 9 May 2011 (final), Case 2008/AR/1841, T.B.H. 2011, 731 (case analysis).
10 Some legal systems have different terminology to distinguish between the shipper who enters into the contract of carriage with the carrier and the 'shipper' who only delivers the goods to the carrier but does not negotiate the contract of carriage with him. Under German law, for instance, the former is called the *Absender*, while the latter is called the *Ablader*.

The Rotterdam Rules have introduced the concept of 'documentary shipper' (Article 1.9), which is not entirely the same, however. A documentary shipper is a person, other than the shipper (the contract partner of the carrier), that accepts to be named as 'shipper' in the transport document. A non-contracting shipper, as the term is used here, refers to the party that physically delivers the goods into the hands of the carrier and that may or may not be named as 'shipper' in the transport document.

pursuant to C's contract with B, but names A as shipper and the goods are delivered for carriage by A.[11] What is then the position of the shipper? Does he have rights against the carrier, and does the carrier have rights against him?[12]

7 Finally, there are those parties that receive and hold the bill of lading as security (e.g. a bank in the context of a documentary credit). From their own perspective, their position is special: they are not interested in the goods *per se*, but only as security for a claim, and will therefore only be enforcing rights under the bill of lading if matters have gone 'wrong', i.e. if their claim has not been paid. Such holders are not concerned with the carriage as such, and would certainly prefer not to acquire any liability towards the carrier.[13] The carrier, on the other hand, would be pleased to have an additional debtor under the bill of lading.

8 The issue has been debated since at least the 19th century,[14] and over the years, a number of theories have been proposed, challenged and defended. To this date, however, no single theory has gained universal acceptance, certainly not on an international level. Before having a more detailed look at the different theories, however, it is important to revisit the functions of the bill of lading. Each of the different functions may be relevant to third parties, but not to the same extent.

---

11 See, for example, *Cho Yang Shipping Co. Ltd v Coral (U.K.) Ltd* [1997] 2 Lloyd's Rep 641 (Court of Appeal, 14–15 April & 15 May 1997). Coral contracted with Nortrop, Nortrop with Interport, and Interport with Cho Yang Shipping, all parties acting as principals. The goods were delivered for shipment by Coral, which was also named as shipper in the bill of lading, which was on Cho Yang's form. The question was whether Coral could be sued for freight by Cho Yang.
See also OLG Rostock 27 November 1996, Case 6 U 113/96, *TranspR* 1997, 113.
12 M. Spanjaart, *Vorderingsrechten uit cognossement*, Zutphen, Uitgeverij Paris, 2012, at p. 148.
13 Compare R. Zwitser, "Het cognossement als zekerheidsinstrument", *NTHR* 2007-2, at p. 84.
14 G. Kirberger, "De positie van den geadresseerde", *Rechtsgeleerd Magazijn* 1898, at p. 41; A. Mesritz, *De Vrachtbrief*, Amsterdam, J.H. de Bussy, 1904, at p. 65; A. Polak, *Historisch-juridisch onderzoek naar den aard van het cognossement*, Amsterdam, Gebroeders Binger, 1865, at p. 121.
The courts at the time also had to deal with the issue. See for instance Rb. Amsterdam, 20 November 1840, *Weekblad van het Regt* N° 144 (4 January 1841), where the position of the holder was important to decide whether or not he was bound by the laytime allowed in the charter party, but not stipulated in the bill of lading. (The Court held that the holder was indeed bound by the charter party's laytime provisions.)

2 The functions of the bill of lading

2.1 Introduction

1 A bill of lading is traditionally said to have three functions: (i) it is a receipt for the cargo, (ii) it is evidence of the existence of a contract of carriage and may be the contract of carriage itself, and (iii) it grants its holder an exclusive right to claim delivery of the cargo, which enables the bill of lading to function as a document of title.[1]

2 These functions are also included in the definitions that are given by some statutes or codes.[2] Art. 506.1 of the Dutch Commercial Code defined the bill of lading as follows:[3]

---

1 J.P. Beurier, *Droits maritimes (Dalloz Action)*, Dalloz, 2009–2010, n° 345.61 at p. 399; J. Cooke et al., *Voyage Charters*, London, Informa, 2007 (3rd Ed.), n° 18.6 at p. 459; I. De Weerdt, *Het verhandelbaar cognossement*, Antwerpen, ETL, 1991, n° 135 at p. 105; T. Eckardt, *The Bolero Bill of Lading Under German and English Law*, München, Sellier European Law Publishers, 2004, at p. 43; T. Falkanger, H.J. Bull and L. Brautaset, *Scandinavian Maritime Law*, Oslo, Universitetsforlaget, 2004 (2nd Ed.), at p. 259; O. Hartenstein and F. Reuschle, *Handbuch des Fachanwalts: Transport- und Speditionsrecht*, Cologne, Luchterhand, 2010, n° 116–122 at pp. 185–186; Ch. Lyon-Caen and L. Renault, *Traité de droit maritime*, Vol. I, Paris, Librairie Cotillon, 1894, n° 696 at p. 463; G. Mangone, *United States Admiralty Law*, The Hague, Kluwer Law International, 1997, at p. 77; C. McLaughlin, "The evolution of the Ocean Bill of Lading", 35 *Yale LJ* 1925–1926, at p. 355; M. Spanjaart, *Vorderingsrechten uit cognossement*, Zutphen, Uitgeverij Paris, 2012, at pp. 268–269; F. Sparka, *Jurisdiction and Arbitration Clauses in Maritime Transport Documents*, Berlin, Springer, 2010, at p. 41; F. Stevens, *Vervoer onder cognossement*, Brussel, Larcier, 2001, n° 43 at p. 22; G. Treitel, "Overseas sales in general", in *Benjamin's Sale of Goods*, London, Sweet & Maxwell, 2006 (7th Ed.), n° 18-012 at pp. 1132–1133; R. Van Delden, *Overzicht van de handelskoop*, Deventer, Kluwer, 1983, at pp. 330–331.

J. Putzeys and M.-A. Rosseels, *Droit des transports et Droit maritime*, Brussels, Bruylant, 1993 (3rd Ed.), n° 498 at p. 278 only mention the receipt and document of title functions.

2 Many statues and codes however do not explicitly define the bill of lading concept. The Belgian, current Dutch, and French Acts for example do not have a definition of the bill of lading. The new German (2013) and Spanish (2014) Maritime Codes do neither.

3 The Dutch Commercial Code was abolished and replaced by the new Civil Code. Book 8 of the Civil Code now deals with shipping and transport law, but does not contain an explicit definition of the bill of lading anymore, for fear that a definition would be too restrictive on the courts (M. Claringbould, *Parlementaire Geschiedenis Boek 8, Verkeersmiddelen en vervoer*, Deventer, Kluwer, 1992, at p. 433).

6 *The functions of the bill of lading*

> "*Het cognossement is een gedagtekend geschrift waarin de vervoerder verklaart, dat hij bepaalde goederen in ontvangst heeft genomen, teneinde die te vervoeren naar een aangewezen bestemmingsplaats en aldaar uit te leveren aan een aangewezen persoon, alsmede onder welke bedingen de uitlevering zal geschieden*".

The bill of lading is a dated document in which the carrier declares that he has received certain goods, to carry them to an indicated place of destination and to deliver them there to an indicated person, as well as the terms under which the delivery will take place.

Section 292 of the Norwegian Maritime Code provides:

> "*By a bill of lading (konnossement) is meant a document*
> 1) *which evidences a contract of carriage by sea and that the carrier has received or loaded the goods, and*
> 2) *which is designated by the term bill of lading or contains a clause to the effect that the carrier undertakes to deliver the goods in exchange for the return of the document only.*"

Article 1.7 of the Hamburg Rules provides:

> "*Bill of lading means a document which evidences a contract of carriage by sea and the taking over or loading of the goods by the carrier, and by which the carrier undertakes to deliver the goods against surrender of the document.*"

Article 1.14 and 1.15 of the Rotterdam Rules provide:

> 14 "*Transport document*" *means a document issued under a contract of carriage by the carrier that:*
> (a) *Evidences the carrier's or a performing party's receipt of goods under a contract of carriage; and*
> (b) *Evidences or contains a contract of carriage.*
>
> 15 "*Negotiable transport document*" *means a transport document that indicates, by wording such as "to order" or "negotiable" or other appropriate wording recognized as having the same effect by the law applicable to the document, that the goods have been consigned to the order of the shipper, to the order of the consignee, or to bearer, and is not explicitly stated as being "non-negotiable" or "not negotiable".*

3 Importantly, however, the bill of lading has never been *created* as a legal instrument presenting these functions; instead, it has grown 'organically' over the course of many years, driven by the customs and practices of merchants.⁴ In 1861, the Dutch author J.G. Kist wrote:

> *The bill of lading, like the bill of exchange, is a commercial instrument created by practice, little aided in its development by legislation and very imperfectly explained by the lawyers. Here also, the customs of the trade conflicted with the opinions of the legal scholars. Here also, incorrect interpretations have caused much confusion. The merchant understood very well what a bill of lading is and which obligations arise from it; the lawyer couldn't find a place for it in his system and tried to explain the nature of the bill of lading in different ways.*⁵

It is submitted that even today, this statement retains some of its truth and force.

2.2 Terminology

4 The *shipper*, in the legal sense of the term, is the party that instructs the carrier and enters into the contract of carriage with him. If the legal shipper is located at the start of the physical carriage, the legal meaning of the word 'shipper' coincides with the day-to-day use of that term. If, on the other hand, the legal shipper is located at the end of the physical carriage (e.g. in case of an FOB sale), there still needs to be someone who delivers the goods to the carrier at the place of departure. That person, in everyday parlance, is also referred to as the 'shipper', but he is not the shipper in the legal sense. For lack of a more elegant term, such person will be called a 'non-contracting shipper'.⁶

5 The *holder* of a bill of lading is the party that physically possesses the bill of lading and is entitled to exercise the rights under it. Both elements are required for someone to be a holder of the bill of lading. The courier who brings a bill of lading from an importer to the shipping agent physically 'holds' the bill of lading, but is not entitled to present it or to claim under it, and therefore is not a

---

4   V.-E. Bokalli, "Crise et avenir du connaissement", *D.M.F.* 1998, at p. 115; S.F. du Toit, "The evolution of the Bill of Lading", 11-2 *Fundamina* 2005, at pp. 12, 15 and 24; K. Grönfors, *Towards Sea Waybills and Electronic Documents*, Gothenburg, Akademiförlaget, 1991, at p. 7; M. Spanjaart, *Vorderingsrechten uit cognossement*, Zutphen, Uitgeverij Paris, 2012, at p. 226.
5   J.G. Kist, *Het Handelspapier, Part 2. Het cognossement*, Amsterdam, J.H. Gebhard & Comp., 1861, at p. 3: "*Het cognoscement is even als de wissel een handelspapier door het gebruik gevormd, tot welks ontwikkeling de wetgevingen weinig hebben toegebragt en hetgeen door de juristen zeer gebrekkig wordt verklaard. Ook hier was het handelsgebruik in strijd met de opvatting der regtsgeleerden. Ook hier hebben verkeerde uitleggingen veel verwarring teweeg gebragt. De koopman begreep zeer goed wat een cognoscement is en welke verbintenissen daaruit ontstaan; de jurist kon er in zijn systeem geene plaats voor vinden en poogde op verschillende wijzen de natuur van het cognoscement te verklaren.*"
6   German law knows the concept of '*Ablader*' (§ 513.(2) HGB), Norwegian law has a similar concept of '*avlaster*' (Sect. 251 Norwegian Maritime Code), defined as the person who delivers the goods to the carrier for carriage. The *Ablader / avlaster* however is not limited to the non-contracting shipper, but also includes the shipper (contract partner of the carrier).

8 *The functions of the bill of lading*

'holder' in the legal sense of the term. The holdership must be regular – with a straight bill of lading, the holder must be the person named in the bill of lading, with an order bill of lading, the holder must be the person to whose order the bill of lading was issued or endorsed, while with a bearer bill of lading, the holder is any person who physically holds the bill of lading – and lawful, i.e. the holder must not be in bad faith.[7]

The holder may be the shipper (in the legal sense), or may be a different person (in that case, he is also known as a 'third-party holder'). The distinction is relevant, as the shipper is a party to the initial contract of carriage with the carrier. If the holder is also the shipper, therefore, not only the bill of lading, but also the initial contract of carriage is relevant.

6 The *consignee* is the person to whom cargo is being consigned. The term may be used to refer to the person named in a straight bill of lading, or more generally, to the ultimate holder of the bill of lading, i.e. the person who presents the bill of lading to the carrier at destination.

2.3 Receipt for the cargo

7 The first and oldest function of the bill of lading is that of a receipt for the cargo.[8]

Most authors trace the origins of today's bill of lading back to the High Middle Ages,[9] although there is some evidence of documents confirming the receipt of

---

7 See on those requirements (regular – lawful) F. Stevens, " 'Consignees' rights in European legal systems", in B. Soyer and A. Tettenborn (Eds), *International Trade and Carriage of Goods*, Oxon, Informa Law, 2017, at pp. 99–108.

8 In France, Emerigon described the bill of lading as a confirmation by the Master of the goods that he had accepted into his custody (B. Emerigon, *Traité des assurances et des contrats a la grosse*, Tome I, Marseille, J. Mossy, 1783, at p. 310: "*Le connoissement, autrement dit police de chargement, est une reconnoissance que le Capitaine donne des marchandises chargées dans le Navire*" – The bill of lading, also called policy of lading, is an acknowledgment that the Master gives of the cargo loaded in the Vessel), a definition that was later copied in Article 222 of the French Commercial Code of 1807 ("*Il est responsable des marchandises dont il se charge. Il en fournit une reconnaissance: cette reconnaissance se nomme connaissement.*" – "He [the Master] is responsible for the cargo that he takes in his charge. He provides an acknowledgement for it: that acknowledgement is called bill of lading").

Early 19th-century Dutch authors have also defined the bill of lading as *only* a receipt for the cargo: A. De Pinto, *Handleiding tot het Wetboek van Koophandel*, 's Gravenhage, Belinfante, 1841, at p. 278; N. Olivier, *Het zeeregt van vroegeren en lateren tijd*, 's Gravenhage, Vervloet, 1831, at p. 400. See also M. Spanjaart, *Vorderingsrechten uit cognossement*, Zutphen, Uitgeverij Paris, 2012, at p. 16.

9 M. Bools, *The Bill of Lading. A Document of Title to Goods. An Anglo-American Comparison*, London, LLP, 1997, at pp. 1–2; R. Rodière, *Traité général de droit maritime*, Tome II, *Les contrats de transport de marchandises*, Paris, Librairie Dalloz, 1968, n° 438 at p. 53; J. Wilson, *Carriage of Goods by Sea*, Harlow, Pearson Longman, 2008 (6th Ed.), at p. 113.

See also P. Bonassies and C. Scapel, *Droit maritime*, Paris, L.G.D.J., 2010 (2nd Ed.), n° 937 at p. 602.

goods to be carried being used by the Romans[10] and the Egyptians,[11] and similar documents may well have been in use with other ancient seafaring people.[12]

8 During the Early Middle Ages, a.k.a. the 'Dark Ages', that followed the fall of the western Roman Empire, the population in western Europe decreased, trade and commerce slowed down, and there is no evidence of the continued use of the shipping documents that the Romans may have known. Early maritime codes such as the Roles d'Oleron (c. 1200) and the Laws of Visby (c. 1266) do not mention bills of lading or similar documents.[13] When the situation improved and the Early Middle Ages gave way to the High Middle Ages (11–13th century), commerce and shipping picked up again, and the need for shipping documentation was again felt.

Initially, the information on the goods carried on board was entered into a 'Book of Lading', which was kept in a single copy on board the carrying ship by the Ship's 'Clerk'.[14] Remarkably, the Clerk was not considered a member of the crew, but was a public officer, subject to severe penalties if he entered incorrect

---

10 See K. Grönfors, *Towards Sea Waybills and Electronic Documents*, Gothenburg, Akademiförlaget, 1991, at p. 10, who cites the text of a Roman 'bill of lading' dating back to 15 A.D.:

"*From Arctus Bibulus, pilot of a public vessel of 2000 artabas burden, whose figure head is an ibis, acting through Sextus Atinius of the 22nd legion, second maniple, to Acusilaus, public collector of corn for the two villages of Lysimachus, deputy of Lucius Marius, freedman of Augustus, greeting:*
I acknowledge that you have embarked into my vessel at the harbour of Ptolemais in the Arsinoite name at Erboreis to the address of Dionysus and Philologis . . . first Syrian wheat, pure, genuine, unadulterated and winnewed, measured in a public brazen measure of Alexandria, of first Syrian corn on thousand seven hundred and eighteen and a half artabas . . . which I will convey to Alexandria and deliver to Dionysus and Philologus or to whomsoever they shall order it to be given, and I have no claim against you (signed) J.H. . . . in the 2nd year of Tiberius Caesar Augustus."

11 In Appendix I of his book on documents of title, H. Purchase reports on a 1924 lecture by Colonel Jackson, D.L., to the Humber District Association of Chartered Shipbrokers, in which the lecturer ". . . *refers to a form of bill of lading before the Christian era which was discovered in Egypt. The lecturer stated that it was not materially different from any bill of lading in use up to about 1850. It was for a cargo of wheat to be carried from the Fayoum by the Nile to a town in Lower Egypt. There was a full provision for lay-days, measuring out the cargo, payment of freight and advances, and even for a gratuity to the master consisting of certain measures of wine.*" (H. Purchase, *The Law Relating to Documents of Title to Goods*, Sweet & Maxwell, 1931, at pp. 207–208.)

12 W.P. Bennett, *The History and Present Position of the Bill of Lading as a Document of Title to Goods*, Cambridge, University Press, 1914, at p. 8; K. Grönfors, *Towards Sea Waybills and Electronic Documents*, Gothenburg, Akademiförlaget, 1991, at p. 10.

13 D. Murray, "History and development of the Bill of Lading", 37 *U. Miami L. Rev.* 1982–1983, fn. 1 at p. 690.

14 A. Lista, *International Commercial Sales: The Sale of Goods on Shipment Terms*, Oxon, Informa Law, 2017, at pp. 77–78; M. Pappenheim, *Handbuch des Seerechts. Sachen des Seerechts. Schuldverhältnisse des Seerechts. I*, Leipzig, Verlag Duncker & Humblot, 1906, at p. 326; W. Reepmaker, *Over de verbindbaarheid der chertepartij voor den cognoscementhouder*, Rotterdam, Kramers, 1873, at p. 7.

10   *The functions of the bill of lading*

information into the Ship's 'Book' or 'Register'.[15] In addition to the information on the goods carried, the contracts made between the merchants and the Master and the moneys received and payments made by the Master were also recorded in the Ship's Book.

The first known mention of the Ship's Clerk and of the Ship's Book is in the *Ordinamenta et Consuetudo Maris* of the Italian city of Trani, which dates back to 1063.[16] The Ship's Book is also mentioned in later maritime Statutes and Codes, such as *Le Fuero Real* of 1255 and the *Consols de la Mar*,[17] a compilation probably created in Barcelona in the 14th century.[18]

As the Clerk was a public officer, it is not surprising that the 'Book of Lading' was given special probative value: the proof that resulted from the Ship's Book could not be rebutted by private documents or witness evidence.[19] Furthermore, if goods were carried without having been entered into the Ship's Book, the Master was not liable for loss of or damage to those goods.[20]

9 Where this single 'Book of Lading' was satisfactory in times when parchment was scarce and merchants travelled together with their goods, the disadvantages of this single Register soon became apparent when around 1250 reliable trading posts and agents had been established and merchants became 'sedentary merchants'.[21] If the Ship's Book was lost (e.g. because of a shipwreck), all evidence of what had been shipped was also lost. In any case, the fact that the Book was kept on board the ship put the merchants at a disadvantage vis-à-vis the shipowners, although the special position of the Ship's Clerk was obviously meant to alleviate the risks. Furthermore, the merchants who now stayed behind wanted copies of

---

15   F. Basset, "Droit français du connaissement", in F. Basset, *Droit romain des avaries communes. Droit français du connaissement*, Paris, Arthur Rousseau, 1889, at pp. 6–7; M. Bools, *The Bill of Lading. A Document of Title to Goods. An Anglo-American Comparison*, London, LLP, 1997, at p. 1; A. Desjardins, *Traité de droit commercial maritime*, Vol. IV, Paris, A. Durand and Pedone-Lauriel, 1885, n° 904 at p. 3; S.F. du Toit, "The evolution of the Bill of Lading", at pp. 16–17; T. Eckardt, *The Bolero Bill of Lading Under German and English Law*, München, Sellier European Law Publishers, 2004, at p. 44 and fn. 225.

16   S.F. du Toit, "The evolution of the Bill of Lading", 11-2 *Fundamina* 2005, at p. 16.
      Some authors, however, doubt the date of 1063 and believe this Code to be one or two centuries younger. See T. Eckardt, *The Bolero Bill of Lading Under German and English Law*, München, Sellier European Law Publishers, 2004, fn. 224 at p. 44.

17   Customs of the Sea.

18   W.P. Bennett, *The History and Present Position of the Bill of Lading as a Document of Title to Goods*, Cambridge, University Press, 1914, at p. 4.

19   W.P. Bennett, *The History and Present Position of the Bill of Lading as a Document of Title to Goods*, Cambridge, University Press, 1914, at pp. 5–6; E. Bensa, *The Early History of Bills of Lading*, Genoa, Stabilimento d'Arti Grafiche Caimo & C., 1925, at p. 6 refers to the jurist Casaregis, who is quoted as saying that "More credit is given to the Register of the mate than to a public instrument".

20   W.P. Bennett, *The History and Present Position of the Bill of Lading as a Document of Title to Goods*, Cambridge, University Press, 1914, at p. 5; T. Eckardt, *The Bolero Bill of Lading Under German and English Law*, München, Sellier European Law Publishers, 2004, at p. 45.

21   S.F. du Toit, "The evolution of the Bill of Lading", 11-2 *Fundamina* 2005, at p. 13.

the cargo information for their own records, and needed a way to inform their overseas factors or agents of what had been shipped to them.[22]

From the mid-13th century, several maritime laws explicitly provide for the merchants' right to obtain a copy of the Ship's Book (Marseilles 1253–1255, Ancona 1397, Genoa 1441).[23] This initial copy then grew into a separate document in its own right.[24] The Statute of Sassari (1316) mentions a "*puliza*" (policy) that was to be given to the merchant,[25] while the Statute of Genoa (1441) uses the term "*apodixia*" for the copy of the Ship's Book,[26] which became the Latin name for the bill of lading. The Statute of Burgos (1538) uses the word "*conosçimiento*", which is still today the term used for bills of lading in continental Europe ("*connaissement*" (French), "*Konnossement*" (German), "*cognossement*" (Dutch), "*conocimiento*" (Spanish).[27] In that same year (1538), the earliest known copy of an English bill of lading was preserved as part of the record in the case of *The Thomas*.[28]

---

22 F. Basset, "Droit français du connaissement", in F. Basset, *Droit romain des avaries communes. Droit français du connaissement. Thèse pour le doctorat*, Paris, Arthur Rousseau, 1889, at p. 7; E. Bensa, *The Early History of Bills of Lading*, Genoa, Stabilimento d'Arti Grafiche Caimo & C., 1925, at p. 7; S.F. du Toit, "The evolution of the Bill of Lading", 11-2 *Fundamina* 2005, at p. 17; T. Eckardt, *The Bolero Bill of Lading Under German and English Law*, München, Sellier European Law Publishers, 2004, at p. 45.

23 S.F. du Toit, "The evolution of the Bill of Lading", 11-2 *Fundamina* 2005, at p. 18.

24 E. Bensa, *The Early History of Bills of Lading*, Genoa, Stabilimento d'Arti Grafiche Caimo & C., 1925, at pp. 7–9 cites three examples of bills of lading from the late 14th century; W. Reepmaker, *Over de verbindbaarheid der chertepartij voor den cognoscementhouder*, Rotterdam, Kramers, 1873, at p. 8.

See however M. Pappenheim, *Handbuch des Seerechts. Schuldverhältnisse des Seerechts. II*, München, Verlag Dunckler & Humblot, 1918, at pp. 211–214, who points out that there are a number of 13th century bills of lading known from Marseille, which apparently existed independently of the Ship's Book.

25 In Italian, a bill of lading is still called "*polizza di carico*" (policy of carriage), and the older French authors sometimes called the bill of lading "*police de chargement*" (policy of loading). The term 'policy' simply refers to a written document in this context (see F. Basset, "Droit français du connaissement", in F. Basset, *Droit romain des avaries communes. Droit français du connaissement. Thèse pour le doctorat*, Paris, Arthur Rousseau, 1889, fn. 1 at p. 90).

26 A. Holtius, *Voorlezingen over Handels- en Zeeregt*, Vol. 2, *Zeerecht*, Utrecht, Kemink en Zoon, 1861, at pp. 281–282.

27 The continental term "*conosçimiento*" and its variants is derived from the Latin verb "*cognoscere*". See, for example, K. Grönfors, *Towards Sea Waybills and Electronic Documents*, Gothenburg, Akademiförlaget, 1991, at p. 8; M. Pappenheim, *Handbuch des Seerechts. Schuldverhältnisse des Seerechts. II*, München, Verlag Dunckler & Humblot, 1918, fn. 1 at p. 210.

In English, the document is known as a "bill of lading", where "*bill*" simply means "document" (A. Knauth, *Ocean Bills of Lading*, Baltimore, American Maritime Cases, 1953 (4th Ed.), at p. 150: "*In plain English, apart from statute or custom, bill of lading signifies a paper (bill) showing that an article had been laden into a vehicle.*")

28 W. Bennett, *The History and Present Position of the Bill of Lading as a Document of Title to Goods*, Cambridge, University Press, 1914, at p. 9; N. Miller, "Bills of lading and factors in nineteenth century English overseas trade", 24 *U. Chi. L. Rev.* 1956–1957, fn. 64 at p. 268; S.F. du Toit, "The evolution of the Bill of Lading", 11-2 *Fundamina* 2005, at p. 22.

12   *The functions of the bill of lading*

By the end of the 16th century, the bill of lading was a well-known and widely used document, both on the continent and in England.[29]

10   The *Ordonnance de la Marine* of 1681 impliedly confirms the receipt function of the bill of lading in Article 1 of Title 2 of Book 3.[30] In the 1807 French Commercial Code, the bill of lading is explicitly defined as a receipt: "*Il est responsable des marchandises dont il se charge. Il en fournit une reconnaissance: cette reconnaissance se nomme connaissement.*".[31] This provision survives to this day in Article 59 of the Belgian Maritime Act, and in a slightly altered form in Article L. 5422–3 of the French Transport Code.[32]

11   The bill of lading in its receipt function, attesting the quantity of goods shipped, their (apparent) condition, their marks, etc., is obviously relevant to third parties, such as the person taking delivery of the goods in the port of destination or the insurer of the goods.[33] They rely on the bill of lading to know which goods have been shipped and are to be delivered.

The question then arises as to whether the carrier is bound vis-à-vis such third parties by what he has stated in the bill of lading, or whether he is allowed to prove against the bill of lading. Under common law, the carrier is in most cases estopped from proving against the bill of lading under the general rule of estoppel

---

29   A. Desjardins, *Traité de droit commercial maritime*, Vol. IV, Paris, A. Durand and Pedone-Lauriel, 1885, n° 904 at p. 4; S.F. du Toit, "The evolution of the Bill of Lading", 11-2 *Fundamina* 2005, at pp. 19, 20 and 22; D. Murray, "History and development of the Bill of Lading", 37 *U. Miami L. Rev.* 1982–1983, at p. 690.

30   "*Les Connoissements, Polices de Chargements, ou reconnaissances des Marchandises chargées dans le Vaisseau, seront signées par le Maitre, ou par l'Ecrivain du Bâtiment.*" (The Bills of Lading, Policies of Lading, or acknowledgements of the Goods loaded in the Vessel shall be signed by the Master or by the Writer of the Vessel.)

Article 9 of Title 1 of Book 2 provides that the Master "*. . . demeurera responsable de toutes les marchandises chargées dans son bâtiment, dont il sera tenu de rendre compte, sur le pied des connoissements*" (shall remain liable for all cargo loaded in his vessel, for which he will be accountable on the basis of the bills of lading).

31   Article 222 of the French Commercial Code of 1807. Translated, these sentences mean: He [the Master] is responsible for the cargo that he takes in his charge. He provides an acknowledgement for it: that acknowledgement is called bill of lading.

32   Article L. 5422–3 provides: "*Le transporteur ou son représentant délivre au chargeur, sur sa demande, un écrit dénommé connaissement. Ce document vaut présomption, sauf preuve contraire, de la réception par le transporteur des marchandises, telles qu'elles y sont décrites.*" (The carrier or his representative deliver to the shipper, at his demand, a document in writing called bill of lading. This document creates a rebuttable presumption of receipt of the goods by the carrier in the condition as described.)

See also § 486.(1) of the German Commercial Code (HGB): "*Der Verfrachter hat demjenigen, der das Gut ablädt, auf dessen Verlangen ein schriftliches Empfangsbekenntnis zu erteilen. Das Empfangsbekenntnis kann auch in einem Konnossement oder Seefrachtbrief erteilt werden.*" (The carrier must provide the person that has shipped the goods, at the latter's request, with a written acknowledgement of receipt. The acknowledgement of receipt can also be part of a bill of lading or sea waybill.)

See also Sect. 259 of the Norwegian Maritime Code: "*The shipper is entitled to demand receipts for the reception of goods as and when they are delivered.*"

33   S.F. du Toit, "The evolution of the Bill of Lading", 11-2 *Fundamina* 2005, fn. 61 at p. 19; M. Spanjaart, *Vorderingsrechten uit cognossement*, Zutphen, Uitgeverij Paris, 2012, at p. 60.

by representation: a person who makes a statement that he knows or ought to know will be relied upon by a third party, will in general be precluded from later asserting that this statement was in fact untrue.[34] On the continent also, the general view was that the carrier is not allowed to prove against the bill of lading vis-à-vis a third-party holder.[35] The Hague Rules, however, provided in Article 3.4 that a bill of lading will only be *prima facie* evidence. The discussions in the *travaux préparatoires* with regard to this provision are somewhat confused, and a number of delegates seem to have been of the opinion that a bill of lading would nevertheless remain conclusive evidence vis-à-vis third parties.[36] That interpretation has later been explicitly confirmed by the Visby Protocol.[37]

---

34 A. Lista, *International Commercial Sales: The Sale of Goods on Shipment Terms*, Oxon, Informa Law, 2017, at pp. 85–90; A. Tettenborn, 'Bills of Lading, multimodal transport documents and other things', in B. Soyer and A. Tettenborn (Eds), *Carriage of Goods by Sea, Land and Air. Unimodal and Multimodal Transport in the 21st Century*, Oxon, Informa Law, 2014, at p. 129.
   See D. Murray, "History and development of the Bill of Lading", 37 *U. Miami L. Rev.* 1982–1983, at pp. 692–716 for an overview of UK and US case law in this respect. See also *The Carso* 43 F.2d 736, 1930 A.M.C. 1743 (S.D. New York, July 17, 1930), for a discussion of how the doctrine of estoppel came to be applied to bills of lading and warehouse receipts (at pp. 738–743).
35 F. Basset, "Droit français du connaissement", in F. Basset, *Droit romain des avaries communes. Droit français du connaissement. Thèse pour le doctorat*, Paris, Arthur Rousseau, 1889, at pp. 60 and 65; R. Cleveringa, "Een stap achterwaarts", *W.P.N.R.* 1921, at p. 542; R. Cleveringa, *Zeerecht*, Zwolle, Tjeenk Willink, 1961 (4th Ed.), fn. 1 at p. 634; Ch. Lyon-Caen and L. Renault, *Traité de droit maritime*, Vol. I, Paris, Librairie Cotillon, 1894, n° 708 at p. 474; C. Smeesters and G. Winkelmolen, *Droit maritime et Droit fluvial*, Vol. I, Brussels, Larcier, 1929 (2nd Ed.), n° 439 at p. 593.
36 The Dutch author, later Professor of maritime law R. Cleveringa published an opinion in the Dutch law journal *W.P.N.R.*, arguing that the Hague Rules were a major step backwards because they sacrificed the absolute evidence rule, accepted in the largest part of the world, for the typically English rule of *prima facie* evidence (R. Cleveringa, "Een stap achterwaarts", *W.P.N.R.* 1921, at pp. 541–543). To this, Roosegaarde Bisschop, a Dutch-speaking London lawyer who had been involved in the drafting of the Hague Rules, replied that the *prima facie* evidence rule was all that was acceptable to the English maritime law community at the time, but that the Hague Rules only set the minimum in this regard, and that the parties themselves or the applicable national law could impose higher standards. In this way, he wrote, the absolute evidence rule could gain dominance, if such was desired by the international community (W. Roosegaarde Bisschop, "Haagsche Conditiën, 1921", *W.P.N.R.* 1922, at pp. 151–152). History has shown that his was a correct analysis of the situation.
37 Article 1.1 of the Visby Protocol added the following sentence to Article 3.4 of the Hague Rules: 'However, proof to the contrary shall not be admissible when the Bill of Lading has been transferred to a third party acting in good faith'.
   Prof. Berlingieri made the following statement with regard to this Amendment: 'I think that most of the Delegations here have stated in their reports that this is not a problem since there is no doubt that the bill of lading has the value of conclusive evidence as regards third parties and on this assumption it has been pointed out that there is no reason to change the wording, but unfortunately in some countries this problem has arisen and there have been many decisions stating that according to the Hague Rules the value of the bill of lading as evidence is just the value of prima facie evidence so that the carrier is allowed also vis-à-vis a bonafide holder of the bill of lading to prove against the wording of the bill of lading.'

12 This issue, however, is not exclusive to bills of lading, and neither is the solution that has been arrived at. Examples of other documents, the contents of which are relevant to third parties, are not hard to find. The class certificates issued by classification societies and the prospectus published by financial institutions are just two possible examples. Here also, third parties rely on the information contained in these documents, and their authors have been held liable for what they stated in their documents.

13 The bill of lading in its receipt function thus has a specific probative value with regard to third parties, but this is not particular to bills of lading, and not limited to the third-party holder of the bill of lading either.[38]

2.4 Evidence of the contract of carriage

14 The bill of lading is also evidence of the fact that a contract of carriage was entered into, and may contain the terms and conditions of the contract of carriage, although that is not necessarily the case.[39]

Initially, the Ship's Book and later the bill of lading served as a simple receipt for the goods. Several of the early bills of lading explicitly set out the quintessential obligations of the carrier (to carry the goods to destination, and to deliver them at destination)[40] and from the 16th century on, some bills of lading contained basic defences,[41] but the bill of lading was not considered the contract of carriage. For a long time, that contract of carriage was a charter party. When the merchants became sedentary merchants and no longer traveled with their goods, they had to enter into contracts with the shipowners for the use of their ships. For centuries, the small capacity of the ships and the irregularity and unpredictability of maritime commerce meant that only one, or at most a few merchants were involved per ship, and the contracts were contracts for the use of the ship rather than contracts for the carriage of goods. In that constellation, the bill of lading

---

38 See also A. Tettenborn, "Bills of Lading, multimodal transport documents and other things", in B. Soyer and A. Tettenborn (Eds), *Carriage of Goods by Sea, Land and Air. Unimodal and Multimodal Transport in the 21st Century*, Oxon, Informa Law, 2014, at p. 129.

39 M. Spanjaart, *Vorderingsrechten uit cognossement*, Zutphen, Uitgeverij Paris, 2012, at p. 16; R. Van Delden, *Overzicht van de handelskoop*, Deventer, Kluwer, 1983, at p. 330.
  See also *The Ardennes* (1951) 1 KB 55, per Goddard CJ: "*a bill of lading is not in itself the contract between the shipowner and the shipper of the goods, though it has been said to be excellent evidence of its terms*".

40 The Roman bill of lading (see fn. 10 above) included the following wording: "*I acknowledge that you have embarked into my vessel* (description of goods) . . . *which I will convey to Alexandria and deliver to Dionysus and Philologus* . . .". Similar wording is also to be found in the English bill of lading in "The Thomas" (W. Bennett, *The History and Present Position of the Bill of Lading as a Document of Title to Goods*, Cambridge, University Press, 1914, at p. 9).

41 D. Murray, "History and development of the Bill of Lading", 37 *U. Miami L. Rev.* 1982–1983, at p. 691, who quotes a 1554 Bill of Lading that read as follows: "[X]v tonne ij ponchions of wyne and a barrel of apples all marked with this marke for to be consigned and well condicioned from this aforesaid toune of Roan unto the citie of London *exceptid the casalties and dangers of the sea*".

only served as evidence that the merchant had handed over and the carrier taken reception of the goods, to be carried in accordance with the terms and provisions of the contract (charter party) between the merchant and the shipowner.[42]

Only in the 19th century, with the advent of steam power and steel ships and the development of liner services,[43] did the bill of lading contract come into being. The ships became bigger and less dependent on the weather, the Industrial Revolution increased the number of products and goods to be carried manifold, and more and more merchants became interested in shipping their goods by sea.[44] When the contracts between the merchants and the shipowner no longer involved the use of the entire ship, or even a large part of the ship, but only concerned the carriage of goods taking up a small part of the ship's capacity, goods

---

42 Malynes' work on the *Lex Mercatoria* (c. 1620) contains the following passage: "*And the Bills of Lading do declare what goods are laden and bindeth the master to deliver them well conditioned to the place of discharge according to the contents of the Charter-Party*" (W. Bennett, *The History and Present Position of the Bill of Lading as a Document of Title to Goods*, Cambridge, University Press, 1914, at pp. 12–13). See also W. Holdsworth, *A History of English Law*, Vol. VIII, London, Methuen & Co. Ltd, 1925, at p. 254.

The commentators of the *Ordonnance de la Marine* also stress the importance of issuing a bill of lading, even if there is a charter party. For instance, the bill of lading serves to prove that the charterer has actually loaded the quantity of goods required under the charter party. P.-S. Boulay-Paty, *Cours de droit commercial maritime*, Tôme I, Brussels, Société belge de Librairie, 1838, at p. 223; B. Emerigon, *Traité des assurances et des contrats a la grosse*, Tome I, Rennes, Molliex, 1827 (2nd Ed.), at p. 317; A. Desjardins, *Traité de droit commercial maritime*, Vol. IV, Paris, A. Durand and Pedone-Lauriel, 1885, n° 904 at p. 3.

See also the definition given of a bill of lading by the Dutch author De Pinto: "*het cognoscement is het schriftelijk bewijs, dat van de zijde der bevrachters voldaan is aan de overeenkomst, de akte, waarbij de schipper erkent de goederen, in de chertepartij vermeld, te hebben ontvangen en ingeladen.*" (the bill of lading is the written evidence that the charterers have complied with the contract, the document in which the Master testifies to have received and loaded the goods indicated in the charter party.) (A. De Pinto, *Handleiding tot het Wetboek van Koophandel*, Vol. 2, Part 2, The Hague, J. Belinfante, 1842, at p. 278). Similarly, in a decision of 26 November 1841, the Dutch Supreme Court held that a bill of lading is only a confirmation by the Master with regard to the loaded goods, and an undertaking to deliver those goods under the terms and conditions of the charter party. The Supreme Court therefore upheld a decision that had held the holder of the bill of lading bound by the laydays provision in the charter party (Hoge Raad, 26 November 1841, *Weekblad van het Regt* N° 249 (6 January 1842) (*De Goede Hoop*)).

See also M. Bools, *The Bill of Lading. A Document of Title to Goods. An Anglo-American Comparison*, London, LLP, 1997, at p. 6; M. Spanjaart, *Vorderingsrechten uit cognossement*, Zutphen, Uitgeverij Paris, 2012, at p. 181.

43 The *Charlotte Dundas*, which in 1802 towed two barges on the Forth and Clyde Canal, is considered the first practical steam vessel. In 1807, the *North River Steamboat* (a.k.a. the *Clermont*), built by Robert Fulton, started a ferry service between New York and Albany. The English Channel was first crossed by a steam powered vessel in 1815, and the Atlantic Ocean in 1827.

Wood was replaced as construction material for ships by iron in the first half of the 19th century. Steel was introduced in the second half of that century.

44 N. Miller, "Bills of lading and factors in nineteenth century English overseas trade", 24 *U. Chi. L. Rev.* 1956–1957, at pp. 256–266; M. Spanjaart, *Vorderingsrechten uit cognossement*, Zutphen, Uitgeverij Paris, 2012, at p. 76.

16 *The functions of the bill of lading*

started to be carried under a bill of lading only, without an underlying charter party.[45] Where the bill of lading is the only document between the merchant and the shipowner, it should come as no surprise that the shipowners then started using this document to lay down in writing and provide evidence of the defences and exculpatory clauses they had agreed with (or imposed on) the merchants.[46] At common law, a common carrier of goods was strictly liable for the loss of or damage to the goods carried, his liability akin to that of an insurer of the goods.[47] Quite understandably, then, the carriers sought to, and were allowed to, reduce this heavy burden of liability by the terms of the contract of carriage.[48] By the end of the 19th century, however, these clauses had become so numerous and so far reaching that the U.S. Congress deemed it necessary to intervene and restore the balance between shipowners and merchants by enacting the Harter Act (1893).[49]

---

45 In 1647 already, Cleirac considered the bill of lading an equal alternative to the charter party for non-commercial shippers and part cargoes (Cleirac, *Us et coustumes de la mer*, Bordeaux, Guillaume Millanges, 1647, at p. 447: "*Le brevet ou connoissement est une escriture privée conçue en moins de termes, & plus succintement que la charte-partie, mais qui a même effet pour le particulier ou partie de la cargaison que la charte-partie pour le total*" – The brevet or bill of lading is a private document drafted in less words & more succinct than the charter party, but having the same effect for individuals or part cargoes as the charter party for the whole).

Holtius writes in 1861 about the regular use of bills of lading without an underlying charter party (A. Holtius, *Voorlezingen over Handels- en Zeeregt*, Vol. 2, *Zeerecht*, Utrecht, Kemink en Zoon, 1861, at p. 284). In 1889, Basset states that shipment under bill of lading, without a charter party, has become the standard practice (F. Basset, "Droit français du connaissement", in F. Basset, *Droit romain des avaries communes. Droit français du connaissement. Thèse pour le doctorat*, Paris, Arthur Rousseau, 1889, at p. 10).

See also M. Spanjaart, *Vorderingsrechten uit cognossement*, Zutphen, Uitgeverij Paris, 2012, at p. 77 and pp. 226–227.

46 K. Grönfors, *Towards Sea Waybills and Electronic Documents*, Gothenburg, Akademiförlaget, 1991, at pp. 8–9.

In *Glyn Mills Currie & Co. v The East and West India Dock Company* (1882) 7 App Cas 591 (House of Lords, 1 August 1882), Lord Selborne remarked that, although the bill of lading by mercantile law and usage is a symbol of the goods, its "*primary office and purpose*" is to express the terms of the contract between the shipper and the shipowner (at p. 596).

Compare R. Aikens, R. Lord and M. Bools, *Bills of Lading*, London, Informa, 2006, n° 1.12–1.25 at pp. 3–6.

47 R. Aikens, R. Lord and M. Bools, *Bills of Lading*, London, Informa, 2006, n° 10.135 at p. 251; J. Beale, "The history of the carrier's liability", in Committee of the Association of American Law Schools (Ed.), *Select Essays in Anglo-American Legal History*, Vol. III, Boston, Little, Brown and Company, 1909, at pp. 148 and 160; S. Girvin, *Carriage of Goods by Sea*, Oxford, Oxford University Press, 2011 (2nd Ed.), n° 14.02 at p. 213; G. Treitel and F. Reynolds, *Carver on Bills of Lading*, London, Sweet & Maxwell, 2011 (3rd Ed.), n° 9-003 at p. 593.

48 Some defences were created by the legislator. The most obvious example is the fire defence, which was granted to the carriers by the UK Fire Statute of 1786 and the US Fire Statute of 1851 (46 USC App. § 182).

49 S. Girvin, *Carriage of Goods by Sea*, Oxford, Oxford University Press, 2011 (2nd Ed.), n° 14.05 at pp. 215–216; D. Murray, "History and development of the Bill of Lading", 37 *U. Miami L. Rev.* 1982–1983, at p. 704.

15 The dichotomy created by this evolution still exists today. Goods are still frequently carried pursuant to a charter party or a volume contract, which may allow for, or impose, the subsequent issuing of bills of lading. In that case, the bill of lading is not the contract between the merchant and the shipowner (although it may have a superseding effect if parties so intended), but it is clear evidence of the fact that a contract for the carriage of the goods was entered into between the merchant and the shipowner.

Equally frequently, however, certainly in the liner trade, goods are carried without a charter party being entered into, with only the bill of lading being issued. Bills of lading today are issued on standard forms, containing a summary or the full text of the carrier's terms and conditions. Even so, however, the bill of lading is still not necessarily the actual contract of carriage between the carrier and the shipper. The bill of lading is only issued after the parties agree on the contract of carriage,[50] often after the goods have been handed over to the carrier, and sometimes even after the ship has already left the port of loading. It is possible, therefore, that the contract of carriage contains different or additional terms and conditions than the ones that later appear in the bill of lading.[51] In *The Ardennes*, for example, the shipowner's agent had promised the shipper that the ship would go directly from Spain to London, which promise however had not been included in the bill of lading. The ship did not go directly to London and thus arrived later than expected, thereby causing economic loss to the shipper. The shipper sued the carrier, invoking the oral promise to proceed directly to London. In defence, the carrier argued that the bill of lading was the entire contract between them and allowed him to call at other ports first. Goddard CJ rejected the carrier's argument, holding that the bill of lading is not in itself the contract between the shipowner and the shipper, and that the latter is allowed to give evidence that the terms of their contract are different than what appears from the bill of lading.[52] It is clear, though, that here also, the bill of lading is 'excellent

---

See also R. Aikens, R. Lord M. Bools, *Bills of Lading*, London, Informa, 2006, n° 10.135 at p. 251.

50 J. Cooke et al., *Voyage Charters*, London, Informa, 2007 (3rd Ed.), n° 18.45 at p. 470; M. Spanjaart, *Vorderingsrechten uit cognossement*, Zutphen, Uitgeverij Paris, 2012, at p. 281.
    Cho Yang Shipping Co. Ltd v Coral (U.K.) Ltd [1997] 2 Lloyd's Rep 641, at p. 643 (per Hobhouse LJ) and p. 646 (per Evans LJ).
51 C. Debattista, *Bills of Lading in Export Trade*, Haywards Heath, Tottel Publishing, 2009 (3rd Ed.), n° 7.5 at pp. 151–152; J. Cooke et al., *Voyage Charters*, London, Informa, 2007 (3rd Ed.), n° 18.46 at p. 470.
52 *SS Ardennes (Cargo Owners) v SS Ardennes (Owners)* [1951] 1 KB 55 (King's Bench Division, 5 July 1950), at p. 59: "*a bill of lading is not in itself the contract between the shipowner and the shipper of the goods, although it has been said to be excellent evidence of its terms (. . .) The contract has come into existence before the bill of lading is signed; the latter is signed by one party only, and handed by him to the shipper usually after the goods have been put on board.*"
    See also *Geofizika DD v MMB International Limited (The Green Island)* [2010] EWCA Civ 459, 2010 WL 1608507 (Court of Appeal, 28 April 2010), in which Thomas LJ pointed out that between the carrier and the shipper, the terms although usually evidenced by the

18 The functions of the bill of lading

evidence' of the fact that a contract of carriage was entered into between the shipper and the shipowner.[53]

Under German law, a bill of lading is deemed to be issued not in performance of the contract of carriage itself, but in performance of a separate contract ('*Begebungsvertrag*' – 'contract to issue'), made between the carrier and the '*Ablader*' (i.e. the party that physically hands over the goods to the carrier, which may or may not be the shipper) or between the carrier and the consignee if the B/L is delivered directly to the consignee.[54] This separate contract requires the carrier to issue the bill of lading, which itself is seen as a negotiable instrument, to the *Ablader* or consignee. As a matter of principle, therefore, the bill of lading in the German view cannot be the contract of carriage, and cannot even be evidence of the terms of the contract of carriage, as it was not issued pursuant to that contract.[55] The German authors do admit, though, that in practice the bill of lading can often be used as evidence, or at least an indication as to the terms and conditions that were agreed.[56]

---

  terms of bill of lading, can be contained in an antecedent agreement such as a booking confirmation (point 21).
  See also *J. Evans & Son (Portsmouth) Ltd v Andrea Merzario Ltd* [1976] 2 Lloyd's Rep 165, [1976] 1 WLR 1078 (Court of Appeal, 13 November 1975), where the shipper had received an oral assurance from his forwarding agent that his goods would not be carried on deck. In reality, however, they were nevertheless carried on deck and swept overboard. When sued by the shipper, the forwarding agent tried to rely on its standard conditions, which allowed it freedom of choice in the arrangement of the carriage. The Court of Appeal however held that the forwarding agent was bound by its oral promise.
  See, however, J. Cooke et al., *Voyage Charters*, London, Informa, 2007 (3rd Ed.), n° 18.46 at p. 471, who are of the opinion that against a third-party holder, the bill of lading is *conclusive* evidence of the terms of the contract.
53 The debate as to whether the bill of lading *is* itself the contract of carriage, or is only proof of the existence of a contract of carriage, is an old one already. The latter position (evidence only) was taken by Lord Bramwell in *Sewell v Burdick (The Zoe)* 10 App.Cas. 74 (House of Lords, 5 December 1884), at p. 105: "*To my mind there is no contract in it. It is a receipt for the goods, stating the terms on which they are delivered to and received by the ship, and therefore excellent evidence of those terms, but it is not a contract.*" For the contrary view, see C. McLaughlin, "The evolution of the Ocean Bill of Lading", 35 *Yale L.J.* 1925–1926, at p. 556.
  If, as some authors do, the bill of lading is seen as evidence not only of the *existence* of the contract of carriage but also of the *terms* of that contract, the distinction between the B/L as the actual contract of cariage and the B/L evidencing existence and terms of the contract becomes very subtle indeed. See E. McKendrick (Ed.), *Goode on Commercial Law*, London, Penguin Books, 2016 (5th Ed.), n° 32.59 at p. 942. See also R. Aikens, R. Lord and M. Bools, *Bills of Lading*, London, Informa, 2006, n° 7.4 at p. 124, who point out that in practice, there rarely are difficulties in this respect.
54 R. Herber (Ed.), *Münchener Kommentar zum Handelsgesetzbuch*, Vol. 7, *Transportrecht*, München, Verlag C.H. Beck, 2014 (3rd Ed.), n° 23 at p. 936.
55 G. Schaps and H. Abraham, *Das Seerecht in der Bundesrepublik Deutschland, Seehandelsrecht*, Vol. 1, Berlin, Walter de Gruyter, 1978 (4th Ed.), n° 10 at p. 748.
56 R. Herber (Ed.), *Münchener Kommentar zum Handelsgesetzbuch*, Vol. 7, *Transportrecht*, München, Verlag C.H. Beck, 2014 (3rd Ed.), n° 3 at pp. 954–955; G. Schaps and H.

The functions of the bill of lading

16 Third parties may be interested in the fact that a contract of carriage was made (a creditor of the carrier may want to attach the freight owed by the shipper, for instance) or the practical consequences thereof (the fact that the goods will be moved from one location to another, for instance), but they are, in essence, not involved with the contract itself or its terms and conditions.[57] As will be shown below, however, a number of theories consider the consignee to be or to become a party to the contract of carriage.

If the bill of lading is simply seen as evidence of the existence of a contract of carriage, that piece of evidence may be used by any party interested in proving the existence of such contract. If, on the other hand, the bill of lading is seen as the contract of carriage itself, as a point of principle or under the specific circumstances of the case, the question arises if and to what extent the position of third parties may be influenced by this contract. That question is, however, hardly new and hardly exclusive to contracts of carriage.

2.5 Document of title

17 Thirdly and finally, the bill of lading also grants its holder the exclusive right to claim delivery of the carried goods.[58] The carrier *must* deliver the goods to the lawful holder of the bill of lading – he has no discretion to refuse to do so –, but he can *only* deliver against presentation (and surrender) of at least one original bill of lading. It is this exclusive right to claim delivery that has allowed the bill of lading to become a document of title,[59] i.e. a document that *represents* the goods described in it, to such extent that the document can be used in lieu of

---

Abraham, *Das Seerecht in der Bundesrepublik Deutschland, Seehandelsrecht*, Vol. 1, Berlin, Walter de Gruyter, 1978 (4th Ed.), n° 10 at p. 748.
[57] Compare I. Arroyo, "Relation entre Charte Partie et Connaissement: La Clause d'Incorporation", *E.T.L.* 1980, 713, at p. 736.
[58] BGH 9 December 1991, Case II ZR 53/91, *TransportR* 1992, 106 (*The Aquila*): "*Das Konnossement verbrieft allein die Verpflichtung des Verfrachters, die zur Beförderung übernommenen Güter an den durch die Urkunde legitimierten Empfänger auszuliefern*" (The bill of lading only incorporates the carrier's obligation to deliver the goods that he accepted for carriage to the person identified by the document).
[59] T. Eckardt, *The Bolero Bill of Lading Under German and English Law*, München, Sellier European Law Publishers, 2004, at p. 56; K. Grönfors, *Towards Sea Waybills and Electronic Documents*, Gothenburg, Akademiförlaget, 1991, at p. 11; M. Spanjaart, *Vorderingsrechten uit cognossement*, Zutphen, Uitgeverij Paris, 2012, at p. 16; P. Todd, *Modern Bills of Lading*, Oxford, Blackwell Scientific Publications, 1990 (2nd Ed.), at p. 3; P. Todd, *Bills of Lading and Bankers' Documentary Credits*, London, LLP, 1993 (2nd Ed.), at pp. 12 and 88.
See also Neill LJ in *Kuwait Petroleum Corp v I&D Oil Carriers Ltd (The Houda)* [1994] CLC 1037, [1994] 2 Lloyd's Rep 541 (Court of Appeal, 21 July 1994) at p. 550: "*The case for the owners is based on the general principle that once a bill of lading has been issued only a holder of the bill can demand delivery of the goods at the port of discharge. It is because of the existence of this principle that a bill of lading can be used as a document of title so that the transfer of the document transfers also the right to demand the cargo from the ship at discharge.*"

the goods themselves,[60] to effect delivery under the sales agreement,[61] to pledge the goods[62] etc.

18 This third function of the bill of lading was the latest to develop, but of its origins and early evolution very little is known. As explained above, the bill of lading grew out of the 'Book' of lading, a single register kept by the ship's clerk. Gradually, the merchants' right to obtain a copy of their entries in the Book of lading was recognized. Later, multiple copies were issued, one of which was sent to the person who would take delivery of the goods in the port of destination. This practice is described in the *Guidon de la Mer*, a collection of maritime customs compiled in Rouen around 1671.[63]

Initially, however, the bill of lading that was sent to the consignee only served to inform him of the upcoming shipment.[64] The Master undertook to deliver the goods to the person agreed upon with the shipper, and holding the bill of lading did not in itself confer any rights. From this initial situation, a twofold development took place. On the one hand, presentation and surrender of the original bill of lading became a requirement to obtain delivery of the goods; on the other hand, it became accepted that the right to demand delivery could be transferred by endorsing the bill of lading.

19 Where the bill of lading was initially only sent to the consignee for informational purposes, it must at a certain point have become necessary to present and surrender the bill of lading to the carrier to obtain delivery of the goods. There is hardly anything known on when or how this change came about, but it was a necessary step. The requirement of physical possession and presentation of the bill of lading was necessary to guarantee the *exclusivity* of the right to demand delivery,

---

60 J. Heenen, *Vente et commerce maritime*, Brussels, Bruylant, 1952, n° 12 at p. 30: '*livrer le connaissement, c'est livrer la chose*' (to deliver the bill of lading is to deliver the goods themselves). See also R. Rodière, *Traité général de droit maritime*, Tome II, *Les contrats de transport de marchandises*, Paris, Librairie Dalloz, 1968, n° 479 at p. 108.

61 This effect is explicitly confirmed in Article 8:417 of the Dutch Civil Code: delivery of the Bill of Lading constitutes delivery of the goods described in the B/L (except when the goods have already been physically delivered when the B/L is transferred, i.e. in case of a 'spent' Bill of Lading). Similar provisions are to be found in § 524 of the German Commercial Code ("*Die Begebung des Konnossements an den darin benannten Empfänger hat, sofern der Verfrachter das Gut im Besitz hat, für den Erwerb von Rechten an dem Gut dieselben Wirkungen wie die Übergabe des Gutes. Gleiches gilt für die Übertragung des Konnossements an Dritte.*") and in Article 251 of the Spanish Navigation Act 14/2014 ("*Conveyance of the bill of lading shall take the same effects as delivery of the goods represented, without prejudice to the relevant criminal and civil actions to which the party illegitimately dispossessed of such may be entitled.*")

62 S. Peel, "The development of the bill of lading: its future in the maritime industry", 2002, thesis submitted to the University of Plymouth, Institute of Marine Studies, at p. 111; P. Todd, *Bills of Lading and Bankers' Documentary Credits*, London, LLP, 1993 (2nd Ed.), at p. 12. G. Treitel, "Overseas Sales in General", in *Benjamin's Sale of Goods*, London, Sweet & Maxwell, 2006 (7th Ed.), n° 18-007 at p. 1127.

63 The text of the *Guidon de la mer* is contained in J.M. Pardessus, *Collection de Lois Maritimes*, Vol. 2, p. 371 et seq.

64 S.F. du Toit, "The evolution of the Bill of Lading", 11-2 *Fundamina* 2005, at p. 20.

The functions of the bill of lading 21

and this exclusivity was necessary to allow the bill of lading to become a symbol of the goods at sea, capable of being traded in lieu of the goods themselves.

As long as the bill of lading served only informational purposes, the addressee of this document could not be certain that he would actually get the goods. The shipper remained at liberty to change its initial instructions to the carrier and have the goods delivered to someone else. Only when possession and surrender of the original bill of lading became required, and conversely, the carrier was only allowed to deliver against presentation of the original bill of lading could the holder of the bill of lading be certain of its position.[65] The experience gained with bills of exchange, which were known to the merchants that were in the business of shipping goods overseas and where the requirement of presentation and surrender of the original document was known as early as the ninth century,[66] may have influenced this evolution. From the early 16th century on, bills of lading start indicating the number of originals issued, and the provision that once the goods have been delivered against one of those originals, the others stand void.[67] This is a clear indication that presentation of at least one original was required to obtain delivery; if the bill of lading only served to inform the consignee, such a provision would have served no purpose.[68] In the facts of *Lickbarrow v Mason*, delivery against production of the bill of lading was mentioned as a known fact, without comment, which would seem to indicate that by then the practice was well established.[69]

Once the exclusivity of the holder's rights had been established and protected by the requirement to possess the original of the bill of lading, this document could then become to be seen as a symbol, uniquely representing the goods themselves. It goes without saying that this view of the bill of lading is entirely dependent upon the exclusivity of the holder's rights.[70] The 'key to the warehouse', as

---

65 The bill of lading is usually issued in a set of originals, but since the number of originals is limited and must be indicated on the bills of lading, it is still possible for the holder to control all originals and to maintain the exclusivity of his rights.
66 E. Jenks, "The early history of negotiable instruments", in Committee of the Association of American Law Schools (Ed.), *Select Essays in Anglo-American Legal History*, Vol. III, Boston, Little, Brown and Company, 1909, at p. 67.
67 W. Bennett, *The History and Present Position of the Bill of Lading as a Document of Title to Goods*, Cambridge, University Press, 1914, at p. 10.
68 W. Bennett, *The history and Present Position of the Bill of Lading as a Document of Title to Goods*, Cambridge, University Press, 1914, at p. 10; S. Peel, "The development of the bill of lading: its future in the maritime industry", 2002, thesis submitted to the University of Plymouth, Institute of Marine Studies, at pp. 114–115.
69 S. Peel, "The development of the bill of lading: its future in the maritime industry", 2002, thesis submitted to the University of Plymouth, Institute of Marine Studies, at p. 112 (fn. 36), p. 117 and p. 129.
70 P. Todd, *Modern Bills of Lading*, Oxford, Blackwell Scientific Publications, 1990 (2nd Ed.), at p. 1.
  See also Neill LJ in *Kuwait Petroleum Corp v I&D Oil Carriers Ltd (The Houda)* [1994] 2 Lloyd's Rep 541 (Court of Appeal, 21 July 1994): "*The case for the owners is based on the general principle that once a bill of lading has been issued only a holder of the bill can demand delivery of the goods at the port of discharge. It is because of the existence of this principle that a*

the bill of lading has been called,[71] is only a thing of value if it is the *only* key; it does not mean anything if other parties also have keys, or if the warehouse is not locked at all.

20 The second development that had to take place was for the bill of lading to become transferable.[72] Here again, the bill of lading may have benefitted from the experience already gained with bills of exchange.[73] Bills of exchange payable 'to bearer' were already known in the 10th century.[74] In Italy, where commerce and commercial and financial law were well developed at the time, the mere possession of such a bearer bill sufficed to prove the holder's entitlement to payment.[75] In other countries, possession of the document was not considered sufficient in itself, but had to be supplemented by a document attesting that the bill of exchange had been transferred to its current holder.[76] Over time, this once separate document probably merged with the bill of exchange itself and became

---

bill of lading can be used as a document of title so that the transfer of the document transfers also the right to demand the cargo from the ship at discharge."

71 In *Sanders Brothers v Maclean & Co.* [1883] 11 QBD 327 (Court of Appeal, 28 April 1883) at p. 341, Bowen LJ held that the bill of lading is ". . . *a key which in the hands of the rightful owner is intended to unlock the door of the warehouse, floating or fixed, in which the goods may chance to be.*" The words 'key to the warehouse' became a stock expression, repeated in later cases such as *Enichem Anic SpA v Ampelos Shipping Co Ltd (The Delfini)* [1990] 1 Lloyd's Rep 252 (Court of Appeal, 28 July 1989) at p. 270 (per Mustill LJ).

There are, however, already examples of the bill of lading being compared to the key to a warehouse in the 18th century in the Netherlands. In 1780, J. M. Barels, an Amsterdam lawyer, published a collection of legal opinions of his fellow lawyers on a number of maritime law issues (J. Barels, *Advysen over den Koophandel en Zeevaert*, Vol. I, Amsterdam, Hendrik Gartman, 1780). Opinion XV (undated, author not identified) uses the key analogy (at p. 82): "*als of iemand met de sleutels (tot zijner securiteit overgeleverd) gaet in de kelder of pakhuis daer de geoppignoreerde goederen of koopmansschappen leggen*" (as if someone with the keys (handed over as his security) goes to the cellar or warehouse where the liened goods or merchandise lie).

72 There is no clear evidence on whether surrender of an original bill of lading first became required, followed by the development of transferability, or whether these developments took place in inverse order, or more or less simultaneously. It is clear, however, that there is hardly any point in a document that only serves informational purposes to become transferable.

73 W. Bennett, *The History and Present Position of the Bill of Lading as a Document of Title to Goods*, Cambridge, University Press, 1914, at p. 11.

74 W. Holdsworth, "Origins & early history of negotiable instruments", 31 *L.Q.Rev.* 1915, at p. 14; E. Jenks, "The early history of negotiable instruments", IX *L. Q. Rev.* 1893, at 70–85, and reprinted in Committee of the Association of American Law Schools (Ed.), *Select Essays in Anglo-American Legal History*, Vol. III, Boston, Little, Brown and Company, 1909, at p. 62.

75 E. Jenks, "The early history of negotiable instruments", IX *L. Q. Rev.* 1893, at pp. 70–85, and reprinted in Committee of the Association of American Law Schools (Ed.), *Select Essays in Anglo-American Legal History*, Vol. III, Boston, Little, Brown and Company, 1909, at pp. 63 and 68.

76 E. Jenks, "The early history of negotiable instruments", IX *L. Q. Rev.* 1893 at, p. 70–85, and reprinted in Committee of the Association of American Law Schools (Ed.), *Select Essays in Anglo-American Legal History*, Vol. III, Boston, Little, Brown and Company, 1909, at p. 68.

an endorsement. The earliest known specimen of endorsed bills of exchange date back to the 14th century,[77] while by the middle of the 17th century, endorsement had become a well-known practice, regulated in detail in the *Ordonnance de Commerce* of 1673.[78]

As regards bills of lading, several examples preserved from the first half of the 16th century allow for delivery to the consignee or to another person, described with terms such as: "*to him that shall do for him*", "*to whom shall be for hym*", "*to said merchant, his factors or assigns*", "*to him that shall have his commission*".[79] Such provisions, however, may have merely given the consignee the possibility to instruct someone to take delivery of the goods on his behalf, rather than allowing a real endorsement to a third party. The 1671 *Guidon de la mer*, although dealing with the bill of lading in quite some detail, is silent on endorsement.[80] In the early 18th century, however, endorsement of bills of lading is mentioned in several legal treatises,[81] and by the end of the 18th century, endorsement had become a well-established and frequently used practice.[82]

21 Once it had become accepted that delivery of the goods could only be claimed by a party possessing and presenting at least one original of the bill of lading, of which only a very limited number of originals exist, and accepted that the bill of lading could be transferred to third parties, all the building blocks were in place for the bill of lading to become a 'symbol of the goods', uniquely representing the actual goods on board, and capable of being traded in the same way as the goods themselves. With the actual goods out of reach during the (long) sea

---

77 T. Eckardt, *The Bolero Bill of Lading Under German and English Law*, München, Sellier European Law Publishers, 2004, at p. 57.
78 W. Holdsworth, "Origins & early history of negotiable instruments", 31 *L.Q.Rev.* 1915, at pp. 182–183; E. Jenks, "The early history of negotiable instruments", IX *L. Q. Rev.* 1893, at pp. 70–85, and reprinted in Committee of the Association of American Law Schools (Ed.), *Select Essays in Anglo-American Legal History*, Vol. III, Boston, Little, Brown and Company, 1909, at p. 71.
79 W. Bennett, *The History and Present Position of the Bill of Lading as a Document of Title to Goods*, Cambridge, University Press, 1914, at pp. 10–11; S. Peel, "The development of the bill of lading: its future in the maritime industry", 2002, thesis submitted to the University of Plymouth, Institute of Marine Studies, at p. 112.
80 S.F. du Toit, "The evolution of the Bill of Lading", 11-2 *Fundamina* 2005, at p. 20.
81 W. Bennett, *The History and Present Position of the Bill of Lading as a Document of Title to Goods*, Cambridge, University Press, 1914, at p. 14, citing Jacob's *Lex Mercatoria or Merchant's Companion* of 1718; S.F. du Toit, "The evolution of the Bill of Lading", 11-2 *Fundamina* 2005, at p. 21, citing Verwer's *Nederlants See-Rechten; Avaryen en Bodemeryen* of 1711, and a book of 1727. See also F. Basset, "Droit français du connaissement", in F. Basset, *Droit romain des avaries communes. Droit français du connaissement. Thèse pour le doctorat*, Paris, Arthur Rousseau, 1889, at p. 87, who states that, even though the *Ordonnance de la Marine* of 1681 does not mention the endorsing of bills of lading, the practice was accepted at that time.
82 W. Bennett, *The History and Present Position of the Bill of Lading as a Document of Title to Goods*, Cambridge, University Press, 1914, at pp. 11 and 15; S.F. du Toit, "The evolution of the Bill of Lading", 11-2 *Fundamina* 2005, at p. 21.

voyage, there was an obvious commercial advantage in nevertheless being able to deal with the goods through the bill of lading.[83]

In the U.K., the document of title function of the bill of lading was recognized in the 1794 case of *Lickbarrow v Mason*,[84] on the basis of 'the custom of merchants'.[85] On the continent, the question whether a bill of lading could be seen and used as a representation of the goods themselves was for quite some time subject to debate.[86] In France, the issue was settled in 1859, when the French Supreme Court (*Cour de Cassation*) held that the title to the goods carried by sea is represented by the bill of lading, and that both the bill of lading and the goods that it represents can be transferred by endorsement.[87] In Germany, the *Allgemeines Deutsches Handelsgesetzbuch* (ADHGB – Uniform German Commercial Code), the drafting of which started around 1849, explicitly provided that the transfer of a bill of lading has the same legal effects as the transfer of the goods themselves.[88] In the Netherlands, a title function was recognized to the bill of

---

83 The position was summed up succinctly by Bowen LJ in *Sanders Brothers v Maclean & Co.* [1883] 11 QBD 327 (Court of Appeal, 28 April 1883), at p. 341: "*A cargo at sea while in the hands of the carrier is necessarily incapable of physical delivery. During this period of transit and voyage, the bill of lading by the law merchant is universally recognized as its symbol, and the indorsement and delivery of the bill of lading operates as a symbolical delivery of the cargo.*"

Along the same lines, Earl Loreburn LC held in *E. Clement Horst Company v Biddell Brothers* [1912] A.C. 18 (House of Lords, 3 November 1911), at pp. 22–23 that "*delivery of the bill of lading when the goods are at sea can be treated as delivery of the goods themselves, this law being so old that I think it is quite unnecessary to refer to authority for it*".

84 *Lickbarrow v Mason* (1794) 5 TR 683.

85 R. Aikens, R. Lord and M. Bools, *Bills of Lading*, London, Informa, 2006, n° 1.28–1.33 at pp. 7–8; G. Treitel and F. Reynolds, *Carver on Bills of Lading*, London, Sweet & Maxwell, 2011 (3rd Ed.), n° 6-002 at pp. 323–324.

86 In 1827, in the second edition of his treatise, Emerigon still wrote that a bill of lading had never been considered a negotiable document in France, thus rejecting Valin's position that goods at sea could be sold by means of the bill of lading (B. Emerigon, *Traité des assurances et des contrats a la grosse*, Tome I, Rennes, Molliex, 1827 (2nd Ed.), at p. 524: "*Le connaissement n'a jamais été considéré parmi nous comme un papier négociable.*") Add R. Rodière, *Traité général de droit maritime*, Tome II, *Les contrats de transport de marchandises*, Paris, Librairie Dalloz, 1968, n° 439 at pp. 55–56.

See on the difference of opinion between Emerigon and Valin also F. Basset, "Droit français du connaissement", in F. Basset, *Droit romain des avaries communes. Droit français du connaissement. Thèse pour le doctorat*, Paris, Arthur Rousseau, 1889, at p. 87.

See also P. Bonassies and C. Scapel, *Droit maritime*, Paris, L.G.D.J., 2006, n° 987 at p. 632.

87 Cass. Fr. 17 August 1859, D. 1859, I, 347, at p. 349: "*la propriété des marchandises, voyageant par la voie de mer, est représentée par le connaissement*" (the ownership of goods travelling by sea is represented by the bill of lading), and "*il* [le connaissement] *se transmet, (. . .), ainsi que les marchandises dont il est la représentation, par la voie de l'endossement*" (the bill of lading, as well as the merchandise of which it is the representation, are transferred by way of endorsement).

F. Basset, "Droit français du connaissement", in F. Basset, *Droit romain des avaries communes. Droit français du connaissement. Thèse pour le doctorat*, Paris, Arthur Rousseau, 1889, unreservedly accepts the bill of lading as "titre représentatif de la marchandise" (at p. 83).

88 M. Pappenheim, *Handbuch des Seerechts. Schuldverhältnisse des Seerechts. II*, München, Verlag Dunckler & Humblot, 1918, at pp. 344–345. The author sees the origins of this concept

lading in the 17th and 18th centuries. In 1780, *Barels Advysen*, a collection of legal opinions by Amsterdam lawyers on a number of maritime law issues, was published.[89] At least two of these opinions clearly point to a document of title function. Opinion XLII, of 1696, deals with the confiscation of goods, sold by Swedish sellers to Dutch buyers, by the Danish authorities. Denmark at the time was at war with Sweden, and considered the goods a legitimate war prize. The opinion, however, argues that since the bill of lading had already been forwarded to the Dutch buyers and since the goods were on board of a vessel chartered by those buyers, the goods were Dutch property and could not be confiscated.[90] Opinion XV (undated) concerns a shipment of brandy by a French merchant to a Dutch factor. The latter had insured the brandy and paid the premium, had accepted a bill of exchange for the price, and had been sent the bill of lading. Before the cargo could be discharged and delivered, however, it was arrested by creditors of the French merchant, who in the meantime had gone bankrupt. The opinion argues that the factor, who held the bill of lading, had possession of the brandy, and that neither the merchant (shipper) nor his creditors could rob him of that possession.[91] At the end of the 18th century and in the early 19th century, however, apparently under French influence, the title function of the bill of lading was called into question again.[92] Finally, the document of title function was explicitly re-confirmed in Article 517a of the 1927 Commercial Code. With regard to this provision the *Travaux Préparatoires* of the Code state that this

---

already in the 17th century (at p. 216). See also M. Pappenheim, *Handbuch des Seerechts. Sachen des Seerechts. Schuldverhältnisse des Seerechts. I*, Leipzig, Verlag Duncker & Humblot, 1906, at pp. 337–338.

89 J. Barels, *Advysen over den Koophandel en Zeevaert*, Vol. I, Amsterdam, Hendrik Gartman, 1780, 464 p.

90 J. Barels, *Advysen over den Koophandel en Zeevaert*, Vol. I, Amsterdam, Hendrik Gartman, 1780, Opinion XLII, p. 214–220.

91 J. Barels, *Advysen over den Koophandel en Zeevaert*, Vol. I, Amsterdam, Hendrik Gartman, 1780, Opinion XV, p. 73–84.

92 CA The Hague 28 November 1817, reprinted in F. Frets, *De kracht van een cognossement, en het regt van den houder*, Rotterdam, F. W. Krieger, 1818, at pp. 77–96. The Court held (at p. 93): "*Overwegende dat een cognossement enkel is een erkentenis van den schipper, dat hij de daarbij vermelde goederen heeft ingeladen en aanneemt die aan de door den inlader opgegeven persoon te zullen uitleveren. Overwegende dat het bloot toezenden van een cognossement of het bezit daarvan mitsdien aan den houder vis-à-vis van den aflader geen regt geeft om zich tegen diens wil, wanneer hij verkiest van dispositie te veranderen, in de possessie van de lading te stellen, of op dezelfde tegen den afzender eenig regt te sustineeren*" (Considering that a bill of lading is only a recognition by the master that he has loaded the goods indicated in the bill and accepts to deliver them to the person indicated by the shipper. Considering that the mere forwarding or possession of a bill of lading does not grant the holder the right as against the shipper to take possession of the cargo or to claim any right on the cargo against the shipper, against the latter's will, if he decides to change his instructions). See also M. Spanjaart, *Vorderingsrechten uit cognossement*, Zutphen, Uitgeverij Paris, 2012, at p. 61.

A. Holtius, *Voorlezingen over Handels- en Zeeregt*, Vol. 2, *Zeerecht*, Utrecht, Kemink en Zoon, 1861, at pp. 284, 290–291 again defends the document of title function of the bill of lading.

26   *The functions of the bill of lading*

function is generally accepted in commerce and trade, but still sometimes questioned in legal circles on theoretical grounds.

22 Several of the modern maritime Codes explicitly confirm this function of the bill of lading. Article 8:417 of the Dutch Civil Code provides:

> *Levering van het cognossement vóór de aflevering van de daarin vermelde zaken door de vervoerder geldt als levering van die zaken.*
>
> Delivery of the bill of lading before the delivery by the carrier of the goods described in the bill of lading counts as delivery of those goods.

Article 251 of the Spanish Act 14/2014 on Maritime Navigation provides:

> *Conveyance of the bill of lading shall take the same effects as delivery of the goods represented, without prejudice to the relevant criminal and civil actions to which the party illegitimately dispossessed of such may be entitled.*[93]

23 The words 'document of title' in essence simply refer to any document dealing with title to goods. A paid invoice, for instance, can in some circumstances be a 'document of title' in this general sense.[94] Although the jury in *Lickbarrow v Mason* did not actually use the words document of title, the case is generally construed as having recognized the bill of lading as such.[95] It is very well possible, though, that when the bill of lading became known as a document of title following *Lickbarrow v Mason*, the term was initially being used in its ordinary sense.[96] At the time, transfer of the bill of lading was indeed thought to *ipso facto* operate transfer of the *title* to the goods described in the bill.[97] As such, the bill of lading was, literally, a 'document of title': it documented the title of the goods passing

---

93 "*La transmisión del conocimiento de embarque producirá los mismos efectos que la entrega de las mercancías representadas, sin perjuicio de las acciones penales y civiles que correspondan a quien hubiese sido desposeído ilegítimamente de aquellas.*"

94 *Merchant Banking Company v Phoenix Bessemer Steel Company* [1877] 5 Ch. D. 205 (Chancery Division, 8 February 1877): "*The invoice contains every element which is required to make it an ordinary document of title on which the purchaser could obtain the goods: [. . .] That is an ordinary document of title, an ordinary invoice sent by a vendor to a purchaser*".

95 P. Todd, *Bills of Lading and Bankers' Documentary Credits*, London, LLP, 1993 (2nd Ed.), at p. 89.

96 Compare E. McKendrick (Ed.), *Goode on Commercial Law*, London, Penguin Books, 2016 (5th Ed.), n° 32.51 at p. 933.

97 In *Meyerstein v Barber* (1869–70) LR 4 HL 317 (House of Lords, 22 February 1870), for instance, Lord Hatherley said: "*if anything could be supposed to be settled in mercantile law, I apprehend it would be this, that when goods are at sea the parting with the bill of lading (. . .) is parting with the ownership of the goods*" (at p. 325) and "*I apprehend that it would shake the course of proceeding between merchants (. . .) if we were to hold that the assignment of the bill of lading, the goods being at the time at sea, does not pass the whole and complete ownership of the goods*" (at p. 326). In that same case, Lord Westbury said: "*no doubt the transfer of it [the bill of lading] for value passes the absolute property in the goods*" (at p. 335).
 The same was true on the Continent. See, for instance, Cass. fr. 13 January 1862, *Pas. fr.* 1862, I, 136, *Sirey* 1862, I, 207: "*la propriété du connaissance à ordre et de la merchandise qu'il représente se transmet par l'endossement*" (the ownership of a bill of lading to order and of the merchandise that it represents is transferred by endorsement).

The functions of the bill of lading 27

from the shipper to the consignee. It was not until the case of *Sanders v Maclean* that the courts recognized that a bill of lading does not transfer title or property, but only (constructive) possession,[98,99] but by then the 'document of title' label had become firmly stuck.

Since those early days, 'document of title' has become a legal concept in its own right, defined to a very large extent on the basis of the characteristics of the bill of lading, which at common law is the only document of title currently in existence.[100] A bill of lading uniquely represents the goods described in it, since possession of the original bill of lading is required to obtain delivery of the goods. Whoever controls the bill of lading controls the goods themselves. In addition, a bill of lading can be transferred to a third party. Any document can, of course, be handed over to someone else, but in case of a bill of lading, endorsement and/or transfer of the document also transfers the right embodied in the document, i.e. the right to claim delivery of the goods. Based on these essential features of the bill of lading, modern definitions of a 'document of title' now focus on the document's ability to transfer constructive possession.[101]

See also L. Pouget, *Principes de droit maritime suivant le Code de commerce français*, Vol. 2, A. Durand, 1858, n° 358 at p. 355: "*Le connaissement prouve la propriété de la marchandise, non seulement entre le capitaine et les chargeurs, mais encore à l'égard des tiers . . .*" (The bill of lading proves the ownership of the goods, not only between the Master and the shippers, but also against third parties . . .)

98 The transfer of (constructive) possession may of course be an element in the transfering of title or property if that is the intention of the parties.
See also A. Lista, *International Commercial Sales: The Sale of Goods on Shipment Terms*, Oxon, Informa Law, 2017, at p. 104.

99 G. Beltjens, *Encyclopédie du Droit Commercial Belge*, Vol. IV, *Le Code Maritime Belge*, Brussels, Bruylant, 1927 (2nd Ed.), n° 296 at p. 427; Ch. Lyon-Caen and L. Renault, *Traité de droit maritime*, Vol. I, Paris, Librairie Cotillon, 1894, n° 715 at p. 481.

100 E. McKendrick (Ed.), *Goode on Commercial Law*, London, Penguin Books, 2016 (5th Ed.), n° 32.51 at p. 933. R. Thomas, "International sale contracts and multimodal transport documents: two issues of significance", in B. Soyer and A. Tettenborn (Eds), *Carriage of Goods by Sea, Land and Air*, Milton Park, Informa Law, 2014, at p. 150.
Other documents could be accepted as documents of title if it is proven that there is a trade custom to that effect. See P. Todd, *Bills of Lading and Bankers' Documentary Credits*, London, LLP, 1993 (2nd Ed.), at p. 94.
Statutory law recognizes additional documents of title. The UK Factors Act 1889 defines the expression 'document of title to include "*. . . any bill of lading, dock warrant, warehouse-keeper's certificate, and warrant or order for the delivery of goods, and any document used in the ordinary course of business as proof of the possession or control of the goods, or authorising or purporting to authorise, either by endorsement or by delivery, the possession of the document to transfer or receive goods thereby represented*" (Sec. 1.4). Along the same lines, Sec. 1–202 (15) of the US Uniform Commercial Code provides that 'document of title' includes: "*. . . bill of lading, dock warrant, dock receipt, warehouse receipt or order for the delivery of the goods, and also any other document which in the regular course of business or financing is treated as adequately evidencing that the person in possession of it is entitled to receive, hold and dispose of the document and the goods it covers.*"

101 See for instance: G. Treitel and F. Reynolds, *Carver on Bills of Lading*, London, Sweet & Maxwell, 2011 (3rd Ed.), n° 6-002 at p. 323: "*a document relating to goods the transfer of which operates as a transfer of the constructive possession of the goods, and may operate as a transfer of the property in them.*"; P. Todd, *Modern Bills of Lading*, Oxford, Blackwell

24 It goes without saying that this third function of the bill of lading is of direct importance to third parties. In fact, the only reason to have a (transferrable) document of title is for use by third parties. The shipper and the carrier, between themselves, have no need for a document of title; their respective positions, rights and obligations are determined by the contract that they made with each other.[102] That being said, however, once a bill of lading has been issued, it also influences the position of the shipper and the carrier. If there is a bill of lading, the shipper can, for example, only modify his instructions to the carrier if he surrenders all originals.

If everything goes well and the goods are delivered in full and without damage to the holder of the bill of lading at the port of destination, the legal position of the holder is not problematic. The exclusive right to claim delivery of the goods has developed in commercial practice and has since been recognized and confirmed in statutory and case law.[103] Problems arise, however, when the goods are delivered with loss or damage, or not at all, and the holder of the bill of lading claims compensation. Which law applies to such claim? Which court has jurisdiction? Is it a contractual claim or a non-contractual claim? The problems become even more acute when it is the carrier that intends to claim costs or compensation from the holder of the bill of lading, wants to invoke his terms and conditions (e.g. a jurisdiction clause) against the holder, etc. On what basis and to what extent can the carrier do so? It is important, therefore, to determine the legal position of a third-party holder of the bill of lading, even if the right to claim delivery of the goods is in itself quite straightforward.

2.6 Conclusions

25 Of the three main functions of the bill of lading, the first two functions – the bill of lading as a receipt for the cargo, and the bill of lading as evidence of the existence of a contract of carriage or as the contract of carriage itself – do not

---

Scientific Publications, 1990 (2nd Ed.), at p. 3: "*As a document of title, the bill of lading represents the consignment of goods, and transfers constructive possession of it.*"; G. Treitel, "Overseas Sales in General", in *Benjamin's Sale of Goods*, London, Sweet & Maxwell, 2006 (7th Ed.), n° 18-007 at p. 1126: "*a document, the transfer of which operates as a transfer of the constructive possession of the goods covered by the document and may, if so intended, operate as a transfer of the property in them.*"

See also *Heskell v Continental Express Ltd*, [1950] 1 All. ER 1033 (King's Bench Division, 03 April 1950) at p. 1042, where Devlin J held that "*the reason why a bill of lading is a document of title is because it contains a statement by the master of a ship that he is in possession of cargo, and an undertaking to deliver it*".

Add S. Peel, "The development of the bill of lading: its future in the maritime industry", 2002, thesis submitted to the University of Plymouth, Institute of Marine Studies, at pp. 105–108.

102 Compare I. Arroyo, "Relation entre Charte Partie et Connaissement: La Clause d'Incorporation", *E.T.L.* 1980, 713, at p. 743.
103 Article 89 of the Belgian Commercial Code, Article 8:441.1 of the Dutch Civil Code, § 519 of the German Commercial Code.

pose particular problems. That is not to say that these functions are not relevant to third parties, but the questions that arise in these respects are not unique to the bill of lading, and the answers and solutions given are not different than those given to similar questions with regard to other documents in other areas of the law.

The uniqueness of the bill of lading lies in its negotiability, and the issues of transferring rights and obligations that come with it. In addition, the bill of lading calls for specific performance rather than generic performance. Negotiable instruments are well known and widely used in the financial sector, but there are very few circumstances that would make the payment of a sum of money difficult or impossible. In contrast, there are many risks and dangers that may make the delivery of the cargo in the same order and condition as they were handed over to the carrier difficult or impossible, and thus more disputes and court cases.[104] Indeed, legal literature and case law on the position of a third-party holder of the bill of lading only took off *after* the bill of lading had become recognized as a document of title. Before that, the bill of lading only received a cursory mention, if at all, in the works of the maritime scholars.

---

104 See also below, n° 60 at p. 191.

3 Contractual theories

1 The theories that are here called 'contractual theories' explain the position of the third-party holder of the bill of lading by starting from the contract of carriage between the shipper and the carrier, to then apply contract law mechanisms to that contract, in order to ultimately arrive at a contractual position for the third-party holder. Within this group, there is a further distinction to be made. A first group of theories, mostly older ones, has the third-party holder step into the shoes of the shipper: the rights and obligations of the holder are the same as those of the shipper. The second group of (more recent) theories still explains the position of the third-party holder within the framework of the contract of carriage, but accepts that the holder has a position of his own ('*un droit propre*'): his rights and obligations are not entirely the same as those of the shipper. An echo of this distinction is found in the European Court of Justice's *Tilly Russ* decision, where the Court arrives at a different result depending on whether the third-party holder has succeeded to the shipper's rights and obligations under the relevant national law or not.[1]

3.1 The first group: the holder steps into the shoes of the shipper

2 The position of the shipper should, in principle, be quite clear. He is the direct contract partner of the carrier, and his rights and obligations are a matter of construction of the contract. Since the holder takes over the bill of lading from the shipper, there is an obvious logic to saying that the holder also takes over the rights and obligations of the shipper.[2] Such an effect is well-known in law. In

---

[1] ECJ 19 June 1984, Case 71/83, *Partenreederei ms. Tilly Russ and Ernest Russ v NV Haven- & Vervoerbedrijf Nova and NV Goeminne Hout* (point 24). The Court later reiterated its position in ECJ 9 November 2000, Case C-387/98, *Coreck Maritime v Handelsveem* (point 23).

[2] See, for example, CA Aix-en-Provence 28 October 1993, *D.M.F.* 1994, 764 (Navire Chang-Ping): "... *au destinataire des marchandises qui, en acquérant le connaissement, a succédé au chargeur dans ses droits et obligations* ..." (... to the consignee of the cargo who, in acquiring the bill of lading, has succeeded the shipper in the latter's rights and obligations).

See also Court Rotterdam 19 April 2006, *S&S* 2008, n° 33 (ms. OPDR Lisboa). In that case, under the applicable conflict law rules, the position of the consignee (a named consignee,

case of subrogation, for example, the subrogated party (e.g. an insurer) acquires the same rights the subrogating party had, with all possible limitations or restrictions that the subrogating party would have been subject to.

3 Thirty years after its *Tilly Russ* decision, the European Court of Justice in *Refcomp/AXA*[3] stated that 'under most legal systems of the Member States which agree on this matter' the holder of a bill of lading becomes the holder of all the rights and obligations of the shipper in relation to the carrier.[4] There are indeed a number of theories that would have the holder of the bill of lading succeed to the shipper – including enforcement of a debtor's claim, agency, assignment and novation, which are discussed in more detail below –, but this is certainly not the majority position in the (maritime) Member States of the EU.[5]

3.1.1 Enforcement of a debtor's claim

(*action oblique, zijdelingse vordering*)

3.1.1.1 The concept

4 The *Code Napoleon*, and the legal systems that are based on that Code,[6] know a special contractual mechanism that allows a claimant, in certain circumstances, to enforce a claim that his debtor has against a third party. If A has a claim against B, and B has a claim against C which he does not enforce, A can step into B's shoes and enforce B's claim against C in his stead.

Both claims – A's claim against B, and B's claim against C – have to be certain and enforceable. Since A does not get a proper right against C, but is actually enforcing B's claim, B can at any time become active again and take over the

---

as the bill of lading was a straight B/L) had to be decided under Portuguese law. The Court found that, under Portuguese law, the consignee succeeds to all rights and obligations of the shipper (point 3.18).

See also F. Scheltema, *Het vervoercontract in het nieuwe zeerecht*, Rotterdam, S.E.T.A., 1925, at p. 17. The author states that the holder of a bill of lading must be considered to step into the shoes of the original shipper, but does not explain or support that statement further.

3 ECJ 7 February 2013, Case C-543/10, *Refcomp SpA v Axa Corporate Solutions Assurance SA*.
4 ECJ, 7 February 2013, Case C-543/10, *Refcomp SpA v Axa Corporate Solutions Assurance SA*, point 35. The Court repeated its position in ECJ 20 April 2016, Case C-366/13, *Profit Investment Sim SpA v Stefano Ossi et al.*, point 33.
5 See below, n° 68 p. 69.
6 In France, Belgium and Luxemburg, the principle of the *action oblique* is laid down in Article 1166 of the Civil Code. The *oblique action* also exists in the Louisiana Civil Code (Article 2044), be it only in case of insolvency of the debtor.

For Belgium, see L. Cornelis, *Algemene theorie van de verbintenis*, Antwerpen, Intersentia, 2000, at pp. 357–360; W. Van Gerven and S. Covemaeker, *Verbintenissenrecht*, Leuven, Acco, 2006 (2nd Ed.), at pp. 242–243.

For France, see Ph. Malaurie, L. Aynès and Ph. Stoffel-Munck, *Les obligations*, Paris, Defrénois, 2011 (5th Ed.), n° 1149–1152 at pp. 643–646.

enforcement started by A. Moreover, if A is successful in enforcing B's claim against C, the proceeds thereof will not go directly to A, but will fall into B's estate. A will then have to use other legal means to transfer these proceeds from B's estate into his own. In doing so, however, A may have to share the proceeds with other creditors of B, or even leave them entirely to other (privileged) creditors.

3.1.1.2 *The holder of the B/L as the enforcer of his debtor's claim*

5 Early French authors have tried to explain the position of the bill of lading holder as an application of the *action oblique*. The holder, when he claims delivery of the goods from the carrier, would in fact be enforcing the shipper's claim under the contract of carriage.[7] It may seem odd to talk about *the shipper's* right to claim delivery, but within the limits of the contract of carriage, the shipper does indeed have that right. He has entered into the contract of carriage with the carrier, and has entrusted the goods to be carried to the latter. If no third party enters the equation, the shipper is clearly entitled to demand that the carrier return the carried goods to him at the port of destination.[8]

6 As the holder of the bill of lading in this theory does not have a proper right against the carrier, but is simply enforcing a claim of the shipper in lieu of the latter, it automatically follows that the carrier can invoke all defences he has against the shipper. On the other hand, as the relation between the holder and the carrier is purely procedural, the carrier does not have a claim against the holder.

3.1.1.3 *When does the relationship come into being?*

7 In this theory, the relationship between the consignee and the carrier is, in fact, purely procedural. The carrier becomes aware of the existence and the identity of the consignee when the latter starts enforcing the shipper's claim under the contract of carriage between the shipper and the carrier, but there is no direct relation between the carrier and the consignee. The relation thus comes into

---

[7] See for a critical description of this theory: L. Josserand, *Les Transports*, Paris, Arthur Rousseau, 1910, n° 381 at p. 322; G. Ripert, *Droit Maritime*, Tôme II, Paris, Editions Rousseau et Cie., 1952 (4th Ed.), n° 1580–1581 at p. 490. See also A. Kpoahoun Amoussou, *Les clauses attributives de compétence dans le transport maritime de marchandises*, Presses Universitaires d'Aix-Marseille, 2002, n° 636 at p. 403.

[8] J. Cahen, *Het cognossement*, Arnhem, Gouda Quint, 1964, at p. 2.
  Compare J. Cooke et al., *Voyage Charters*, London, Informa, 2007 (3rd Ed.), n° 18.88 at p. 485.
  It has sometimes been argued that a shipper under a contract of carriage or a charterer under a (voyage) charter party is not entitled to claim return of the goods from the carrier, unless a bill of lading is issued and the shipper or charterer is able to surrender that bill of lading to the carrier. It is submitted, however, that that position is untenable. The carrier cannot claim proprietary rights to the cargo; he must ultimately return the goods to someone.

being when the consignee, in lieu of the shipper, demands delivery of the goods from the carrier.

3.1.1.4 Intermediate holders

8 There is, in the *action oblique* analysis, no role to play for intermediate holders of the bill of lading. As only the actual claiming of delivery gives rise to a (limited) relation between the holder and the carrier, simply holding the bill of lading does not, in itself, create any rights or obligations of the holder vis-à-vis the carrier.

3.1.1.5 The non-contracting shipper

9 If the contract of carriage is made by the consignee, as in the case of an FOB sale, there is no contractual relation between the 'shipper' – understood as the party that physically delivers the goods to the carrier for transport – and the carrier, but the non-contracting shipper will ordinarily still receive the bill of lading from the carrier, to transfer it to the consignee once he has received payment for the goods. If he does not receive payment, or if something else goes wrong and the non-contracting shipper needs to enforce the rights under the bill of lading, the *action oblique* concept could explain why he can do so. The (contractual) shipper/consignee clearly has a claim against the carrier under the contract of carriage and/or the bill of lading. Since the consignee, in this hypothesis, has not obtained the bill of lading, he has not been able to enforce his claim against the carrier. Since matters did not work out between the non-contracting shipper and the consignee, the non-contracting shipper most likely has a claim against the consignee, for example under the sales contract. The non-contracting shipper thus has a claim against the consignee, and the consignee has a claim against the carrier. If the consignee does not enforce that claim, even if that is because he is unable to enforce it for lack of the bill of lading, the *action oblique* concept would allow the non-contracting shipper to exercise the consignee's claim against the carrier.

3.1.1.6 Appraisal

10 More recent authors have not had too much trouble in pointing out the difficulties with this theory. First of all, the consignee is not necessarily a creditor of the shipper. He may have a claim for delivery of the goods under the sales contract, but that is not always the case. The consignee might well be an agent or a forwarder, who is not itself the buyer of the goods, and not contractually engaged vis-à-vis the shipper. If the consignee does not have a claim against the shipper, an *action oblique* is not possible.

11 Furthermore, the *action oblique* is not tied in with the bill of lading. *Any* creditor of the shipper could exercise the *action oblique*, step into the shipper's shoes and claim delivery of the goods from the carrier. Possession of the bill of lading would no longer provide the holder with an exclusive right to claim delivery, which would destroy the bill of lading's ability to function as a symbol of the goods.

12 Also, the *action oblique* does not provide the consignee with a right of his own: he is enforcing the action of the shipper, because the latter neglects to do so. That means, however, that the shipper could at any time step in again and take over the action commenced by the consignee.

13 Finally, as an *action oblique* is the shipper's own action, the proceeds of this action fall into the shipper's estate, and not the consignee's estate. The consignee will then have to use other legal means to transfer these proceeds from the shipper's estate to his own, but may be hindered or even prevented from doing so by other creditors of the shipper, who also can lay claim to the shipper's estate.

3.1.2 Agency

(*mandat, lastgeving, Stellvertretung*)

3.1.2.1 The concept

14 Agency is the situation where one person (the agent) acts on behalf of another person (the principal).

15 The concept of agency is known in both civil law and common law. Civil law generally defines agency as the agreement whereby a person (the *principal*) instructs and authorizes another person (the *agent*) to perform acts with legal consequences on his behalf.[9] Common law generally defines agency as the relationship that exists between two persons when one, called the *agent*, is considered in law to represent the other, called the *principal*, in such way as to be able

---

[9] Article 1984 of the Belgian and French Civil Codes defines agency as follows: "*Le mandat ou procuration est un acte par lequel une personne donne à une autre le pouvoir de faire quelque chose pour le mandant et en son nom. Le contrat ne se forme que par l'acceptation du mandataire.*" (Agency is the act by which a person entrusts another with the power to do something for the principal and in the latter's name. The contract only comes into being by the acceptance of the agent.)

Article 7:414 of the Dutch Civil Code provides the following definition: "*Lastgeving is de overeenkomst van opdracht waarbij de ene partij, de lasthebber, zich jegens de andere partij, de lastgever, verbindt voor rekening van de lastgever een of meer rechtshandelingen te verrichten.*" (Agency is a contract for the provisions of services in which one party, the agent, undertakes against the other party, the principal, to perform one or more legal transactions on behalf of the principal.) Dutch law however distinguishes between the actual agency relation, between the principal and the agent ('*lastgeving*'), and the resulting powers of the agent vis-à-vis third parties ('*vertegenwoordiging*'). Article 3:60 of the Dutch Civil Code has a separate definition of the '*volmacht*', i.e. the power of an agent to act on behalf of a disclosed, named principal.

See also F. Terré, Ph. Simler and Y. Lequette, *Droit civil. Les obligations*, Paris, Dalloz, 2009 (10th Ed.), n° 173 at p. 182; B. Tilleman, *Lastgeving*, A.P.R., Gent, Story-Scientia, 1997, n° 1–4 at pp. 2–3.

to affect the principal's legal position in respect of third parties.[10] The principal may be 'disclosed', in which case the third party knows that the party it is dealing with is an agent, or 'undisclosed', in which case the third party is unaware that the party it is dealing with is acting on behalf of someone else. Where the principal is disclosed, there is a further distinction depending on whether the identity of the principal is revealed (a 'named' principal) or not.[11]

All three forms of relationship are known in both common and civil law. Common law, however, sees all three of them as agency, whereas civil law generally only sees the disclosed principal situations as agency. Agents for an undisclosed principal ('*commissionaire*', '*mittelbare Stellvertreter*') do exist, certainly in practice, but are not always recognized as (true) agents.[12]

16 With regard to an agent for a disclosed principal, civil law and common law are very similar. Where the agent acts within the scope of his authority, his actions are immediately and directly attributed to the principal.[13] A contract that the agent makes with a third party is a contract between the third party and the principal; the agent itself is not a party to the contract, and not personally liable thereunder.[14] Where the agent acted outside the scope of his authority, the principal is not bound by his actions, but may ratify them afterwards.[15] If there is no subsequent ratification by the principal, the agent is liable for the damage caused by his acting beyond the scope of his authority.[16]

---

10 G. Fridman, *The Law of Agency*, London, Butterworths, 1996 (7th Ed.), at p. 11; P. Bugden and S. Lamont-Black, *Goods in Transit and Freight Forwarding*, London, Sweet & Maxwell, 2010 (2nd Ed.), n° 2-01 at p. 25.
11 G. Fridman, *The Law of Agency*, London, Butterworths, 1996 (7th Ed.), at p. 215; F. Terré, Ph. Simler and Y. Lequette, *Droit civil. Les obligations*, Paris, Dalloz, 2009 (10th Ed.), n° 181 at p. 187; T. Tjong Tjin Tai, *Asser 7-IV*, Deventer, Kluwer, 2014, n° 228.
12 But see B. Tilleman, *Lastgeving*, A.P.R., Gent, Story-Scientia, 1997, n° 3 at p. 3, who points out that the difference between a *commissionaire* and a 'true' agent is mainly an issue of categorization rather than a fundamental divergence.
13 S. Kortmann, *Asser 2-I*, Deventer, Kluwer, 2004 (8th Ed.); n° 75; C. Schubert, *Münchener Kommentar zum BGB, Band 1: Allgemeiner Teil*, München, C.H. Beck, 2015 (7th Ed.), § 164 Rn. 230; F. Terré, Ph. Simler and Y. Lequette, *Droit civil. Les obligations*, Paris, Dalloz, 2009 (10th Ed.), n° 175 at p. 183; B. Tilleman, *Lastgeving*, A.P.R., Gent, Story-Scientia, 1997, n° 342 at p. 171.
14 F. Terré, Ph. Simler and Y. Lequette, *Droit civil. Les obligations*, Paris, Dalloz, 2009 (10th Ed.), n° 180 at p. 187; B. Tilleman, *Lastgeving*, A.P.R., Gent, Story-Scientia, 1997, n° 371 at p. 185.
15 S. Kortmann, *Asser 2-I*, Deventer, Kluwer, 2004 (8th Ed.); n° 83; C. Schubert, *Münchener Kommentar zum BGB, Band 1: Allgemeiner Teil*, München, C.H. Beck, 2015 (7th Ed.), § 177 Rn. 30; B. Tilleman, *Lastgeving*, A.P.R., Gent, Story-Scientia, 1997, n° 397 at p. 203. Civil law accepts ratification not only when the agent exceeded the limits of his authority, but also when there was no (valid) authority at all.
16 S. Kortmann, *Asser 2-I*, Deventer, Kluwer, 2004 (8th Ed.); n° 97; C. Schubert, *Münchener Kommentar zum BGB, Band 1: Allgemeiner Teil*, München, C.H. Beck, 2015 (7th Ed.), § 177 Rn. 55; B. Tilleman, *Lastgeving*, A.P.R., Gent, Story-Scientia, 1997, n° 385 at p. 198.

17 With regard to an agent for an undisclosed principal, however, civil law and common law provide different solutions. Under civil law, the agent is a party to and personally liable under the contract he makes with a third party.[17] The undisclosed principal is not a party to this contract, and cannot sue nor be sued on it.[18] Under common law on the other hand, if the agency relationship is proven, the contract is a contract with the undisclosed principal, who will be able to sue and be sued on the contract.[19] The agent is, in principle, taken out of the equation, with the proviso however that he remains liable to the other party until the latter has elected to hold the undisclosed principal liable.[20]

18 Common law furthermore stresses the fact that agency is a legal concept, that applies whenever the conditions are met, even if the parties themselves did not use agency wording, or did not even realize that they were, in fact, creating an agency relationship.[21] The U.S. Restatement (Second) of Agency for example provided:

> *Agency is a legal concept which depends upon the existence of required factual elements: the manifestation by the principal that the agent shall act for him, the agent's acceptance of the undertaking and the understanding of the parties that the principal is to be in control of the undertaking. The relation which the law calls agency does not depend upon the intent of the parties to create it, nor their belief that they have done so. To constitute the relation, there must be an agreement, but not necessarily a contract, between the parties; if the agreement results in the factual relation between them to which are attached the legal consequences of agency, an agency exists although the parties did not call it agency and did not intend the legal consequences of the relation to follow.*[22]

---

17 F. Terré, Ph. Simler and Y. Lequette, *Droit civil. Les obligations*, Paris, Dalloz, 2009 (10th Ed.), n° 181 at p. 187; B. Tilleman, *Lastgeving*, A.P.R., Gent, Story-Scientia, 1997, n° 493 at p. 271; C. Schubert, *Münchener Kommentar zum BGB, Band 1: Allgemeiner Teil*, München, C.H. Beck, 2015 (7th Ed.), § 164 Rn. 40; T. Tjong Tjin Tai, *Asser 7-IV*, Deventer, Kluwer, 2014, n° 244.
18 B. Tilleman, *Lastgeving*, A.P.R., Gent, Story-Scientia, 1997, n° 497–498 at pp. 274–276.
  Under Dutch law, however, the undisclosed principal can in certain circumstances acquire direct rights against the third party or, conversely, become directly liable to the third party (Article 7:420 and 7:421 of the Dutch Civil Code).
19 P. Bugden and S. Lamont-Black, *Goods in Transit and Freight Forwarding*, London, Sweet & Maxwell, 2010 (2nd Ed.), n° 2-06 at pp. 29–30.
20 P. Bugden and S. Lamont-Black, *Goods in Transit and Freight Forwarding*, London, Sweet & Maxwell, 2010 (2nd Ed.), n° 3-05 at p. 66.
21 G. Fridman, *The Law of Agency*, London, Butterworths, 1996 (7th Ed.), at p. 13: "*It is the effect in law of the way parties have conducted themselves, and not the conduct of parties considered apart from the law, or the language used by the parties, that must be investigated, in order to determine whether the agency relationship has come into existence.*" See also P. Bugden & S. Lamont-Black, *Goods in Transit and Freight Forwarding*, London, Sweet & Maxwell, 2010 (2nd Ed.), n° 2-03 at p. 26.
22 Restatement (Second) of Agency (1958), § 1, Comment b.

The Restatement (Third) of Agency has elevated this principle to a separate rule (§ 1.02 – Parties' Labeling and Popular Usage Not Controlling). In essence, there is nothing original or remarkable to this principle, which is also known in civil law.[23] If a party accepts to part with the property of an object in exchange for a sum of money to be paid by another party, they have entered into a sales agreement, whether they expressly use the word 'sale' or not, and whether they are aware of the legal concept of sale or not. Common law, however, seems quite willing to read an agency relationship into the facts of a case, whereas civil law focuses more on the parties' intention and agreement to create an agency relationship, even if implicit agreements and implicit authority are not entirely excluded.[24]

3.1.2.2 The consignee as the agent of the shipper

19 In the early days of maritime commerce, the merchants travelled together with their goods. In such scenario, there is no consignee; once arrived at destination, the merchant arranged everything himself. Later, with the establishment of permanent trading posts, it became more efficient for the merchants to stay at home and to ship their goods to their agents in the trading posts. The Industrial Revolution then brought mass production and a substantial increase in maritime commerce. Initially, the manufacturers had their own commercial agents in their export markets to which they shipped their products. Later on, manufacturers predominantly consigned their goods to commission merchants or factors, who shipped the goods to their agents abroad, to be commercialized and sold on behalf of the manufacturers.[25] In those days, the local agents of the manufacturers or factors were, indeed, agents of the shipper.[26] They presented the bill of lading to the Master, received the goods and sold them, but on behalf of the shipper. They did not themselves have a proprietary interest in the goods, and were accountable to their principal.

---

23 See, in general, J.-F. van Drooghenbroeck, "La requalification judiciaire du contrat et des pretensions qui en découlent", in S. Stijns and P. Wéry (Eds), *Le juge et le contrat. De rol van de rechter in het contract*, Brugge, die Keure, 2014, 1–73.
24 See, for example, Comm. Court Gent 26 April 1994, *T.G.R.* 1998, 223. If the insured leaves the handling of a claim to his insurer, and does not react or protest against letters of the insurer informing him about the handling of the case, the insured has implicitly made the insurer his agent, and is bound by the latter's actions in handling the case.
25 N. Miller, "Bills of lading and factors in nineteenth century English overseas trade", 24 *U. Chi. L. Rev.* 1956–1957, at pp. 256–260.
26 Compare R. Rodière, *Traité général de droit maritime*, Tome II, *Les contrats de transport de marchandises*, Paris, Librairie Dalloz, 1968, n° 438 at p. 55.
  See, for an example of such situation, Opinion XV in J. Barels, *Advysen over den Koophandel en Zeevaert*, Vol. I, Amsterdam, Hendrik Gartman, 1780, at pp. 73–84. Anthony Huigla, a spirits merchant in Bordeaux, shipped 60 barrels of brandy to Guilliam and Jean Pels, his agents in Amsterdam. The latter arranged for and paid the cargo insurance, and accepted the draft covering the price of the brandy.

38 *Contractual theories*

20 In addition, the French *Code de Commerce* of 1807 explicitly provided that an improper endorsement of a bill of exchange did not transfer the property of the bill of exchange to the endorsee, but only served as an authority to the latter to collect on the bill on behalf of the endorsing party.[27] Although these provisions were part of the title on bills of exchange, the principle was accepted to apply to all documents capable of being endorsed.[28] Thus, an invalid endorsement of a bill of lading, such as an endorsement of a straight bill of lading or an endorsement that didn't satisfy the legal requirements,[29] was only considered authorization for the endorsee to take delivery of the goods as an agent for the shipper.[30]

21 Construing the consignee as the agent of the shipper thus has a basis in history. With the evolution of the underlying realities, however, the theory largely faded into history. In France, Ripert still mentioned the consignee acting as an agent of the shipper as a possible theory to explain the position of the consignee in 1952, if only to immediately reject it.[31] If indeed the consignee were only an agent of the shipper, he would be subject to all of the defences that the carrier could invoke against the shipper, and creditors of the shipper could simply take

---

27 Section I, § VI of Title VIII on Bills of Exchange specifically deals with endorsement and provides as follows:

> Article 136. La propriété d'une lettre de change se transmet par la voie de l'endossement. (The ownership of a bill of exchange is transferred by way of endorsement.)
>
> Article 137. L'endossement est daté. Il exprime la valeur fournie. Il énonce le nom à l'ordre de qui il est passé. (The endorsement is dated. It expresses the consideration provided. It indicates the name to whose order it is made.)
>
> Article 138. Si l'endossement n'est pas conforme aux dispositions de l'article précédent, il n'opère pas le transport; il n'est qu'une procuration. (If the endorsement does not comply with the provisions of the previous article, it does not operate a transfer; it is only a power of attorney.)
>
> Article 139. Il est défendu d'antidater les ordres à peine de faux. (It is forbidden to pre-date the orders on penalty of falsehood.)

28 Cass. (fr.), 1 March 1843, *S.* 1843, 1.188. F. Basset, "Droit français du connaissement", in F. Basset, *Droit romain des avaries communes. Droit français du connaissement. Thèse pour le doctorat*, Paris, Arthur Rousseau, 1889, n° 33 at p. 99; A. Desjardins, *Traité de droit commercial maritime*, Vol. IV, Paris, A. Durand and Pedone-Lauriel, 1885, at p. 69 and 71.
29 An endorsement in blank, for instance, did not satisfy the requirements of Article 137 of the Code de Commerce. In 1889, however, Basset argued that an endorsement in blank should nevertheless be accepted as valid when the bill of lading is one of "... *those new bills of lading that bear an order clause but do not indicate the name of the consignee*". (F. Basset, "Droit français du connaissement", in F. Basset, *Droit romain des avaries communes. Droit français du connaissement. Thèse pour le doctorat*, Paris, Arthur Rousseau, 1889, at p. 102).
30 F. Basset, "Droit français du connaissement", in F. Basset, *Droit romain des avaries communes. Droit français du connaissement. Thèse pour le doctorat*, Paris, Arthur Rousseau, 1889, at pp. 99–100; A. Desjardins, *Traité de droit commercial maritime*, Vol. IV, Paris, A. Durand and Pedone-Lauriel, 1885, at pp. 68 and 71.
31 G. Ripert, *Droit Maritime*, Tôme II, Paris, Editions Rousseau et Cie., 1952 (4th Ed.), n° 1580–1581 at p. 490. See also A. Kpoahoun Amoussou, *Les clauses attributives de compétence dans le transport maritime de marchandises*, Presses Universitaires d'Aix-Marseille, 2002, n° 636 p. 403.

away the goods from him. As Ripert correctly pointed out, such consequences run afoul of commercial practices and expectations. In *Pyrene Co. LD. v Scindia Navigation Co. LD.*,[32] Devlin J considered it a possibility for the consignee – FOB buyer, who had negotiated the contract of carriage with the carrier, to have acted as an agent for the shipper – FOB seller, if it had been the parties' intention for the shipper to become a party to the *whole* of the contract of carriage, but did not find such intention in the case at hand.

3.1.2.3 The shipper as the agent of the consignee

22 Agency was also used to construe the position of the shipper, who was seen as acting on behalf of the consignee when entering into the contract of carriage with the carrier. Here also, this construction had a basis in history. When with the advent of the Industrial Revolution and steam ships overseas trade started to develop, merchants and manufacturers not only had agents and factors to sell finished products for them, but also agents to buy raw materials and goods and ship them to their principals. In such case, the shipper was indeed the consignee's agent, and acted as such in making the contract of carriage.

23 In addition, the common law in the UK from a very early stage developed a presumption that a contract of carriage is made by the *owner* of the carried goods.[33] The starting point of this development is the question as to which party has title to sue the carrier.[34] In such early cases as *Evans v Martell* (1697),[35] *Snee v Prescott* (1745)[36] and *Dawes v Peck* (1799),[37] it was held that the party that owns the carried goods or at least has a proprietary interest in them and thus sustains the loss in case of an incident during the carriage, is the proper party to sue the carrier. Very often, the party owning the goods and sustaining the loss would be the consignee rather than the shipper. In a contract for the sale of goods that had to be shipped to the buyer, the delivery of the goods to the carrier was seen as delivery to the buyer, which vested the property of the goods in the buyer. Also,

---

32 *Pyrene Co. LD. v Scindia Navigation Co. LD.* [1954] 2 WLR 1005, [1954] 2 QB 402 (Queen's Bench Division, 14 April 1954).
   See also M. Spanjaart, *Vorderingsrechten uit cognossement*, Zutphen, Uitgeverij Paris, 2012, at pp. 279–280.
33 See C. Cashmore, *Parties to a Contract of Carriage, or Who Can Sue on a Contract of Carriage of Goods?* London, Lloyd's of London Press, 1990, for a very detailed research and analysis of this issue.
34 See, for instance, Brandon J. in *Owners of Cargo Laden on Board the Albacruz v Owners of the Albazero (The Albazero)* [1976] 3 WLR 419, [1977] A.C. 774 (House of Lords, 28 July 1976), who starts off his discussion of the issue by stating: "On this I was referred to a large number of authorities going back many years, *in which the question of title to sue a carrier for loss of or damage to goods arose.*"
35 *Evans v Martell* (1697) 1 Ld. Raym. 272, 12 Mod. 156, 3 Salk. 290.
36 *Snee v Prescott* (1745) 1 Atk. 239.
37 *Dawes v Peck* (1799) 8 T.R. 330, 101 ER 1417.

in the early days of negotiable bills of lading, the endorsement of a bill of lading was thought to *ipso facto* operate a transfer of property. In most cases, therefore, it was the consignee that was considered the proper party to sue the carrier. In order to allow him to do so on a contractual basis, however, the privity of contract doctrine made it necessary for the consignee to be a party to the contract of carriage. This then led to a presumption, even a presumption *of law*,[38] that a contract of carriage is made between the carrier and the consignee.[39] If such a presumption is accepted, however, the involvement of the shipper and his contacts and negotiations with the carrier become problematic. Why is the shipper dealing with the carrier if it is the consignee that enters into the contract of carriage? A solution was not hard to devise: the shipper must have been acting as the *agent* of the consignee.[40]

This theory was quite largely accepted in the late 19th and early 20th century, and is explicitly espoused in a number of decisions of that era. In *Cork Distilleries v Gt. S. & W. Ry. of Ireland*, for instance, Mellor J held that: "*The contract of carriage is between the carrier and the consignee, the consignor being the agent for the consignee to make it.*"[41] A different result could be reached, though, if under the terms and conditions of the sales contract the property and risk in the goods

---

38 A presumption or inference of law is an inference that a court *must* draw when certain elements are present. If, for instance, there is a marriage and a child born into that marriage, the courts *must* infer that the husband is the father of the child. A presumption or inference of fact, on the other hand, refers to a fact that a court deduces from the presence of other facts, based on logic, experience, etc. If, for instance, several cars, well maintained and properly operated, have their engines explode after buying fuel from the same fuel station, a court *may* infer from those facts that the fuel must have been defective.
39 P. Bugden and S. Lamont-Black, *Goods in Transit and Freight Forwarding*, London, Sweet & Maxwell, 2010 (2nd Ed.), n° 8-01 at p. 134; C. Cashmore, *Parties to a Contract of Carriage, or Who Can Sue on a Contract of Carriage of Goods?* London, Lloyd's of London Press, 1990, at p. 111 and fn. 4 at p. 130.
40 C. Cashmore, *Parties to a Contract of Carriage, or Who Can Sue on a Contract of Carriage of Goods?* London, Lloyd's of London Press, 1990, at p. 130: "*Indeed if the legal presumption be that the consignee/owner is, as principal, the correct person to sue upon the contract of carriage, then it should be axiomatic that the consignor/seller is his agent to make it.*"
41 *Cork Distilleries v Gt. S. & W. Ry. of Ireland* (1874) LR 7 HL 269.
  Other cases include *Gt. E. Ry. v Nix* (1895) 39 Sol. J. 709: "*The contract with the carrier is, therefore, made by the seller as agent for the purchaser.*" (per Grantham J.), *John Wallis v Gt. N. Ry. of Ireland* (1903) 12 Ry. & Can. Tr. Cas. 38: "*Where the consignee is owner the contract is presumed (...) to have been made by the consignor as his agent.*" (per Gibson J.), and *Brown, McFarlane & Co. v Shaw, Lovell and Sons* (1921) 7 Ll.L. Rep 36: "*The contract (...) is made on behalf of the buyer (by the seller).*" (per Rowlatt J.).
  See also *Houlder Brothers & Co., Limited v Commissioner of Public Works* 1908 A.C. 276 (Privy Council, 2 April 1908), at p. 290: "*It may well be that, under a normal c.i.f. contract, the vendor who charters a ship for the carriage of the goods sold acts in so doing as the agent of the consignee (...)*". The Privy Council however held that the contracts in the case at bar were not 'normal' c.i.f. contracts, and also held that, unless the vendor acts as a commission agent, there is no trust or contract of agency between the vendor and the consignee.
  See also C. Cashmore, *Parties to a Contract of Carriage, or Who Can Sue on a Contract of Carriage of Goods?* London, Lloyd's of London Press, 1990, at p. 131.

remained with the seller/shipper, or if the shipper had entered into a 'special contract' with the carrier, for instance by engaging himself to pay the freight.[42]

The agency theory has survived to this very day. It was passionately defended by Chris Cashmore in his 1990 book on the parties to a contract of carriage[43] and is occasionally still argued in modern day cases.[44] In *Texas Instruments v Nason (Europe)*, a 1990 CMR case, Evans J held that 'business efficacy' requires that a seller who makes a contract with a carrier for the carriage of goods to the buyer does so on behalf of the buyer.[45] With regard to bills of lading, it was mentioned (though apparently limited to *straight* bills of lading) by Lord Hobhouse in *The Berge Sisar*.[46] In *The Dunelmia*,[47] however, the buyer of a consignment of

---

42 P. Bugden and S. Lamont-Black, *Goods in Transit and Freight Forwarding*, London, Sweet & Maxwell, 2010 (2nd Ed.), n° 8-01 at p. 134.
43 C. Cashmore, *Parties to a Contract of Carriage, or Who Can Sue on a Contract of Carriage of Goods?* London, Lloyd's of London Press, 1990, 246 p.
   See also R. Aikens, R. Lord and M. Bools, *Bills of Lading*, London, Informa, 2006, n° 7.73 at p. 143.
44 See, for instance, *The Athanasia Comninos and Georges Chr. Lemos*, [1990] 1 Lloyd's Rep 277 (Queen's Bench Division, Commercial Court, 21 December 1979). The claimants argued that CEGB, the FOB buyer which had chartered the vessel, had been made a party to the bill of lading contract through Devco, the FOB seller, acting as its agent. Mustill J. however held that "*I can see nothing in the circumstances of the case justifying the inference that either Mr. Lorway* [shipping agent] *or Devco were authorized by CEGB to make the latter parties to the bill of lading. They already had a contract for the carriage of the goods, in the shape of the charter party. They had no need of another, and they were concerned with the bill of lading only in its character as a receipt for the goods.*"
   In *Hispanica de Petroleos S.A. and Compania Iberica Refinadera S.A. v Vencedora Oceanica Navegacion S.A. (The Kapetan Markos N.L. (No. 2))* [1987] 2 Lloyd's Rep 321 (Court of Appeal, 28–30 April and 1 and 5 May 1987), the possibility of the shipper (Sumed) being the agent of the owner of the cargo (Petroliber) was discussed but not accepted, not in the least because the cargo owner himself never claimed that the shipper had been his agent. Mustill LJ held in this respect: "*On the face of it, this is an attractive proposition. Sumed never had title to the goods, and they had no commercial interest in their transportation to La Coruna. Petroliber did have the property, and were going to retain it throughout, and they played a part in arranging the transportation. It would not ordinarily be difficult to infer in such circumstances that Sumed acted as agents only, and that Petroliber were parties to the bill of lading throughout. Such an inference would correspond with commercial reality (...). This proposition has, however, never been pleaded or even suggested by Petroliber, and was indeed disclaimed on their behalf...*".
45 *Texas Instruments Ltd v Europe Cargo Ltd*, The Financial Times, July 6, 1990. Sub nom. *Texas Instruments v Nason (Europe)* [1991] 1 Lloyd's Rep 146. See also C. Cashmore, "Case Comment. Title to sue in contract of carriage: land", *J.B.L.* 1991, July, 362–364.
   The decision is remarkable, as the CMR Convention explicitly provides that the consignee (the buyer in the case) is entitled to sue the carrier (Article 13.1 CMR), thus removing any need for an agency construction.
46 *Borealis AB v Stargas Ltd and others and Bergesen D.Y. A/S (The Berge Sisar)* [2001] UKHL 17, [2001] 2 All ER 193 (House of Lords, 22 March 2001): "*Where there is a named consignee it may be inferred that the contracting party is the consignee not the shipper*".
   See also M. Davies and A. Dickey, *Shipping Law*, Lawbook Co., 2004 (3th Ed.), at p. 250.
47 *The President of India v Metcalfe Shipping Co Ltd (The Dunelmia)* [1969] 3 WLR 1120, [1970] 1 QB 289.

42 Contractual theories

fertilizer had chartered that vessel to carry the fertilizer from Italy to India. Upon delivering the cargo to the vessel, the seller received a bill of lading, which, having received payment, it then endorsed to the buyer/charterer. The goods were delivered short, and the buyer/charterer intended to sue the carrier for their loss. The question, however, was whether they had to do so under the charter party (which contained an arbitration clause) or under the bill of lading (which did not contain a similar clause). That question was referred to an arbitrator. The buyer/charterer argued that the seller, in delivering the fertilizer to the vessel, had acted as its agent. This argument, however, was rejected by the arbitrator:[48]

> "*I hold that A.N.I.C. [seller] shipped on the* Dunelmia *urea (and bags) which were at that time their own property and that in doing so they did not act as the charterer's agents. The charterer had bound himself to the owners to ship the cargo, but that did not necessitate employing his own agents (and I find that he did not) to fulfill this obligation. The ship had bound herself to give certain notices and advices (. . .) to A.N.I.C., Milan and Ravenna agents and I have no doubt that the notice was duly given to, inter alia, A.N.I.C. at Ravenna, but that does not make A.N.I.C. the charterer's agents to ship the cargo. A.N.I.C. shipped the cargo because they had contracted with the charterer (as seller) to do that thing.*"

In *TICC Ltd. v COSCO (UK) Ltd.*, the consignee argued that he was in fact the contracting party through the agency of the shippers in Hong Kong. Under the circumstances of the case, that led to a more favourable result for the consignee (TICC), as notice of certain surcharges had been given to the shippers, but not to the consignee, who on the contrary had been assured by the carrier's UK office that no surcharges would be applied. The County Court had upheld this argument. On appeal, however, the Court of Appeal, Rix LJ writing, held:[49]

> "*I will assume that it may be possible that TICC is to be regarded as the Hong Kong shippers' principal and thus as the true original party to the bill of lading contracts. It has to be said, however, that that is an unusual situation. The normal rule is that a party who procures a shipment for the ultimate benefit of a consignee does not thereby contract with the carrier as agent for the consignee. Thus a cif seller is not an agent for his buyer in procuring a contract of carriage.*"

In *Fortis Bank, Stemcor UK Ltd v Indian Overseas Bank*, it was the shipper who argued that he had acted as an agent for the consignee, again because under the

---

48 Point 16 of the arbitrator's decision, as quoted in *The President of India v Metcalfe Shipping Co Ltd (The Dunelmia)* [1969] 3 WLR 1120, [1970] 1 QB 289, at p. 294.
49 *TICC LtdLtd v COSCO (UK) Ltd* [2001] EWCA Civ 1862; [2002] CLC 346 (Court of Appeal, 5 December 2001), at § 17.
See also J. Cooke et al., *Voyage Charters*, London, Informa, 2007 (3rd Ed.), n° 18.77 at p. 481.

circumstances of the case that would have been beneficial. The shipper (Stemcor) indeed had been made to pay demurrage charges to the carrier, and now sought to recover those sums from the consignee (IOB). Here also, the court rejected the argument:[50]

> "The L/Cs required in field 46A that the bills of lading be consigned to the order of IOB. I do not consider that by making this requirement, it can be inferred that IOB was authorising Stemcor to enter into a contract on its behalf in terms of the bills of lading. If Mr Young's submission is correct, it would seem to follow that whenever a bank requires in a letter of credit that it is named as consignee in the bill of lading, it must be inferred that it is authorising the shipper to contract on its behalf. Such a conclusion would run contrary to the regime established by COGSA and open banks up to potentially enormous liabilities. I would add that in my judgment Stemcor did not even purport to contract on behalf of IOB. The contracts it made were as shipper and principal in its own right."

24 The early UK cases also influenced the courts in the U.S.A., and the agency theory was adopted in a number of 19th century decisions. One of the stronger expressions of the theory is to be found in the New York Supreme Court's decision in *Green v Clark*, where Allen J held:[51]

> "When the consignee is the general owner of the goods, or when by the delivery of the goods to the carrier the property vests in the consignee, it is an inference

---

50 *Fortis Bank S.A./N.V., Stemcor UK Ltd v Indian Overseas Bank* [2011] EWHC 538 (Comm); 2011 WL 806786 (Queen's Bench Division (Commercial Court), 17 March 2011), at § 67.
51 *Green v Clark* 13 Barb. 57 (Supreme Court, New York, April 5, 1852).
  Other cases include: *Smith v Lewis* 3 B.Mon. 229, 42 Ky. 229, 1842 WL 3315 (Court of Appeals of Kentucky, October 25, 1842): "*a general consignment, nothing else appearing, imports that the consignee is the owner of the property, and therefore, the contract to carry is, prima facie, presumed to have been made with him. (. . .) And although this contract is here a covenant, and must therefore operate according to its own intrinsic import, still, upon the principle already suggested, it implies that the consignees were the owners of the goods. (. . .) it is a covenant to the consignees through the consignor, as their presumed agent in obtaining it, for it is not expressly with the consignor, but so far as he is concerned, only acknowledges a receipt of the goods from him, and therefore may be understood, so far as it is a covenant, to be an express one, with and to the consignees. The carrier's receipt, promising to deliver goods to the consignee, generally is a covenant with the consignee through the consignor as his presumed agent on which consignee may and should sue.*", *Madison, I. & P.R. Co. v Whitesel* 11 Ind. 55, 1858 WL 4096 (Supreme Court of Indiana, November 22, 1858): "*it must be assumed that the property in the goods vested in the consignees upon their delivery to the carriers; and that, for safe carriage, the contract is between the defendants and the consignees, who are, consequently, the real party in interest.*", *Blum v the Caddo* 1 Woods 64, 3 F.Cas. 753 (Circuit Court D. Louisiana, 1870): "*it has been repeatedly held that the vendor in making the contract with the carrier acts merely as the agent of the vendee*".
  See also J. Angell, *A Treatise on the Law of Carriers of Goods and Passengers, by Land and by Water*, Boston, Little, Brown and Company, 1877 (5th Ed.), § 499 at p. 447; C. Cashmore, *Parties to a Contract of Carriage, or Who Can Sue on a Contract of Carriage of Goods?*

44 Contractual theories

> *of law and not a presumption of fact that the contract for the safe carriage is between the carrier and the consignee, and consequently the latter has the legal right of action. This is true notwithstanding the freight, as in this case, is to be paid by the consignor and not by the consignee."*

Nevertheless, the 19th century also saw a number of decisions that explicitly rejected the agency view and favoured a contract-based approach. The origins of this alternative approach are probably to be found in the dissenting opinion of Gibson J in *Griffith v Ingledew*.[52] Against the majority of the court, which had held that the bill of lading vests the property of the carried goods in the consignee, thereby enabling him to sue the carrier, Gibson J argued that a court should analyse whether the contract of carriage was made by the consignor in his own right, in which case the consignor can and must sue, or by the consignor as agent for the consignee, in which case title to sue lies with the consignee.[53] This approach was later taken up and elaborated by the Supreme Court of Massachusetts in *Blanchard v Page*[54] and *Menzo W. Finn v Western Railroad Corp*.[55] In *Blanchard v Page*, Chief Justice Shaw expressed the opinion that earlier cases had placed too much importance on the question who owned the goods, or who was to pay the freight, and that "*... the question, who were the parties to the contract, and the nature of that contract, have not been sufficiently regarded*".[56] He then held, after having reviewed several of the older cases, that the contract for carriage is between the shipper and the carrier.[57] Along the same lines, Wells J held in *Menzo W. Finn v Western Railroad Corp.* that the contract of carriage is made with the person requiring the carrier to perform the carriage, and that it does not become a contract with another person by reason of subsequent events. He then went on to explicitly reject the agency theory by holding that:

> *"One who forwards goods in execution of an order or agreement for sale is not a mere agent of the purchaser in doing so. He is acting in his own interest and behalf, and his dealings with the carrier are in his own right and upon his own*

London, Lloyd's of London Press, 1990, at pp. 132–133; R. Hutchinson, *A Treatise on the Law of Carriers*, Vol. III, Chicago, Callaghan and Company, 1906 (3rd Ed.), Sec. 1307 at p. 1555.
52 *Griffith v Ingledew* 1821 WL 1807, 9 Am.Dec. 444, 6 Serg. & Rawle 429 (Supreme Court of Pennsylvania, April, 1821).
53 *Griffith v Ingledew* 1821 WL 1807, 9 Am.Dec. 444, 6 Serg. & Rawle 429 (Supreme Court of Pennsylvania, April, 1821), at p. 9.
54 *Blanchard v Page* 8 Gray 281, 74 Mass. 281, 1857 WL 5865 (Supreme Court of Massachusetts, March Term, 1857).
55 *Menzo W. Finn v Western Railroad Corp.* 112 Mass. 524, 1873 WL 9026 (Supreme Court of Massachusetts, September Term, 1873).
56 *Blanchard v Page* 8 Gray 281, 74 Mass. 281, 1857 WL 5865 (Supreme Court of Massachusetts, March Term, 1857), at p. 288.
57 *Blanchard v Page* 8 Gray 281, 74 Mass. 281, 1857 WL 5865 (Supreme Court of Massachusetts, March Term, 1857), at pp. 293 and 295.

responsibility, unless he has some special authority or directions from the purchaser, upon which he acts."[58]

In the late 19th and 20th century, the agency theory disappeared below the radar, only to resurface again in the 1990's. By that time, several decisions had held that 'federal maritime law embraces the general principles of agency law', mostly in relation to the question whether a freight forwarder or NVOCC should be considered an agent of the shipper.[59] In the 1992 decision in *Nebraska Wine & Spirits, Inc. v Burlington Northern Railroad Co.*,[60] the court extended this maxim to the relation between shipper and consignee, holding that the purchase of a consignment of wine to be shipped from Italy to the USA included authorization to the seller and importer to arrange the shipment of the wine, thus making the latter the agents of the buyer/consignee.[61] Three years later, the court in *U.S. v M/V Santa Clara*[62] went even further by citing and applying Saul Sorkin's position in his book on *Goods in Transit* that:

> "*The general rule is that where a consignee purchases merchandise from a seller and authorizes the seller to ship the goods, the seller as shipper or consignor is the consignee's agent for the purpose of shipping. The shipper or consignor is impliedly authorized to enter into the usual and customary transportation contract with the carrier, and the consignee is bound by such terms.*[63]

This 'general rule' was subsequently also accepted and applied in *The Burlington Northern and Santa Fe Railway Co. v Interdom Partners Ltd.*[64] and *Taisheng International Ltd. v Eagle Maritime Services, Inc.*[65]

---

58 *Menzo W. Finn v Western Railroad Corp.* 112 Mass. 524, 1873 WL 9026 (Supreme Court of Massachusetts, September Term, 1873), at p. 534.
59 See, for instance, *Kirno Hill Corp. v Holt* 618 F.2d 982 (C.A.N.Y., 31 March 1980), *West India Industries, Inc. v Vance & Sons AMC-Jeep* 671 F.2d 1384 (C.A.Tex., 9 April 1982), *Naviera Neptuno S.A. v All Intern. Freight Forwarders, Inc.* 709 F.2d 663 (C.A.Fla., 11 July 1983).
60 *Nebraska Wine & Spirits, Inc. v Burlington Northern Railroad Co.* 1992 WL 328938 (W.D.Missouri, 29 September 1992).
61 See also *Kanematsu Corp. v M/V Gretchen W* 897 F.Supp. 1314 (D. Oregon, 15 September 1995), where the Magistrate Judge found that the shipper had acted as an agent for the consignee, because the sales contract between the shipper and the consignee required the shipper to ship the goods to the consignee.
62 *United States v M/V Santa Clara I* 887 F.Supp. 825, 41 ERC 1101, 1996 A.M.C. 910, 64 USLW 2016, 26 Envtl. L. Rep 20,624 (D.South Carolina, 8 May 1995).
63 The text is a quote from S. Sorkin, *Goods in Transit*, Vol. 1, Matthew Bender, loose-leaf, § 2.01[9].
64 *The Burlington Northern and Santa Fe Railway Co. v Interdom Partners LtdLtd* 2004 WL 734081 (N.D.Tex. 26 March 2004).
65 *Taisheng International Ltd v Eagle Maritime Services, Inc.* 2006 WL 846380 (S.D.Tex. 30 March 2006).

46   *Contractual theories*

In 2004, however, the U.S. Supreme Court in *Norfolk Southern Railway Co. v Kirby*, having to decide on the position of a transport intermediary, explicitly rejected the respondents suggestion to fashion a rule from general agency law principles and stated that reliance on agency law was misplaced.[66] The Court held that the traditional indicia of agency, a fiduciary relationship and effective control by the principal, did not exist between the shipper and the intermediary, and that the latter could only be considered the agent of the shipper for a single, limited purpose: to agree on limitation of liability with subsequent carriers.

Following *Kirby*, the court in *In re M/V Rickmers Genoa Litigation* explicitly held that agency can only be assumed in the limited context identified in *Kirby* and does not extend to consignor/consignee relationships.[67] Similarly, in *APL Co. Pte. Ltd. v Kemira Water Solutions, Inc.* the court held that a purchase agreement, although imposing certain obligations on the seller related to the shipment of the goods, does not in and of itself establish an agency relationship.[68]

25 The agency theory as it existed in the UK and the USA has never held much sway on the continent, with some limited exceptions. In the Netherlands, the Amsterdam Court in 1840 held that 'as a general rule', the shipper of the goods is to be considered the agent of the consignee.[69] The consignee was therefore

---

66   *Norfolk Southern Railway Co. v Kirby* 543 US 14 (Supreme Court, 9 November 2004), at p. 34.
67   *In re M/V Rickmers Genoa Litigation* 622 F.Supp.2d 56, 2009 A.M.C. 609 (S.D. New York, 31 March 2009), fn. 23: "*As an aside, I reject the Non-Moving Parties' argument that I should automatically assume an agency relationship existed between* [consignee] *and* [shipper]. *It is true that intermediaries, such as NVOCCs, may be assumed to be acting as agents for shippers, but only insofar as the agents contract to limit carriers' liability downstream. See Norfolk, 543 US at 33, 125 S.Ct. 385. Agency is only to be assumed in this limited context, and the assumption does not extend to consignor/consignee relationships. (. . .) If taken literally, the notion that consignors and consignees can be assumed to be in a principal/agent relationship would expose consignees to potentially limitless liability for the conduct and contracts of their consignors. Clearly that cannot be the case. Rather, agency theories of liability must be considered on a case-by-case basis and should not be assumed.*"
68   *APL Co. Pte. Ltd v Kemira Water Solutions, Inc.* 890 F.Supp.2d 360 (S.D.N.Y., 22 August 2012). The court in support of its decision cites *Professional Communications, Inc. v Contract Freighters, Inc.* 171 F.Supp.2d 546 (D.Md. 17 October 2001), a road carriage case in which the court held that "*A mere contract to ship goods does not establish an agency relationship*".
    See also S. Geense, "De 'merchant-clausule'", *NTHR* 2011-5, 190, at pp. 200–201.
69   A.R. Amsterdam, 20 November 1840, *W* N° 144 (4 January 1841) (*De Goede Hoop*): "*dat ook een contract van be- en vervrachting ten opzigte van de geconsigneerden eener lading eene verbindtenis is tusschen derden aangegaan, daar toch in den algemeinen regel en behoudens enkele uitzonderingen, die ten deze niet bestaan, de bevrachters of afzenders eener lading als lasthebbers der ontvangers of geconsigneerden moeten beschouwd worden, en bij gevolg hunne lastgevers jegens den schipper door de cherte-partij verbinden*" (that furthermore a charter party contract is a contract between third parties as regards the consignees of a cargo, since in general and save for some exceptions, that are not present here, the charterers or shippers of a cargo must be considered the agents of the consignees, and thus bind their principals vis-à-vis the Master by the charter party).
    See also M. Spanjaart, *Vorderingsrechten uit cognossement*, Zutphen, Uitgeverij Paris, 2012, at p. 34.

considered bound by the laytime provisions that the shipper had agreed with the carrier, but were not included in the bill of lading. The decision was confirmed by the Dutch Supreme Court (*Hoge Raad*), but on slightly different grounds and without an express repetition or confirmation of the agency theory.[70] The contemporary authors were divided. De Pinto approved the agency solution,[71] while Polak rejected it as a general rule, although allowing the agency concept a role in certain specific circumstances.[72] In France also, the shipper has occasionally been held to be the agent of the consignee.[73] In Germany, the agency theory has been proposed in the Staub/Canaris Commentary to the Commercial Code,[74] but their position has remained an isolated one.[75]

---

70 HR 26 November 1841, *W* 249 (6 January 1842) (*De Goede Hoop*). The Supreme Court held that the carrier's undertaking to deliver the goods to the consignee is subject to the condition that the carrier will be paid by the consignee the freight and other charges that the carrier agreed with the shipper, even if that agreement only appears in the charter party and not in the bill of lading.
71 A. De Pinto, *Handleiding tot het Wetboek van Koophandel*, Vol. 2, Part 2, The Hague, J. Belinfante, 1842, at pp. 254–255.
72 A. Polak, *Historisch-juridisch onderzoek naar den aard van het cognossement*, Amsterdam, Gebroeders Binger, 1865, at p. 263.
73 Trib. civ. Tunis, 14 November 1889, *RIDM* Vol. V (1889–90) 698: "*qu'en signant le connaissement l'expéditeur agit et stipule pour le compte du destinataire; que celui-ci, en acceptant le connaissement et en se présentant porteur de cet acte, pour réclamer la marchandise, accepte par cela même de se substituer à l'expéditeur vis-à-vis de la Compagnie des transports*" (that in signing the bill of lading the shipper acts and provides on behalf of the consignee; that the latter, by accepting the bill of lading and by presenting that document to claim delivery of the goods, thereby accepts to succeed to the shipper vis-à-vis the transport company).
   Cour d'Appel d'Alger, 7 February 1891, *RIDM* Vol. VII (1891–92) 23. The Court explicitly holds the shipper to be the agent of the consignee, but only to create the legal link required for the consignee to claim delivery from the carrier and for the carrier to claim payment of the freight from the consignee, not to accept a jurisdiction clause: "*Considérant que si cette clause lie le chargeur et la compagnie qui l'ont signée, elle ne saurait, étrangère au destinataire, être invoquée contre lui, le chargeur n'ayant mandat ni légal, ni conventionnel pour consentir à son encontre cette dérogation aux lois de compétence; qu'il convient de dire que si les effets du connaissement se trouvent nécessairement limités entre transporteur et destinataire, dans l'obligation pour le transporteur de faire remise de la marchandise au destinataire, et, pour ce dernier, d'en payer le fret, c'est pour la seule création de ce lien de droit que le chargeur représente le destinataire, et que son mandat ainsi limité ne saurait être étendu à des stipulations auxquelles le destinataire demeurerait étranger.*" (Considering that although this clause binds the shipper and the company that have signed it, it could not bind the consignee, who is a stranger to it; the shipper does not have the power, neither in law nor contractually, to agree to this derogation from the laws on jurisdiction; it must be said that the effects of the bill of lading between the carrier and the consignee are necessarily limited to the obligation for the carrier to deliver the goods to the consignee, and for the latter to pay the freight, it is only to create that legal relationship that the shipper represents the consignee, and his power, thus limited, could not be extended to provisions to which the consignee remains a stranger).
74 C.-W. Canaris, W. Schilling and P. Ulmer (Eds), *Handelsgesetzbuch Großkommentar, begründet von Hermann Staub*, Berlin, De Gruyter, 2001 (4th Ed.), § 363 n° 58–59 at pp. 64–65.
75 W. Bayer, *Der Vertrag zugunsten Dritter*, Tübingen, J.C.B. Mohr (Paul Siebeck), 1995, at pp. 179–180; R. Herber (Ed.), *Münchener Kommentar zum Handelsgesetzbuch*, Vol. 7, *Transportrecht*, München, Verlag C.H. Beck, 2014 (3rd Ed.), n° 9 at p. 984.

48 *Contractual theories*

26 A peculiar variation of the agency theory is to be found in France, where the majority position is that the contract of carriage is a three-party contract, involving the shipper, the carrier and the consignee.[76] Usually, the contract of carriage is thought to *become* a three-party contract at some stage in its existence, but there are also authors who see the contract of carriage as a three-party contract from the very moment it comes into being. In practice, however, the consignee is not physically present during the making of the contract. That difficulty is solved by having the shipper act as the agent of the consignee.[77] In this theory, therefore, the shipper acts in a *double* capacity when entering into the contract of carriage: he makes the contract both on his own behalf, as shipper, *and* on behalf of the consignee, as agent of the latter.[78]

27 Finally, in a number of cases the shipper has been considered the agent or trustee of the consignee in filing a (cargo) claim against and recovering damages from the carrier.[79] This position, however, has more to do with protecting the carrier against a second suit, should it turn out that it was in fact the consignee who was the real party in interest, than with explaining the legal position of the bill of lading holder.

3.1.2.4 *When does the relationship come into being?*

28 Under the law of agency, the agent acts on behalf of the principal. The agent's actions are imputed to the principal, and the legal relationship immediately and directly comes into being between the principal and the party that the agent has dealt with.

In a bill of lading context, this means that there is not first a contract of carriage between the agent and the carrier, which is then at a later stage somehow transferred to or taken over by the principal. The contract of carriage, negotiated by the shipper as agent of the consignee, is from the very start a contract between

---

76 See below, n° 104 p. 99.
77 V.-E. Bokalli, "Crise et avenir du connaissement", *D.M.F.* 1998, at p. 125.
    See also C. Smeesters and G. Winkelmolen, *Droit maritime et Droit fluvial*, Vol. I, Brussels, Larcier, 1929 (2nd Ed.), n° 444 at p. 603: "*Mais si, d'une part, l'affreteur seul a contracté avec le capitaine, d'autre part, en adressant la marchandise au destinataire, il stipule non seulement pour lui-même, mais aussi pour le destinataire, dont il est le mandataire, le negotiorum gestor.*" (But if, on the one hand, only the shipper has contracted with the Master, on the other hand, by shipping the goods to the consignee, he contracts not only for himself, but also for the consignee, of whom he is the agent, the *negotiorum gestor*.)
78 Compare P. Rodière, "Cass. fr. 21 November 1978", *La Semaine Juridique, JCP* 1980, 643 (note), at p. 645.
79 *Menzo W. Finn v Western Railroad Corp.* 112 Mass. 524, 1873 WL 9026 (Supreme Court of Massachusetts, September Term, 1873).
    See also W. Tetley, *Marine Cargo Claims*, Vol. 1, Cowansville, Les Editions Yvon Blais, 2008 (4th Ed.), at p. 455.
    Contra: C. Cashmore, *Parties to a Contract of Carriage, or Who Can Sue on a Contract of Carriage of Goods?* London, Lloyd's of London Press, 1990, at p. 124.

Contractual theories 49

the carrier and the consignee. The shipper (agent) on the other hand is *not* a party to the contract of carriage, unless explicitly agreed otherwise.

3.1.2.5 Intermediate holders

29 The agency theory does not have an easy answer for the position of intermediate holders. In the first version of the theory, where the consignee is considered to be the agent of the shipper, this arrangement would ordinarily preclude the consignee from selling on the goods and the bill of lading. Even if, in theory, the consignee's authority as agent could conceivably extend to selling the goods, that would then give rise to a contract of sale between the shipper and the ultimate buyer, with no legal basis or reason to construe the latter as an agent of the shipper. The ultimate buyer will claim delivery of the goods at destination, but on his own behalf, because he has bought the goods from the shipper.

30 The second version of the agency theory, where the shipper is considered to be the agent of the consignee, is based on the inference that a contract of carriage is made by the owner of the goods, and a second inference that the consignee is the owner of the goods. That is, however, not necessarily correct, not even in a 'simple' situation with only a shipper and a consignee.[80] The presence of intermediate holders only exacerbates the problem. It is one thing to say that when A sells goods to B, B as (prospective) owner of the goods is the party that makes the contract of carriage with the carrier, with A acting as his agent for the negotiation of the contract, it is another thing still to say that if B sells on the goods to C and C to D, A is then supposed to have acted as an agent for D, whose identity and even existence was completely unknown to A at the time of his dealing with the carrier, and may well remain unknown to A forever. That would be a very strange form of agency indeed. In this view, there are only three parties involved: the ultimate consignee, the carrier and the shipper. Intermediate holders of the bill of lading are left out of the picture entirely; they are not parties to the contract of carriage, and thus have no rights or obligations under this contract. The alternative view would be to say that the contract of carriage is presumed to be made by the party to which the shipper/seller sells the goods and transfers the title, i.e. the *first* intermediate holder of the bill of lading (B). The contract of carriage would then be made by B with the carrier, with the shipper (A) acting as B's agent. If that is correct, however, what is then the position of the later and ultimate holders of the bill of lading (C and D)? They are not contracting parties

---

80 See for a discussion of the problems that this causes for the agency theory C. Cashmore, *Parties to a Contract of Carriage, or Who Can Sue on a Contract of Carriage of Goods?* London, Lloyd's of London Press, 1990, at pp. 113–121. The shipper is presumed to act as an agent for the owner of the goods, but the owner at which point in time? The owner of the goods at the time the shipper makes the contract of carriage, at the time the goods are handed over to the carrier, at the time of the loss or damage, or at the time of delivery? None of these possibilities perfectly solves the problem.

50 *Contractual theories*

of the carrier, and they can hardly be considered agents of B either. Their position cannot be explained by the agency theory.

3.1.2.6 *Appraisal*

31 It is, of course, possible, and it undoubtedly happens in practice even today that the shipper is indeed the agent of the consignee or vice versa.[81] Imagine, for instance, a company that ships goods to or from a subsidiary. In such circumstances, it may be that the subsidiary is, in law, acting as an agent for the parent company, although even then, it will have to be shown that the parent company intended to grant authority to the subsidiary to act on its behalf. As a general theory to explain the position of a third-party holder, however, the agency theory is not satisfactory.[82]

32 In this respect, it should be pointed out that the agency theory did not start out as a theory to explain the position of the third-party holder of the bill of lading. The agency theory, initially, was a solution developed to solve the problem of title to sue.[83] In the early days of commercial shipping, it was more often than not the shipper who actually negotiated the contract of carriage with the carrier (if only because the means of communication at the time did not allow the consignee to efficiently arrange the carriage from his end). If, however, the shipper was the contracting party of the carrier, the privity rules of the common law, together with the fact that a contract of carriage was not assignable under common law, meant that only the shipper could have sued the carrier for loss of or damage to the carried goods, and not the consignee. In those early days of less sophisticated sales contracts, however, title and risk to the goods commonly passed to the buyer/consignee upon delivery of the goods to the carrier. The end result thus would have been that the shipper could sue the carrier, but did not suffer the loss, while the consignee, who did suffer the loss, could not sue the carrier. It is in order to solve this problem that the presumption developed that a contract of carriage is made by the owner of the goods, i.e. generally the consignee. If it is indeed the consignee that is the contracting party of the carrier, then obviously the consignee has title to sue the carrier for loss of or damage to his goods. This solution to the title to sue problem however created another problem. If it is the consignee that enters into the contract of carriage, what then

---

81 Compare *Evergreen Marine Corporation v Aldgate Warehouse (Wholesale) Ltd* [2003] EWHC 667, 2003 WL 1610235 (Queen's Bench Division (Commercial Court), 28 March 2003), at n° 29: "*In general it can be presumed that the contract of carriage is made with the person named as shipper, but the evidence may show that the nominal shipper contracted as agent for a third party, in which case the contract will be with his principal.*"
82 Compare J. Cooke et al., *Voyage Charters*, London, Informa, 2007 (3rd Ed.), n° 18.77 at p. 481: "(. . .) *it may sometimes be inferred that the shipper acts as agent for the named consignee. However, the general rule is that a party who procures shipment for the ultimate benefit of a consignee does not thereby contract with the carrier as agent of the consignee.*"
83 S. Peel, "The development of the bill of lading: its future in the maritime industry", 2002, thesis submitted to the University of Plymouth, Institute of Marine Studies, at p. 143.

is the role of the shipper? This (secondary) problem was conveniently solved by making the shipper into an agent of the consignee. This, of course, is a very biased approach.[84] It does not start with an analysis of the legal position of the different parties, to then deduct from that position their rights and obligations (including title to sue), it starts with the clear intention to grant one of the parties (the consignee) title to sue, to then look for legal theories that will allow this predefined result.

33 Agency, furthermore, must be proven. It must be shown that the principal granted actual or implied authority to the agent to act on his behalf, and that the agent accepted to act on the principal's behalf. The fact that the actions of a party also benefit, or even exclusively benefit another party does not in and of itself prove that this party acts as an agent. A car salesman who informs a potential buyer of the financing possibilities with a selected bank, and maybe even helps his customer to fill out the forms, does not by doing so become an agent, in the legal sense of the term, of the bank, although his actions are clearly beneficial to the bank. It is true, of course, that the courts have the power to apply the correct legal qualification to the relationship that exists between two parties, and that the courts may indeed find an agency relationship even if the parties themselves did not term their relationship that way, or maybe even didn't realize that they were creating an agency relationship between themselves,[85] but this power is limited to correctly *qualifying* an existing relationship between the parties. The courts cannot *create* a legal relationship that did not exist before.

In a bill of lading context, it is clear that the shipper's actions in making the contract of carriage with the carrier also benefit the consignee. Without a contract of carriage, the goods that he is expecting would not arrive at destination. From there, it is not too big a step to argue that the consignee, in accepting to buy goods that have to be shipped, has impliedly given authority to the seller to enter into a contract of carriage on his behalf. It is submitted, however, that this does not correspond to the real intentions of the parties, certainly not when they have agreed in the contract of sale that the seller would take care of the carriage.[86] When the goods are sold during the voyage, i.e. at a time that the contract of carriage has already been made, it is even more difficult to explain how the later buyer/holder of the bill of lading could have given authority to the shipper to negotiate a contract of carriage at a time when he was not interested yet in the

---

84 Compare *Menzo W. Finn v Western Railroad Corp.* 112 Mass. 524, 1873 WL 9026 (Supreme Court of Massachusetts, September Term, 1873) at p. 531: "*In discussing the grounds of decision it seems to have been assumed by various judges, as we think, erroneously, that the right of recovery necessarily involved the question with whom the original contract of service was made. And the effort to make the inference of law as to that contract conform to what was deemed the proper decision as to the right to recover for injury, has led to some statements of legal inference which appear to us to be somewhat overstrained.*"
85 See also above, n° 66.
86 Compare G. Ripert, *Droit Maritime*, Tôme II, Paris, Editions Rousseau et Cie., 1952 (4th Ed.), n° 1586 at p. 494.

goods or their carriage.[87] Furthermore, it is worth mentioning that even a (limited) involvement of the consignee in the performance of the carriage does not necessarily prove that the consignee acted as principal. In *Evergreen Marine Corporation v Aldgate Warehouse (Wholesale) Ltd*, Moore-Bick J held that the fact that from time to time the consignee gave instructions about the handling of the goods and the stuffing of containers did not support the conclusion that the consignee was the original contracting party, but simply reflected the fact that the consignee, as buyer and ultimate receiver, had an interest in ensuring that the consignment was dispatched in an appropriate manner.[88]

34 It is sometimes argued in defence of the agency theory that the carrier 'knows nothing' about the shipper, and only knows the consignee.[89] By making the consignee the principal and thus the party to have contracted with the carrier, the agency theory would in fact serve to protect the interests of the carrier. It is submitted that this is a historic argument, which no longer holds true in this day and age. On the contrary, the carrier today is probably more aware of the status and financial position of the shipper than of that of the consignee, who usually collects the goods from a stevedore or storage company some time after the ship has already left the port.

35 Another argument to support the agency theory is based on Sect. 32 of the UK Sale of Goods Act 1979. Sect. 32 (1) provides that where the seller is authorized or required to send the goods to the buyer, the delivery of the goods to the carrier is presumed to be a delivery to the buyer.[90] The carriage, therefore, is carried out on behalf of the buyer. In addition, section 32 (2) expressly provides that the seller must make a contract with the carrier "... *on behalf of the buyer*".[91] These provisions confirm, it is argued, that the shipper, when he makes the contract of carriage, does so as an agent of the consignee. The focus of the Act, however, is on the sale of goods and the rights and obligations of the parties under the contract of sale, and not on ancillary contracts that have to be made to

---

87 R. De Wit, *Multimodal Transport: Carrier Liability and Documentation*, London, Lloyd's of London Press, 1995, n° 5.2 at p. 244.
   See also above, n° 77–78, on the difficulties that intermediate holders pose under the agency theory.
88 *Evergreen Marine Corporation v Aldgate Warehouse (Wholesale) Ltd* [2003] EWHC 667, 2003 WL 1610235 (Queen's Bench Division (Commercial Court), 28 March 2003), at n° 39.
89 C. Cashmore, *Parties to a Contract of Carriage, or Who Can Sue on a Contract of Carriage of Goods?* London, Lloyd's of London Press, 1990, at p. 106.
90 Sect. 32 (1) of the Sales of Goods Act 1979 reads as follows: "*Where, in pursuance of a contract of sale, the seller is authorised or required to send the goods to the buyer, delivery of the goods to a carrier (whether named by the buyer or not) for the purpose of transmission to the buyer is prima facie deemed to be a delivery of the goods to the buyer.*"
91 Sect. 32 (2) of the Sales of Goods Act 1979 reads as follows: "*Unless otherwise authorised by the buyer, the seller must make such contract with the carrier on behalf of the buyer as may be reasonable having regard to the nature of the goods and the other circumstances of the case; and if the seller omits to do so, and the goods are lost or damaged in course of transit, the buyer may decline to treat the delivery to the carrier as a delivery to himself or may hold the seller responsible in damages.*"

perform certain obligations under the contract of sale. Where the Act speaks of the contract of carriage being made 'on behalf of the buyer', it uses those words in a general, commercial sense, not to provide that, by law, the seller/ shipper is to be seen as the agent of the buyer.[92]

36 The agency theory, furthermore, has the disadvantage of taking the shipper out of the equation. If indeed the shipper is making the contract of carriage as agent for a disclosed principal (the consignee), he himself is *not* a party to the contract of carriage, and thus cannot sue nor be sued upon this contract. From the carrier's point of view, who may want to sue the shipper for freight, demurrage or other costs, this problem could be solved by explicitly providing in the contract that the agent (the shipper) will personally be liable, together with his principal, for the obligations under the contract of carriage. Most bills of lading do, in fact, contain a 'Merchant Clause' that seeks to make as large a group of people as possible liable under the bill of lading. From the shipper's point of view, who may want to sue the carrier for loss or damage in case the consignee is unable to do so, the problem could, in theory, also be solved contractually – except that in practice, clauses to such effect are very uncommon, if they exist at all. Also, if the bill of lading were to provide that the agent (shipper) is both personally liable under the bill of lading and entitled to sue upon the bill of lading, the end result would be closer to a three-party contract than to an agency situation.

37 Finally, the agency theory has a hard time explaining how the shipper can have the right to redirect the goods or even to stop them during transit, if he is only an agent of the consignee. It goes without saying that an agent cannot act against the instructions of his principal, or at least will not be vindicated in court if he does try to do so. The shipper, on the other hand, as long as he continues to hold the bill of lading, is generally accepted to have the right to give instructions to the carrier, even over opposition of the consignee. The right of 'stoppage in transitu' is a prime example of this power. Such power, however, would not have come into being and would not have become generally accepted if, as a general rule, the shipper was only the agent of the consignee.[93]

---

[92] Compare M. Bridge, *The Sale of Goods*, Oxford, Oxford University Press, 2009 (2nd Ed.), n° 4.16 at p. 164: "*Section 32(2) should apply regardless of whether the seller contracts with the carrier as principal or as agent for the buyer.*" If there is a possibility for the seller to be acting as principal, then Sect. 32 (2) cannot mean that the seller should, by law, be considered the agent of the buyer.
  G. Treitel, "Overseas sales in general", in *Benjamin's Sale of Goods*, London, Sweet & Maxwell, 2006 (7th Ed.), *Benjamin's Sale of Goods*, London, Sweet & Maxwell, 1987 (3rd Ed.) n° 18–245 at p. 1352 mentions that under some FOB contracts, the buyer may become a party to the contract of carriage, even though this contract was made by the seller (referring to *Pyrene Co. Ltd v Scindia Navigation Co. Ltd*), but without expressly stating that this would be because the seller acts as an agent for the buyer.

[93] Compare G. Treitel, "Overseas sales in general", in *Benjamin's Sale of Goods*, London, Sweet & Maxwell, 2006 (7th Ed.), n° 18–021 at p. 1140.

3.1.3 Assignment of rights

(cession (de créance), overdracht (van schuldvordering), Abtretung)

3.1.3.1 The concept

38 Assignment refers to the transfer of contractual rights, and possibly contractual obligations, from one party to another.

39 Both civil law and common law allow the parties to a contract to assign rights under this contract to a third party. Assigning obligations or burdens, on the other hand, is in principle not possible, although there are (quasi-) exceptions to this rule.

40 Civil law sees rights and claims under a contract as (non-corporeal) assets of a person, that can be sold and transferred as corporeal assets can be.[94] So for instance the seller of goods who assigns his right to be paid the sales price to a credit company. Consent of the debtor (the buyer in the example) is not required,[95] but the assignment must be notified to the debtor for him to be bound by the assignment. Before the notification, the debtor validly discharges his obligation by paying to the original creditor.[96] In several legal systems, the requirements regarding the notification have become less stringent over time, with basically now any form of (provable) notification being acceptable.[97] Assignment of rights is, in principle, always possible, except in case of a contract *intuitu personae*, i.e. a contract in which the identity of the one party is relevant and of interest to the other party, or when the law or the contract itself precludes assignment of the rights under the contract.[98] Assignment implies a *transfer* of rights from the assignor (the seller in the example) to the assignee (the credit company). The assignor thus no longer has these rights, and the assignee takes them as they

---

[94] L. Cornelis, *Algemene theorie van de verbintenis*, Antwerpen, Intersentia, 2000, at p. 397; W. Van Gerven and S. Covemaeker, *Verbintenissenrecht*, Leuven, Acco, 2006 (2nd Ed.), at pp. 566–567.

[95] W. Van Gerven and S. Covemaeker, *Verbintenissenrecht*, Leuven, Acco, 2006 (2nd Ed.), at p. 565.

[96] Ph. Malaurie, L. Aynès and Ph. Stoffel-Munck, *Les obligations*, Paris, Defrénois, 2011 (5th Ed.), n° 1414 at p. 762; W. Van Gerven and S. Covemaeker, *Verbintenissenrecht*, Leuven, Acco, 2006 (2nd Ed.), at p. 575.

[97] Before 1994, Article 1690 of the Belgian Civil Code required the assignment to be served upon the debtor or to be accepted by him in a notarized document. This provision was amended by the Act of 6 July 1994, and now only requires that the debtor be informed of the assignment or that the assignment be accepted by the debtor.

See L. Cornelis, *Algemene theorie van de verbintenis*, Antwerpen, Intersentia, 2000, at pp. 421–422; W. Van Gerven and S. Covemaeker, *Verbintenissenrecht*, Leuven, Acco, 2006 (2nd Ed.), at pp. 569–571.

In France, Article 1690 still survives in its original form. See Ph. Malaurie, L. Aynès and Ph. Stoffel-Munck, *Les obligations*, Paris, Defrénois, 2011 (5th Ed.), n° 1411 at p. 760.

[98] L. Cornelis, *Algemene theorie van de verbintenis*, Antwerpen, Intersentia, 2000, at pp. 413–414; W. Van Gerven and S. Covemaeker, *Verbintenissenrecht*, Leuven, Acco, 2006 (2nd Ed.), at p. 565.

This principle is confirmed in Article 3:83 of the Dutch Civil Code.

existed for the assignor, with their characteristics (such as contractual time bars) and 'defects' (such as defences available to the debtor).[99]

41 With regard to the assignment of obligations, civil law distinguishes between a 'complete' or 'perfect' assignment and an 'incomplete' or 'imperfect' assignment. A 'complete' assignment requires the consent of the creditor, and entirely replaces the original debtor with the new debtor, thus releasing the original debtor from his obligations under the contract. The contract continues to exist as it was made, but with a new debtor.[100] It thus follows that the new debtor can invoke all contractual defences that the original debtor could have invoked. An 'incomplete' assignment on the other hand does not require the creditor's consent, but does not release the original debtor. The assignment of the obligation is valid and binding between the assignor (the original debtor) and the assignee (the new debtor), but does not bind the creditor.[101] The original debtor remains liable under the contract and can be actioned by the creditor if the assignee does not correctly perform the obligation. On the other hand, the assignment cannot be invoked by the creditor either. The creditor does not have an action against the assignee, unless the assignment contains a third-party beneficiary clause in favour of the creditor. Even an 'incomplete' assignment is not possible, however, in case of a contract *intuitu personae*.

42 Finally, civil law knows the concept of 'delegation'. In the delegation scenario, the original debtor (B) nominates an additional debtor (C). If C accepts this nomination, a new relation springs up between C (the 'delegated debtor') and the creditor (A), but the original contract between A and B also remains in place.[102],[103]

---

99 Belgium: L. Cornelis, *Algemene theorie van de verbintenis*, Antwerpen, Intersentia, 2000, at p. 397 and p. 415; W. Van Gerven and S. Covemaeker, *Verbintenissenrecht*, Leuven, Acco, 2006 (2nd Ed.), at p. 575.
    France: Ph. Malaurie, L. Aynès and Ph. Stoffel-Munck, *Les obligations*, Paris, Defrénois, 2011 (5th Ed.), n° 1417 at pp. 765–766.
    The Netherlands: Article 6:145 of the Dutch Civil Code; J. Cahen, *Algemeen deel van het verbintenissenrecht*, Deel 4 van Pitlo, *Het Nederlands burgerlijk recht*, Deventer, Kluwer, 2002 (9e Ed.), n° 129 at pp. 114–117.
100 Belgium: W. Van Gerven and S. Covemaeker, *Verbintenissenrecht*, Leuven, Acco, 2006 (2nd Ed.), at p. 582.
    Netherlands: Article 6:155 of the Dutch Civil Code; J. Cahen, *Algemeen deel van het verbintenissenrecht*, Deel 4 van Pitlo, *Het Nederlands burgerlijk recht*, Deventer, Kluwer, 2002 (9th Ed.), n° 138 at p. 121 and n° 140 at pp. 122–123.
101 L. Cornelis, *Algemene theorie van de verbintenis*, Antwerpen, Intersentia, 2000, at p. 397; W. Van Gerven and S. Covemaeker, *Verbintenissenrecht*, Leuven, Acco, 2006 (2nd Ed.), at pp. 581–582.
    Ph. Malaurie, L. Aynès and Ph. Stoffel-Munck, *Les obligations*, Paris, Defrénois, 2011 (5th Ed.), n° 799 at p. 411; B. Starck, H. Roland and L. Boyer, *Obligations*, Vol. 2, *Contrat*, Paris, Litec, 1993 (4th Ed.), n° 1376 at p. 575.
102 This is where a delegation differs from a 'complete' assignment. With a 'complete' assignment, the original obligation continues to exist but is swapped over from the original debtor (B) to the new debtor (C), whereas with a delegation the original obligation continues to exist between the creditor (A) and the original debtor (B) and a *new* obligation (be it identical or largely similar in terms to the original obligation) is created between the creditor (A) and the new debtor (C).
103 Belgium: W. Van Gerven and S. Covemaeker, *Verbintenissenrecht*, Leuven, Acco, 2006 (2nd Ed.), at p. 583.

56 *Contractual theories*

The end result is thus a three party and three contract situation: there is the original contract between the creditor (A) and the original ('delegating') debtor (B), there is the new contract that springs up between the creditor (A) and the new ('delegated') debtor (C), and there is the underlying contract between B and C that is the cause of C's accepting to become a debtor. The new contract between A and C is independent from the original contract between A and B. The new debtor (C) is thus not entitled to invoke defences arising from the original contract.[104]

43 Common law initially did not know the assignment of 'things (choses) in action', i.e. intangible personal property rights that can only be claimed or enforced by legal action, or essentially a right to sue (as opposed to 'things in possession', i.e. tangible property that can be physically possessed).[105] In 1873, however, statutory assignment of such rights was made possible by section 25(6) of the Judicature Act, now re-enacted by section 136 of the Law of Property Act 1925. Equitable assignment had already been accepted before the Judicature Act, and remains possible to this date.[106] Consent of the debtor is not required,[107] but the assignment must be notified to the debtor for him to be bound by it. As per the text of section 136 of the Law of Property Act 1925, a statutory assignment must be in writing and notified to the debtor in writing to be valid.[108] The validity of an equitable assignment on the other hand does not require a written notice, but a debtor who was not given notice validly pays to the original creditor.[109] Assignment is not possible when the contract itself or statute or public policy exclude assignment, or when the contract is *intuitu personae*.[110] Assignment, once notified, transfers the claim from the original creditor to the new creditor,

---

Netherlands: J. Cahen, *Algemeen deel van het verbintenissenrecht*, Deel 4 van Pitlo, *Het Nederlands burgerlijk recht*, Deventer, Kluwer, 2002 (9th Ed.), n° 141 at p. 125 (who mentions the concept, but without using the term 'delegation').

104 W. Van Gerven and S. Covemaeker, *Verbintenissenrecht*, Leuven, Acco, 2006 (2nd Ed.), at p. 583.
105 G. Tolhurst, *The Assignment of Contractual Rights*, Oxford, Hart Publishing, 2006, at pp. 19–28.
106 *Chitty on Contracts*, Vol. 1, *General Principles*, London, Sweet & Maxwell, 1989 (26th Ed.), n° 1393 at pp. 864–865; A. Guest, *The Law of Assignment*, London, Sweet & Maxwell, 2012, at p. 60 and at p. 85 et seq.; G. Tolhurst, *The Assignment of Contractual Rights*, Oxford, Hart Publishing, 2006, at pp. 65 et seq.
  See also C. Cashmore, *Parties to a Contract of Carriage, or Who Can Sue on a Contract of Carriage of Goods?* London, Lloyd's of London Press, 1990, fn. 31 at p. 83.
107 *Chitty on Contracts*, Vol. 1, *General Principles*, London, Sweet & Maxwell, 1989 (26th Ed.), n° 1427 at p. 894.
108 *Chitty on Contracts*, Vol. 1, *General Principles*, London, Sweet & Maxwell, 1989 (26th Ed.), n° 1399 at pp. 870–871; A. Guest, *The Law of Assignment*, London, Sweet & Maxwell, 2012, n° 2–21 at p. 77.
109 *Chitty on Contracts*, Vol. 1, *General Principles*, London, Sweet & Maxwell, 1989 (26th Ed.), n° 1401 at p. 872; A. Guest, *The Law of Assignment*, London, Sweet & Maxwell, 2012, n° 3–58 at pp. 130–131; G. Tolhurst, *The Assignment of Contractual Rights*, Oxford, Hart Publishing, 2006, n° 8.06 at p. 386.
110 *Chitty on Contracts*, Vol. 1, *General Principles*, London, Sweet & Maxwell, 1989 (26th Ed.), n° 1412–1418 at pp. 882–889; A. Guest, *The Law of Assignment*, London, Sweet &

who takes it 'subject to equities',[111] meaning (in general) that a set-off or counterclaim that the debtor could have invoked against the original creditor before the notification can also be invoked against the new creditor.[112]

44 With regard to the assignment of obligations, common law is in substance very similar to civil law, but with a different terminology. As in civil law, a debtor cannot simply substitute another debtor and expect the creditor to be bound by such substitution. The transfer of a debt or burden, with release of the original debtor, requires the consent of the creditor.[113] Whereas civil law sees such a 'complete' or 'perfect' assignment as a transfer of the original, existing contract to a new debtor, however, common law rather conceptualizes this operation as a novation: the original contract between the creditor and the original debtor is extinguished and replaced by a new contract between the creditor and the new debtor.[114] As the new debtor is bound by a new contract, the terms and conditions of this new contract may be different from those that had been agreed between the creditor and the original debtor. The 'incomplete' or 'imperfect' assignment of the civil law is known as 'vicarious performance' in common law. Unless the contract is *intuitu personae*, the debtor can agree with a third party that the latter will perform the debtor's obligations under his contract with the creditor.[115] Such an agreement is valid and binding between the debtor and the third party, but does not bind the creditor, whose consent to the operation is not required.

3.1.3.2 The bill of lading holder as the assignee of the shipper

45 In civil law countries, assignment is occasionally mentioned as a possible solution to explain the position of the bill of lading holder, but usually without much

---

Maxwell, 2012, at pp. 135 et seq.; G. Tolhurst, *The Assignment of Contractual Rights*, Oxford, Hart Publishing, 2006, at pp. 187 et seq.
111 *Chitty on Contracts*, Vol. 1, *General Principles*, London, Sweet & Maxwell, 1989 (26th Ed.), n° 1428 at p. 894; G. Tolhurst, *The Assignment of Contractual Rights*, Oxford, Hart Publishing, 2006, n° 8.49 at p. 426.
112 *Chitty on Contracts*, Vol. 1, *General Principles*, London, Sweet & Maxwell, 1989 (26th Ed.), n° 1428 at pp. 895–896; A. Guest, *The Law of Assignment*, London, Sweet & Maxwell, 2012, at pp. 261 et seq. See also A. Tettenborn, "Assignees, equities and cross-claims: principle and confusion", *LMCLQ* 2002, 485.
113 *Chitty on Contracts*, Vol. 1, *General Principles*, London, Sweet & Maxwell, 1989 (26th Ed.), n° 1430 at p. 897; A. Guest, *The Law of Assignment*, London, Sweet & Maxwell, 2012, n° 9-01 at p. 325.
114 *Chitty on Contracts*, Vol. 1, *General Principles*, London, Sweet & Maxwell, 1989 (26th Ed.), n° 1436 at p. 902; A. Guest, *The Law of Assignment*, London, Sweet & Maxwell, 2012, n° 1-64 at pp. 41–42 and n° 9-01 at p. 325; G. Tolhurst, *The Assignment of Contractual Rights*, Oxford, Hart Publishing, 2006, n° 6.123 at p. 303.
115 *Chitty on Contracts*, Vol. 1, *General Principles*, London, Sweet & Maxwell, 1989 (26th Ed.), n° 1432 at pp. 899–900; A. Guest, *The Law of Assignment*, London, Sweet & Maxwell, 2012, n° 9.16 at pp. 335–337; G. Tolhurst, *The Assignment of Contractual Rights*, Oxford, Hart Publishing, 2006, n° 3.08 at p. 35.

58 *Contractual theories*

conviction.[116] The authors are quicker to point out the difficulties that this theory faces than to defend it. Assignment of rights or claims is often possible in civil law systems, but does not suffice; the holder of the bill of lading not only has rights against the carrier, but is also obliged towards him. Assignment of obligations is less accepted, and requires the consent of the creditor, i.e. the carrier in the case of a contract of carriage. Every negotiation of the bill of lading would thus require the carrier's consent. Assignment of a contract – to the extent that this is considered a separate concept, that is something more or different than an assignment of rights plus an assignment of obligations – also requires the creditor's consent. Furthermore, even a 'simple' assignment of rights requires a notification to the creditor (carrier), and may require a formal agreement between the assignor (the initial holder of the B/L) and the assignee (the subsequent holder). In practice, the negotiation of a bill of lading often does not involve a separate agreement, and notice to the carrier is never given.

46 In the United Kingdom, assignment before the 1873 Judicature Act only existed in equity, and was explicitly rejected with regard to bills of lading. In *Sanders v Vanzeller*,[117] where the consignee was sued by the carrier in payment of freight, Tindal C.J held that the contract of carriage is not transferred together with the property in the goods carried. In *Thompson v Dominy*,[118] the court held that the endorsement of a bill of lading only transfers the property in the goods carried under the bill of lading,[119] but does not transfer the contract and does not enable the consignee to bring an action upon the bill of lading. In *Howard*

---

116 F. Basset, "Droit français du connaissement", in F. Basset, *Droit romain des avaries communes. Droit français du connaissement. Thèse pour le doctorat*, Paris, Arthur Rousseau, 1889, at p. 64; C. Paulin, *Droits des transports*, Paris, Litec, 2005, fn. 69 at p. 232; M. Spanjaart, "The Konnossementsbegebungsvertrag – a suggestion for further reformation", *TransportR* 2011, at p. 336; F. Sparka, *Jurisdiction and Arbitration Clauses in Maritime Transport Documents*, Berlin, Springer, 2010, at p. 178; R. Van Delden, *Overzicht van de handelskoop*, Deventer, Kluwer, 1983, at pp. 418–419.

 R. De Wit, *Multimodal Transport. Carrier Liability and Documentation*, London, Lloyd's of London Press, 1995, n° 5.9–5.10 at pp. 249–250 and n° 5.11 at p. 251 is more positive, selecting the transfer of contract concept as the most sensible answer in civil law systems. J. Trappe, "Zur Schiedsgerichtsklausel im Konnossement", in R. Lagoni and M. Paschke (Eds), *Seehandelsrecht und Seerecht. Festschrift für Rolf Herber zum 70. Geburtstag*, Hamburg, LIT Verlag, 1999, at p. 314 sees the endorsement of a bill of lading as an assignment of both the rights and the obligations of the shipper to the holder of the bill of lading.

 J. Cahen, *Het cognossement*, Arnhem, Gouda Quint, 1964, at p. 5 arrives at an assignment, because he sees the transfer of a negotiable instrument (the bill of lading) as a special form of assignment.

 Ph. Delebecque, *Droit maritime*, Paris, Dalloz, 2014 (13th Ed.), n° 731 at p. 511, simply states that the consignee is not the assignee of the shipper, without further elaboration.

117 *Sanders v Vanzeller* 114 ER 897, 4 QBR 260 (Exchequer Chamber, 2 February 1843).
118 *Thompson v Dominy* 153 ER 532, 14 M7W 403 (Court of Exchequer, 20 June 1845).
119 In those days, the endorsement of a bill of lading was thought to *ipso facto* transfer the property in the goods described in the bill of lading. Only by the end of the 19th century did it become accepted that a bill of lading only represents *possession* of the goods, and that transfer of possession only transfers title if such was the intention of the parties.

v Shepherd,[120] where the consignee sued the carrier for wrongful delivery of the goods to another person, Maule J held that it is perfectly clear that a contract cannot be transferred so as to enable the transferee to sue upon it.[121] As this state of affairs was considered undesirable, however, the Bills of Lading Act was passed in 1855 with the express purpose to have the rights under the contract of carriage passed to the consignee.[122] This Act, although not solving every problem,[123] to a large extent did away with the need for an assignment scenario.[124] Recent authors,[125] however, have pointed out that assignment might still be useful in situations that fall outside the scope of the Bills of Lading Act or its successor, the Carriage of Goods by Sea Act 1992, but not without also pointing out the obstacles that confront the assignment theory. A statutory assignment, for instance, must be in writing, and it is not clear whether an endorsement of the bill of lading satisfies this requirement. Further, notice to the debtor (carrier) must be given with a statutory assignment and is desirable with an equitable assignment, but is in practice never given when a bill of lading is transferred. The assignee takes the rights 'subject to equities', meaning that the carrier will be able to invoke against the assignee the defences he could have invoked against the assignor (shipper). Finally, an assignment is generally an assignment of rights; assignment of liabilities is much less straightforward.

3.1.3.3 *When does the relationship come into being?*

47 Between the assignor (shipper) and assignee (new holder of the bill of lading), an assignment of rights takes effect from the time these parties agree on the assignment or, the case being, from the effective date they agree between themselves. For the debtor (carrier) and other third parties, the assignment is only

---

120 *Howard v Shepherd* 137 ER 907, 9 C.B. 297 (Court of Common Pleas, 16 February 1850).
121 See also *Brandt v Liverpool, Brazil and River Plate Steam Navigation Co. Ltd* [1924] 1 K.B. 575 (Court of Appeal, 19 November 1923), where Scrutton LJ when speaking about the pre 1855 situation said: "*Before the Bills of Lading Act, 1855, was passed, by the custom of merchants the indorsement of the bill of lading passed the property in the goods contained therein, but it did not assign the contract contained therein, and therefore the person who by indorsement became the owner of the goods did not by the same indorsement acquire a right to sue the shipowner upon his contract, which was evidenced in the bill of lading*".
122 The Preamble to the Bills of Lading Act 1855 reads: "*WHEREAS by the Custom of Merchants a Bill of Lading of Goods being transferable by Endorsement the Property in the Goods may thereby pass to the Endorsee, but nevertheless all Rights in respect of the Contract contained in the Bill of Lading continue in the original Shipper or Owner, and it is expedient that such Rights should pass with the Property*".
123 See below, n° 18 p. 157.
124 But see *Glyn Mills Currie & Co. v The East and West India Dock Company* (1882) 7 App Cas 591 (House of Lords, 1 August 1882), where Lord Selborne explicitly explains the transfer of a bill of lading in terms of an assignment (at p. 596).
125 G. Treitel, "Overseas Sales in General", in *Benjamin's Sale of Goods*, London, Sweet & Maxwell, 2006 (7th Ed.), n° 18–097 at pp. 1224–1225 and n° 18–147 at pp. 1275–1277.

binding once they have been notified thereof. For as long as the debtor has not been notified of the assignment, he validly pays to the original creditor.

An assignment of liabilities or of the contract as a whole requires the consent of all parties involved (shipper, new holder of the bill of lading, carrier). It only takes effect upon the agreement of all of these parties, but is then automatically and immediately effective against the carrier also.

3.1.3.4 Intermediate holders

48 If the transfer of a bill of lading is seen as the assignment of rights, intermediate holders do not create much of a problem. The shipper assigns his rights to a first holder (A), who in turn assigns those same rights to a subsequent holder (B), who assigns them to the final holder (C). In principle, each of these assignments should be notified to the carrier, but as only the final holder will be claiming delivery, it is conceivable that only the last assignment to the final holder is notified to carrier. In that case, however, the notification will have to be given by the shipper and the final holder, which in practice might be difficult. Once the intermediate holders have re-assigned the rights to the next holder, they have no rights against the carrier anymore, but no liabilities either. The liabilities under the bill of lading remain always and only with the shipper.

If the transfer of a bill of lading is seen as also an assignment of liabilities, or as the assignment of the contract as a whole, the consent of the carrier is required. Each subsequent assignment has to be agreed to by the carrier. In principle, an assignment of liabilities or of the contract implies that the assignor is released of his obligations and substituted by the assignee, but the parties can agree that the assignor will remain bound as a co-debtor. If the assignor is released, all rights and liabilities under the bill of lading will come to lie exclusively with the final holder. If the assignor is not released, the rights and liabilities under the bill of lading will also lie with the final holder, but the shipper and all intermediate holders will be co-debtors of the liabilities under the B/L. The carrier won't object to this outcome (in fact, the 'Merchant Clause' in many bills of lading is meant to produce exactly this effect), but for the intermediate holders, the position is less acceptable, as they remain bound under a bill of lading from which they no longer derive rights.

3.1.3.5 The non-contracting shipper

49 The assignment theory does not provide a very good solution for the position of the non-contracting shipper. In theory, of course, the consignee could, after having made the contract of carriage with the carrier, demand of the shipper that he accepts to be bound by the liabilities under the bill of lading. If the shipper does indeed accept and the carrier is notified, the shipper and the consignee are then co-debtors of the liabilities under the bill of lading. Why, however, would the consignee make such a demand, which only benefits the carrier, and even more crucially, why would the shipper accept to become bound? It would for him be a burden without a benefit, all the more so since he did not want to arrange the carriage in the first place.

3.1.3.6 Appraisal

50 Assignment is not a very popular theory to explain the position of a third-party holder of the bill of lading. The agreement between assignor and assignee, the notification of the debtor and the difficulties with the assignment of liabilities are just a few of the obstacles.[126] Nevertheless, a more modern approach to assignment could solve several of these problems. Assignment clearly requires an agreement between assignor and assignee, but the real question is whether there are any formal requirements regarding this agreement. If not, the fact itself that an order bill is endorsed or a bearer bill is handed over could be considered sufficient proof of the required agreement. With regard to the notification of the debtor, a separate, formal notification is never given in the day-to-day practice. Several legal systems have, however, relaxed their previously strict requirements to now allow any provable form of notification. In that case, the presentation of the bill of lading to the carrier at destination could be seen as also a notification to the carrier that the rights (and liabilities) under the bill of lading were assigned to the current holder.[127] Finally, the opinions have also changed regarding the assignment of liabilities. Once considered pure heresy, it has become more and more accepted that liabilities can indeed be assigned. Such assignment is in any case binding between assignor and assignee, but only binds the creditor if he agreed to it. If the creditor (carrier) does not agree, or is not even aware of the assignment of the liabilities under the bill of lading, the original shipper remains obliged vis-à-vis the carrier. That then results in the holder of the bill of lading being obliged to assume the liabilities under the B/L because of his agreement with the shipper or the previous holder, but with the carrier still able to go against the original shipper should the holder of the B/L not live up to his obligations.[128]

51 There are, however, issues that are not easily overcome. Assignment indeed implies that the assignee (the holder of the B/L) steps into the shoes of the assignor (the shipper). Any agreements that the shipper may have made with the

---

126 R. De Wit, *Multimodal Transport: Carrier Liability and Documentation*, London, Lloyd's of London Press, 1995, n° 5.5 at p. 246 and n° 5.10 at pp. 250–251. See also H. Logmans, *Zekerheid op lading*, Zutphen, Uitgeverij Paris, 2011, at p. 267.
127 This route, however, will not fully work in legal systems where notification to the debtor is a constitutive requirement for the assignee's right to come into being. In that case, indeed, the assignee must first give notice to the debtor (carrier) before he can re-assign the rights under the bill of lading to a subsequent holder.
128 Not asking for the carrier's consent thus solves the problem pointed out by R. De Wit, *Multimodal Transport: Carrier Liability and Documentation*, London, Lloyd's of London Press, 1995, n° 5.10 at p. 250, that some of the shipper's liabilities should remain with him, if only subsidiarily. Such result is, of course, not entirely indisposable, but rather an (understandable) concern of the carriers, which prefer to have a fall-back position should the holder of the bill of lading not pay what is due.

carrier, any specific knowledge that the shipper may have had will thus be binding on the holder of the B/L, even if such agreements or knowledge are not apparent from the bill of lading itself. In *Higgins v Anglo-Algerian S.S. Co. Limited*[129] for instance, a carrier had issued a clean bill of lading at the request of the shipper and in exchange for a letter of indemnity, although he knew and had noted in the mate's receipts that the goods were wet damaged upon receipt for shipment. When sued by the later holder of the B/L, the carrier tried to rely on the actual condition of the goods, claiming that the holder of the bill of lading is the assignee of the shipper. The court declared itself 'unimpressed' by the argument, all the more so since it considered the carrier's actions in this case not merely negligent, but fraudulent. It has indeed been accepted for quite some time now that a third-party holder of the bill of lading is not bound by agreements or knowledge of the shipper that do not appear from the bill of lading itself. With regard to the condition of the goods, that position was expressly confirmed in the Visby Protocol, and had already been accepted in several countries even before the Protocol.[130] Furthermore, following the *Tilly Russ* decision of the EU Court of Justice,[131] both the Belgian and the French Supreme Courts held that the holder of a bill of lading does not succeed to the rights and obligations of the shipper.[132] Commercial and legal practice thus accepts that a third-party holder of a bill of lading does not (fully) step into the shoes of the shipper, which in itself is sufficient to exclude assignment as an explanatory theory.[133]

One could, however, try to overcome this obstacle by arguing that the shipper has, in fact, two pairs of shoes, one being his 'real' position vis-à-vis the carrier, including all special arrangements and knowledge that may exist between them, and the second being the position as confined to the bill of lading. By transferring the bill of lading, the shipper would only make the subsequent holder step into his 'second pair of shoes', by only assigning his rights and liabilities as laid down in the bill of lading.[134] *Which* rights and liabilities are assigned indeed depends on the agreement between the assignor and the assignee; the assignor can assign only certain rights and liabilities while retaining other rights and liabilities for himself. Such a 'limited assignment' theory, however, cannot work in situations where there is a preexisting contract between the shipper and the carrier (charter party,

---

129 *Higgins v Anglo-Algerian S.S. Co. Limited* 248 F. 386 (Court of Appeals 2nd Circ., 13 February 1918).
130 See above, n° 11 p. 12.
131 ECJ 19 June 1984, Case 71/83, *Partenreederei ms. Tilly Russ and Ernest Russ v NV Haven- & Vervoerbedrijf Nova and NV Goeminne Hout.*
132 Belgium: Cass. 18 September 1987, R.H.A. 1987, 175 (ms. Regina). See also: Comm. Court Antwerp 1 June 1992, R.H.A. 1995, (48), at p. 56 (ms. Nordic Stream).
    France: Cass. com., 4 March 2003, *D.M.F.* 2003, 556 (Navire Houston Express), note Ph. Delebecque; *JCP* ed. G 2004, II, 10071, note A. Sinay-Cytermann.
133 Compare R. Zwitser, "Toetreden tot de vervoersovereenkomst; het Contship America", *T.V.R.* 2000, at pp. 38–39.
134 Compare J.-P. Tosi, "L'adhésion du destinataire au contrat de transport", in X., *Mélanges Christian Mouly*, Paris, Litec, 1998, fn. 29 at p. 182.

volume contract, etc.).[135] In that case, the bill of lading for the shipper and carrier only serves as a receipt, with the rights and liabilities of the shipper being defined in the preexisting contract. An assignment, even a limited assignment, could only be an assignment of rights and liabilities under the charter party, volume contract or the like. This result is clearly not in line with the way bills of lading are perceived and used in legal and commercial practice.

52 Assignment also means that rights (and obligations) are transferred from one party to another. After the assignment, the transferring party (the shipper) no longer has the rights or obligations it had before. This, again, is not in line with practice.[136] Unless explicitly agreed otherwise, the shipper remains bound to the carrier even after the bill of lading has been transferred to a third-party holder.[137]

53 A further issue with the assignment theory is the situation where the loss of or damage to the carried goods has already occurred at the time of the assignment. What is assigned then is in fact a *right to sue*. Assignments of rights to sue, however, are frowned upon in most legal systems, as they were feared to encourage litigation.[138] The assignment might be void altogether, or the debtor might be able to escape further liabilities by reimbursing to the assignee the price the latter has paid to the assignor. With regard to bills of lading, however, the problem is probably not really acute.[139] In most cases, the parties will not have been aware of the fact that the loss of or damage to the goods had already occurred and that they were thus assigning rights to sue. Furthermore, the consignee has a genuine commercial interest in the goods and their fate, and thus also in the claim against the carrier if things go wrong. Finally, there is no encouraging of litigation that would not have existed otherwise. If the cargo claim against the

---

135 R. Zwitser, "Toetreden tot de vervoersovereenkomst; het Contship America", *T.V.R.* 2000, at p. 39.
136 H. Logmans, *Zekerheid op lading*, Zutphen, Uitgeverij Paris, 2011, at p. 268.
137 Comm. C. Antwerp 18 June 2002, *R.H.A.* 2003, 156, at p. 169 (ms. MSC Dymphna).
138 Common law knows the concepts of maintenance and champerty, which were succinctly defined by Steyn LJ in *Giles v Thompson* (1993) WL 963259, 143 NLJ 284 (Court of Appeal, 11 January 1993) as follows: ". . . maintenance is the support of litigation by a stranger without just cause. Champerty is an aggravated form of maintenance. The distinguishing feature of champerty is the support of litigation by a stranger in return for a share of the proceeds." Although maintenance and champerty are no longer crimes since the Criminal Law Act 1967, they still exist and can result in a contract or assignment being declared void. See, for instance, *Jennifer Simpson (as assignee of Alan Catchpole) v Norfolk & Norwich University Hospital NHS Trust* [2011] EWCA Civ 1149, WL 4706949 (Court of Appeal, 12 October 2011), where the assignment of a right to sue for personal injury was considered champertous and therefore void. See also P. Bugden and S. Lamont-Black, *Goods in Transit and Freight Forwarding*, London, Sweet & Maxwell, 2010 (2nd Ed.), n° 13-05 at pp. 229–230.

Article 1699 of the Belgian and French Civil Codes provides that a debtor, against whom a contested right has been assigned, can escape liability by reimbursing to the assignee the price the latter has paid for the assignment, plus costs and interests. For the purposes of this provision, a right is only 'contested' when proceedings have been started (Article 1700).
139 Compare C. Cashmore, *Parties to a Contract of Carriage, or Who Can Sue on a Contract of Carriage of Goods?* London, Lloyd's of London Press, 1990, at pp. 136–138.

carrier is not assigned to and made by the consignee, it would be made by the shipper.

A related issue is loss or damage that occurs after the assignment. Some authors have argued that if the transfer of a bill of lading is an assignment, the subsequent holder of the B/L could only sue for loss suffered by the assignor, but not for loss suffered by himself.[140] That position, however, is clearly incorrect. An assignment of rights does not make the assigned rights immutable, certainly not when they are rights under a contract that is still being performed. From the time of the assignment, the subsequent holder steps into the shoes of the shipper and obtains the latter's right to claim delivery. If later the goods are lost or damaged, the B/L holder's right to delivery is converted to a right to sue.

54 A weak point of the assignment theory is further that it necessarily depends on the agreement between the assignor (shipper) and the assignee (the subsequent holder). This means that, if the shipper's agreement to assign is invalid – e.g. because the assignment was made shortly before the shipper's bankruptcy and is voidable under bankruptcy law, or because the shipper was legally incapable of agreeing to an assignment –, the holder of the B/L does not have any rights against the carrier, even though he is holding the original bill of lading. Also, since the assignee steps into the shoes of the assignor, any encumbrances on the assignor's rights (such as liens, pledges, creditor rights, etc.) will have effect against the assignee.[141]

55 In addition, it must be pointed out that the assignment theory in fact undermines the position of the bill of lading as a trade instrument.[142] What would happen, indeed, if the shipper transferred the bill of lading to A, and then explicitly assigned his rights against the carrier to B, giving formal notice of this assignment to the carrier? It is clear that this conflict would eventually be resolved in favour of either A or B, but such resolution takes time, and during that time the position of the holder of the B/L is compromised.

56 Finally, some older authors have complained that assignment only explains (imperfectly) *how* the holder of the B/L gets rights against the carrier, but not

---

140 R. Rodière, *Traité général de droit maritime*, Tome II, *Les contrats de transport de marchandises*, Paris, Librairie Dalloz, 1967, n° 407 at p. 26; R. Rodière, *Droit des transports. Transports terrestres et aériens*, Paris, Sirey, 1977 (2nd Ed.), n° 364 at p. 421. See also A. Kpoahoun Amoussou, *Les clauses attributives de compétence dans le transport maritime de marchandises*, Presses Universitaires d'Aix-Marseille, 2002, n° 638 at p. 404.

See also F. Smeele, "The bill of lading contracts under European national laws (civil law approaches to explaining the legal position of the consignee under bills of lading), in R. Thomas (Ed.), *The Evolving Law and Practice of Voyage Charterparties*, London, Informa, 2009, n° 12.36 at p. 269, who points out that assignment cannot explain that the holder can sue for damage suffered by himself.

141 R. Rodière, *Traité général de droit maritime*, Tome II, *Les contrats de transport de marchandises*, Paris, Librairie Dalloz, 1968, n° 407 at p. 26; A. Kpoahoun Amoussou, *Les clauses attributives de compétence dans le transport maritime de marchandises*, Presses Universitaires d'Aix-Marseille, n° 638 at p. 404.

142 G. Treitel, "Overseas sales in general", in *Benjamin's Sale of Goods*, London, Sweet & Maxwell, 2006 (7th Ed.), n° 18.147 at p. 1277.

why he does so.[143] This critique, however, is no longer valid today. Few today would indeed contest that it is desirable and efficient for the holder of the bill of lading to have rights against the carrier.

3.1.4 Novation

3.1.4.1 The concept

57 Novation is the termination of an existing contract and the replacement of it by a new, modified contract.

58 Novation originated in Roman law, and from there found its way to both civil and common law. In Roman law, the identity of the contracting parties was considered an essential element of the contract, which prevented the assignment of the rights (or liabilities) under the contract to another party.[144] The only way to 'transfer' a contract from one party to another was to annul the existing contract and to create a new contract between the desired parties. With the acceptance of assignments and party autonomy in general, novation has lost much of its importance, even though it has not completely disappeared. Novation today is mainly used when X starts doing business with A but through circumstances continues that business with B; the concept of novation then protects both X and B.[145] Novation is also argued in order to escape unwanted accessories of the original contract.

59 As novation implies the dissolution of the existing contract and the creation of a new contract, the agreement of all parties involved is required.[146] Their agreement must include an intention to novate ('*animus novandi*'), be it that the agreement and the intention need not be express but may be inferred from acts and conduct when appropriate.[147] Since the existing contract is dissolved, the

---

143 G. Kirberger, "De positie van den geadresseerde", *Rechtsgeleerd Magazijn* 1898, at p. 50; A. Mesritz, *De Vrachtbrief*, Amsterdam, J.H. de Bussy, 1904, at pp. 67–68. See also M. Spanjaart, *Vorderingsrechten uit cognossement*, Zutphen, Uitgeverij Paris, 2012, at p. 34.

144 Ph. Malaurie, L. Aynès and Ph. Stoffel-Munck, *Les obligations*, Paris, Défrenois, 2011 (5th Ed.), n° 1181 at p. 660; W. Van Gerven and S. Covemaeker, *Verbintenissenrecht*, Leuven, Acco, 2006 (2nd Ed.), at p. 627.

145 Such circumstances may for example arise in case of amalgamation of companies, changes in partnership firms, etc. In *Scarf v Jardine* 7 App.Cas. 345 (House of Lords, 13 June 1882) for instance, Jardine had been doing business with W.H. Rogers & Co., a partnership originally between Rogers and Scarf, but later transformed, unbeknownst to Jardine, to a partnership between Rogers and Beech. Without novation, there would not be a contract between Jardine and the 'new' partnership.

See also *Chitty on Contracts*, Vol. 1, *General Principles*, London, Sweet & Maxwell, 1989 (26th Ed.), n° 1436 at p. 902.

146 *Chitty on Contracts*, Vol. 1, *General Principles*, London, Sweet & Maxwell, 1989 (26th Ed.), n° 1436 at p. 902 and n° 1598 at p. 1002.

147 T. Eckardt, *The Bolero Bill of Lading Under German and English Law*, München, Sellier European Law Publishers, 2004, at p. 92; Ph. Malaurie, L. Aynès and Ph. Stoffel-Munck,

securities, time bars, defences etc. linked to the existing contract also disappear, unless the new parties take care to recreate them.[148]

The principles above apply in both common law and civil law. The two systems differ, however, in that common law primarily sees novation as a way to change the parties to the contract,[149] whereas in civil law novation is used to change not only the parties but also the subject of the contract, the parties remaining the same.[150]

3.1.4.2 *The transfer of a bill of lading seen as novation*

60 Novation is not unknown in transport law. The concept has been used by some to argue that the pre-existing charter party is novated when the bill of lading is issued, be it that this point of view has never been very successful. It has also been used to explain how and why previous agreements between the shipper and the carrier (the booking note, the mate's receipt) are novated by the bill of lading.[151]

61 As a theory to explain the position of the B/L holder, however, novation has never been very prominent. In the U.K., the Bills of Lading Act 1855 (described by some as a form of 'statutory novation'[152]) and later COGSA 1992 provided a basis for the holder's rights and liabilities. On the continent, the civil law had made the contract into a very flexible instrument, that could be assigned, amended, extended to additional parties, etc. Novation was not needed very often anymore. Remarkably, novation has gained new popularity with the advent of the electronic bill of lading. The authors of the 1999 BOLERO Legal Feasibility Study indicated that under some legal systems, a contract of carriage is novated

---

Les obligations, Paris, Defrénois, 2011 (5th Ed.), n° 1184 at p. 663; W. Van Gerven and S. Covemaeker, *Verbintenissenrecht*, Leuven, Acco, 2006 (2nd Ed.), at p. 630.

Seakom Limited, Seakom International Limited v Knowledgepool Group Limited [2013] EWHC 4007 (High Court of Justice Chancery Division, 18 December 2013), at § 147.

148 L. Cornelis, *Algemene theorie van de verbintenis*, Antwerpen, Intersentia, 2000, n° 664 at p. 860; W. Van Gerven and S. Covemaeker, *Verbintenissenrecht*, Leuven, Acco, 2006 (2nd Ed.), at p. 627 and p. 630.

149 A. Guest, *The Law of Assignment*, London, Sweet & Maxwell, 2012, n° 1–62 at p. 40.
    See also *Chitty on Contracts*, Vol. 1, *General Principles*, London, Sweet & Maxwell, 1989 (26th Ed.), n° 1598 at p. 1002. The authors, however, refer to *Scarf v Jardine* 7 App.Cas. 345 (House of Lords, 13 June 1882), 351, where the court allowed the possibility for the new contract to be between the same parties.

150 The three possibilities (change of creditor, change of debtor, change of subject) are explicitly mentioned in Article 1271 of the Belgian and French Civil Codes.
    L. Cornelis, *Algemene theorie van de verbintenis*, Antwerpen, Intersentia, 2000, n° 658 at pp. 853–854; W. Van Gerven and S. Covemaeker, *Verbintenissenrecht*, Leuven, Acco, 2006 (2nd Ed.), at pp. 628–629.

151 H. Sanders, *Het cognossement*, 's Gravenhage, Martinus Nijhoff, 1912, at p. 73.

152 M. Bridge, L. Gullifer, G. McMeel and S. Worthington, *The Law of Personal Property*, London, Sweet & Maxwell, 2013, n° 30-019 at p. 823. The more common view, however, is that historically the Bills of Lading Act 1855 and now COGSA 1992 provide for a 'statutory assignment' (see below, n° 32 p. 171).

to the consignee when he becomes a transferee of a bill of lading,[153] and in the BOLERO Rulebook, novation is selected as the mechanism to transfer the rights and liabilities to the new holder. That choice is supported by several authors that have written on the subject of electronic bills of lading. The absence of a statutory regime for electronic bills of lading to take care of the transfer of rights and liabilities is one of the reasons to use the concept of novation. Another reason is the fact that several legal systems have formal requirements for assignments that are difficult or impossible to satisfy in an electronic environment, which rules out assignment as a possible solution.[154]

62 Novation is dealt with in the first group of contractual theories, which has the consignee step into the shoes of the shipper. That, of course, is only true to the extent that the novation is only used to change the identity of the holder of the B/L. Novation would also allow the contents of the contract of carriage to be changed between holders, in which case the ultimate holder no longer has the same rights and liabilities as the shipper.

3.1.4.3 *When does the relationship come into being?*

63 As set out above, novation requires the consent of all three parties involved: the current holder of the B/L, the carrier and the proposed new holder. In principle, the relationship between the carrier and the new holder comes into being when the parties reach agreement, although they could (in theory) agree that the new contract with the new holder will only come into force at a later date.

3.1.4.4 *Intermediate holders*

64 In a novation approach, there are in fact no intermediate holders. As the existing contract is terminated, the previous holder no longer has any rights or liabilities vis-a-vis the carrier. Only the new holder has rights and liabilities under the novated contract with the carrier. The identity of the previous holders can be retraced, but they are no longer involved in the contract of carriage.

3.1.4.5 *The non-contracting shipper*

65 Novation does not really have an answer for the position of the non-contracting shipper. In theory, of course, it would be possible for the consignee and the carrier to agree to terminate their existing contract of carriage and replace it with a new contract between the carrier and the shipper, but such an exercise would be pointless. The goods are en route to their destination, to be received by the consignee (or a subsequent holder of the B/L); novating the bill of lading to the non-contracting shipper thus makes no sense.

---

153 Without identifying the legal systems they were referring to, though.
154 T. Eckardt, *The Bolero Bill of Lading Under German and English Law*, München, Sellier European Law Publishers, 2004, at p. 76.

3.1.4.6 Appraisal

66 There is a certain appeal to the novation theory, particularly the common law variant of novation where only one of the parties is changed, but not the terms and conditions of the contract. Novation would seem a simple and straightforward way to transfer the rights and liabilities, as initially agreed to by the carrier, to subsequent holders.

There are, however, a number of drawbacks to this theory. Firstly, the carrier's consent is required for each and every novation. Not only does this create an administrative overhead, it also means that the carrier is aware of all transactions with the bill of lading. The fact itself that this information is (necessarily) available to the carrier might already be undesirable, but it may also put the carrier in a difficult spot, for example when a transaction is envisaged that is allowed under the laws of the current and proposed new holder, but illegal under the laws of the carrier. Also, novation implies that the existing contract is *terminated*, and a new contract created. This fact could have consequences with regard to time bars, applicable rates, etc.[155] Problems can also arise when it can be shown that the damage found at destination had already occurred *before* the novation. Since in a novation approach the holder of the bill of lading is always a direct contracting partner of the carrier, the rule prohibiting proof against the bill of lading[156] does not apply, and the carrier is allowed to prove that the condition of the goods at the start of the contract was not as described in the bill of lading. Thirdly, since novation implies that the existing contract is terminated, there are never more than two parties involved. That is not a problem from a theoretical point of view, but it is not in line with commercial practice. Carriers prefer to have their initial contracting party remain liable as a safeguard against non-performance by the ultimate holder, and it is generally accepted that this is indeed the case, unless explicitly agreed otherwise.[157]

3.2 The second group: the holder has a position of his own

67 The first group of contractual theories, discussed above, had the subsequent holders step into the shoes of the shipper.[158] From a purely legal point of

---

155 See, for example, Cass. (Fr.) 7 July 2009 (B 08–17.375), *E.T.L.* 2009, 641, where containers had been shipped by SCTI from Marseille to Anger. Afterwards, the carrier at the request of SCTI issued a second Bill of Lading, indicating a different shipper and a different consignee. The containers were never picked up, and the carrier sued SCTI for detention charges. The French Supreme Court, however, held that the carrier, by issuing the new bill of lading, had novated the contract of carriage and thus released SCTI from all of its obligations under the first bill of lading.
156 As laid down in Article 3, paragraph 4 of the Hague Visby Rules.
157 Compare R. De Wit, *Multimodal Transport: Carrier Liability and Documentation*, London, Lloyd's of London Press, 1995, n° 5.6 at p. 247.
158 The 'shipper' taken as the party that originally made the contract of carriage with the carrier, which is not necessarily the party that delivers the goods to the carrier in the port of loading.

view, such a succession of parties is perfectly possible. A subrogated insurer, for instance, steps into the shoes of his insured, and takes the latter's claim against the liable party with all of its 'deficiencies'. If the claim of the insured has become time barred, it will also be time barred for the subrogated insurer. With regard to bills of lading, however, it was soon realized that such approach would reduce the commercial value of the bill of lading. Trade on bills of lading would not have developed the way it has if the carrier had been allowed to disprove the condition of the goods described in the bill of lading against a third-party holder, if a third-party holder had been held to agreements made by the shipper but not apparent from the bill of lading, etc. From this, only one conclusion was possible: although the holder's position stems from the shipper's position, the holder does not have, and *should* not have, exactly the same rights and liabilities as the shipper.[159]

In *The Helene*, for instance, casks of oil had been overstowed with wool and rags, which heated up during the voyage and caused the casks to leak, thus resulting in a very considerable loss of oil. The shipper was well aware of the way the cargo was stowed, as he had been personally present on board during the loading, and had not objected to it. The Court, however, held that this knowledge, even if it might have estopped the shipper from claiming against the carrier, did not stop the consignee.[160] Similarly, in *Leduc v Ward*, the bill of lading was for a voyage from Fiume to Dunkirk. The ship however deviated to Glasgow and sank en route. If the deviation was not allowed under the contract, the carrier, under the law at the time, would lose the right to invoke the excepted perils clause. The carrier argued that the deviation to Glasgow had been agreed with the shipper and was therefore allowed by the contract. The Court of Appeal however held that such agreement, which did not appear from the bill of lading, could not bind a third-party holder of the bill of lading.[161]

Furthermore, if the holder steps into the shoes of the shipper, he could be exposed to unexpected but very substantial liabilities. If for instance the shipper fails to (properly) declare dangerous cargo, which later damage the ship and other cargo, the holder succeeding to the shipper's liabilities would be faced with important claims, even though he was probably not aware of the shipper's negligence and not personally negligent in any way.[162]

68 In its *Tilly Russ* decision, the ECJ held that the applicable national law would have to decide whether the third party, upon acquiring the bill of lading, succeeds to the shipper's rights and obligations. Thirty years later, in *Refcomp/ AXA* (a non-maritime case), the Court expressed the opinion that 'under most

---

159 A. Kpoahoun Amoussou, *Les clauses attributives de compétence dans le transport maritime de marchandises*, Presses Universitaires d'Aix-Marseille, 2002, n° 621 at p. 394; G. Ripert, *Droit Maritime*, Tôme II, Paris, Editions Rousseau et Cie., 1952 (4th Ed.), n° 1585 at pp. 492–493; H. Sanders, *Het cognossement*, 's Gravenhage, Martinus Nijhoff, 1912, at p. 1.
160 *The Helene* Br. & L. 415, 167 ER 426 (High Court of Admiralty, 3 March 1865).
161 *Leduc v Ward* 20 QBD 475 (Court of Appeal, 13 February 1888).
162 Compare The Law Commission and The Scottish Law Commission, *Rights of Suit in Respect of Carriage of Goods by Sea*, 19 March 1991, (LAW COM No 196 and SCOT LAW COM No 130), n° 3.7 at p. 30.

legal systems of the Member States which agree on this matter' the third party becomes the holder of *all* the rights and obligations of the shipper in relation to the carrier.[163] In the later case of *Profit Investment*, again a non-maritime case, the Court somewhat elaborated its earlier, rather surprising, position by stating that a bill of lading is an instrument of a very specific nature, which is intended to govern a relationship involving at least three persons.[164] The Advocate General in his Opinion explicitly referred to a tripartite contract in this respect.[165] Remarkably, however, neither the Court itself nor the Advocates General in either of these two cases cited any sources in support of their statement that a bill of lading creates a tripartite contract or relationship, with the holder of the bill of lading taking over all rights and obligations of the shipper. In fact, the position is quite the opposite. Most EU maritime law systems take the position that the holder of the bill of lading does not succeed to all of the shipper's rights and obligations, but has a position of his own.[166] The Belgian Supreme Court in its decision of 18 September 1987 explicitly held that a third-party holder of the bill of lading does not step into the shoes of the shipper but has a separate position.[167] This decision has been unanimously accepted by the lower courts and the authors, and has never been recalled into question since.[168] In France also, the Supreme Court has explicitly held that a third-party holder does not succeed to the rights and obligations of the shipper.[169] In Germany and the Netherlands, the relevant Codes provide that the carrier can only invoke against a third-party holder those defences and conditions that appear from the bill of lading itself (Art. 8:441. (2) of the Dutch Civil Code – § 522.(1) of the German Commercial Code).[170]

163 ECJ 7 February 2013, Case C-543/10, *Refcomp SpA v Axa Corporate Solutions Assurance SA*, point 35.
164 ECJ 20 April 2016, Case C-366/13, *Profit Investment Sim SpA v Stefano Ossi et al.*, point 33.
165 Opinion of Advocate General Bot, Case C-366/13, point 55.
166 Compare J. Eckoldt, *De forumkeuze in het zeevervoer*, Zutphen, Uitgeverij Paris, 2014, at pp. 152–156; P. Kuypers, *Forumkeuze in het Nederlandse internationaal privaatrecht*, Deventer, Kluwer, 2008, at pp. 210–211.
167 Cass. 18 September 1987, *Arr.Cass.* 1987–88, 82, *E.T.L.* 1987, 529, *Pas.* 1988, I, 75, *R.H.A.* 1987, 175, *R.W.* 1987–88, 714, *R.D.C.* 1988, 376 (ms. Regina).
168 See, for instance, CA Antwerp, 4th Division, 18 January 2016, *not reported*, Case N° 2013/AR/3097; CA Antwerp 13 February 2006, *R.H.A.* 2007, 162 (ms. Ocean Island / ms. Sri Arika).

J. Putzeys and M.-A. Rosseels, *Droit des transports et Droit maritime*, Brussels, Bruylant, 1993 (3rd Ed.), n° 139 at p. 93 and n° 504 at p. 283.
169 Cass.com. 4 March 2003, *D.M.F.* 2003, 556, note Ph. Delebecque, *J.C.P.* G 2004 II, 10071, note A. Sinay-Cytermann (Navire Houston Express). See also Ph. Delebecque, "La clause attributive de compétence stipulée dans un connaissement et dûment convenue entre le chargeur et le transporteur est-elle de plein droit opposable au destinataire?", *D.M.F.* 2000, at p. 14; P.-Y. Nicolas, "CA Paris 29 November 2000 (Navire Nuevo Leon)", *D.M.F.* 2001, 689–696 (note), n° 14 at p. 694.
170 In addition, both Codes explicitly deal with references in the bill of lading to external content. Under Dutch law, such references only work if the external content is 'readily knowable' (*duidelijk kenbaar*) (Article 8:415.(1) of the Dutch Civil Code). Under German

Similarly, the Norwegian Maritime Code[171] in Section 325 provides with regard to tramp bills of lading that it is the bill of lading that governs the conditions of carriage and delivery of the goods and not the charter party, unless the provisions of the charter party are included in the bill of lading or at least referred to in the bill of lading. From these provisions, it is clear that the position of the holder is determined by the bill of lading, and is only identical to the position of the shipper if the bill of lading exhaustively describes the rights and obligations of the shipper. The holder of the bill of lading does not succeed to rights or obligations of the shipper that do not appear from the bill of lading.

Spain is an exception in this respect. Article 251 of the Spanish Act 14/2014 on Maritime Navigation provides that "the acquirer of the bill of lading shall acquire all the rights and actions of the conveyor to the goods", with the exception however of agreements regarding jurisdiction and arbitration, which must be specifically accepted by the acquirer of the bill of lading.[172]

69 If, however, the holder of the bill of lading does not succeed to the rights and obligations of the shipper, while it is still considered necessary for him to be in a *contractual* relation with the carrier, new theories had to be found to explain the holder's position. The concepts of a third-party beneficiary clause and of multi-party contracts are often used in this respect.

3.2.1 *Third-party beneficiary clause*

(*stipulation pour autrui, derdenbeding, Vertrag zugunsten Dritter*)

3.2.1.1 *The concept*

70 A third-party beneficiary clause is a contractual clause, by which the parties to the contract create a right (benefit) for a third party.

71 Under Roman law, contracts could only be made directly between the parties involved. The contracting parties could not assign their contractual rights to other parties, and agency did not exist: a person could not enter into a contract through the intermediary of another free person (*per liberam personam nihil acquiri potest*). A third-party beneficiary, therefore, could not obtain rights, as he had not been personally involved in the making of the contract.[173] Between the parties to the contract, the third-party clause was often unenforceable, unless the promisee had a personal pecuniary interest in the promisor performing the

---

law, references to external content do not work at all (§ 522.(1) of the German Commercial Code).
171 The Norwegian Maritime Code of 24 June 1994, as amended, is available online in an English translation from different websites.
172 "*El adquirente del conocimiento de embarque adquirirá todos los derechos y acciones del transmitente sobre las mercancías, excepción hecha de los acuerdos en materia de jurisdicción y arbitraje, que requerirán el consentimiento del adquirente en los términos señalados en el capítulo I del título IX.*"
173 N. Carette, *Derdenbeding*, Antwerp, Intersentia, 2011, n° 185 at p. 176.

72   *Contractual theories*

third-party clause.[174] These principles survived until the Middle Ages, but were increasingly questioned from the 16th century on. The *Code Napoleon* of 1804, although confirming the principle that, in general, a party only stipulates for itself (Art. 1119),[175] explicitly allowed a third-party beneficiary clause, if that clause was a condition or charge for a stipulation that the promisee had obtained to his own advantage (Art. 1121).[176] From there, similar provisions found their way into the other civil law Codes. Furthermore, subsequent practice has taken a very benevolent view to third-party beneficiary clauses, and has refused or removed almost all restrictions that could be read into the rather succinct provision of Art. 1121. In the U.K., third-party beneficiary clauses have been longer in the making, but were eventually recognized by the Contracts (Rights of Third Parties) Act 1999.[177]

72 A third-party beneficiary clause is a contractual stipulation, and thus requires a valid contract between the promisee and the promisor. If, for some reason, this underlying contract is annulled or dissolved, the third-party beneficiary clause also disappears. For there to be a third-party beneficiary clause, the promisee and the promisor must have intended to create a legally enforceable right for the third party.[178] The fact that a contract may have beneficial (side) effects for a third party does not, in itself, mean that the contract contains a third-party beneficiary

---

174 N. Carette, *Derdenbeding*, Antwerp, Intersentia, 2011, n° 184 at p. 175 and n° 186 at p. 176–178.
175 "*On ne peut, en général, s'engager ni stipuler en son propre nom, que pour soi-même.*" (One can in general only undertake something or provide for something in one's own name on one's own behalf.)
176 "*On peut pareillement stipuler au profit d'un tiers, lorsque telle est la condition d'une stipulation que l'on fait pour soi-même ou d'une donation que l'on fait à un autre.*" (One can also provide for the benefit of a third party, if such is the condition of a provision that one has made for oneself or of a gift that one gives to someone else.)
177 The Contracts (Rights of Third Parties) Act 1999 explicitly does not apply to contracts for the carriage of goods by sea, contained in or evidenced by a bill of lading (ss 6.(5) and 6.(6)).
178 This requirement is apparent from the modern definitions of a third-party beneficiary clause.
    Sections 1.(1) and 1.(2) of the UK Contracts (Rights of Third Parties) Act 1999 provide:
    "*1.(1) Subject to the provisions of this Act, a person who is not a party to a contract (a "third party") may in his own right enforce a term of the contract if –*
    (a) the contract expressly provides that he may, or
    (b) subject to subsection (2), the term purports to confer a benefit on him.
    (2) Subsection (1)(b) does not apply if on a proper construction of the contract it appears that the parties did not intend the term to be enforceable by the third party."
    Article 6.110 (1) of the Principles of European Contract Law (PECL) 2002 provides:
    "*A third party may require performance of a contractual obligation when its right to do so has been expressly agreed upon between the promisor and the promisee, or when such agreement is to be inferred from the purpose of the contract or the circumstances of the case.*"

clause. As the clause is created by the promisee and the promisor, it are these parties that freely decide what the contents and the limits will be of the right that is granted to the third party.[179] It is entirely possible, therefore, even probable, that the rights of the third party will not be identical to the rights of the promisee. In many legal systems, a third-party beneficiary clause is thought to give rise to a separate relationship between the promisor and the third party, distinct from the original relationship between the promisor and the promisee.[180] Dutch law is an exception in this respect, in that Article 6:254.(1) of the Dutch Civil Code provides that the third party, by accepting the clause, becomes a party to the contract between the promisee and the promisor. In principle, as the name implies, the third party can only benefit from the clause. Parties cannot impose obligations on a third party, at least not without that third party's consent. With the increasing use and acceptance of third-party beneficiary clauses, however, it has become more accepted that the promisee and promisor can subject the benefit to certain conditions.[181] It are, indeed, the contracting parties that decide what the benefit for the third party will be. Furthermore, a benefit minus a condition is still a net

---

Article 5.2.1.(1) of the UNIDROIT Principles of International Commercial Contracts 2010 provides:

"*The parties (the "promisor" and the "promisee") may confer by express or implied agreement a right on a third party (the "beneficiary").*"

179 UK Contracts (Rights of Third Parties) Act 1999, Sec. 1.(4):

"*This section does not confer a right on a third party to enforce a term of a contract otherwise than subject to and in accordance with any other relevant terms of the contract.*"

Article II – 9.301 (2) of the Draft Common Frame of Reference (DCFR) provides

"*The nature and content of the third party's right or benefit are determined by the contract and are subject to any conditions or other limitations under the contract.*"

Article 5.2.1.(2) of the UNIDROIT Principles of International Commercial Contracts 2010 provides:

"*The existence and content of the beneficiary's right against the promisor are determined by the agreement of the parties and are subject to any conditions or other limitations under the agreement.*"

180 J. Ghestin, C. Jamin and M. Billiau, *Traité de droit civil. Les effets du contrat*, Paris, L.G.D.J. 1994 (2nd Ed.), n° 636 at p. 694: "*Le bénéficiaire n'est donc pas partie au contrat dont son droit est issu et ne le devient pas par son acceptation*" (the beneficiary is thus not a party to the contract that is the source of his right and does not become a party by his acceptance). J.-P. Tosi, "L'adhésion du destinataire au contrat de transport", in X., *Mélanges Christian Mouly*, Paris, Litec, 1998, at p. 185:" . . . *affubler le tiers qui en bénéficie de la qualité de partie est en effet une contradiction dans les termes car, par construction même, il est extérieur au contrat*" (. . . to put the label of contract party to the third party that benefits is indeed a contradiction in terms, because by definition, he is a stranger to the contract).
181 N. Carette, *Derdenbeding*, Antwerp, Intersentia, 2011, at pp. 723–746; H. Gaudemet-Tallon, "Cass. fr. 10 January and 4 April 1995", *Rev. crit. dr. internat. privé* 1995, 610 (note), at p. 615.

74 Contractual theories

benefit, and the third party is free to decide whether he will accept the benefit plus condition or not. Finally, a valid third-party beneficiary clauses requires that the third party be identified, or at least identifiable.

73 A valid third-party beneficiary clause creates a separate, new right for the third party, which has a direct action against the promisor to enforce the term in its favour. This right immediately belongs to the third party; it does not come from or transit via the promisee. Once the third party has accepted the clause in its favour, it becomes irrevocable. Up to the acceptance, however, the promisee and the promisor can agree to modify or withdraw the third-party beneficiary clause.[182] Against an enforcement action by the third party, the promisor can invoke the defences that stem from the clause itself or from his relation with the third party, but also the defences that stem from the contract between the promisor and the promisee.[183]

3.2.1.2 *The bill of lading holder as a third-party beneficiary*

74 The contract of carriage between the shipper and the carrier produces, at the very least, a *factual* benefit for the consignee. It is thanks to this contract of carriage that the goods are shipped to destination, where they can be delivered to the consignee. It need not surprise, then, that a contract of carriage was and is seen as containing a third-party beneficiary clause.

Cass. fr. 21 November 1978, *Recueil Dalloz Sirey* 1980, 309: a bank had entered into a contract with an armored carrier to carry money from supermarkets to the bank, but the cost of those transports had to be paid by the supermarkets. When a consignment of money was stolen, the supermarket involved sued the armored carrier, arguing that the contract between the bank and the carrier contained a third-party beneficiary clause in its favour. The carrier's counterargument that it could not be a third-party beneficiary clause because a burden was imposed on the beneficiary (the payment of the carriage invoices) was rejected by the French Supreme Court.

CA The Hague 26 June 2008, *S&S* 2008, n° 115, ms. *OPDR Lisboa*, point 2.17: "*Dat aanvaarding van een derdenbeding ook verplichtingen mee kan brengen, behoeft uiteraard geen betoog*" (That the acceptance of a third-party beneficiary clause can result in obligations obviously needs no explaining).

182 The promisor could undertake, or the promisor and promisee could agree that the clause will be 'irrevocable'. Since that 'irrevocability' is based on the will of the parties, however, they could change their minds and make the clause revocable again. Other legal theories (estoppel, protection of a third party in good faith, etc.) are then required to make the clause really irrevocable.

183 Article II – 9.302 (b) of the Draft Common Frame of Reference (DCFR) provides
"*the contracting party may assert against the third party all defences which the contracting party could assert against the other party to the contract.*"

Article 5.2.4 of the UNIDROIT Principles of International Commercial Contracts 2010 provides:

"*The promisor may assert against the beneficiary all defences which the promisor could assert against the promisee.*"

Contractual theories

The third-party beneficiary solution has been proposed by Belgian and French authors of the late 19th and early 20th century,[184] but has never been really successful in these countries,[185] mainly because of the (at that time) very strictly conceived rule that a third-party beneficiary clause can only confer benefits, but cannot impose burdens on the third party.[186] The holder of a bill of lading, however, does get the benefit of constructive possession of the goods and being able to claim delivery, but may also have obligations vis-à-vis the carrier. In the traditional view of the third-party beneficiary clause, such obligations are difficult, even impossible to explain.[187]

---

184 Belgium: L. Fredericq, *Handboek van Belgisch Handelsrecht*, Vol. III, Brussels, Bruylant, 1980 (2nd Ed.), n° 1580 at p. 202 ; C. Smeesters and G. Winkelmolen, *Droit maritime et Droit fluvial*, Vol. I, Brussels, Larcier, 1929 (2nd Ed.), n° 444 at pp. 603–604, who only touch briefly upon the subject and see in the contract of carriage a mechanism *similar to* a third-party beneficiary clause; J. Van Ryn and J. Heenen, *Principes de Droit Commercial*, Vol. IV, Brussels, Bruylant, 1988 (2nd Ed.), n° 763 at p. 626.

See also, on inland shipping bills of lading: G. Van Bladel, *Le contrat de transport par bateaux d'intérieur et l'affrètement en séjour*, Vol. I, Antwerp, Lloyd Anversois, s.d., n° 165 at pp. 86–87. Comm. C. Antwerp, 9 October 1941, *J.P.A.* 1941, (337), 345.

France: F. Basset, "Droit français du connaissement", in F. Basset, *Droit romain des avaries communes. Droit français du connaissement. Thèse pour le doctorat*, Paris, Arthur Rousseau, 1889, at p. 63 and p. 115; P. Bonassies, *Cass. com. 29 November 1994 (Navires Harmony et Nagasaki)*, *D.M.F.* 1995, 209 (note), at p. 215; L. Josserand, *Les Transports*, Paris, Arthur Rousseau, 1910, n° 383–384 at pp. 323–326; L. Josserand, *Cours de Droit Civil positif français*, Vol. II, *Théorie générale des obligations*, Paris, Sirey, 1939 (3rd Ed.), n° 274 at p. 156; Ch. Lyon-Caen and L. Renault, *Traité de droit maritime*, Vol. I, Paris, Librairie Cotillon, 1894, n° 750 at p. 516. See also M. Rèmond-Gouilloud, "Des clauses de connaissements maritimes attribuant compétence à une juridiction étrangère: essai de démystification", *D.M.F.* 1995, at p. 348; G. Ripert, *Droit Maritime*, Tôme II, Paris, Editions Rousseau et Cie., 1952 (4th Ed.), n° 1583–1584 at pp. 491–492; R. Rodière, *Traité général de droit maritime*, Tome II, *Les contrats de transport de marchandises*, Paris, Librairie Dalloz, n° 407 at p. 27; J.-P. Tosi, "L'adhésion du destinataire au contrat de transport", in X., *Mélanges Christian Mouly*, Paris, Litec, 1998, at p. 176.

Cass. (fr.) 20 May 1912, *R.I.D.M.* XXVIII, 326.

See also Y. Tassel, *Cass. com. 29 November 1994 (Navire Stolt Osprey)*, *D.M.F.* 1995, 218 (note), at p. 223, who seems to prefer the third-party beneficiary concept to the three-party contract (see below, para 3.2.2), but does not elaborate his position.

185 See for instance G. Ripert, *Droit Maritime*, Tôme II, Paris, Editions Rousseau et Cie., 1952 (4th Ed.), n° 1583–1584 at pp. 491–492; R. Rodière, *Traité général de droit maritime*, Tome II, *Les contrats de transport de marchandises*, Paris, Librairie Dalloz, 1968, n° 407 at p. 27.

See also CA Ghent 28 November 1996, *R.W.* 1996-97, (1441), at p. 1442, which explicitly rejects the third-party beneficiary concept, be it without further explaining its position.

186 C. Carreau, "Cass. fr. 21 November 1978", *Recueil Dalloz Sirey* 1980, 309 (note), at p. 312; P. Rodière, "Cass. fr. 21 November 1978", *La Semaine Juridique, JCP* 1980, 643 (note), at p. 645.

187 Ph. Delebecque, *Droit maritime*, Paris, Dalloz, 2014 (13th Ed.), n° 731 at p. 511; R. De Wit, *Multimodal Transport: Carrier Liability and Documentation*, London, Lloyd's of London Press, 1995, n° 5.4 at p. 245; G. Ripert, *Droit Maritime*, Tôme II, Paris, Editions Rousseau et Cie., 1952 (4th Ed.), n° 1584 at p. 492; F. Stevens, *Vervoer onder cognossement*, Brussel, Larcier, 2001, n° 349 at p. 203.

76 Contractual theories

In Germany[188] and the Netherlands,[189] on the other hand, the third-party beneficiary solution has been much more successful and is today the majority

---

188 J. Basedow, *Der Transportvertrag*, Tübingen, J.C.B. Mohr (Paul Siebeck), 1987, at p. 322; D. Rabe, *Seehandelsrecht*, München, Verlag C.H. Beck, 2000 (4th Ed.), n° 2 at p. 626; G. Schaps and H. Abraham, *Das Seerecht in der Bundesrepublik Deutschland, Seehandelsrecht*, Vol. 1, Berlin, Walter de Gruyter, 1978 (4th Ed.), n° 15 at p. 750; F. Sparka, *Jurisdiction and Arbitration Clauses in Maritime Transport Documents*, Berlin, Springer, 2010, at p. 176.
  BGH 27 October 1960 (Case N° II ZR 127/59), NJW 1961, 665; BGH 25 September 1986 (Case N° II ZR 26/86), *N.J.W.* 1987, 588.
  For a critical appraisal of the majority view, see C.-W. Canaris, W. Schilling and P. Ulmer (Eds), *Handelsgesetzbuch Großkommentar, begründet von Hermann Staub*, Berlin, De Gruyter, 2001 (4th Ed.), § 363 n° 58–60 at pp. 64–65.
  See also T. Eckardt, *The Bolero Bill of Lading Under German and English Law*, München, Sellier European Law Publishers, 2004, at p. 64; M. Spanjaart, *Vorderingsrechten uit cognossement*, Zutphen, Uitgeverij Paris, 2012, at pp. 240–241.
189 R. Cleveringa, *Zeerecht*, Zwolle, Tjeenk Willink, 1961 (4th Ed.), at p. 599; T. Dorhout Mees and A. Van Empel, *Nederlands handels- en faillissementsrecht*, IV, *Vervoer*, Arnhem, Gouda Quint, 1980 (7th Ed.), n° 8.11 at p. 6; S. Geense, "De 'merchant-clausule', 190 *NTHR* 2011-5, at p. 197; R. Japikse, *Verkeersmiddelen en Vervoer. Deel I. Algemene bepalingen en rederij*, Asser Serie, Deventer, Kluwer, 2004, n° 216 at p. 121; A. Korthals Altes and J.J. Wiarda, *Vervoerrecht*, Serie Recht en Praktijk, Deventer, Kluwer, 1980, at p. 52; H. Logmans, *Zekerheid op lading*, Zutphen, Uitgeverij Paris, 2011, at p. 267; W. Molengraaff, *Leidraad bij de beoefening van het Nederlandsche Handelsrecht*, Haarlem, De Erven F. Bohn, 1912 (2nd Ed.), at p. 370; W. Oostwouder, *Hoofdzaken Boek 8 BW. Verkeersmiddelen en vervoer*, Deventer, Kluwer, 2001 (3th Ed.), at p. 73; P. Seck, *Reisbevrachting en cognossementsvervoer*, Zutphen, Uitgeverij Paris, 2011, at p. 186; M. Spanjaart, *Vorderingsrechten uit cognossement*, Zutphen, Uitgeverij Paris, 2012, at p. 98; P. van Huizen, "Het incasso (endossement) in het vervoer", 71 *T.V.R.* 1999, at p. 71; R. Zwitser, "Toetreden tot de vervoersovereenkomst; het Contship America", 33 *T.V.R.* 2000, at p. 35 and p. 39; R. Zwitser, "De cognossementhouder als derde uit derdenbeding", *T.V.R.* 2002, at p. 157; R. Zwitser, "Het cognossement als zekerheidsinstrument", 83 *NTHR* 2007-2, at p. 90.
  When Book 8 of the Dutch Civil Code was introduced, the competent Minister was asked whether the holder of a bill of lading becomes a party to the contract of carriage. In his answer, the Minister pointed out that the Code defines the rights and obligations of the holder in quite some detail in order to avoid the need for such questions, but then added that the obligations of the carrier to the holder of the B/L correspond to a third-party beneficiary clause (M. Claringbould, *Parlementaire Geschiedenis Boek 8, Verkeersmiddelen en vervoer*, Deventer, Kluwer, 1992, at p. 474.)
  See for a very peculiar (but incorrect) position M. Claringbould, "Het cognossement", in *Preadvies van de Vereeniging Handelsrecht en de Nederlandse Vereniging voor zee- en vervoerrecht. Vervoersrecht in Boek 8 BW*, Zwolle, Tjeenk Willink, 1997, at pp. 138–139. The author argues that the third-party beneficiary clause is actually part of the *bill of lading contract*, which exists between the carrier and the bill of lading holder. In this view, however, the holder of the bill of lading is at the same time a contracting party *and* the third-party party beneficiary.
  HR 22 September 2000, *N.J.* 2001, 44, *S&S* 2001, 37 (*ms Eendracht*); HR 29 November 2002, *N.J.* 2003, 374, *S&S* 2003, 62 (*ms Ladoga 15*); CA 's Gravenhage 26 June 2008, *S&S* 2008, 115 (*ms OPDR Lisboa*), point 2.17; Court Rotterdam 10 October 2012, *S&S* 2013, 38 (*ms MSC Daniela*).
  Contra: H. Boonk, *Zeevervoer onder cognossement*, Arnhem, Gouda Quint, 1993, at pp. 11–12; J. Cahen, *Het cognossement*, Arnhem, Gouda Quint, 1964, at p. 5; J. Loeff, *Vervoer ter zee*, Deel I, Zwolle, Tjeenk Willink, 1981, n° 70–71 at p. 48; E. van Beukering-Rosmuller, "De ontvangstexpediteur als cognossementshouder", 61 *T.V.R.* 2000, at p. 64.

view. German law has an additional twist to the theory, because it distinguishes between the contract of carriage, which is made between the shipper and the carrier, and the so-called *Begebungsvertrag*, or contract to issue the bill of lading, which is made between the carrier and the initial holder of the bill of lading. The rights under the bill of lading are, at least in theory, strictly separated from the rights under the contract of carriage.[190] Both the contract of carriage and the *Begebungsvertrag* can contain a third-party beneficiary clause.[191] Where the contract of carriage is relevant, e.g. because no bill of lading was issued, the contract of carriage is deemed to contain a third-party beneficiary clause in favour of the consignee. Where the bill of lading is relevant, the *Begebungsvertrag* between the carrier and the first holder is deemed to contain a third-party beneficiary clause in favour of the subsequent holders of the bill of lading.

In the U.K., third-party beneficiary clauses remained problematic until they were formally recognized and regulated by the Contracts (Rights of Third Parties) Act 1999, which however excludes bills of lading from its scope of application (Sec. 6.(5) and 6.(6)). Unsurprisingly, then, the third-party beneficiary clause concept has not been very popular in the context of bills of lading in the U.K., although not entirely without advocates either.[192] In the U.S.A., on the other hand, the courts from the 19th century onwards started to recognize that parties in their contract could indeed grant enforceable rights to third parties,[193] and third-party beneficiary clauses were included in the *Restatement of Contracts*

---

190 O. Hartenstein and F. Reuschle, *Handbuch des Fachanwalts: Transport- und Speditionsrecht*, Cologne, Luchterhand, 2010, n° 74 at p. 178; R. Herber, *Seehandelsrecht: Systematische Darstellung*, Berlin, De Gruyter, 2016 (2nd Ed.), at p. 247 and p. 307; G. Schaps and H. Abraham, *Das Seerecht in der Bundesrepublik Deutschland, Seehandelsrecht*, Berlin, Walter de Gruyter, 1978 (4th Ed.), Vol. 2, N° 2 at p. 814; C. Stumm, *Der Ablader im Seehandelsrecht: Eine rechtsvergleichende Darstellung des deutschen und des amerikanischen Rechts*, Berlin, LIT Verlag, 2010, at pp. 45, 68 and 74.

191 W. Bayer, *Der Vertrag zugunsten Dritter*, Tübingen, J.C.B. Mohr (Paul Siebeck), 1995, at p. 173 (regarding the contract of carriage) and at p. 179 (regarding the *Begebungsvertrag*); C.-W. Canaris, W. Schilling and P. Ulmer (Eds), *Handelsgesetzbuch Großkommentar, begründet von Hermann Staub*, Berlin, De Gruyter, 2001 (4th Ed.) § 363 n° 60 at p. 65 (regarding the *Begebungsvertrag*); H. Gramm, *Das neue Deutsche Seefrachtrecht nach den Haager Regeln*, Berlin, E.S. Mittler & Sohn, 1938, at p. 152 (regarding the *Begebungsvertrag*); R. Herber, *Seehandelsrecht: Systematische Darstellung*, Berlin, De Gruyter, 2016 (2nd Ed.), at p. 236 and p. 243 (regarding the contract of carriage) and at p. 315 (regarding the *Begebungsvertrag*); D. Rabe, *Seehandelsrecht*, München, Verlag C.H. Beck, 2000 (4th Ed.), n° 14 at p. 304 (general), n° 49 at p. 316 (regarding the contract of carriage) and n° 10 at p. 731 (regarding the *Begebungsvertrag*); G. Schaps and H. Abraham, *Das Seerecht in der Bundesrepublik Deutschland, Seehandelsrecht*, Vol. 1, Berlin, Walter de Gruyter, 1978 (4th Ed.), n° 14 at p. 438 (regarding the contract of carriage).
See also M. Spanjaart, *Vorderingsrechten uit cognossement*, Zutphen, Uitgeverij Paris, 2012, at p. 241.

192 R. Bradgate and F. White, "The Carriage of Goods by Sea Act 1992", 56 *Mod. L. Rev.* at p. 207 ("*The contract for sea carriage is an example* par excellence *of a contract for the benefit of a third party*").

193 D. Summers, "Third party beneficiaries and the Restatement (second) of contracts", 880 *Cornell L. Rev.* 1982, at p. 881 and fn. 15.

from their first edition (1932).[194] The possibility of construing the holder of the bill of lading as a third-party beneficiary was already discussed in *Griffith v Ingledew*,[195] and has survived as a possible explanation ever since, although the courts also point out that a third-party beneficiary clause cannot create obligations on the part of the beneficiary.[196]

3.2.1.3 *When does the relationship come into being?*

75 In order to determine at what time the relationship between the promisor (carrier) and the third-party beneficiary (B/L holder) comes into being, a distinction has to be made between the Dutch concept of a third-party beneficiary clause and the concept as it exists in many other legal systems. Generally, the third party's right comes into being the moment the contract between the promisee and the promisor is made. The intended third party obviously has the option never to use the right, but it exists. Acceptance of the right by the third party only makes the right irrevocable, but is not required for the right to exist. Under Dutch law, on the other hand, acceptance by the third party is required for the right to come into being. The contract between the promisee and the promisor only creates a possibility: the intended third party can, if he chooses to do so, bring the right to life by accepting the third-party beneficiary clause.

76 In the majority view, a further distinction has to be made depending on whether the beneficiary is identified or not. For the validity of the third-party beneficiary clause, it is not required that the intended beneficiary is uniquely identified or even exists at the time the contract is made. It is sufficient that he is identifiable at the relevant time. In the bill of lading context, the intended beneficiary is known in case of a straight bill of lading. He is also known, but with

---

194 D. Summers, "Third party beneficiaries and the restatement (second) of contracts", 880 *Cornell L. Rev.* 1982, at p. 883.

195 *Griffith v Ingledew* 1821 WL 1807, 9 Am.Dec. 444, 6 Serg. & Rawle 429 (Supreme Court of Pennsylvania, April 1821), per Tilghman C.J.: "*The question, then, is reduced to a single point: If one man, in consideration of value received from another, promises to do a thing for the benefit of a third, can that third person support an action? And that he can, was long ago decided in the case of Dutton and Wife v Pool (cit. omitted) and Starkey v Mill (cit. omitted). (...) So, in the case before us, a promise in law may be said to have been made to the plaintiff, that the goods should be carried safely; indeed, it might almost be said, that a promise in fact was made to the plaintiff, for the bill of lading does not expressly make a promise to any body.*"

See also *Polo Ralph Lauren L.P. v Tropical Shipping & Construction Co. Ltd* 215 F.3d 1217 (11th Circuit, 21 June 2000), where the owner of the shipped goods, which was not mentioned in the bill of lading, was considered a possible third-party beneficiary of the bill of lading.

196 *In re m/v Rickmers Genoa litigation*, 622 F.Supp.2d 56, 2009 AMC 609 (S.D. New York, 31 March 2009), at p. 72: "*Of course, common law third-party beneficiary principles may be applicable when interpreting bills of lading. Generally, the Restatement says that to the extent a third party qualifies as an intended beneficiary, it may enforce contract terms in its favour. However, qualifying as an intended beneficiary in no way creates contractual obligations on the part of the intended beneficiary.*"

the possibility of substitution, in case of an order bill of lading,[197] and he is not known in case of a bearer bill of lading. That in turn means that, with a straight bill of lading, the relationship between the holder and the carrier comes into being when the contract of carriage is made between the shipper and the carrier. With order and bearer bills, the answer is more complex. In general, when the intended beneficiary is not immediately known, the relationship with the promisor only comes into being once the beneficiary can indeed be uniquely identified, although it is also argued that this identification has a retroactive effect to the date the contract was made.[198] The question then is at what time the intended beneficiary of an order or bearer bill can be positively identified? That question raises a preliminary question, viz. *who exactly* did the shipper and the carrier intend to be the beneficiary?[199] Is the intended beneficiary simply the lawful holder of the bill of lading,[200] i.e. the endorsee of an order bill of lading or the physical holder of a bearer bill of lading, or is it only the lawful holder who actually presents the bill of lading to the carrier to obtain delivery of the goods? Contracts of carriage usually do not contain an explicit third-party beneficiary clause – the third-party beneficiary character is a construction of the courts and legal scholars –, and thus do not explicitly define who is the intended beneficiary. The authors that advocate the third-party beneficiary solution hardly touch upon this issue either. If the intended beneficiary is any 'third-party' holder, i.e. any holder who did not make the contract of carriage himself, the relation between the carrier and the holder comes into being when the bill of lading is endorsed or physically transferred to the third-party holder. If, on the other hand, it is accepted that the intended beneficiary is only the 'final' holder, who presents the bill of lading to the carrier for delivery, the relation between the carrier and the holder comes into being in the port of delivery, at the time of presentation.

77 In the Dutch view, the contract between the promisee (shipper) and the promisor (carrier) does not immediately create a *right* for the intended beneficiary. It only creates a *possibility* for the latter to bring this right into being by accepting the clause.[201] In general, there are no formal requirements regarding the required

---

197 With order bills of lading, there is a special case when the bill is simply 'to order', without specifically naming a consignee. In that case, the bill of lading is considered to be to order of the shipper. The shipper, however, is the contract partner of the carrier, and thus cannot be a third-party beneficiary.
198 N. Carette, *Derdenbeding*, Antwerp, Intersentia, 2011, n° 544 at p. 455 and n° 557–565 at pp. 462–468.
199 Compare H. Logmans, *Zekerheid op lading*, Zutphen, Uitgeverij Paris, 2011, at p. 268.
200 Compare R. Zwitser, "De cognossementhouder als derde uit derdenbeding", *T.V.R.* 2002, at p. 159: "*Een 'gewoon' derdenbeding is gericht tot een met name genoemde persoon. Bij het cognossement daarentegen strekt het derdenbeding ten voordele van een in kwaliteit aangeduide persoon, namelijk de rechthebbende op het cognossement.*" (A 'standard' third-party beneficiary clause benefits a person identified by name. In the bill of lading on the other hand the third-party beneficiary clause benefits a person identified by quality, viz. the person entitled to the bill of lading.)
201 The existence of a right, simply because of the contract between the promisee and the promisor and without intervention of the beneficiary, is seen as a violation of the privity of contract, even if it is only a right and thus a benefit for the third party.

acceptance, which can be by notification to the promisor, by conduct, etc.[202] As regards bills of lading, however, the majority view is that acceptance only takes place – and the relation between the carrier and the holder thus only comes into being – when the holder presents the bill of lading to the carrier and claims delivery.[203] The acquisition of the bill of lading from the shipper or from a previous holder provides the new holder with the possibility to claim delivery, but is not in itself an acceptance of the third-party beneficiary clause.[204] A few authors, however, have argued that the holder of a bill of lading already accepts the third-party beneficiary clause by taking over the bill of lading from a previous holder.[205] Remarkably, they mostly do so to solve specific problems. Dorhout Mees has the holder enter into a relation with the carrier upon taking over the bill of lading to

---

HR 13 February 1924, *N.J.* 1924, 711 (*Gouda / Ontvanger der Registratie*). See also R. Zwitser, "De cognossementhouder als derde uit derdenbeding", *T.V.R.* 2002, at p. 158.

202 A. Korthals Altes and J.J. Wiarda, *Vervoerrecht*, Serie Recht en Praktijk, Deventer, Kluwer, 1980, at p. 52.

203 H. Boonk, "HR 29 november 2002 RvdW 2002, 197 (Ladoga 15): de grondslag van de rechtsverkrijging door de derde cognossementhouder", *T.V.R.* 2003, at p. 136; M. Claringbould, "Het cognossement", in *Preadvies van de Vereeniging Handelsrecht en de Nederlandse Vereniging voor zee- en vervoerrecht. Vervoersrecht in Boek 8 BW*, Zwolle, Tjeenk Willink, 1997, at p. 139 (the author bases his argument on the requirement for the third party to notify his acceptance to the carrier); J. Eckoldt, *De forumkeuze in het zeevervoer*, Zutphen, Uitgeverij Paris, 2014, at p. 163; S. Geense, "De 'merchant-clausule'", *NTHR* 2011–5, at p. 197; H. Logmans, *Zekerheid op lading*, Zutphen, Uitgeverij Paris, 2011, at p. 267; R. Japikse, "Boekbeschouwing: Mr. G.J. van der Ziel, Het cognossement, naar een functionele benadering", *RM Themis* 2000/5, at p. 194 (the author bases his position primarily on the necessity for the carrier to know who his counterparty is); M. Spanjaart, *Vorderingsrechten uit cognossement*, at p. 91, p. 151 and fn. 496; A. Van Oven, *Handelsrecht*, Zwolle, Tjeenk Willink, 1981, n° 123 at p. 255; Zwitser (2000), at pp. 40–42 (the author makes an exception for a straight bill of lading, where the acquisition of the B/L does create the relationship).

204 H. Boonk, "HR 29 november 2002 RvdW 2002, 197 (Ladoga 15): de grondslag van de rechtsverkrijging door de derde cognossementhouder", 132 *T.V.R.* 2003, at p. 136.

205 R. Van Delden, *Overzicht van de handelskoop*, Deventer, Kluwer, 1983, fn. 3 at p. 330.
  See for an overview S. Geense, "De 'merchant-clausule'", *NTHR* 2011–5, at p. 197. In fn. 92 at p. 198, the author refers to case law that would have supported this position. None of the cited decisions clearly do so, however. In the *Nedlloyd Kyoto* (Court of Rotterdam 12 May 1980, *S&S* 1981, n° 6), the contract of carriage had been made by an agent of the shipper, thus binding the shipper to the contract made on his behalf. In the *Sennar* (Court of Rotterdam 27 June 1977, *S&S* 1977, n° 97), an intermediate holder had sold on the goods to the ultimate buyer, but as a result of the annulment of that sale, had again become the holder of the B/L and claimed as such against the carrier. In the *John Schehr* (Court of Rotterdam 19 June 1973, *S&S* 1973, 73), the Court does say that when a party becomes the holder of the B/L, it also becomes a party to the contract, but since the claimant in that case had also presented the B/L to the carrier, it is not clear whether the Court meant that accepting the B/L always creates a contractual relationship, even if the party does not afterwards present the B/L. Similarly, in the *Velswijk* (CA The Hague, 27 June 1975, *S&S* 1976, n° 3), the Court mentions the acquisition of the B/L, which in that case occurred in the port of destination and was followed by the delivery of the cargo. The *OPDR Lisboa* (CA The Hague 26 June 2008, *S&S* 2008, n° 115) finally does not concern the legal consequences of the acquisition of the B/L.

refuse him the possibility to walk away from the cargo (and more importantly, the associated costs) by simply not presenting the bill of lading at destination.[206] Van der Ziel also has the relation start from the moment of acquisition of the bill of lading, to explain how the holder of the bill of lading can give instructions to the carrier.[207] The problem, of course, is that the carrier is often unaware of the fact that the bill of lading has been acquired by a new holder, and may never know that X or Y has been the holder of the bill of lading for a period of time.[208] Finally, a compromise position is proposed by Zwitser, who argues that acceptance of the third-party beneficiary clause is in principle by the presentation of the bill of lading, but that it can also be earlier, if such early acceptance is what the shipper and the carrier provided for or made possible in the contract of carriage.[209] Whatever the position taken, however, it is clear that in the Dutch view of a third-party beneficiary clause the relationship only comes into being once the beneficiary has actually received the bill of lading.[210] In the majority view on the other hand, the relationship comes into being once the beneficiary is identified.

78 The Dutch Supreme Court in the *Eendracht*[211] has held that presentation of the bill of lading to the carrier is not the only possible way of accepting the third-party beneficiary clause. In this case, a cargo of beer tanks had been shipped for Malta, but suffered weather damage early in the voyage. Shipper, carrier and consignee all agreed to have the ship return to port and the tanks repaired by the manufacturer. When the consignee sued the carrier for the repair costs, however,

---

See also J. Basedow, *Der Transportvertrag*, Tübingen, J.C.B. Mohr (Paul Siebeck), 1987, at p. 324, who requires an explicit provision in the B/L that makes 'the holder' liable for freight or other obligations.

206 T. Dorhout Mees and A. Van Empel, *Nederlands handels- en faillissementsrecht*, IV, *Vervoer*, Arnhem, Gouda Quint, 1980 (7th Ed.), at p. 6.
 In an earlier version of this book, the author had also pointed out that a third-party beneficiary clause can be revoked as long as the beneficiary has not accepted it. Thus, the earlier the consignee is deemed to accept the clause, the quicker it becomes irrevocable. Compare J. Loeff, *Vervoer ter zee*, Deel I, Zwolle, Tjeenk Willink, 1981, n° 71 at pp. 48–49.

207 G.J. van der Ziel, *Het cognossement, naar een functionele benadering*, Deventer, Kluwer, 1999, at p. 6. In his review of this publication, Japikse pointed out that a holder of the bill of lading, if he wants to give instructions during the voyage, will often have to 'present' the B/L, i.e. will have to prove to the carrier that he holds all originals of the B/L (R. Japikse, "Boekbeschouwing: Mr. G.J. van der Ziel, Het cognossement, naar een functionele benadering", *RM Themis* 2000/5, at p. 193).

208 H. Boonk, "HR 29 november 2002 RvdW 2002, 197 (Ladoga 15): de grondslag van de rechtsverkrijging door de derde cognossementhouder", 132 *T.V.R.* 2003, at p. 136; R. Japikse, "Boekbeschouwing: Mr. G.J. van der Ziel, Het cognossement, naar een functionele benadering", *RM Themis* 2000/5, at pp. 193–194.

209 R. Zwitser, "De cognossementhouder als derde uit derdenbeding", *T.V.R.* 2002, at p. 163.

210 H. Boonk, "HR 29 November 2002 RvdW 2002, 197 (Ladoga 15): de grondslag van de rechtsverkrijging door de derde cognossementhouder", *T.V.R.* 2003, at p. 138.

211 Hoge Raad 22 September 2000, case C98/320HR, *RvdW* 2000, 188, *S&S* 2001, 37, *NJ* 2001, 44 (case note K. Haak).

the carrier argued that the consignee had not presented the bill of lading,[212] thus had not accepted the third-party beneficiary clause and therefore did not have title to sue. The Court of Appeal of the Hague rejected the argument and held that the consignee had accepted the third-party beneficiary clause and become a party to the contract through the parties' joint agreement to have the ship return to port. That decision was later confirmed by the Supreme Court. Two years later, however, in *Ladoga 15*,[213] the Supreme Court cautioned that its earlier *Eendracht* decision doesn't mean that the third-party beneficiary clause can be accepted at any time and in any form whatsoever. In the *Ladoga 15* case, goods had to be shipped from Antwerp to Moscow via Saint Petersburg. Due to problems with the inland leg (St Petersburg – Moscow), all parties agreed to end the carriage in Saint Petersburg and to leave it to the buyer to arrange the further carriage to Moscow. As the carrier initially had to carry the goods on to Moscow, he had already sent one original of the bill of lading to the road carrier in Saint Petersburg, to receive the goods from the vessel and clear them with customs. Following the change in transport plans, the shipper instructed the carrier not to release the goods, as they had not yet been paid for by the buyer. Notwithstanding these instructions, the carrier did in fact release the goods to the road carrier (who in the meantime had been instructed by the buyer) against presentation of the original bill of lading that the road carrier had in his possession. The buyer disappeared, the goods were never paid for and the shipper sued the carrier for damages. As a defence, the carrier argued that the buyer/consignee had accepted the third-party beneficiary clause in his favour and had thus become the lawful holder of the bill of lading, to whom the carrier was entitled and obliged to deliver the goods. The Supreme Court, however, held that in such (admittedly peculiar) circumstances the buyer could not simply choose to accept the third-party beneficiary clause. The end result, that the buyer did not have a valid claim to delivery, is very acceptable in light of the circumstances of the case, but the reasoning is surprising. After all, the buyer had indeed *presented* the bill of lading to the carrier (through an agent, but that is not relevant from a legal point of view), and presentation of the bill of lading is seen as the most obvious way, and for some the only way, to accept the third-party beneficiary clause and become a party to the contract.[214] Such result is not entirely unique, though. In *MSC*

---

212 The consignee had eventually received the bills of lading, but only after the tanks had already been returned to the port of shipment and discharged.
213 Hoge Raad 29 November 2002, case C01/105HR, *RvdW* 2002, 197, *S&S* 2003, 62, *NJ* 2003, 374 (case note K. Haak).
214 It would seem that the Supreme Court actually intended to say that the buyer acquired the bill of lading under circumstances that did not *allow* it to present it to the carrier and demand delivery. The buyer had not received the bill of lading from the seller, and the road carrier, which had received the bill of lading in another context, should not have 'released' the bill of lading to the buyer (which in fact it did by presenting the bill of lading on behalf of the buyer). The Court's playing field, however, is shaped and delimited by the arguments of the parties, and the parties apparently constructed their arguments very much in light of the Court's decision in the *Eendracht*.

Claudia, the Court of Appeal of The Hague also concluded that the named consignee, who had obtained delivery of the goods, nevertheless had not become a party to the contract (and thus apparently had not accepted the third-party beneficiary clause in his favour). Caterpillar had instructed Skelton to arrange the carriage of two underground loaders on flat racks from Melbourne to Rotterdam. Skelton booked the sea voyage with MSC, which issued a straight bill of lading, indicating Skelton as the shipper and Wilmink, the company with which Skelton worked in the Netherlands, as consignee. Wilmink had received a copy of the MSC bill of lading from Skelton and took delivery of the goods after Skelton had presented the original bill of lading to MSC. When the flat racks went missing and Wilmink was sued by MSC, however, both the Rotterdam Court[215] and the Court of Appeal of the Hague[216] held that Wilmink was not bound by the provisions of the bill of lading and could not be held liable by MSC, because it had not become a party to the contract. In light of the fact that the bill of lading was a straight bill of lading and that the named consignee had indeed claimed and obtained delivery, this is a rather surprising decision. It is true that the bill of lading was physically presented to the carrier by Skelton, but it is clear that it did so on behalf of Wilmink, to enable Wilmink to take delivery of the goods.[217] To summarize, the basic rule is that the holder of the bill of lading accepts the third-party beneficiary clause and enters into a contractual relationship with the carrier when he presents the bill of lading and claims delivery. Under the right circumstances, however, other actions or conduct of the holder can also constitute acceptance of the third-party beneficiary clause, while on the other hand, actual presentation of the bill of lading does not always and necessarily mean that the holder has indeed accepted the third-party clause.

3.2.1.4 *Intermediate holders*

79 What is the position of intermediate holders in the third-party beneficiary construction? The answer to this question again depends on the answer to the earlier question, *viz.* who exactly is the intended beneficiary?[218] If the intended beneficiary is only the party that holds the bill of lading and actually presents it to the carrier to obtain delivery, intermediate holders do not have a legal position vis-à-vis the carrier. They are not the intended beneficiary and thus cannot accept the third-party beneficiary clause. As a consequence, they neither have rights nor

---

215 Court of Rotterdam 3 November 2004, *S&S* 2005, n° 86.
216 CA The Hague 28 July 2009, *S&S* 2010, n° 108 (ms. *MSC Claudia / Kapitan Kudlay*).
217 The alternative interpretation, that Skelton itself presented the bill of lading *as shipper*, while Wilmink only acted as a subcontractor for Skelton, may well be what actually happened or was intended in practice, but is not in line with how the bill of lading was made out. The bill was a straight bill of lading, naming Wilmink as the consignee, which means that the carrier was only entitled to deliver to Wilmink.
218 See also above, n° 76 p. 78.

obligations to the carrier.[219] If, on the other hand, the intended beneficiary is any party that acquires the bill of lading, the first party to indeed acquire the bill of lading will enter into a legal relationship with the carrier.[220] The question then is, however, how this first holder transfers its rights and obligations to the subsequent holder(s) and to the ultimate holder. Such transfer must follow from and be based on the underlying contract between the holder at a certain point and the subsequent holder, which could mean that defences that the carrier had against the first holder are transferred to subsequent holders. An alternative (though rather exceptional) approach would be to consider *every* holder of the bill of lading an intended beneficiary, allowing all of them to accept the third-party beneficiary clause and become parties to the contract.[221] If the bill of lading is transferred several times, the end result would be that the carrier has multiple contract partners. In practice, of course, the carrier is often unaware of the existence or the identity of the intermediate holders, which simple fact will suffice to shield them from claims or actions by the carrier. From a legal point of view, however, it is important to know whether the intermediate holders are indeed in a contractual relationship with the carrier. It is quite clear that intermediate holders no longer have the right to claim delivery (or compensation) since they no longer hold the bill of lading. If intermediate holders remain bound, however, they could be sued by the carrier for freight, costs, etc. if the primary targets for such claims are unavailable or insolvent. Most authors, however, are of the opinion that intermediate holders are *not* bound once they have parted with the bill of lading.[222]

---

219 In that sense, R. Japikse, "Boekbeschouwing: Mr. G.J. van der Ziel, Het cognossement, naar een functionele benadering", *RM Themis* 2000/5, at p. 194.
220 Compare S. Geense, "De 'merchant-clausule'", *NTHR* 2011-5, at p. 199, who argues that accepting a bill of lading and transferring it to a third party implies acceptance of the third-party beneficiary clause and thus the creation of a contractual relationship with the carrier. The Supreme Court decision that he cites in support of this position (HR 15 February 1980, *S&S* 1980, n° 63, ms. *Agatha*) does not (clearly) say so, though. A forwarding company (Atlas) had been instructed by the importer of chemical products to arrange their carriage from Rotterdam to Mannheim by inland vessel. Atlas instructed a shipping company (Stasse), which in turn instructed another shipping company (NPRC), which issued a bill of lading listing Atlas as the shipper. Atlas had paid the freight and demurrage to its immediate contract partner Stasse, which then went bankrupt and did not pay NPRC. NPRC then sued Atlas under the bill of lading in payment of freight and demurrage. The Supreme Court held that Atlas was the principal ('*Auftraggeber*') under the bill of lading, and thus could be sued by NPRC. The Supreme Court also held that the fact that Atlas had already paid the freight to Stasse was not a defence against NPRC under the bill of lading, and ordered Atlas to pay a second time. The Court, however, does not say that Atlas was to be considered the principal ('*Auftraggeber*'), because it had accepted the bill of lading and forwarded it to the consignee in Germany; it is in fact not even clear from the decision whether Atlas had ever received the B/L.
221 R. Zwitser, "De cognossementhouder als derde uit derdenbeding", *T.V.R.* 2002, at p. 159 and p. 163.
222 M. Claringbould, "Het cognossement", in *Preadvies van de Vereeniging Handelsrecht en de Nederlandse Vereniging voor zee- en vervoerrecht. Vervoersrecht in Boek 8 BW*, Zwolle, Tjeenk Willink, 1997, at p. 140; M. Spanjaart, *Vorderingsrechten uit cognossement*, Zutphen,

3.2.1.5 *The non-contracting shipper*

80 Can the third-party beneficiary concept provide a solution for the position of the non-contracting shipper, when the contract of carriage is made between the carrier and the consignee? Theoretically, it is of course possible for the carrier and the consignee to decide to create a benefit for a third party (the shipper).[223] It is, however, rather hard to see what that benefit would be. If the contract of carriage is made by the consignee, it follows that the shipper is not interested in the carriage as such. He only has to deliver the goods to the vessel; what happens thereafter does not concern him. What benefit could the carrier and consignee confer to the non-contracting shipper in those circumstances? It does have to be a *benefit*; contracting parties cannot impose *obligations* on third parties.

81 Some authors have suggested that the benefit conferred is the right to obtain the bill of lading. That, however, is a very debatable point of view.[224] To the non-contracting shipper, the bill of lading is simply a receipt, proof that the shipper did indeed deliver the goods to the carrier. If goods are handed over to another party, the right to obtain a receipt is a basic right that does not depend upon or need to be created by other parties. Obviously, the underlying sales agreement or the payment arrangements will often require the seller/shipper to obtain a bill of lading. This is, however, because the buyer wants or needs a negotiable document. The seller/shipper only needs to prove that he has satisfied his obligation to deliver the sold goods. To this, one could object that the non-contracting shipper may need to use the bill of lading as a document of title, if the underlying transaction doesn't go through and he needs to recover the goods from the carrier. Such a situation may indeed occur, but here also, the right for a party to recover what he has already 'paid' (in the largest sense of the term) if the deal falls apart is elementary and does not need to be specifically created by other parties. In most cases, therefore, there is no (relevant) benefit that the carrier and consignee could confer to the non-contracting shipper, which in turn means that the third-party beneficiary construction cannot really explain the position of the non-contracting shipper.[225]

Uitgeverij Paris, 2012, at p. 91 and fn. 280; R. Zwitser, "Toetreden tot de vervoersovereenkomst; het Contship America", *T.V.R.* 2000, at p. 42.

223 M. Claringbould, *Het schip en zijn cognossementen*, Deventer, Kluwer, 1996, p. 32–33; R. Zwitser, "Toetreden tot de vervoersovereenkomst; het Contship America", *T.V.R.* 2000, at p. 40; R. Zwitser, "De cognossementhouder als derde uit derdenbeding", *T.V.R.* 2002, at p. 158.
Compare S. Geense, "De 'merchant-clausule'", *NTHR* 2011-5, at p. 202; M. Spanjaart, *Vorderingsrechten uit cognossement*, Zutphen, Uitgeverij Paris, at p. 148.

224 Compare M. Spanjaart, *Vorderingsrechten uit cognossement*, Zutphen, Uitgeverij Paris, at pp. 148–149.
See also R. Herber, *Seehandelsrecht: Systematische Darstellung*, Berlin, De Gruyter, 2016 (2nd Ed.), at p. 242: the *Ablader* (non-contracting shipper) is not a party to the contract of carriage, even though under German law he is entitled to demand a bill of lading (§ 513. (1) HGB) and is subject to certain liabilities (§ 488.(3) HGB).

225 Compare H. Boonk, *Zeevervoer onder cognossement*, Arnhem, Gouda Quint, 1993, at p. 12; C. Paulin, *Droits des transports*, Paris, Litec, 2005, n° 434 at p. 225.

86 *Contractual theories*

82 In addition, even if it is accepted that the consignee and the carrier include a third-party beneficiary clause in favour of the non-contracting shipper in their contract of carriage, the question remains which benefit exactly is conferred. A third-party beneficiary clause has no fixed or predefined content. It is up to the contract parties to decide which right(s) they intend to bestow upon the beneficiary. If the benefit is only the right to obtain a bill of lading as proof of delivery of the goods to the carrier, the theory explains that the non-contracting shipper is named as 'shipper' on the bill of lading and receives the bill of lading from the carrier, but does not automatically explain how the non-contracting shipper can become the proper and lawful holder of the bill of lading, entitled to enforce the rights under the bill of lading. Unless it is a bearer bill or a bill of lading simply 'to order', the party named as shipper on the document is not the party entitled to claim under the bill of lading. From a theoretical point of view, of course, the problem can be solved by construing an elaborate third-party beneficiary clause, covering all possible scenarios in which a non-contracting shipper might need to act against the carrier, but the end result then is more legal fiction than a real intention of the contract parties.

3.2.1.6 Appraisal

83 Carriage of goods almost always involves a third party. The contract of carriage is made between the carrier and a shipper, but the goods are collected at destination by someone else. It is hardly surprising then that the legal concept of a third-party beneficiary clause comes to mind. This is particularly so for contracts of carriage where the transport documents used are not negotiable documents of title. In such case, the third party (consignee) is identified by the contract of carriage and the transport document, and can only be changed by a joint decision of the shipper and the carrier, i.e. the original parties to the contract. Even in that situation, however, where there is an obvious analogy to a traditional third-party beneficiary clause, the consignee's position must not necessarily or unavoidably be construed on the basis of a third-party beneficiary clause. In carriage situations where the transport document used is a negotiable document of title, the parallel is less clear and there are quite a number of difficulties with applying the third-party beneficiary concept.

84 A third-party beneficiary clause, first of all, requires the intention of the contracting parties (carrier and shipper) to create a benefit for a third party, that can be legally enforced by that third party. Such intention is not always present, however.[226] In case of an FOB sale, the contract of carriage is made by the consignee, who has no intention to create a benefit for someone else.[227] The FOB

---

226 Compare R. De Wit, *Multimodal Transport: Carrier Liability and Documentation*, London, Lloyd's of London Press, 1995, n° 5.4 at p. 245; P. Seck, *Reisbevrachting en cognossementsvervoer*, Zutphen, Uitgeverij Paris, 2011, at p. 199; G. Treitel and F. Reynolds, *Carver on Bills of Lading*, London, Sweet & Maxwell, 2011 (3rd Ed.), n° 5–002 at p. 210.
227 On the theory that the consignee and the carrier intend to confer the right to obtain the bill of lading, see above, n° 81–82 p. 85–86.

buyer/consignee intends to take delivery of the goods himself. Nevertheless, if the consignee changes his mind (e.g. because there are technical problems at the plant and he cannot use the goods at that time) and decides to sell on the goods and transfer the bill of lading, he can do so without any problem. He does not first have to exchange the 'bill of lading *without* a third-party beneficiary clause' for a 'bill of lading *with* a third-party beneficiary clause' or renegotiate with the carrier to have the contract of carriage amended. The bill of lading, even though there was no initial intention to create a benefit for a third party, will function like any other bill of lading. On a theoretical level, this problem could perhaps be solved by arguing that, when parties allow a bill of lading to be issued, they must be assumed to have included a third-party beneficiary clause, even if they did not in fact realize that they were doing so. As the example shows, the consignee may at some stage need to transfer the bill of lading to a third party, even if he did not originally intend to so. The argument is not entirely convincing, though. There are indeed cases where it is very clear that the parties did *not* intend to create a benefit for a third party by issuing a bill of lading. In the *Pietersgracht*,[228] a German company manufacturing brewery equipment had sold a new plant to a Mexican brewer. The company arranged road carriage to the port of Antwerp itself, and then instructed Samskip to arrange sea carriage to Mexico and oncarriage by road to the location of the new plant, where it would be put together and installed by the German manufacturer. The ocean carrier issued a bill of lading, which (apparently) the Mexican road carrier used to take delivery of the equipment. Samskip itself however also issued an ocean bill of lading, although that document was not needed for the performance of the carriage, solely *for customs purposes*. The Mexican brewer needed the Samskip bill of lading to be able to declare the equipment with the Mexican customs. It is clear that in such circumstances, there is no actual intention to create an enforceable right for a third party, and that an assumed intention to that effect would be little more than a fiction. To the parties, the bill of lading was simply an administrative document.[229] Nevertheless, should the need have arisen to sell the equipment (e.g. in case of a bankruptcy of the Mexican brewer), the bill of lading could have been used for that purpose. An (actual or presumed) intention of the original parties is thus not required for the bill of lading to function.

85 The essential object of a third-party beneficiary clause is to create an enforceable right for a third party. That supposes, of course, that the third party is identified or at least identifiable. This is not an issue with a straight bill of lading,

---

228 CA Antwerp 5 October 2009, *T.B.H.* 2010, 93 (*Pietersgracht*).
229 For a comparable case, see CA Paris 22 October 2003, *D.M.F.* 2004, 601 (*Navire Theophano*). A French shipper of industrial equipment had contracted with the company SCAC for carriage from France to Qatar. SCAC in turn had made a booking with Bonyad, for which the latter had issued a bill of lading. As the parties apparently needed a French bill of lading, however, SCAC had also requested the French shipping company Delmas to issue a bill of lading, which it did. The Paris Court of Appeal held that the Delmas bill of lading, which only served 'organisational purposes', was not evidence of a contract of carriage and could not serve as a basis to hold Delmas liable for the cargo damage.

88 Contractual theories

where there is a named consignee, but it is a problem with order and bearer bills of lading.[230] Is the intended beneficiary any party which happens to be the holder of the bill of lading at a given moment, or is the intended beneficiary only the ultimate holder at destination? What if party A, who holds the bill of lading in January, instructs the carrier to deliver the cargo in Hamburg instead of in Antwerp as initially foreseen, and then sells the goods and transfers the bill of lading to party B, who takes delivery in Hamburg in February? A and B must both be intended beneficiaries and must both have accepted the third-party beneficiary clause in their favour. If not, then either A could not have instructed the carrier to change the port of delivery or B could not have claimed delivery of the cargo.[231] There could be situations where even more parties have interacted with the carrier under the bill of lading. It is also possible that the different originals of the bill of lading are in the hands of different parties, which then all are entitled to claim delivery, as long as they do so first. The answer therefore must be that the intended beneficiary is any lawful holder of the bill of lading.

Being an *intended* beneficiary, however, does not necessarily or automatically mean that one will actually enter into a relationship with the carrier. The intended beneficiary must accept the right that the promisee and promisor have created for him and must notify the promisee and/or promisor of his acceptance. How exactly the beneficiary can or must accept is not clear, though. Presentation of the bill of lading to obtain delivery is often mentioned as an (obvious) way to accept the third-party beneficiary clause, but in the *Eendracht*, the Dutch Supreme Court held that this is not the only way. On the other hand, in *Ladoga 15*, the Dutch Supreme Court held that, although the consignee had actually presented the bill of lading (through an agent), the third-party beneficiary clause cannot be accepted in any way and at any time whatsoever.[232] The correct answer would seem to be that the beneficiary accepts by enforcing a right under the bill of lading against the carrier (or possibly the shipper, although that is unlikely in practice). Enforcing a right is an unmistakable indication that the intended beneficiary has indeed accepted the right, and by enforcing it against the promisor, the latter is necessarily made aware of this acceptance. The right to claim delivery is the most obvious right under the bill of lading, and presenting the bill of lading to the carrier to obtain delivery of the cargo is the most obvious way for the holder to accept the third-party beneficiary clause, but it is not the only right under the bill of lading and not the only way to accept. Any time a lawful holder

---

230 See above, n° 76 p. 78.
231 An alternative answer would be to say that, in a situation as described, there are two distinct bills of lading: the first (original) one, of which A is the beneficiary, and a second (amended) one, of which B is the beneficiary.
232 Admittedly, *Ladoga 15* is a fact-specific case and not very helpful when determining the general principles. The decision would have been clearer and easier to understand if the Court had held that, under the circumstances of the case, the consignee had not become a *lawful* holder of the B/L, and therefore was not entitled to accept the third-party beneficiary clause, rather than holding that such clause cannot be accepted in any way and at any time whatsoever. See also above, n° 78 p. 81.

of the bill of lading enforces a right under it (such as the right to give instructions) against the carrier, he must be deemed to have accepted the third-party beneficiary clause. The consequence is, of course, that multiple beneficiaries can accept the third-party beneficiary clause and thus enter into a relationship with the carrier. In the example above, both A and B have enforced rights under the bill of lading and entered into a relationship with the carrier. This also means that if the carrier is owed money under the bill of lading, he can recover from both A and B. If on the other hand a party has simply held the bill of lading at a certain time, but without enforcing rights under it, that party has not accepted the third-party beneficiary clause and not entered into a relationship with the carrier, and thus cannot be held liable by the carrier.

86 A further problem with the third-party beneficiary construction is that such clause is necessarily based upon a contract between the promisee and the promisor. If that contract is annulled or terminated, the third-party beneficiary clause cannot survive. This will not happen very often in practice, but it is not impossible either. Suppose, for instance, that the contract of carriage is made shortly before the shipper is declared bankrupt, and the trustee in bankruptcy successfully challenges the validity of the contract (e.g. to recover the freight paid by the shipper). The disappearance of the contract of carriage means that also the third-party beneficiary clause disappears, which would render the bill of lading worthless. Since the third-party beneficiary clause no longer exists, the intended beneficiary can no longer accept it. Nevertheless, the German authors in particular are very clear that the bill of lading and the obligations under it remain valid even if the contract of carriage is annulled,[233] and many other legal systems would probably also protect the holder of the bill of lading, if the issue came up.[234] Protection of the third-party holder in such case is necessary, or at the very least warranted to protect the bill of lading's commercial functions, but is hard to reconcile with the pure third-party beneficiary clause concept. Additional concepts or theories such as the protection of third parties in good faith or the law of negotiable instruments are required to arrive at the desired result.

---

233 G. Schaps and H. Abraham, *Das Seerecht in der Bundesrepublik Deutschland, Seehandelsrecht*, Vol. 1, Berlin, Walter de Gruyter, 1978 (4th Ed.), n° 14 at p. 750; C. Stumm, *Der Ablader im Seehandelsrecht: Eine rechtsvergleichende Darstellung des deutschen und des amerikanischen Rechts*, Berlin, LIT Verlag, 2010, at p. 75.

234 Compare R. Zwitser, "De cognossementhouder als derde uit derdenbeding", *T.V.R.* 2002, at p. 158.

See also, in an insurance context, the *Zürich / Lebosch* decision of the Dutch Supreme Court (HR 19 April 2002, *RvdW* 2002, 73, *S&S* 2002, 126, *NJ* 2002, 456 (Zürich / Lebosch)). Lebosch, the consignee of a cargo of milk powder, had received an insurance certificate, issued under a cargo policy taken out by Traconro. The milk powder never arrived at destination, and Lebosch claimed against the insurers. The latter however refused payment, arguing that the underlying policy was void for misrepresentations and concealments by Traconro. The Supreme Court rejected this argument, holding that defences from the underlying policy cannot be invoked against a holder in good faith of the insurance certificate (which was explicitly considered to be a negotiable instrument (*waardepapier*)).

87 Another major problem with the third-party beneficiary construction is that, as long as the clause has not been accepted by the intended beneficiary, it can be revoked if the promisee and promisor agree to do so.[235] As discussed above, the beneficiary accepts the clause by enforcing a right under the bill of lading. Occasionally, this may happen while the goods are still at sea, but most often, it will only be at the end of the voyage, in the port of destination. Until that time, the shipper and the carrier could agree to withdraw their third-party beneficiary clause, which would leave the holder of the bill of lading without any rights at all. Such result, of course, is unacceptable,[236] as it would rob the bill of lading of its commercial value. As soon as the bill of lading is transferred to a third party, the third-party beneficiary clause must become irrevocable. Loeff tries to explain this by arguing that the object of the third-party beneficiary clause is, in fact, the issuing by the carrier of an irrevocable *offer* (in the form of a bill of lading) to the ultimate consignee.[237] This theory, however, makes the third-party beneficiary clause disappear. There is, in Loeff's view, a direct contractual obligation between the shipper and the carrier, obliging the latter to issue an irrevocable offer. Whomever is the beneficiary of that offer will depend on the terms of the offer, not on a third-party beneficiary clause in the contract between the shipper and the carrier, and the beneficiary of the offer derives its rights from the offer itself, not from a third-party beneficiary clause in the contract between the shipper and the carrier. Once the offer has been accepted, there is a separate contractual relationship between the carrier and the party that has accepted the offer. This is, in other words, no longer a third-party beneficiary clause at all.[238] The third-party beneficiary concept cannot really explain how the clause can become irrevocable as soon as the bill of lading is in the hands of a third party, even if that third party has not accepted the clause yet.[239]

88 The third-party beneficiary clause construction would, in principle, also entail that the promisor (carrier) can invoke the defences he has under his contract

---

235 In a 'standard' contract of carriage, not under bill of lading, that is indeed the case: the shipper can modify his instructions to the carrier or cancel the carriage altogether as long as the goods have not been delivered (see, for example, Article 12.(1) CMR, Article 12 Montreal Convention, Article 14.(1) CMNI, Article 18.1 CIM).
236 Compare M. Spanjaart, *Vorderingsrechten uit cognossement*, Zutphen, Uitgeverij Paris, 2012, at p. 213.
237 J. Loeff, *Vervoer ter zee*, Deel I, Zwolle, Tjeenk Willink, 1981, n° 71 at p. 49.
238 One could try to rescue the argument by saying that the enforceable right which is given to the third party is the right to have an offer issued to him and/or a contract made with him (compare N. Carette, *Derdenbeding*, Antwerp, Intersentia, 2011, n° 806 at pp. 737–745). The problem, however, is that the identification of the intended beneficiary then becomes difficult: the intended beneficiary has the right to have a B/L issued to him, but the B/L must have been issued to determine who is the intended beneficiary.
239 R. De Wit, *Multimodal Transport: Carrier Liability and Documentation*, London, Lloyd's of London Press, 1995, n° 5.4 at p. 246.

with the promisee (shipper) against the third party. Under a volume contract, for example, the carrier would in a standard third-party beneficiary setting be able to invoke the shipper's failure to provide the agreed volumes against the holder of the bill of lading. Most authors agree, however, that the carrier cannot invoke such defences, unless they are incorporated in or at least referred to in the bill of lading itself.[240] Also, the bill of lading, even if maybe not entirely a negotiable instrument,[241] at least has certain characteristics of a negotiable instrument. It would be rather surprising if defences from an underlying contract could be invoked against the holder of a negotiable instrument.[242]

89 A common counterargument against the third-party beneficiary concept is that the contracting parties can only grant rights to a third party, but not impose obligations on the third party. In a bill of lading context, however, the holder not only gets the right to claim under the bill of lading, but may also become liable, e.g. for freight, demurrage, costs, etc. For several authors, this is a sufficient reason to dismiss the third-party beneficiary concept.[243] The issue may however be surmountable, especially in a more modern view of the third-party

---

240 R. De Wit, *Multimodal Transport: Carrier Liability and Documentation*, London, Lloyd's of London Press, 1995, n° 5.38 at p. 271.
   See also BGH 25 September 1986 (Case N° II ZR 26/86), *N.J.W.* 1987, 588. The claimant had bought five cars from a car dealer, to be shipped from Germany to Jeddah. The car dealer had instructed a forwarder, who had booked space with a carrier. The carrier had issued 'shipped' bills of lading, while in truth, the cars had not been loaded. The claimant paid the sales price to the car dealer in exchange for an original bill of lading, but never received the cars as they had not been shipped. The claimant then sued the carrier for having issued an incorrect bill of lading. The carrier argued that this is not a standard cargo claim under the bill of lading, that the holder is only protected to the same extent as the '*Ablader*', and that the '*Ablader*' knew that the cars had not actually been shipped. The German Supreme Court rejected the argument, holding that the holder of the bill of lading must be able to rely on the bill of lading, which precludes the carrier from invoking defences that do not appear from the bill of lading itself, even if the claim is not a claim under the bill of lading as such.
241 See below, para 4.4.2.
242 R. De Wit, *Multimodal Transport: Carrier Liability and Documentation*, London, Lloyd's of London Press, 1995, n° 5.4 at p. 245.
243 J. Cahen, *Het cognossement*, Arnhem, Gouda Quint, 1964, at pp. 6–7; R. Cleton, *Hoofdlijnen van het vervoerrecht*, Zwolle, Tjeenk Willink, 1994, at p. 145; R. De Wit, *Multimodal Transport: Carrier Liability and Documentation*, London, Lloyd's of London Press, 1995, n° 5.4 at p. 245; E. Dirix, *Obligatoire verhoudingen tussen contractanten en derden*, 1984, n° 88 at p. 71; G. Ripert, *Droit Maritime*, Tôme II, Paris, Editions Rousseau et Cie., 1952 (4th Ed.), n° 1583–1584 at p. 492; R. Rodière, *Traité général de droit maritime*, Tome II, *Les contrats de transport de marchandises*, Paris, Librairie Dalloz, n° 407 at p. 27; M. Tilche, A. Chao and P. Berthod, "Contrat de transport. Adhésion du destinataire?", *BT* N° 2484, 20 July 1992, at p. 471; A. Van Oven, *Handelsrecht*, Zwolle, Tjeenk Willink, 1981, n° 123 at pp. 253–254.
   Compare R. Zwitser, "De cognossementhouder als derde uit derdenbeding", *T.V.R.* 2002, at p. 159.

beneficiary clause.[244] Dutch[245] and French[246] law recognize the possibility of a third-party beneficiary clause 'with a burden' (*derdenbeding met last, stipulation pour autrui avec charge*). In France, the Supreme Court in 1987 held that the concept of a third-party beneficiary clause does not exclude that the beneficiary becomes bound by certain obligations, if he accepts the clause.[247] The majority of the French authors, however, construes the obligation of the beneficiary as the result of a contract between the beneficiary and the promisor, and not as a result of the third-party beneficiary clause as such.[248] Some see this contract as a voluntary addition on top of the third-party contract, others change the object of the third-party beneficiary clause: the promisor no longer promises a benefit directly, but promises to enter into a contract (or at least to enter into good faith negotiations) regarding the benefit (*stipulation de contrat pour autrui*).[249] This last approach would in fact turn the bill of lading into a contract offer by the carrier to the holder.[250] English and German law distinguish between 'conditional benefits' (*Obliegenheiten*), which are possible, and 'burdens' (*Drittbelastungen*), which are not possible.[251] The difference is that a conditional benefit only gives rise to a defence if the condition is not met, whereas a burden can be enforced by the promisor against the beneficiary. The third-party beneficiary clause could thus provide that the holder of the bill of lading is only entitled to receive the goods if he first pays the freight. If the holder does not pay the freight, the carrier is not obliged to provide the benefit (delivery of the goods), but he cannot force the holder to pay the freight. The clause could not provide, on the other hand, that the holder will be liable for all unpaid costs under the contract of carriage.

---

244 J.-P. Tosi, "L'adhésion du destinataire au contrat de transport", in X., *Mélanges Christian Mouly*, Paris, Litec, 1998, at pp. 178 and 188.
    Compare A. Mesritz, *De Vrachtbrief*, Amsterdam, J.H. de Bussy, 1904, at pp. 70–74. The author explains the obligations of the holder by having him accede to the contract of carriage, with such rights and obligations as determined by the shipper and carrier, but also invokes the lien of the carrier on the cargo as an argument to support the obligations of the holder.
245 A. Hartkamp and C. Sieburgh, *Mr. C. Assers Handleiding tot de beoefening van het Nederlands Burgerlijk Recht. 6. Verbintenissenrecht. Deel III. Algemeen overeenkomstenrecht*, Deventer, Kluwer, 2014 (14th Ed.), n° 564 and n° 575.
246 Ph. Malaurie, L. Aynès and Ph. Stoffel-Munck, *Les obligations*, Paris, Defrénois, 2011 (5th Ed.), n° 819 at p. 427.
247 Cass. fr. 8 December 1987, *Bull. civ.* I, n° 343.
248 Compare A. Kpoahoun Amoussou, *Les clauses attributives de compétence dans le transport maritime de marchandises*, Presses Universitaires d'Aix-Marseille, 2002, n° 647 at p. 412. The author rejects the possibility of a third-party beneficiary clause 'with burden', because a third-party beneficiary does not become a party to the contract, whereas the majority opinion in France does see the consignee as a party to the contract of carriage.
249 N. Carette, *Derdenbeding*, Antwerp, Intersentia, 2011, n° 788–789 at pp. 727–728; J.-P. Tosi, "L'adhésion du destinataire au contrat de transport", in X., *Mélanges Christian Mouly*, Paris, Litec, 1998, at p. 186.
250 See below, para 3.2.3.1.
251 W. Bayer, *Der Vertrag zugunsten Dritter*, Tübingen, J.C.B. Mohr (Paul Siebeck), 1995, at p. 228; N. Carette, *Derdenbeding*, Antwerp, Intersentia, 2011, n° 785 at p. 725.

Although more modern views on the third-party beneficiary concept could thus explain certain obligations of the holder, a full explanation of his position still requires the help of other theories beside the third-party beneficiary clause.

90 In addition to the issues discussed above, there have also been other points of criticism which are less founded or not founded at all. Some authors have argued against the third-party beneficiary concept because often, the position of the holder (beneficiary) is not identical to the position of the shipper (promisee).[252] It has correctly been pointed out, though, that there is no requirement for these positions to be identical.[253] The rights and obligations of the beneficiary do not automatically derive from the rights and obligations of either the promisee or the promisor, but have to be specifically determined by them. The promisee and promisor are free to grant the beneficiary whichever rights they want.

91 It has also been argued that the third-party beneficiary concept cannot explain how the shipper loses certain rights (most importantly the right to claim delivery) to the holder of the bill of lading.[254] It is not evident, however, that the shipper (promisee) actually 'loses' rights to the holder (beneficiary). It is perfectly possible for the contract between the promisee and the promisor to contain obligations to the promisee,[255] and the promisee in any case has a contractual claim against the promisor for performance of the third-party beneficiary clause.[256] It is possible, therefore, to structure the 'contract of carriage with third-party beneficiary clause' in such way as to give both the shipper and the holder of the bill of lading the rights they need.

92 Boonk, who advocates the contract accession theory, points out that in many cases, several parties become involved with the (contract of) carriage: sub-carriers, the shipowner or charterer who has not issued the bill of lading but can nevertheless be sued under the applicable law, stevedores, forwarders, etc.[257] All of these parties may have rights or obligations under the bill of lading. Having these parties accede to the contract of carriage is quite difficult, but considering all of them third-party beneficiaries is even more difficult and farfetched.[258]

---

252 H. Boonk, *Zeevervoer onder cognossement*, Arnhem, Gouda Quint, 1993, at pp. 11–12; R. De Wit, *Multimodal Transport: Carrier Liability and Documentation*, London, Lloyd's of London Press, 1995, n° 5.4 at p. 245; G. Ripert, *Droit Maritime*, Tôme II, Paris, Editions Rousseau et Cie., 1952 (4th Ed.), n° 1585 at p. 493.

253 R. Zwitser, "Toetreden tot de vervoersovereenkomst; het Contship America", *T.V.R.* 2000, at p. 40; R. Zwitser, "De cognossementhouder als derde uit derdenbeding", *T.V.R.* 2002, at p. 158.

254 M. Spanjaart, "The Konnossementsbegebungsvertrag – a suggestion for further reformation", *TransportR* 2011, at p. 336.

255 Some authors even consider the existence of obligations to the promisee a necessary requirement, and only accept an *accessory* third-party beneficiary clause.

256 N. Carette, *Derdenbeding*, Antwerp, Intersentia, 2011, at p. 141.

257 H. Boonk, *Zeevervoer onder cognossement*, Arnhem, Gouda Quint, 1993, at pp. 12–13.

258 See for a (partial) reply R. Zwitser, "Toetreden tot de vervoersovereenkomst; het Contship America", *T.V.R.* 2000, at p. 40. The author points out that the fact that the law holds certain parties liable (e.g. the shipowner in several legal systems) does not imply that the original contract parties could not have inserted third-party beneficiary clauses in favour of

93 Cahen rejects the third-party beneficiary construction because in his opinion, the contract law claim of the holder of the bill of lading must fail before the property law claim of the owner of the goods. In the author's view, the holder of the bill of lading can only enforce his claim for delivery if he has property rights to the carried goods. A third-party beneficiary clause can only transfer contractual rights, but not property rights, and thus cannot explain how the holder of the bill of lading acquires all the rights he needs to claim delivery.[259] This argument, of course, entirely depends on the author's position that property rights to the goods trump the contractual claim for delivery, which is simply incorrect. The carrier is not concerned with the property rights in the carried goods; his obligation to deliver the carried goods is exclusively to the (lawful) holder of the bill of lading. It is obviously possible for there to be property law disputes between the holder of the bill of lading and another party (e.g. the real owner of the goods), but such disputes will have to be fought and decided between the holder and the other party, not by the carrier.

94 Korthalss Altes and Wiarda point out that the applicable law sometimes leaves very little freedom of contract to the promisee and the promisor to decide what the rights of the beneficiary will be. In the carriage of goods by sea, the rights of the consignee are indeed to a large extent determined by international conventions and/or mandatory national law. From this, they conclude that a third-party beneficiary clause in this context is at least of a peculiar kind, and may no longer be a third-party beneficiary clause at all.[260] The fact that the legislator has stepped in to determine the rights, or certain rights, of a party does not mean, however, that the origin of those rights could not be a third-party beneficiary clause.

95 Ripert sees an objection in the fact that the concept of a third-party beneficiary clause is of a younger date than the rights of the consignee against the carrier.[261] That, however, is not a very strong argument. The rights of the consignee only came into full being at the end of the 19th century,[262] and by that time, the concept of a third-party beneficiary clause was certainly known, even if not as accepted and broadly applied as today.[263] Also, legal concepts generally do not appear out of thin air. Even if a third-party beneficiary clause did not exist yet as

---

    other parties. This is correct, of course, but not an answer to Boonk's point that such legally liable parties can (if one insists) be considered to have acceded to the contract by force of law, but can hardly be considered third-party beneficiaries.
259 J. Cahen, *Het cognossement*, Arnhem, Gouda Quint, 1964, at pp. 7–8.
260 A. Korthals Altes and J.J. Wiarda, *Vervoerrecht*, Serie Recht en Praktijk, Deventer, Kluwer, 1980, at p. 53.
261 G. Ripert, *Droit Maritime*, Tôme II, Paris, Editions Rousseau et Cie., 1952 (4th Ed.), n° 1583–1584 at p. 492.
262 See above, n° 36.
263 N. Carette, *Derdenbeding*, Antwerp, Intersentia, 2011, n° 183–208 at pp. 175–189; F. Terré, Ph. Simler and Y. Lequette, *Droit civil: Les obligations*, Paris, Dalloz, 2009 (10th Ed.), n° 513–514 at pp. 530–531.

a formal legal concept, the rights of the consignee against the carrier may have been one of the elements that led to its appearance.[264]

96 Ripert also points out that a third-party beneficiary clause can only be an accessory to a stipulation that the promisee makes for himself. In a contract of carriage, however, there is not one stipulation for the promisee (shipper) and a different stipulation for the third party (consignee). There is only one common stipulation, for the carriage of the goods.[265] The position has indeed been defended that the benefit for the third party cannot be the only object of the contract between the promisee and the promisor.[266] More recent authors, however, have questioned this position and defended the possibility of a 'solitary' third-party beneficiary clause, i.e. a contract in which the promisee and promisor only agree to create a right for a third party.[267] If this more recent view of the third-party beneficiary clause is accepted, Ripert's criticism is no longer relevant.

97 Seck sees a problem in the fact that the third-party beneficiary clause is a concept of national law, the boundaries and contents of which differ from country to country, and thus hardly compatible with the universal nature of the bill of lading.[268] The bill of lading itself, however, is also subject to national differences of interpretation, while on the other hand the third-party beneficiary concept is sufficiently uniform to be included in the Principles of European Contract Law (PECL), the Draft Common Framework of Reference (DCFR) and the UNIDROIT Principles of International Commercial Contracts. It is correct that Dutch law, the author's national law, does have a particular approach to third-party beneficiary clauses, in that the Dutch Civil Code explicitly has the beneficiary accede to the contract between the promisee and the promisor,[269] but even this particularity does not make it impossible to see the third-party beneficiary clause as a common legal basis across the nations.

98 Seck further objects that, when a bill of lading is issued under a charter party, the bill of lading initially does not have a contractual function – it only acquires that contractual function once it has been transferred to a third party, thereby giving rise to two separate contracts: the charter party on the one hand, and the bill of lading on the other hand. According to the author, such cannot be the result of a third-party beneficiary clause.[270] This is not correct, however. On the contrary, the mechanism is the archetype of a third-party beneficiary clause.

---

264 Compare P. Bonassies and C. Scapel, *Droit maritime*, Paris, L.G.D.J., 2010 (2nd Ed.), n° 931 at pp. 634–635.
265 G. Ripert, *Droit Maritime*, Tôme II, Paris, Editions Rousseau et Cie., 1952 (4th Ed.), n° 1583–1584 at p. 492.
266 N. Carette, *Derdenbeding*, Antwerp, Intersentia, 2011, n° 222 at p. 197 *et seq.*
267 N. Carette, *Derdenbeding*, Antwerp, Intersentia, 2011, n° 277–278 at pp. 230–233. See also Ph. Malaurie, L. Aynès and Ph. Stoffel-Munck, *Les obligations*, Paris, Defrénois, 2011 (5th Ed.), n° 809 at pp. 419–420; F. Terré, Ph. Simler and Y. Lequette, *Droit civil: Les obligations*, Paris, Dalloz, 2009 (10th Ed.), n° 516 at pp. 532–534.
268 P. Seck, *Reisbevrachting en cognossementsvervoer*, Zutphen, Uitgeverij Paris, 2011, at p. 192.
269 Article 6:254 (1) Dutch Civil Code.
270 P. Seck, *Reisbevrachting en cognossementsvervoer*, Zutphen, Uitgeverij Paris, 2011, at p. 195.

96 *Contractual theories*

The promisee (charterer) and the promisor (owner) enter into an initial contract (the charter party), in which they agree to grant certain specific rights (as listed in the bill of lading) to a third party. Once the third party has accepted the stipulation in his favour, the promisor (owner) has one set of obligations vis-à-vis the promisee (charterer) under the charter party and another set of obligations vis-à-vis the beneficiary (holder) under the bill of lading. The fact that *the law* may introduce other parties into the contractual sphere – e.g. the shipowner, who may be liable as carrier even when the charter party was not made by the owner – does not change the analysis. The liability of such other parties is, by definition, a legal liability, not a contractual one.

99 As discussed above, the third-party beneficiary concept when applied to bills of lading has a number of (sometimes major) issues. Moreover, applying this concept hardly results in answers. In many legal systems, the provisions on third-party beneficiary clauses basically only confirm that such clause, as an exception to privity or relativity of contract, is indeed possible and valid. The consequences of such clause, the exact rights and obligations of the parties involved, etc. are left for the courts and the legal doctrine to ponder and decide.[271] Dutch law is, to a certain extent, an exception, in that the Dutch Civil Code expressly provides that the beneficiary who accepts the clause in his favour becomes a party to the contract between the promisee and the promisor. That means, however, that under Dutch law, a third-party beneficiary clause is in fact simply a form of accession to a contract, resulting in a multi-party contract.[272] Zwitser, who strongly defends the third-party beneficiary construction, readily admits that the holder of the bill of lading accedes to the contract of carriage between the shipper and the carrier, turning this contract into a three-party contract. In truth, therefore, the Dutch majority position, although nominally based on the third-party beneficiary concept, is in fact based on contract accession and explains the position of the third-party holder on the basis of his becoming a party to the contract of carriage.[273] In Germany, where the third-party beneficiary concept is also often proposed, the third-party beneficiary clause is primarily seen as the (legal) cause of the carrier's issuing a negotiable instrument (*Wertpapier*), and the holder's position is mainly appreciated and explained in light of the law of negotiable instruments. Ultimately, therefore, invoking the third-party beneficiary concept does not really solve anything.

---

271 Compare G.J. van der Ziel, *Het cognossement, naar een functionele benadering*, Deventer, Kluwer, 1999, at p. 7, who rejects the third-party beneficiary approach because it does not answer the question which provisions of the contract of carriage can be invoked against the holder, and which cannot.
272 N. Carette, *Derdenbeding*, Antwerp, Intersentia, 2011, n° 165 at p. 164; R. Zwitser, "Toetreden tot de vervoersovereenkomst; het Contship America", *T.V.R.* 2000, at p. 40; R. Zwitser, "De cognossementhouder als derde uit derdenbeding", *T.V.R.* 2002, at p. 158.
273 On the bill of lading as a multi-party contract, see Section 3.2.2.2.

3.2.2 Multi-party contracts – accession

3.2.2.1 The concept

100 A multi-party contract is a contract with more than two parties. A contract can be multi-party from the start, or can become multi-party afterwards through the accession of additional parties to an existing contract.

101 A contract typically is a two-party affair.[274] Contracts of sale or rent, contracts for services, etc. are made between two parties. Nevertheless, there are also contracts that involve more parties, particularly in the commercial context. A contract can be multi-party from the very beginning, when more than two parties enter into a contract with each other, or can become multi-party at a later stage, through the accession (*adhésion, toetreding, Beitritt*) of a new party to the existing contract. Accession of a new party to the contract is a well-known concept in civil law countries.[275] If for example A owns a car and allows B to drive it, B accedes to the insurance contract that A has with his insurer for the car.[276] If B gets involved in an accident while driving the car, he will be able to claim under A's insurance policy, but conversely, the insurance company will also be able to sue B under the policy. Also, if A is living in a leased apartment and is later joined there by B, B accedes to the lease agreement between A and the landlord.[277] Accession to an existing contract requires the consent of all parties involved. The acceding party obviously intends and accepts to become a party to the contract, but also the original parties must accept the accession of a new party. It is possible, however, that the consent of the original parties has already been given (implicitly) at an earlier stage, or even from the very making of the contract.[278] The original parties can explicitly determine the rights and obligations of the acceding party. If they have not done so, those rights and obligations will have to be deduced from the original contract. In general, the acceding party must accept

---

[274] Also, the (traditional) legislators tend to only deal with two-party contracts. (E. Dirix, "De Meerpartijenovereenkomst", *T.P.R.* 1983, at p. 757).

[275] E. Dirix, *Obligatoire verhoudingen tussen contractanten en derden*, Antwerpen, 1984, n° 85–98 at pp. 68–74; W. Van Gerven and S. Covemaeker, *Verbintenissenrecht*, Leuven, Acco, 2006 (2nd Ed.), at p. 232.
  The Italian Civil Code explicitly refers to contract accession in its Article 1332.
  The European Commission explicitly provides for later accession of new contractors to existing research programmes: see Commission Decision C(2003) 3834 of 23 October 2003, Form A (Accession to the contract) and Form B (Request for accession of new contractor).

[276] E. Dirix, *Obligatoire verhoudingen tussen contractanten en derden*, Antwerpen, 1984, n° 90 at p. 72.

[277] E. Dirix, *Obligatoire verhoudingen tussen contractanten en derden*, Antwerpen, 1984, n° 85 at p. 68.

[278] E. Dirix, *Obligatoire verhoudingen tussen contractanten en derden*, Antwerpen, 1984, n° 98 at p. 74; W. Van Gerven and S. Covemaeker, *Verbintenissenrecht*, Leuven, Acco, 2006 (2nd Ed.), at p. 232.

98 *Contractual theories*

the contract as it exists between and is understood by the original parties.[279] This does not mean, however, that the position of the acceding party must always be exactly the same as the position of one of the original parties.[280] Adding a new party to a contract could also be achieved through novation, but the fundamental difference is that with novation, the existing contract is terminated and a new contract is entered into, whereas accession leaves the existing contract intact, with its original starting date, periods of limitation, etc.

102 The English scholars passingly mention contracts that are multipartite from the beginning,[281] but hardly ever discuss accession of a new party to an existing contract. For there to be a valid contract, English law traditionally requires an offer, acceptance of this offer, and consideration by the promisee, and accession of a new party to an existing contract is not (always) easy to fit into these slots.[282] This is not to say, however, that accession to a contract does not exist at all under English law. In *The Zephyr*,[283] Hobhouse J pointed out that "*The Satanita*[284] *recognizes the legal efficacy of multilateral contracts of accession whereby one document, the yacht club sailing rules, can be acceded to by a number of individuals in succession so as to put them all in contractual relations with each other*",[285] and held that

279 E. Dirix, "De Meerpartijenovereenkomst", *T.P.R.* 1983, n° 19 at p. 773.
280 E. Dirix, "De Meerpartijenovereenkomst", *T.P.R.* 1983, n° 4 at p. 759; E. Dirix, *Obligatoire verhoudingen tussen contractanten en derden*, Antwerpen, 1984, n° 86 at p. 69.
281 C. Thorpe and J. Bailey, *Commercial Contracts. A Practical Guide to Deals, Contracts, Agreements & Promises*, London, Kogan Page Limited, 1999, at pp. 27–28.
282 In *New Zealand Shipping Co. Ltd Appellant v A. M. Satterthwaite & Co. Ltd (The Eurymedon)* [1974] 2 WLR 865, [1975] A.C. 154 (Privy Council, 25 February 1974), Lord Wilberforce remarked that "... *English law, having committed itself to a rather technical and schematic doctrine of contract, in application takes a practical approach, often at the cost of forcing the facts to fit uneasily into the marked slots of offer, acceptance and consideration*" (at p. 167).
283 *General Accident Fire and Life Assurance Corporation and others v Peter William Tanter and others (The Zephyr)* [1984] 1 Lloyd's Rep 58 (Queen's Bench Division (Commercial Court), 12 July 1983). The decision was partially appealed against and reversed by the Court of Appeal (*General Accident Fire and Life Assurance Corporation and others v Peter William Tanter and others (The Zephyr)* [1985] 2 Lloyd's Rep 529 (Court of Appeal, 20–23 May 1985)), but not on the points that are relevant here.
284 *Clarke v Earl of Dunraven (The Satanita)* [1897] A.C. 59 (House of Lords, 19 November 1896). The parties in this case entered their yachts for a club race, each owner undertaking to be bound by the club's sailing and racing rules. The *Satanita*, in breach of one of these sailing rules, ran into and sank the *Valkyrie*. The main issue in the case was whether the club rules excluded the possibility of limitation of liability, but Lords Halsbury and Herschell readily and without further explanation accepted that the yacht owners were in a contractual relationship with each other. "*I cannot entertain any doubt that there was a contractual relation between the parties to this litigation. The effect of their entering for the race, and undertaking to be bound by these rules to the knowledge of each other, is sufficient, I think, where those rules indicate a liability on the part of the one to the other, to create a contractual obligation to discharge that liability*" (per Lord Herschell, at p. 63).
285 *General Accident Fire and Life Assurance Corporation and others v Peter William Tanter and others (The Zephyr)* [1984] 1 Lloyd's Rep 58 (Queen's Bench Division (Commercial Court), 12 July 1983), at p. 72.

a marine reinsurance slip creates a contractual and distinct relationship between each reinsured and each reinsurer.[286]

3.2.2.2 The bill of lading as a multi-party contract

103 The multi-party contract approach has been used quite often to explain the position of the third-party holder of the bill of lading. There are, in fact, at least three sub-approaches possible. The first sub-approach is to consider the contract of carriage as a three-party contract from the very start, with the holder of the bill of lading immediately a party to the contract. The second sub-approach is to have the holder accede to the contract of carriage *as made between the shipper and the carrier*, and the third sub-approach is to have the holder accede to the contract of carriage *as laid down in the bill of lading*. It is possible, of course, that the bill of lading exactly describes the contract of carriage as made between the shipper and the carrier. In that case, the second and the third sub-approach are identical. The bill of lading does not necessarily contain the contract as made between the shipper and the carrier, though. There may be additional agreements that are not included in the bill of lading, or even an entirely different contract (such as a charter party).

104 French maritime scholars have often seen the contract of carriage as essentially a three-party contract, bringing together the shipper, the carrier and the consignee.[287] Rodière was adamant that the consignee does not become a party

---

286 *General Accident Fire and Life Assurance Corporation and others v Peter William Tanter and others (The Zephyr)* [1984] 1 Lloyd's Rep 58 (Queen's Bench Division (Commercial Court), 12 July 1983), at p. 71.
  See also *Michael Toth v Emirates* [2011] EWPCC 18, 2011 WL 900254 (Patents County Court, 13 June 2011). Mr. Toth had registered the domain name 'emirates.co.uk' with Nominet, the UK domain names authority. This registration was later challenged by the Emirates airline as abusive. In point 35 of his judgment, Birss J said: "[Claimant] *also submitted, for what it is worth, that not only is this contract* [the contract between Mr. Toth and Nominet] *binding on Mr. Toth and on Nominet, but, having submitted themselves to the procedure, it is also binding on Emirates on the principle in the Mudhook regatta case Clarke v Dunraven [1897] AC 59. It does not seem to me to matter but in my judgment, it is probably correct.*"
287 V.-E. Bokalli, "Crise et avenir du connaissement", *D.M.F.* 1998, at p. 125; P. Bonassies and C. Scapel, *Droit maritime*, Paris, L.G.D.J., 2010 (2nd Ed.), n° 931 at p. 634; C. Carreau, "Cass. fr. 21 November 1978", *Recueil Dalloz Sirey* 1980, 309 (note), at p. 312; H. Gaudemet-Tallon, "Cass. fr. 10 January and 4 April 1995", *Rev. crit. dr. internat. privé* 1995, 610 (note), at p. 614; A. Kpoahoun Amoussou, *Les clauses attributives de compétence dans le transport maritime de marchandises*, Presses Universitaires d'Aix-Marseille, 2002, at p. 371; M. Rémond-Gouilloud, *Le contrat de transport*, Paris, Dalloz, 1993, at p. 34; P. Rodière, "Cass. fr. 21 November 1978", *La Semaine Juridique, JCP* 1980, 643 (note), at p. 645; M. Tilche, A. Chao and P. Berthod, "Contrat de transport. Adhésion du destinataire?", *BT* N° 2484, 20 July 1992, at p. 471.
  More critical: Ph. Delebecque, *Droit maritime*, Paris, Dalloz, 2014 (13th Ed.), n° 731 at p. 511, who sees the contract of carriage as initially a two-party contract, which sometimes

100 *Contractual theories*

later on, but is a party from the start.[288] The problem is, of course, that the consignee is almost never physically present when the contract of carriage is made. In order to solve this problem, it has been argued that the shipper (who is present) not only acts on his own behalf, but also as an agent for the consignee,[289] or that he promises that the consignee will ratify the contract (*convention de porte-fort, sterkmaking, Porte-Fort-Versprechen*).[290] Such a 'promise of ratification' means that A negotiates a contract with B, promising that a third party (C) will actually enter into that contract with B.[291] If C then accepts what A has negotiated with B and does indeed enter into the contract, the contract comes into being directly between B and C. A has performed what he had promised to do, and is no longer involved in the contract between B and C.[292] If on the other hand C refuses to accept what A has negotiated and does not enter into the contract, there is no contract between B and C, but A has then failed to perform his promise to B and is thus in breach. In principle, A is in that situation not liable to perform the negotiated contract himself (instead of C), but is only liable for damages, but A and B could agree otherwise. Applying this concept to the bill of lading means that the shipper negotiates a contract of carriage with the carrier, promising that, at destination, a third party (the consignee) will enter into that contract of carriage. If the consignee presents the bill of lading and claims delivery of the cargo, that is then seen as an (implicit) acceptance of the contract negotiated by the shipper. The consignee becomes a party to the contract of carriage with retroactive effect, i.e. from the time the contract of carriage was made between the shipper and the carrier. The shipper has performed his promise and is released of his obligations as *porte-fort*, though of course not of the obligations that he has personally assumed

---

    remains a two-party contract, but often *becomes* a three-party contract by the accession of the consignee.
    Contra: J.-P. Tosi, "L'adhésion du destinataire au contrat de transport", in X., *Mélanges Christian Mouly*, Paris, Litec, 1998, at p. 183 and 185, who insists that the contract of carriage is initially a two-party contract which does not involve the consignee.
288 R. Rodière, *Traité général de droit maritime*, Tome II, *Les contrats de transport de marchandises*, Paris, Librairie Dalloz, 1967, n° 408 at p. 28: "*Le destinataire n'est pas un personnage qui s'associe plus tard à l'opération. Il y est partie dès le début.*" (The consignee is not a character that becomes associated to the operation at a later stage. He is a party from the very start.)
289 V.-E. Bokalli, "Crise et avenir du connaissement", *D.M.F.* 1998, at p. 125. See also above, n° 26 p. 48.
290 V.-E. Bokalli, "Crise et avenir du connaissement", *D.M.F.* 1998, at p. 125; M. Rèmond-Gouilloud, *Le contrat de transport*, Paris, Dalloz, 1993, at pp. 34–35.
291 N. Carette, *Derdenbeding*, Antwerp, Intersentia, 2011, n° 48 at p. 38. The concept dates back to the *Code Napoléon*, and is currently found in Article 1120 of the Belgian and French Civil Codes.
    An example would be, for instance, that A, who knows that his cousin C is interested in paintings by a certain artist, walks past an art gallery and sees a painting by that artist for sale. He enters the gallery and negotiates a price and other conditions with the gallery owner B, and promises him that his cousin C will buy the painting for that price and under those conditions.
292 Unless explicitly agreed otherwise between A and B.

as shipper. If, on the other hand, the bill of lading is not presented at destination, there is no consignee that becomes a party to the contract of carriage, but the shipper will be in breach of its obligation towards the carrier and will be liable for damages. It has also been argued that the consignee is a party simply because that is the nature of a contract of carriage involving a bill of lading.[293] Kpoahoun Amoussou, who strongly defends the idea that a contract of carriage is a three-party contract from the beginning, even applies this concept to bills of lading issued pursuant to a charter party. In his view, the charter party is a two-party contract between the charterer and the owner. Once the bill of lading is transferred to a third party, however, a new three-party bill of lading contract springs to life, between the shipper, the carrier and the holder of the bill of lading.[294]

The position that the holder of the bill of lading later accedes to the contract of carriage, either immediately by acquiring the bill of lading,[295] only by enforcing rights under the bill of lading,[296] or at the latest by presenting the bill of lading and claiming delivery,[297] is also defended in France.[298] In two decisions of

---

293 R. Rodière, *Traité général de droit maritime*, Tome II, *Les contrats de transport de marchandises*, Paris, Librairie Dalloz, 1967, n° 408 at p. 28. Rodière refers to G. Ripert, *Droit Maritime*, Tôme II, Paris, Editions Rousseau et Cie., 1952 (4th Ed.), n° 1585 at p. 494, who had written that if the holder of a bill of lading has rights and obligations, it is simply because of and through the bill of lading.
  See also A. Kpoahoun Amoussou, *Les clauses attributives de compétence dans le transport maritime de marchandises*, Presses Universitaires d'Aix-Marseille, 2002, n° 639 at p 405 and n° 645–652 at pp. 410–415.
294 A. Kpoahoun Amoussou, *Les clauses attributives de compétence dans le transport maritime de marchandises*, Presses Universitaires d'Aix-Marseille, 2002, n° 648 at pp. 412–413.
295 C. Paulin, *Droits des transports*, Paris, Litec, 2005, n° 440 at p. 229 and fn. 69 at p. 232.
  Compare CA Pau 18 May 2011, n° 10/05093 (*Navire Sava Ocean*): "*Au demeurant, la SAS FERTINAGRO en tant que destinataire et notify au connaissement a accepté la clause compromissoire puisque la transmission du connaissement au destinataire fait présumer l'acceptation de la clause compromissoire*" (Furthermore, SAS FERTINAGRO as consignee and notify party under the bill of lading has accepted the arbitration clause since the forwarding of the bill of lading to the consignee creates a presumption of acceptance of the arbitration clause).
296 M. Tilche, A. Chao and P. Berthod, "Contrat de transport. Adhésion du destinataire?", *BT* N° 2484, 20 July 1992, at p. 471.
297 P. Bonassies and C. Scapel, *Droit maritime*, Paris, L.G.D.J., 2010 (2nd Ed.), n° 932 at p. 635; P.-Y. Nicolas, "CA Paris 29 November 2000 (*Navire Nuevo Leon*)", *D.M.F.* 2001, 689–696 (note), n° 11 at p. 693 and n° n° 14 at p. 694. Compare Ph. Delebecque, "Nouvelles précisions et nouvelles interrogations sur le régime des clauses attributives de juridiction", *D.M.F.* 2003, n° 8 at p. 561.
  See also Cass. (ch. des requêtes) 19 October 1891, *R.I.D.M.* Vol. VII (1891–1892), 385: "*Attendu que les stipulations du contrat intervenu entre le chargeur et le transporteur profitent et s'imposent au destinataire qui, agissant en justice en vertu du connaissement, est soumis à l'exécution des clauses licites qui y sont insérées*". (Considering that the provisions of the contract made between the shipper and the carrier benefit and bind the consignee who, filing suit on the basis of the bill of lading, is subject to the effects of the lawful clauses that it contains.)
298 See also J.-P. Tosi, "L'adhésion du destinataire au contrat de transport", in X., *Mélanges Christian Mouly*, Paris, Litec, 1998, at p. 182.

102 *Contractual theories*

29 November 1994, the French Supreme Court held that the consignee accedes to the contract of carriage by taking delivery of the goods.[299] Conversely, then, a holder who refuses to take delivery (because the bill of lading had been antedated and the goods shipped later than agreed) is not bound by the provisions of the bill of lading.[300] The Supreme Court however does not specify whether this contract of carriage is the contract of the carriage as made between the shipper and the carrier (in one of the two decisions, that contract was a charter party[301]) or the contract as incorporated in the bill of lading.[302] In the literature, both positions are defended: for Bokalli, the consignee accedes to the contract as made between the shipper and the carrier,[303] while Tosi takes the position that the consignee, by acceding, enters into a separate relationship with the carrier that is distinct from the latter's relationship with the shipper.[304] Other authors have argued that the consignee accedes to the contract between the shipper and the carrier, but nevertheless only accepts those clauses that are part of the 'economy of the contract' ('*l'économie du contrat*'), i.e. clauses that 'naturally' belong in a contract of

---

[299] Cass. com. 29 November 1994, *D.M.F.* 1995, 209 (*Navires Harmony et Nagasaki*), note P. Bonassies.
Cass. com. 29 November 1994, *D.M.F.* 1995, 219 (*Navire Stolt Osprey*), note Y. Tassel.
In both decisions, the Court held that the jurisdiction clause in the bill of lading had to be specifically accepted by the consignee at the latest when ". . . *recevant livraison de la marchandise, il avait adhéré au contrat de transport*" (. . . taking receipt of the goods, he had adhered to the contract of carriage).
In his case note, Bonassies tries to rescue the concept of the contract of carriage as a three-party contract from the beginning, by describing the consignee as a 'virtual' party until the time he accepts to become a 'real' party. "*Il est plus malaisé d'apprécier la portée de la présente décision sur la théorie du contrat de transport maritime, contrat dès l'origine à trois personnes. Il semble cependant que cette théorie ne soit pas condamnée. (. . .) On peut très bien concevoir le contrat de transport comme un contrat dès l'origine à trois personnes, transporteur, chargeur et destinataire, étant considéré que le destinataire ne sera intégré à ce contrat le jour où, personnellement, il y aura donné son consentement (ou, comme le dit la Cour de cassation, le jour où il y aura «adhéré»).*" Unless the acceptance is considered to have a retroactive effect, however, this capacity of 'virtual' party has no legal relevance.
Rèmond-Gouilloud also regrets that the three-party approach has been unable to convince the Supreme Court, and that the consignee is now seen as an acceding party, whereas he is, according to the author, not only a party to but even the cause of the contract of carriage (M. Rèmond-Gouilloud, "CA Caen 20 March 1997 (Navire Westfield)", *D.M.F.* 1997, 716 (note), at p. 721).
[300] CA Aix-en-Provence 28 April 1976, *D.M.F.* 1977, 27 (*Navire Talita*).
[301] Cass. com. 29 November 1994, *D.M.F.* 1995, 219 (*Navire Stolt Osprey*), note Y. Tassel.
[302] Y. Tassel, *Cass. com. 29 November 1994 (Navire Stolt Osprey)*, *D.M.F.* 1995, 218 (note), at p. 221.
J.-P. Tosi, "L'adhésion du destinataire au contrat de transport", in X., *Mélanges Christian Mouly*, Paris, Litec, 1998, at pp. 190–191 is of the opinion that the holder of the bill of lading accedes to a separate contract with the carrier.
[303] V.-E. Bokalli, "Crise et avenir du connaissement", *D.M.F.* 1998, at p. 125.
[304] J.-P. Tosi, "L'adhésion du destinataire au contrat de transport", in X., *Mélanges Christian Mouly*, Paris, Litec, 1998, at p. 190.

carriage.[305] 'Special' or 'exorbitant' clauses are not automatically binding on the consignee, but have to be specifically accepted by him.[306] A clause has been said to be 'special' if it deviates from standard legal solutions or rights and imposes a particular obligation.[307]

105 In the Netherlands, the majority position is that the consignee is a third-party beneficiary.[308] However, as the Dutch Civil Code (Art. 6:251.(1)) explicitly provides that the beneficiary, when he accepts, becomes a party to the contract between the promisee and the promisor,[309] Dutch maritime law actually construes the position of the consignee on the basis of his accession to the contract of carriage. Zwitser very explicitly argues that a third-party beneficiary clause is nothing more than a way to create a multi-party contract; the end result is that the holder of the bill of lading becomes a party to the contract of carriage.[310] The majority of the Dutch authors agree that the holder of a bill of lading indeed

---

305 Ph. Delebecque, "Cass. com. 16 January 1996 (Navire Monte Cervantes)", *D.M.F.* 1996, 629 (note); Ph. Delebecque, "La validité des clauses de compétence doit s'apprécier en application de la loi du contrat: une solution de droit commun qui froisse le particularisme du droit des transports maritimes", *D.M.F.* 2001, n° 6 at p. 997.
  See also CA Aix-en-Provence 9 November 2011, n° 10/22956 (*Navire Elbfeeder*): "*la société Unima Europe, (. . .) le tiers porteur du connaissement, n'a pas accepté expressément la clause 26 : « Law and Juridiction » ; que cette clause ne tend pas à définir un élément ressortissant à l'économie générale du contrat de transport, mais tend à faire régir la totalité du contrat par un droit national déterminé*" (the company Unima Europe (. . .) third-party holder of the bill of lading, has not explicitly accepted Clause 26 "Law and Jurisdiction"; that the purpose of this clause is not to define an element belonging to the general economy of the contract of carriage, but to subject the entire contract to a specific national law).
306 C. Paulin, *Droits des transports*, Paris, Litec, 2005, n° 449 at p. 233; M. Rèmond-Gouilloud, "CA Caen 20 March 1997 (Navire Westfield)", *D.M.F.* 1997, 716 (note), at p. 722; J.-P. Tosi, "L'adhésion du destinataire au contrat de transport", in X., *Mélanges Christian Mouly*, Paris, Litec, 1998, at p. 177 and p. 181.
  Cass. com. 16 January 1996, *D.M.F.* 1996, 627 (*Navire Monte Cervantes*) (a contrario).
307 CA Caen 20 March 1997, *D.M.F.* 1997, 714 (*Navire Westfield*): "*. . . une clause spéciale de ce contrat de transport, dérogatoire au droit commun et lui imposant une obligation particulière*".
308 See above, n° 74 p. 74.
309 Article 6:254.(1) of the Dutch Civil Code provides: "*Nadat de derde het beding heeft aanvaard, geldt hij als partij bij de overeenkomst.*" (Once the third party has accepted the clause, he is a party to the contract.)
310 R. Zwitser, "Toetreden tot de vervoersovereenkomst; het Contship America", *T.V.R.* 2000, at p. 40: "*Te weinig wordt nog ingezien dat het derdenbeding niets anders is dan een bijzondere vorm van een gewone driepartijenovereenkomst.*" (It is realised too seldomly that a third-party beneficiary clause is nothing else than a specific form of a standard three-party agreement.)
  R. Zwitser, "Het cognossement als zekerheidsinstrument", *NTHR* 2007–2, at p. 90: "*Ik zie daarin graag de werking van een derdenbeding, maar ik bedoel daarmee niet iets anders te zeggen dan degenen die zonder die rechtsfiguur te noemen willen spreken van toetreding zonder meer.*" (I prefer to see that as the effects of a third-party beneficiary clause, but in doing so, I do not intend to say something else than those who, without naming that clause, talk about accession without more.)

accedes to the contract of carriage.³¹¹ The Dutch courts also regularly confirm that the consignee accedes to the contract of carriage, without always explicitly referring to a third-party beneficiary clause.³¹²

Because of Art. 6:251.(1) of the Dutch Civil Code, the holder should in principle become a party to the contract of carriage *as made between the shipper and the carrier*, that is including all particular arrangements between those parties.³¹³ This article indeed provides that the beneficiary becomes a party to 'the contract', which in the context of a typical third-party beneficiary clause can only mean the contract between the promisee and the promisor. The Dutch Supreme Court has held, in a non-carriage case, that a party that accedes to a pre-existing contract must take the contract as it is construed and applied by the original parties and has an obligation to enquire with the original parties as to what exactly the contents of the contract are.³¹⁴ Although this is a fairly obvious rule – the opposite rule, that each acceding party could take the contract to mean what it thinks it

---

311 H. Boonk, *Zeevervoer onder cognossement*, Arnhem, Gouda Quint, 1993, at p. 10; H. Boonk, "Cognossement en cognossementhouder", *NTBR* 2007-9, at p. 373; J. Eckoldt, *De forumkeuze in het zeevervoer*, Zutphen, Uitgeverij Paris, 2014, fn. 624 at p. 141 and at pp. 152–153; R. Japikse, *Verkeersmiddelen en Vervoer. Deel I. Algemene bepalingen en rederij*, Asser Serie, Deventer, Kluwer, 2004, n° 216 at p. 121; M. Spanjaart, *Vorderingsrechten uit cognossement*, Zutphen, Uitgeverij Paris, 2012, at pp. 104–105; A. Van Oven, *Handelsrecht*, Zwolle, Tjeenk Willink, 1981, at pp. 252–253.

See also CA The Hague 26 June 2008, *S&S* 2008, 115 (ms. OPDR Lisboa), point 2.17.

Contra: J. Huizink, "De derde-cognossementshouder wordt geen partij", *T.V.R.* 1998, at pp. 15–16 (the author rejects the accession theory because the holder has no intention to accede and because it is not necessary to have him accede); P. Seck, *Reisbevrachting en cognossementsvervoer*, Zutphen, Uitgeverij Paris, 2011, at p. 143 (specifically with regard to charter parties and bills of lading: the holder does not accede to the charter party, but is a party to the separate bill of lading contract).

312 See, for example, Court of Rotterdam, 24 June 2015 (ECLI:NL:RBROT:2015:5032), point 5.5.

With reference to a third-party beneficiary clause: Court of Rotterdam, 10 October 2012, *S&S* 2013, 38 (*ms MSC Daniela*), point 4.9.

313 M. Claringbould, "Het cognossement", in *Preadvies van de Vereeniging Handelsrecht en de Nederlandse Vereniging voor zee- en vervoerrecht. Vervoersrecht in Boek 8 BW*, Zwolle, Tjeenk Willink, 1997, at pp. 140–142. The author correctly points out, however, that certain clauses in the contract between the shipper and the carrier may be worded in such way that they simply do not apply to the holder of the bill of lading, and thus cannot be invoked by him or against him, even if he becomes a party to the contract.

F. Smeele, "The bill of lading contracts under European national laws (civil law approaches to explaining the legal position of the consignee under bills of lading)", in R. Thomas (Ed.), *The Evolving Law and Practice of Voyage Charterparties*, London, Informa, 2009, n° 12.46 at p. 273.

314 HR 15 April 1977, *N.J.* 1978, 163 (*Staalcom '66 BV / Neher Nederland BV*). A construction company had acceded to an existing agreement between other construction companies. The agreement provided, *inter alia*, that the members would resolve possible differences amicably and would not sue each other. The acceding company did eventually sue one of the other members, arguing that it did not know about this rule and had certainly not accepted it. Both the Court of Appeal and the Supreme Court held that the acceding company should have enquired with the existing parties and should have been aware of the rule.

should mean would hardly be acceptable –, the Dutch authors are reluctant to accept it when it comes to bills of lading. Molengraaaff wrote that the holder accedes to the contract between the shipper and the carrier, which he must accept as a whole.[315] The holder may assume, however, that the bill of lading *is* the contract as it exists between the shipper and the carrier. From there, it is only a small step to saying that the holder accedes to the contract of carriage incorporated in the bill of lading.[316] Korthals Altes and Wiarda are of the opinion that the holder of the bill of lading accedes to the contract between the shipper and the carrier, but only to that part of that contract that is 'relevant' for the holder at destination.[317] Spanjaart confirms that the holder becomes a party to the contract of carriage between the shipper and the carrier, even if that contract is a charter party, but argues that the holder is not bound by those provisions that he did not know or could not have known,[318] both because the bill of lading is a negotiable instrument but primarily because the holder, as a third party in good faith, is entitled to assume that the bill of lading is the entire contract of carriage.[319]

See also HR 21 January 1966, ECLI:NL:HR:1966:AC4621, *N.J.* 1966, 183 (*Booy / Wisman*). A party that intends to enter into a contract must take reasonable measures to avoid being mistaken about the contents of that contract.

See also C. du Perron, *HR 18 October 2002 (Butter / Besix)*, *N.J.* 2003, N° 503 (note), at p. 3918: "*Zowel bij de toepassing van art. 3:35 als van art. 3:36 zal op de derde doorgaans een onderzoeksplicht rusten naar de inhoud van de rechtsbetrekking (. . .) De omvang van de onderzoeksplicht zal vooral afhangen van de aard van de overeenkomst*" (Both under Article 3:35 and under Article 3:36 the third party will ordinarily have a duty to investigate the contents of the legal relation (. . .). The extent of that duty will primarily depend on the nature of the agreement).

315 W. Molengraaff, *Leidraad bij de beoefening van het Nederlandsche Handelsrecht*, Haarlem, De Erven F. Bohn, 1912 (2nd Ed.), at p. 371 and p. 372.

316 W. Molengraaff, *Leidraad bij de beoefening van het Nederlandsche Handelsrecht*, Haarlem, De Erven F. Bohn, 1912 (2nd Ed.), at p. 521 ("*door zich met het cognossement aan te melden, treedt hij toe tot de in dit stuk omschreven vervoerovereenkomst, waardoor alsdan zoowel zijne rechten als verplichtingen worden bepaald*"). See also J. Loeff, *Vervoer ter zee*, Deel I, Zwolle, Tjeenk Willink, 1981, n° 70 at p. 48; M. Spanjaart, "The Konnossementsbegebungsvertrag – a suggestion for further reformation", *TransportR* 2011, at p. 336. Compare H. Boonk, *Zeevervoer onder cognossement*, Arnhem, Gouda Quint, 1993, at p. 11.

317 A. Korthals Altes and J.J. Wiarda, *Vervoerrecht*, Serie Recht en Praktijk, Deventer, Kluwer, 1980, at p. 51.

318 M. Spanjaart, *Vorderingsrechten uit cognossement*, Zutphen, Uitgeverij Paris, 2012, at p. 108. Compare B. van Bockel, "De positie van de geadresseerde in het wegvervoer, de binnenvaart en het gecombineerd vervoer", *T.V.R.* 2002/3, at pp. 86–87.

The exception if the holder *could not have known* a certain provision is in line with the 1977 decision of the Dutch Supreme Court (above, fn. 439), where the Court accepted that it would be relevant if the acceding party had tried to obtain information but had been left in the dark or had been deceived by the existing parties. The exception if the holder simply *was not aware* of a certain provision, on the other hand, is hard to reconcile with the acceding party's duty to enquire.

319 M. Spanjaart, *Vorderingsrechten uit cognossement*, Zutphen, Uitgeverij Paris, 2012, at pp. 109–110.

106 Contractual theories

There are, however, also authors that take the position that the holder accedes to the contract of carriage *as incorporated in the bill of lading*.[320] Their position is (at least partially) supported by Article 8:441.(2) and Article 8:415.(1) of the Dutch Civil Code. Article 8:441.(2) provides that against a third holder of the bill of lading, the carrier is bound by and can invoke the provisions of the bill of lading.[321] Article 8:415.(1) provides that when a bill of lading refers to another document, such referral only incorporates those provisions of this other document that are 'readily knowable' for the holder of the bill of lading.[322] It is clear from these provisions that the contents of the bill of lading itself are primordial in determining the position of the third-party holder. When Art. 8:441 of the Dutch Civil Code was introduced, the competent Minister stated that the holder of a bill of lading becomes a party to the contract of carriage 'to the extent it is reproduced in the bill of lading'.[323] This position has also had its echoes in the Dutch case law.[324]

---

320 H. Boonk, "Cognossement en cognossementhouder", *NTBR* 2007–9, at p. 373 (*"De ontvanger treedt door presentatie van het cognossement als partij toe tot de in het cognossement neergelegde vervoerovereenkomst"* – By presenting the bill of lading, the consignee becomes a party to the contract of carriage incorporated in the bill of lading) and p. 379; J. Cahen, *Het cognossement*, Arnhem, Gouda Quint, 1964, at pp. 10–11; P. Seck, *Reisbevrachting en cognossementsvervoer*, Zutphen, Uitgeverij Paris, 2011, at pp. 185–186; R. Zwitser, "Toetreden tot de vervoersovereenkomst; het Contship America", *T.V.R.* 2000, at p. 40.
   See also W. Molengraaf, *Kort begrip van het Nieuwe Nederlandsche Zeerecht*, Haarlem, De Erven F. Bohn, 1928, at p. 205.

321 Article 8:441.2: *"Jegens de houder van het cognossement, die niet de afzender was, is de vervoerder onder cognossement gehouden aan en kan hij een beroep doen op de bedingen van dit cognossement."* (As regards the holder of the bill of lading, who was not the shipper, the carrier under the bill of lading is bound by, and can invoke, the terms of the bill of lading.)

322 Article 8:415.1: *"Verwijzingen in het cognossement worden geacht slechts die bedingen daarin in te voegen, die voor degeen, jegens wie daarop een beroep wordt gedaan, duidelijk kenbaar zijn."* (References in the bill of lading are deemed to only incorporate such terms that are readily knowable to him, against whom these terms are invoked.)
   See S. Geense, "De 'merchant-clausule'", *NTHR* 2011–5, at p. 203.

323 M. Claringbould, *Parlementaire Geschiedenis Boek 8, Verkeersmiddelen en vervoer*, Deventer, Kluwer, 1992, at p. 474: "... *dat de cognossementshouder partij wordt bij de vervoerovereenkomst, voor zover in het cognossement weergegeven*" (... that the holder of the bill of lading becomes a party to the contract of carriage, to the extent that it appears from the bill of lading).

324 In *Condorcamp / Bosman* (HR 26 November 1993, RvdW 1993, 237, S&S 1994, 25, NJ 1995, 446), the Dutch Supreme Court held that a third-party holder of the bill of lading is not bound by provisions of the carriage or other contracts, if he is not himself a party to those contracts and those provisions are not apparent from the bill of lading (*"De regel strookt met de in die bepalingen vervatte bescherming van de regelmatige cognossementhouder (...) die niet gebonden is aan vervoers- of andere overeenkomsten, waarbij hij geen partij is en waarvan uit het cognossement niet blijkt."*)
   See also Court of Rotterdam 4 April 2007, S&S 2008, 126 (*ms Svanetiya*), point 7.4: *"De derde-cognossementhouder treedt in het algemeen tot de in het cognossement neergelegde vervoerovereenkomst toe."* (In general, the third-party holder of the bill of lading accedes to the contract of carriage incorporated in the bill of lading.)

106 In Belgium, the Antwerp Commercial Court has during a number of years clearly defended the position that the third-party holder 'obviously' and 'by definition' accedes to the contract of carriage as incorporated in the bill of lading by presenting the bill of lading to the carrier.[325] The Court has also pointed out that the holder must accede to the bill of lading, because he would not have title to sue if he didn't, since Article 89 of the Belgian Maritime Act exclusively limits title to sue to the holder of the bill of lading.[326] In other decisions, the Court has said that in order to be a third-party holder accession to the bill of lading is required,[327] that accession to the bill of lading is required for the holder to be protected by the Hague-Visby Rules,[328] and that the holder accedes to the

---

Along the same lines: Court of Rotterdam 19 June 1973, S&S 1973, 73 (*ms. John Schehr*); Court of Rotterdam 27 June 1977, S&S 1977, 97 (*ms. Sennar*); Court of Rotterdam 12 May 1980, S&S 1981, 6 (*ms. Nedlloyd Kyoto*); Court of Rotterdam 6 January 1984, S&S 1984, 58, (*ms. François*).

[325] Comm. C. Antwerp 1 June 1992, R.H.A. 1995, (48), at p. 56 (*ms. Nordic Stream*): "*De derde cognossementhouder treedt per definitie toe tot het cognossement (voor- en achterkant). Door het cognossement ter bestemming aan de zeevervoerder aan te bieden, treedt hij toe tot de vervoerovereenkomst, zoals in het cognossement neergelegd.*" (The third-party holder of the bill of lading by definition accedes to the bill of lading (front and backside). By presenting the bill of lading at destination to the carrier, he accedes to the contract of carriage, as incorporated in the bill of lading.)

In the same sense: Comm. C. Antwerp 20 February 1995 R.H.A. 1995, (165), at p. 171 (*ms. Nordfels*); Comm. C. Antwerp 18 June 2002, R.H.A. 2003, (156), at p. 169 (*ms. MSC Dymphna*), in which case the Court indicates that the 'contract of carriage' was a voyage charter party; Comm. C. Antwerp 19 June 2007, *unreported*, Case N° A/05/2148 and A/05/4054.

See also Comm. C. Antwerp 6 March 2013, E.T.L. 2013, (418), at p. 422 (*ms. Atlantic Trader*). In this case, the carriage was under a sea waybill, which under Belgian law is not protected by mandatory legislation. The Court held that the accession to the contract of carriage follows from the fact that a cargo claim was filed against the carrier.

See also J. Loyens, "Noot: Castelletti t./ Trumpy: geen wijziging van de rechtspositie van de derde-houder van het cognossement", E.T.L. 1999, at p. 667 (accession to the contract made by the shipper).

[326] Comm. C. Antwerp 1 June 1992, R.H.A. 1995, (48), at p. 57 (*ms. Nordic Stream*). Article 89 of the Belgian Maritime Act provides that only the holder of the bill of lading can claim delivery of the goods. That is generally taken to mean that also the right to claim damages is exclusive to the holder of the bill of lading. It does not follow, however, that the holder of the bill of lading must 'accede to the bill of lading' to be able to claim damages.

[327] Comm. C. Antwerp 20 February 1995 R.H.A. 1995, (165), at p. 171 (*ms. Nordfels*): "*de derde-cognossementhouder treedt per definitie toe tot het cognossement en, ergo, tot de voorwaarden van het cognossement. Wat is anders een 'derde-cognossementhouder'?*" (the third-party holder of the bill of lading by definition accedes to the bill of lading and therefore to the terms of the bill of lading. What else is a 'third-party holder of the bill of lading'?)) Identical motivation in Comm. C. Antwerp 9 February 2000, *Transportrechtspr.* BVZ n° 587a.

[328] Comm. C. Antwerp 20 February 1995 R.H.A. 1995, (165), at p. 171 (*ms. Nordfels*): "*En hoe zou die derde de bescherming van het Brussels cognossementsverdrag (Haags-Visbysche regels) genieten als hij niet tot het cognossement zou toetreden?*" (And how would that third party enjoy the protection of the Brussels Convention on Bills of Lading (Hague-Visby

108   Contractual theories

bill of lading because the holder's cargo claim is based on the bill of lading.[329] Although the Court in some decisions explicitly refers to the contract of carriage, and in one decision identifies this contract of carriage as a voyage charter party, the Court's reasoning leads to think that it (also) sees the bill of lading as an 'institution'[330] and in fact holds that the holder of a bill of lading must 'accede' to that institution and must accept the 'position' of holder, in order to be able to exercise the rights of a holder.

On the appellate level, the position that the holder of the bill of lading accedes to the contract of carriage has both been accepted[331] and rejected,[332] be it in both cases with little or no supportive reasoning. The Belgian authors are also divided.[333] Insel, who supports the accession theory, is of the opinion that the holder

---

Rules) if he did not accede to the bill of lading?) Identical motivation in Comm. C. Antwerp 9 February 2000, *Transportrechtspr. BVZ* n° 587a.
329   Comm. C. Antwerp 9 February 2000, *Transportrechtspr. BVZ* n° 587a.
330   See below, para 4.3.3.3.
331   CA Antwerp 13 February 2006, *R.H.A.* 2007, (162), at p. 176 (*ms. Ocean Island / ms. Sri Arika*): "*De derde houder van een cognossement volgt de verscheper niet op in diens rechten, maar treedt toe tot de bepalingen van het cognossement*" (The third-party holder of a bill of lading does not succeed to the shipper's rights, but accedes to the terms of the bill of lading). The Court, however, then goes on to hold that there is no proof that the holder, even though he has *acceded* to the provisions of the bill of lading, has accepted the jurisdiction clause of the bill of lading. How a party can have acceded to a contract, but nevertheless not have accepted one of the clauses of that contract, remains unexplained.
    CA Antwerp 7 January 2013, *unreported*, Case N° 2011/AR/1401, point V.A.2: "*Geïntimeerde sub 1 (. . .) heeft de cognossementen in eigen naam aangeboden (. . .) en is dus in eigen naam toegetreden tot de vervoerovereenkomsten, zoals neergelegd in de cognossementen.*" (Defendant sub 1 (. . .) has presented the bills of lading in his own name (. . .) and has therefore acceded in his own name tot the contracts of carriage, as incorporated in the bills of lading).
    CA Antwerp, 4th Division, 18 January 2016, *unreported*, Case N° 2013/AR/3097, at p. 7: "*Het forumbeding (. . .) kan niet worden tegengeworpen aan Dongnam Chemical, nu deze een derde is die toegetreden is tot de vervoerovereenkomst en geen rechtsopvolger is van verscheper Helm AG.*" (The jurisdiction clause (. . .) does not bind Dongnam Chemical, since this is a third party that has acceded to the contract of carriage and does not succeed to the rights and obligations of shipper Helm AG).
332   CA Ghent 28 November 1996, *R.W.* 1996-97, (1441), at p. 1442: "*Dientengevolge beweren appellanten ten onrechte dat geïntimeerden, door aanbieding van het cognossement in de haven van bestemming, tot alle bepalingen van het cognossement toegetreden zijn.*" (The appellants therefore incorrectly argue that the defendants, by presenting the bill of lading in the port of destination, have acceded to all terms of the bill of lading).
    CA Antwerp 6 November 2006, *unreported*, Case N° 2005/AR/1955: "*. . . er tussen de derde-houder en de zeevervoerder geen contractuele relatie bestaat*". (. . . there is no contractual relationship between the third-party holder and the ocean carrier).
333   Pro accession: B. Insel, "Commentaar op recente transportrechtelijke uitspraken", *R.H.A.* 1996, (105), at pp. 116–117; P. Verguts, "De overeenkomst van zeevervoer", in A. Poelmans (Ed.), "Overzicht van rechtspraak. Vervoersrecht 1976–2012", *T.P.R.* 2013, n° 28 at p. 2179 and n° 58 at p. 2200.
    Contra: K. Maes, "Het statuut van het naamcognossement in het zeevervoer", *E.T.L.* 2008, n° 121 at p. 649; F. Stevens, *Vervoer onder cognossement*, Gent, Larcier, 2001, n° 352

of the bill of lading must accede to the contract of carriage in order to be able to claim delivery of the goods. Conversely, for the carrier the accession of the holder means that the latter can be held liable under the contract of carriage.[334]

In 2011, however, the Belgian Supreme Court held that a third-party holder of the bill of lading cannot be seen as a party to the contract.[335] Two years later, in 2013, the Supreme Court held that a third-party holder of the bill of lading does not accept the jurisdiction clause simply by presenting the bill of lading to obtain delivery, and that the argument that the holder obviously accedes to the contract of carriage as incorporated in the bill of lading is not valid either.[336] From these two decisions, it is quite clear that the Supreme Court has rejected the accession theory.[337]

107 German law sees the rights and obligations under the contract of carriage on the one hand, and the rights and obligations under the bill of lading on the other hand, as entirely separate.[338] The former are created when the contract of

---

at p. 205; F. Stevens, "Treedt de cognossementhouder toe tot de vervoerovereenkomst?", (note, *Cass.* 12 September 2013), *R.A.B.G.* 2014, (598), n° 6–8 at pp. 600–601.
334 B. Insel, "Commentaar op recente transportrechtelijke uitspraken", *R.H.A.* 1996, (105), at p. 117.
335 Cass. 7 January 2011, Case N° C.09.611.N, *R.A.B.G.* 2012/12, 836, *R.H.A.* 2010, 238: "*De grieven die ervan uitgaan dat de derde houder van een cognossement geldt als een der contractanten of in de rechten getreden is van een der contractpartijen, berust op een onjuiste rechtsopvatting.*" (The arguments that start from the position that the third-party holder of the bill of lading is one of the contracting parties or succeeds to the rights of one of the contracting parties, are based on an incorrect understanding of the law.)
336 Cass. 12 September 2013, Case N° C.13.0089.N, *Pas.* 2013, 1642; *R.A.B.G.* 2014, 597: "*De appelrechters oordelen op grond van eigen redengeving en deze van de eerste rechter waarnaar zij verwijzen en die zij overnemen dat, krachtens het door hen toegepaste Belgische recht,* "door het cognossement aan te bieden, de derde houder uiteraard [toetreedt] tot de voorwaarden van de vervoerovereenkomst die in het cognossement zijn neergelegd" *zodat* "alle clausules van het cognossement hem dus kunnen worden tegengeworpen". *De appelrechters die op deze gronden oordelen dat het bevoegdheidsbeding in het cognossement aan de eiseressen als derde-houders van het cognossement* "rechtsgeldig, tegenstelbaar en bindend is", *verantwoorden hun beslissing niet naar recht.*" (The appeal court holds, on the basis of its own reasoning and that of the first judge which is referred to and adopted, that under Belgian law which they apply "the third-party holder by presenting the bill of lading obviously [accedes] to the terms of the contract of carriage incorporated in the bill of lading", so that "all clauses of the bill of lading can be invoked against him". The appeal court which on these grounds holds that the jurisdiction clause in the bill of lading is "valid and binding" on claimants as third-party holders of the bill of lading does not provide a sufficient legal basis for its decision.)
337 F. Stevens, "Bevoegdheidsbedingen in cognossementen en de internationale handelsgewoonten", *T.B.H.* 2012, n° 17 at p. 748; F. Stevens, "Treedt de cognossementhouder toe tot de vervoerovereenkomst?", (note, *Cass.* 12 September 2013), *R.A.B.G.* 2014, n° 5 at p. 600.
338 BGH 23 November 1978, *BGHZ* 73, 4, *NJW* 1979, 1102 (Case II ZR 27/77): "*... dass das Konnossement und der Frachtvertrag zwei völlig getrennte Rechtsverhältnisse darstellen*" (... that the bill of lading and the contract of carriage constitue two completely separate legal relations); BGH 10 October 1957, *BGHZ* 25, 300, *NJW* 1957, 1917 (Case II ZR 278/56): the carrier's claim against the consignee in payment of freight is "*... einen durch*

carriage is made between the shipper and the carrier, the latter come into being when the bill of lading is issued by the carrier.[339] By issuing the bill of lading, the carrier enters into an (implicit) contract with the person to whom he hands over the bill of lading (called '*Begebungsvertrag*'), undertaking to deliver the goods described in the bill of lading at destination.[340] There are different theories as to what happens when the first holder forwards the bill of lading to a subsequent holder. It has been argued that the first holder assigns his rights under the bill of lading to the subsequent holder, or transfers them by means of a third-party beneficiary clause in the *Begebungsvertrag*. A more modern view is that the carrier's undertaking is not only to the first holder, but also, and directly, to all possible subsequent holders. In that view, subsequent holders have rights of their own, which are not derived from or influenced by the rights of the first holder.[341] In this constellation, there is of course no need and no reason for the holder to become a party to the contract of carriage. Nevertheless, also in Germany the position has been taken that the transfer of the bill of lading transfers the contract of carriage, to the extent at least that the terms of that contract have been incorporated in the bill of lading.[342]

108 In the USA, the courts have repeatedly held that, although the third-party holder is not an initial party to the bill of lading, he can nevertheless be bound by its terms if he has accepted these terms.[343] The holder at the very least accepts

---

die Annahme des Gutes entstehenden gesetzlichen Anspruch, der vom Frachtvertrag und seinem Inhalt völlig unabhängig ist" (. . . a statutory claim that comes into being by taking receipt of the goods, which is completely independent from the contract of carriage and its contents).

    C. Stumm, *Der Ablader im Seehandelsrecht. Eine rechtsvergleichende Darstellung des deutschen und des amerikanischen Rechts*, Berlin, LIT Verlag, 2010, at p. 42 and p. 45.

    Critical: H.-J. Puttfarken, *Seehandelsrecht*, Heidelberg, Verlag Recht und Wirtschaft, 1997, n° 92 at p. 35.

339 C. Stumm, *Der Ablader im Seehandelsrecht. Eine rechtsvergleichende Darstellung des deutschen und des amerikanischen Rechts*, Berlin, LIT Verlag, 2010, at p. 38.

340 This presumed contract between the carrier and the first holder is a pure fiction, of course, and not needed at all. The clearest illustration is that if the *Begebungsvertrag* is held to be invalid for some reason or other, a subsequent holder in good faith will nevertheless acquire rights against the carrier (C. Stumm, *Der Ablader im Seehandelsrecht: Eine rechtsvergleichende Darstellung des deutschen und des amerikanischen Rechts*, Berlin, LIT Verlag, 2010, at p. 46).

341 C. Stumm, *Der Ablader im Seehandelsrecht: Eine rechtsvergleichende Darstellung des deutschen und des amerikanischen Rechts*, Berlin, LIT Verlag, 2010, at p. 46.

342 H.-J. Puttfarken, *Seehandelsrecht*, Heidelberg, Verlag Recht und Wirtschaft, 1997, n° 106 at p. 39.

343 *All Pacific Trading, Inc. v M/V Hanjin Yosu* 7 F.3d 1427 (9th Circuit, 22 October 1993), at p. 1432. The Court explicitly refers to the bill of lading as a contract, and invokes the basic rule of contract interpretation that a party may accept a contract by filing suit on it (17A Am.Jur.2d Contracts § 456).

    See also *APL Co. PTE Ltd v Kemira Water Solutions Inc.* 890 F.Supp.2d 360 (S.D. New York, 22 August 2012): "*Although sea waybills or bills of lading are contracts between a shipper and a carrier, there is ample precedent for binding a consignee to these contracts under the theory that the non-signatory consignee accepted their terms.*" and *Kawasaki Kisen Kaisha Ltd*

the terms of the bill of lading if he files suit under it,[344] but his acceptance can also be earlier and in a different form.[345] When the holder accepts the terms of the bill of lading, he must accept them as a whole; he cannot pick and choose among the clauses.[346] Terms from the contract of carriage between the shipper and the carrier can also be binding on the holder of the bill of lading, if he had at least constructive knowledge of these terms.[347]

In addition to this view which has the consignee accede to the bill of lading if he takes action upon it, there are also a number of cases which seem to consider the bill of lading an *ipso facto* contract between the carrier and the consignee. In *Louisville & N.R. Co. v Central Iron & Coal Co.*, the U.S. Supreme Court held that a bill of lading '*serves both as a receipt and as a contract*'.[348] Although the case was about the liability of a non-contracting shipper to pay freight for a rail carriage, and although the Court found that, on the facts of the case, the bill of lading was irrelevant as the non-contracting shipper had not signed it and was not described in it as the consignor, some later decisions have relied on this dictum of the Supreme Court to hold that the bill of lading is a contract between the carrier and the holder of the bill of lading. In *States Marine International v Seattle-First National Bank*, the Ninth Circuit quoted *Louisville* and held that courts examine the bill of lading to determine a consignee's contractual liability.[349] Similarly, in *Ivaran Lines v Sutex Paper & Cellulose Corp.*, the District Court quoted *Louisville* and would apparently have held the consignee liable to pay freight, if the bill of

---

    v Plano Moulding Co. 2012 A.M.C. 2611 (7th Circuit, 29 August 2012): "*Although a bill of lading is a contract between a shipper and a carrier, it can nonetheless bind a non-party buyer where there is consent to be bound.*"
344 *All Pacific Trading, Inc. v M/V Hanjin Yosu* 7 F.3d 1427 (9th Circuit, 22 October 1993); *Mitsui & Co (USA) Inc. v M/V Mira* 111 F.3d 33 (5th Circuit, 28 April 1997); *Kukje Hwajae Insurance Co Ltd v M/V Hyundai Liberty* 408 F.3d 1250 (9th Circuit, 26 May 2005).
    Kanematsu Corp. v M/V Gretchen W 897 F.Supp. 1314 (D. Oregon, 15 September 1995); *Metallia USA Inc. v M/V Buyalyk* 1999 WL 717642 (E.D. Louisiana, 13 September 1999); *F.D. Import & Export Corp. v M/V Reefer Sun* 248 F.Supp.2d 240 (S.D. New York, 4 December 2002); *APL Co. PTE Ltd v Kemira Water Solutions Inc.* 890 F.Supp.2d 360 (S.D. New York, 22 August 2012).
345 *All Pacific Trading, Inc. v M/V Hanjin Yosu* 7 F.3d 1427 (9th Circuit, 22 October 1993), at p. 1432; *Taisheng International Ltd v Eagle Maritime Services* 2006 WL 846380 (S.D. Texas, 30 March 2006): "*. . . acceptance of a bill of lading can take many forms. The filing of a lawsuit under the bill of lading is one form of acceptance explicitly recognized by the Fifth Circuit.*"
346 *F.D. Import & Export Corp. v M/V Reefer Sun* 248 F.Supp.2d 240 (S.D. New York, 4 December 2002), at p. 248.
347 *Steel Warehouse Co. v Abalone Shipping Ltd* 141 F.3d 234 (5th Circuit, 21 May 1998), at p. 237; *F.D. Import & Export Corp. v M/V Reefer Sun* 248 F.Supp.2d 240 (S.D. New York, 4 December 2002), at pp. 247–248.
348 *Louisville & N.R. Co. v Central Iron & Coal Co.* 44 S.Ct. 441 (US Supreme Court, 5 May 1924), at p. 443.
349 *States Marine International v Seattle-First National Bank* 524 F.2d 245 (9th Circuit, 16 October 1975), at p. 248.
    See also *A/S Dampskibsselskabet Torm v Beaumont Oil Ltd* 927 F.2d 713, 1991 A.M.C. 1573 (2nd Circuit, 11 March 1991), citing both *Louisville* and *States Marine*.

lading had contained a clause to that effect (which it did not).[350] In *Ataei v M/V/ Barber Tonsberg*, there is no reference to *Louisville*, but the District Court simply held that the defendant, since he was the consignee, was a party to the contract.[351]

109 In the U.K., Lord Ellenborough in *Cock v Taylor* (1811) held that "*The defendants, by becoming assignees of the bill of lading and receiving the goods, adopt the contract. They were aware on what terms the goods were to be delivered, and by accepting them they accede to those terms.*"[352] Subsequent cases rather went in the direction of a new, implied contract between the carrier and the consignee,[353] and in 1855, the Bills of Lading Act provided a statutory position for many holders of bills of lading.[354]

3.2.2.3 When does the relationship come into being?

110 When the contract of carriage is seen as a multi-party contract from the start, the necessary consequence is that the relationship between the carrier and the consignee immediately comes into being when the contract of carriage is made,[355] even if the consignee at that time hasn't seen or received the bill of lading or isn't even aware yet that a contract of carriage has been made.

111 If the holder of the bill of lading is seen as later acceding to the contract of carriage, the answer is, in principle, simple and straightforward: the relationship between the carrier and the holder of the bill of lading comes into being at the moment the latter accedes to the contract. This answer, however, only replaces the initial question with a second one: when does the holder accede to the contract? There are, in general, three answers possible: at the time the holder presents the bill of lading to the carrier, at the time the holder exercises a right under the bill of lading, or at the time the holder receives the bill of lading from the shipper or from a previous holder.[356]

112 There is not always a distinction between the first two possibilities. Claiming delivery is indeed the most obvious right for the holder to exercise, and the courts that hold that the holder accedes by presenting the bill of lading to the carrier and claiming delivery do not necessarily imply that the holder could not

---

350 *Ivaran Lines v Sutex Paper & Cellulose Corp.* 1987 A.M.C. 690 (S.D. Florida, 12 February 1985).
　See also *Korea Express Usa, Inc. v K.K.D. Imports, Inc.* 2002 A.M.C. 2446 (D. New Jersey, 28 August 2002).
351 *Ataei v M/V/ Barber Tonsberg* 639 F.Supp. 993 (S.D. New York, 2 July 1986), at p. 1003.
352 *Cock v Taylor* 2 Camp. 587, 170 ER 1261 (Nisi Prius, 26 February 1811), at pp. 588–589.
　Later proceedings at 13 East 399, 104 ER 424 (King's Bench, 2 May 1811).
353 Such implied contracts later became known as *Brandt v Liverpool* contracts. See below, para 3.2.3.2.
354 See below, n° 17 p. 155.
355 Compare M. Remond-Gouilloud, *Le contrat de transport*, Paris, Dalloz, 1993, at p. 35. The author sees the shipper as '*porte-fort*' for the consignee. The latter's subsequent ratification of the actions of the '*porte-fort*' has retroactive effect.
356 Compare S. Geense, "De 'merchant-clausule', *NTHR* 2011-5, at p. 197.

accede before presentation, if he had exercised another right under the bill of lading earlier – that issue simply did not come up in the case they had to decide.

113 The majority view in the Netherlands is that the holder only accedes to the contract by presenting the bill of lading to the carrier (or by exercising another right under the bill of lading[357]), and not already by simply receiving the bill of lading.[358] In France, the standard position is that the holder accedes by taking delivery of the goods,[359] which in fact presupposes the presentation of the bill of lading to the carrier.

114 It has been said that a distinct action by the holder vis-à-vis the carrier is required, as the carrier would otherwise not be aware of who his contract partner is.[360] That argument is not really convincing, though. It is true, of course, that in practice, the carrier will often be unaware of who is holding the bill of lading at a given moment, and will only learn the identity of the holder when the latter at a given time interacts with the carrier, but that does not mean that, from a legal point of view, that holder could not have acceded to the contract immediately when he received the bill of lading. Conversely, when it is the carrier who wants or needs to know who was the holder of the bill of lading at a certain time, it might be possible for the carrier to retrace the chain of transfers and find that

---

357 Such as the right to modify the instructions to the carrier, or the right to demand delivery of the goods before they have arrived at destination (see, for example, Article 50–51 Rotterdam Rules, Article 8:440 Dutch Civil Code).

358 H. Boonk, "Cognossement en cognossementhouder", 372 *NTBR* 2007-9, at p. 374; M. Claringbould, "Het cognossement", in *Preadvies van de Vereeniging Handelsrecht en de Nederlandse Vereniging voor zee- en vervoerrecht: Vervoersrecht in Boek 8 BW*, Zwolle, Tjeenk Willink, 1997, at p. 139; P. Seck, *Reisbevrachting en cognossementsvervoer*, Zutphen, Uitgeverij Paris, 2011, at pp. 154–155 and p. 217; A. Van Oven, *Handelsrecht*, Zwolle, Tjeenk Willink, 1981, at pp. 254–255.

Court of Rotterdam 4 April 2007, Case N° 30664/HAZA94-3345, *S&S* 2008, 126 (*ms. Svanetiya*).

Zwitser initially supported the majority position (R. Zwitser, "Toetreden tot de vervoersovereenkomst; het Contship America", 33 *T.V.R.* 2000, at p. 41), but later changed to the position that the holder accedes by accepting the bill of lading or having it endorsed to him (R. Zwitser, "Het cognossement als zekerheidsinstrument", *NTHR* 2007-2, (83), at p. 88 and p. 90; R. Zwitser, *De rol van het cognossement als waardepapier in het handelsverkeer*, Zutphen, Uitgeverij Paris, 2012, § 5.7 at pp. 107–111).

359 Ph. Delebecque, *Droit maritime*, Paris, Dalloz, 2014 (13th Ed.), n° 731 at p. 511; Y. Tassel, *Cass. com. 29 November 1994 (Navire Stolt Osprey)*, *D.M.F.* 1995, 218 (note), at p. 220; J.-P. Tosi, "L'adhésion du destinataire au contrat de transport", in X., *Mélanges Christian Mouly*, Paris, Litec, 1998, at p. 177 and p. 180; R. Rodière, *Traité général de droit maritime*, Tome II, *Les contrats de transport de marchandises*, Paris, Librairie Dalloz, 1967, n° 405 at p. 25.

Cass. fr. 29 November 1994, Pourvoi N° 92-19987, *D.M.F.* 1995, 209 (*Navires Harmony and Nagasaki*); Cass. fr. 29 November 1994, Pourvoi N° 92-14920, *D.M.F.* 1995, 218 (*Navire Stolt Osprey*).

360 H. Boonk, "HR 29 november 2002 RvdW 2002, 197 (Ladoga 15): de grondslag van de rechtsverkrijging door de derde cognossementhouder", 132 *T.V.R.* 2003, at p. 136. Compare R. Japikse, "Boekbeschouwing: Mr. G.J. van der Ziel, Het cognossement, naar een functionele benadering", 193 *RM Themis* 2000/5, at p. 194.

information. Clearly, therefore, the fact that the carrier is not aware of the transfer of the bill of lading should not impede the holder's accession to the contract. Under Dutch law, however, there is an additional argument in the provisions of Art. 3:33 and 3:37.(3) of the Dutch Civil Code. Acceding to a contract is, without doubt, a juridical act (*rechtshandeling*). As purely private thoughts and intentions are irrelevant to the law, a juridical act requires a public declaration of will (Art. 3:33). If such declaration is addressed to a specific person, it must have reached that person in order to be effective (Art. 3:37.(3)). A declaration of accession addressed to the carrier thus must have reached the carrier. If simply acquiring the bill of lading can be seen as a 'declaration' of will at all, that declaration in any case does not reach the carrier.

115 It has also been argued that accession requires an 'active' act (presentation of the bill of lading), and that a 'passive' act (accepting the bill of lading) does not suffice. Again, this argument is not really convincing. There is no objective yardstick to determine when an act is 'active' rather than 'passive', and in any case, it is not self-evident that accepting a bill of lading is a 'passive' act. Bills of lading are not handed out like flyers in the street; in order to obtain a bill of lading, the prospective holder does need to take action (such as entering into a purchase agreement). Finally, a number of Dutch authors have argued that, since Article 8:481 of the Dutch Civil Code explicitly requires the holder to surrender the bill of lading to the carrier in order to obtain delivery of the goods, this is the moment that the holder accedes to the contract of carriage.[361] This is a *non sequitur*, however. The holder does indeed need to surrender the bill of lading to the carrier to prove that he is the holder and to prevent the bill of lading from circulating further, but that does not mean that the holder cannot have acceded to the contract earlier. It is perfectly possible for someone to be a party to a contract, but nevertheless only able to exercise certain rights from a point of time in the future, e.g. after a condition has been met.

116 Does the holder have to actually possess the bill of lading to accede to the contract? With a bearer bill of lading, the answer is clearly affirmative, as the capacity of 'holder' then depends on physically holding the bill of lading. With an order bill of lading, however, the prospective holder may already be known from an endorsement before that party has physically received the bill of lading. With a straight bill of lading, the prospective holder is known from the start. In theory, therefore, such identified prospective holders could accede to the contract of carriage before physically being the holder of the bill of lading. If, however, the position is taken that the holder only accedes by presenting the bill of lading to the carrier, physical holdership is an implicit requirement. A party that does not physically hold the bill of lading cannot present it to the carrier. In 2000, however, the Dutch Supreme Court in *Eendracht* held that presentation of the bill of lading – a straight bill of lading in that case – is not the only possible way to

---

[361] R. Japikse, "Boekbeschouwing: Mr. G.J. van der Ziel, Het cognossement, naar een functionele benadering", *RM Themis* 2000/5, at p. 194.

accede to the contract of carriage.³⁶² When a cargo of beer tanks was damaged shortly after departure, the shipper, carrier and consignee all agreed to have the equipment returned to the shipper for repairs. This agreement, and the negotiations leading up to it, were seen by the Supreme Court as an accession by the consignee (accepted by the shipper and the carrier), even though he had not yet received the bill of lading at that time.³⁶³ Two years later, however, in *Ladoga 15*, the Supreme Court cautioned that the holder of a bill of lading (again a straight bill) cannot accede to the contract of carriage 'at any time and in any way whatsoever'.³⁶⁴ This is, of course, not a very clear or helpful guideline.³⁶⁵ It is clear, however, from these decisions that, under the right circumstances, the prospective holder of the bill of lading can accede to the contract of carriage before receiving the physical bill of lading.³⁶⁶

117 The minority view, both in the Netherlands and in France, is that the holder immediately accedes to the contract when he receives and accepts the bill of lading. For van der Ziel, the reason is that the holder usually pays for and/or acquires rights on the goods when he receives the bill of lading, and therefore must be able to give instructions to the carrier with respect to the goods.³⁶⁷ Notice of the accession must not necessarily be given to the carrier, but can also be given to the shipper (or, presumably, to the previous holder if that is not the shipper). Further, by having the holder accede to the contract upon receipt of the bill of lading, the carrier can act against the holder even if the latter does not claim the goods.³⁶⁸ For Bokalli, the reason is that the holder benefits from the bill of lading and remains liable under it, even if he transfers it to another party later on.³⁶⁹ For

---

362 HR 22 september 2000, *N.J.* 2001, 44 (*ms. Eendracht*).
363 Two originals were in the mail, the third was in the ship's bag when the decision was made to have the ship return.
364 HR 29 November 2002, *RvdW* 2002, 197 (*ms. Ladoga 15*).
365 The *Ladoga 15* decision is quite remarkable, in that the consignee had actually *presented* the bill of lading (through an agent). The issue however was that the agent had started out as the agent of the shipper, and had received the bill of lading in that capacity. He then changed hats and became the agent of the consignee, and presented the bill of lading on behalf of the consignee. The decision would probably have been clearer if the Court had held that in those circumstances the consignee (through his then agent) had not *lawfully* become the holder of the bill of lading and therefore could not, or at least not in good faith, exercise the rights under it.
366 It has been pointed out, and quite correctly, that in practice, the right circumstances will only rarely occur. (K. Haak, "HR 29 November 2002 (Ladoga 15)", *N.J.* 2003, 374 (note)).
  See also Court of Rotterdam 3 November 2004, *S&S* 2005, 86 (*MSC / Wilmink Air & Ocean*), where the court held that, in principle, a party must hold the bill of lading to be bound by it.
367 G.J. van der Ziel, *Het cognossement, naar een functionele benadering*, Deventer, Kluwer, 1999, at pp. 6–7.
368 G.J. van der Ziel, *Het cognossement, naar een functionele benadering*, Deventer, Kluwer, 1999, at p. 7.
369 V.-E. Bokalli, "Crise et avenir du connaissement", *D.M.F.* 1998, at p. 123: "*En bénéficiant du connaissement, cette société rentre en effet dans l'opération; en l'endossant à son tour, s'il*

116 *Contractual theories*

the author, the consequence is that intermediate holders have title to sue the carrier for cargo loss or damage.[370]

3.2.2.4 Intermediate holders

118 When the contract of carriage is seen as a multi-party contract from the start, the (implied) understanding is that the third party to the contract is the consignee, i.e. the ultimate holder who presents the bill of lading at destination. There is no attention and no explanation for the position of intermediate holders in this view.

119 If the holder of the bill of lading accedes afterwards to the contract, the position of intermediate holders depends on the answer that is given to the previous question, viz. at what time does the holder accede to the contract? If the holder accedes by presenting the bill of lading to the carrier and claiming delivery, then only the ultimate holder can accede. Previous holders do no become a party to the contract of carriage, and do not have a legal position under the multi-party concept.[371] If on the other hand the holder accedes by exercising rights under the bill of lading, multiple holders can become parties to the contract. Suppose, for instance, that party A, which then holds the bill of lading, instructs the carrier to change the port of destination, and afterwards endorses the bill of lading to party B, which ultimately presents the bill of lading and claims delivery. In that case, both A and B would have become a party to the contract of carriage. In practice, however, such scenario will probably not occur very often.[372] If, finally,

---

est vrai que par cet acte, elle transmet tous ses droits à son acquéreur, elle ne sort pas pour autant de cette opération dont du reste elle continue d'assumer la responsabilité." (By benefitting from the bill of lading, that company indeed becomes part of the operation; by again endorsing it, even if it is true that by that act it transfers all of its rights to the acquirer, it does not step out again of the operation, for which it remains liable.)

370 The author refers to the *Ramona* case (CA Poitiers, 30 June 1993, unreported, confirmed by Cass. com. 19 December 1995, *D.M.F.* 1996, 389), where an intermediate holder (Agrocéan) had endorsed the bill of lading to the ultimate buyer. At destination, the cargo was delivered with a considerable shortage. The buyer, however, only had to pay by weight delivered and thus did not suffer a loss. Agrocéan, which did suffer the loss, saw its claim against the carrier rejected for lack of title to sue.

371 R. Zwitser, "Toetreden tot de vervoersovereenkomst; het Contship America", *T.V.R.* 2000, at p. 42.

But see M. Claringbould, "Het cognossement", in *Preadvies van de Vereeniging Handelsrecht en de Nederlandse Vereniging voor zee- en vervoerrecht. Vervoersrecht in Boek 8 BW*, Zwolle, Tjeenk Willink, 1997, at p. 140. For the author, holding the bill of lading provides the right and the possibility to accede, but actual accession requires a notice to that effect to the carrier. See also H. Boonk, "Cognossement en cognossementhouder", *NTBR* 2007-9, at p. 376, who construes the position of the holder which hasn't acceded to the contract yet as a 'property law position'. The holder of the bill of lading has the possibility to claim delivery (which gives him power over the carried goods), but only accedes to the contract when he actually does so.

372 The carrier can quite easily prevent such scenario by demanding the return of all originals of the existing bill of lading before he accepts the modified instructions, and by then issuing

the holder accedes simply by accepting the bill of lading, then every holder of the bill of lading will become a party to the contract of carriage, even if he later transfers the bill of lading to another party. As bills of lading are often transferred in practice, this view would mean that contracts of carriage are frequently 'many-party contracts'.[373] For the intermediate holders, this is not the most enviable position. There are not that many rights under a contract of carriage that can be exercised by a party not in possession of the bill of lading, but – being a party to the contract – it will still be subject to the obligations and liabilities of the contract of carriage. For the carrier, this would only be a result by law that he often tries to achieve by contract, through the Merchant Clause.

3.2.2.5 *The non-contracting shipper*

120 The multi-party contract concept should, in principle, have no problems accommodating the non-contracting shipper, who is clearly involved with the contract of carriage. His participation is, in fact, crucial for the performance of the contract of carriage; if he does not supply the goods, then the carrier cannot carry them to destination. It will often also be the non-contracting shipper who collects the bill of lading from the carrier. One would expect, therefore, the non-contracting shipper to accede to the contract when he delivers the goods to the carrier or when he receives the bill of lading from the carrier.[374] The authors who consider the position of the non-contracting shipper, however, rather deny his becoming a party to the contract of carriage, primarily because the non-contracting shipper is thought not to have a (real) *intention* to become a party and/or because the parties to the contract would not mean for the non-contracting

---

a new bill of lading reflecting the modified instructions. The German Commercial Code (HGB) explicitly confirms this principle in § 520.(1): "*Der Verfrachter darf Weisungen nur gegen Vorlage sämtlicher Ausfertigungen des Konnossements ausführen.*" (The carrier is only obliged to make changes against presentation of all copies of the bill of lading.)

373 Compare R. Zwitser, "De cognossementhouder als derde uit derdenbeding", *T.V.R.* 2002, at p. 159, who explicitly considers it possible that subsequent holders all accede to the contract of carriage, possibly even with different rights and obligations from one to another. ("*In de eerste plaats is het mogelijk dat opeenvolgende houders allemaal toetreden tot de vervoerovereenkomst en wellicht zelfs niet allemaal met precies dezelfde rechten en plichten (. . .)*")

374 In that sense: *The Athanasia Comninos and Georges Chr. Lemos*, [1990] 1 Lloyd's Rep 277 (Queen's Bench Division, Commercial Court, 21 December 1979). A shipment of coal had been sold by Devco (Australia) to CEGB (UK) on FOB basis. CEGB, as FOB buyer, had chartered the vessel, and Devco had been named as shipper on the bill of lading. The coal having damaged the carrying vessel, Devco was later sued by the shipowner under the bill of lading. Devco argued that the contract of carriage had been made by CEGB and that they (Devco) were not a party to that contract. Mustill J however held: "*The original documents were routed to Devco, for onward transmission to CEGB under the contract of sale. No objection was taken by Devco to their designation as shippers, which is not surprising, since that is what they were. It seems to me quite plain that Devco were bound by the contract contained in the bill of lading.*"

shipper to accede to their contract.[375] Why the consignee would intend to become a party to the contract of carriage, but not the non-contracting shipper, or why the parties to the contract would mean for the consignee to accede but not the non-contracting shipper is not immediately clear and is not further explained.[376]

121 The German courts have had to deal with the position of the non-contracting shipper several times. The OLG Bremen has held that a non-contracting shipper, which requests to be named as 'Shipper' in the bill of lading, thereby accepts to become (co-)debtor of the freight. The non-contracting shipper is indeed aware of the terms of the bill of lading, and knows, or must know, that his request to be named as 'Shipper' will be understood by the carrier as an intention or acceptance to be bound by the terms of the bill of lading.[377] The OLG München, however, in a 1988 decision at length rejects this point of view.[378] The non-contracting shipper wants to be named as Shipper in order to keep control over the goods until he has been paid, or to be able to use the bill of lading to obtain payment under a documentary credit. His request to be so named is therefore not indicative of an intention to become a co-debtor of the freight or to enter into an obligatory relationship with the carrier, and is not in contradiction with an intention *not* to become indebted under the bill of lading. Furthermore, without specific circumstances, the carrier cannot reasonably assume or expect such intention on the part of the non-contracting

---

375 M. Spanjaart, *Vorderingsrechten uit cognossement*, Zutphen, Uitgeverij Paris, 2012, at pp. 148–149. The author also argues that accession requires an 'active' act, and can only take the form of presentation of the bill of lading (also at p. 151). It has already been pointed out that neither of these arguments is really convincing (above, n° 163).

See also *The Roseline* [1987] 1 Lloyd's Rep 18 (Federal Court of Canada, 23 March 1984), at p. 22. The ship had been chartered by the buyer of a cargo of sulphur. The seller (Petrosul) had provided some information to the carrier to be entered into the bill of lading, and had later received the bill from the carrier. The ship's holds were damaged by the sulphur and the carrier sued Petrosul. In those circumstances, Reed J held that: "... [Petrosul's] *only interest in the bill of lading was to be able to use it as one of the documents that was required to be delivered to the bank in order to obtain payment for the sulphur under the letter of credit. Thus the bill of lading in its hands partook of the nature of a receipt or a document of title. Use for this purpose does not make the document a contractual one as far as the defendant* [Petrosul] *is concerned. It does not make the defendant a party to the contract of carriage.*"

376 See also n° 121 p. 119 and fn. 387 p. 121.

377 OLG München 3 November 1988, Case 24 U 814/87, *NJW-RR* 1989, 803, refers to unreported case law of the LG and OLG Bremen: "*Das LG Bremen und das OLG Bremen haben in dem Rechtsstreit 11 O 402/80 = 2 U 110/81 die Rechtsauffassung vertreten, die vom Exporteur veranlaßte "Shipper"-Stellung begründe ohne weiteres eine Frachtzahlungspflicht.*" (The LG Bremen and the OLG Bremen in the cases 11 O 402/80 and 2 U 110/81 have expressed the opinion that the identification as 'Shipper' by the exporter is in itself sufficient to create an obligation to pay freight.)

See also OLG Bremen 2 November 1978, Case 2 U 55/78, *VersR* 1979, 667.

378 OLG München 3 November 1988, Case 24 U 814/87, NJW-RR 1989, 803, VersR 1990, 998, RIW 1989, 650.

shipper either. The OLG München has since been followed by a number of other courts.[379]

3.2.2.6 Appraisal

122 Accession is a way to enter into a contract; it requires the will and the intention of the acceding party to indeed enter into a contractual relationship with other parties. Contracts are voluntary: a party cannot be *forced* to enter into a 'contract'.[380] The law can of course grant certain rights to or impose obligations on a party, but such 'legal' position is not contractual. In order to say, therefore, that the holder of the bill of lading has acceded to the contract, it must be proven that the holder *actually intended* to enter into a contract with the carrier (and the shipper). Several authors simply assume this necessary intention from the fact that the holder has claimed and taken delivery of the carried goods.[381] That assumption, however, is questionable – to say the least. There is, indeed, a difference between exercising a right (claiming delivery) and the intention to accede to a contract.[382] One could probably say that there is a hierarchy going from having a right pure and simple, without burdens, over having a right with conditions attached to it, to acceding to and becoming a full party to a contract. The holder of a bill of lading obviously has rights, but does not go all the way to becoming a full party to the contract.

First, the holder of the bill of lading is, in reality, not at liberty to decide whether or not he will present the bill of lading. He *must* do so to obtain the carried goods, which may be his property, or which he must collect and deliver to his principal, etc. This *de facto* obligation to present the bill of lading does influence the analysis of the act of presentation. If a party makes an (open) offer and another party freely decides to accept it – e.g. a reduction coupon in an newspaper, which is cut out and presented by a shopper – it is not impossible to construe such conduct as an intention to contract under the given terms (i.e.

---

379 OLG Düsseldorf 26 October 1995, Case N° 18 U 46/95, *NJW-RR* 1996, 1380, *TranspR* 1996, 165; OLG Rostock 27 November 1996, Case N° 6 U 113/96, *TransR* 1997, 113; LG Bremen 10 October 2007, Case 11 O 381/05, *BeckRS* 2010, 25028.
380 P. Bonassies, *Cass. com. 29 November 1994 (Navires Harmony et Nagasaki)*, D.M.F. 1995, 209 (note), at p. 216; R. Rodière, *Traité général de droit maritime*, Tome II, *Les contrats de transport de marchandises*, Paris, Librairie Dalloz, 1967, n° 405 at p. 25; J.-P. Tosi, "L'adhésion du destinataire au contrat de transport", in X., *Mélanges Christian Mouly*, Paris, Litec, 1998, at p. 187.
381 J.-P. Tosi, "L'adhésion du destinataire au contrat de transport", in X., *Mélanges Christian Mouly*, Paris, Litec, 1998, at p. 192.
382 CA Caen 20 March 1997, *D.M.F.* 1997, 714 (*Navire Westfield*), at p. 715: "*Attendu cependant que s'il n'est pas douteux que le destinataire a manifesté sa volonté de bénéficier des droits essentiels nés du contrat en prenant possession de la marchandise, son consentement à une clause spéciale (. . .) n'est pas pour autant démontré*" (Considering however that even if there is no doubt that the consignee manifested his will to benefit from the essential rights deriving from the contract by taking possession of the goods, his consent to a special clause (. . .) is not thereby automatically proven).

the conditions of the coupon).[383] If, on the other hand, conduct is forced by the circumstances, it is much more difficult to construe such conduct as an intention to (voluntarily) enter into a contract. The simple fact that the holder presented the bill of lading and claimed delivery therefore does not prove that he intended to enter into a contract with the carrier (and the shipper).[384]

Second, it seems safe to say that, in truth, the holder most often has no intention at all to accede to the contract of carriage.[385] This is very clear when goods are sold and shipped on a CIF or similar basis, where the seller of the goods has to arrange the shipping. If the holder of the bill of lading expressly agreed with the seller that the latter would take care of the carriage, why would he then accede to the contract of carriage after all? And even if the holder did not make it clear in the underlying agreement that he did not want to be involved in the carriage, why would he want to become a party to the contract of carriage? What would be the advantage to him of that course of action, certainly considering that at the time of his accession the largest part of the contract has already been performed: the goods have been carried to destination, discharged from the ship, etc. All

---

[383] Even then, it could be argued that the shopper who presents the coupon does not really intend to enter into a contract, but simply wants to collect what is, in his mind, already his.

[384] Compare CA Antwerp, 4th Division, 6 November 2006, *unreported*, Case N° 2005/AR/1955. The Court held that presenting the bill of lading to obtain delivery, without reservation as to the provisions of the bill lading, does not prove that the holder (implicitly) accepted these provisions.

See also Comm. C. Antwerp 18 December 2003, *R.H.A.* 2005, 67, at p. 79: "*Overwegende immers dat zo het juist is dat cognossementen sedert meer dan een eeuw voorwaarden inhouden en een forumbeding daarvan gebruikelijk deel uitmaakt, de cognossementhouder die de goederen gekocht heeft en die niet anders kan dan het cognossement presenteren om deze in ontvangst te kunnen nemen, weliswaar kennis neemt van deze voorwaarden doch niet bij machte is deze te negociëren en deze hem in feite worden opgelegd; overwegende dat dan ook van enige stilzwijgende aanvaarding van de cognossementsclausules zoals gedaagden aanvoeren, geen sprake kan zijn*" (Considering that even if it is true that since more than a century, bills of lading contain clauses, which usually include a forum selection clause, the holder of the bill of lading, who has bought the goods and has no other option than to present the bill of lading to take delivery of those goods, is indeed aware of those clauses, but is not able to negotiate them; they are in fact forced upon him; considering therefore that a tacit acceptance of those clauses, as argued by the defendants, cannot be accepted).

Compare *Hispanica de Petroleos S.A. and Compania Iberica Refinadera S.A. v Vencedora Oceanica Navegacion S.A. (The Kapetan Markos N.L. (No. 2))* [1987] 2 Lloyd's Rep 321 (Court of Appeal, 28–30 April and 1 and 5 May 1987), at p. 332: "... *in many cases, it would be hard to regard the act of becoming endorsees as referable to an acceptance of the open offer* [allegedly contained in the bill of lading], *since it would be very often (although not in this particular case) be an act done because the contract of sale requires the endorsee to take up and pay for the documents when duly tendered.*"

Compare also the opinion of Advocate General Gordon Slynn in the *Tilly Russ* case (ECJ 19 June 1984, Case 71/83, *Partenreederei ms. Tilly Russ and Ernest Russ v NV Haven- & Vervoerbedrijf Nova and NV Goeminne Hout*): "*It does not seem to me that the mere presentation by the holder of the bill, who has already purchased the goods, to the carrier would in itself constitute such an agreement or evidence of an agreement for the purposes of Article 17.*"

[385] Compare J. Huizink, "De derde-cognossementshouder wordt geen partij", *T.V.R.* 1998, at p. 15; F. Stevens, *Vervoer onder cognossement*, Brussel, Larcier, 2001, n° 352 at p. 205.

that is left is for them to be collected by the consignee. The most obvious answer would be that the holder 'wants' (or rather, needs) to become a party to the contract in order to be able to claim delivery or compensation. That answer, however, is hardly convincing.[386] Accession to the contract of carriage thus is hardly beneficial to the holder. On the contrary, accession to the contract opens up the possibility of obligations and liabilities. It is quite remarkable in this respect that authors that are adamant that the consignee accedes to the contract of carriage are equally adamant that intermediate holders and the non-contracting shipper do *not* accede to the contract since they have no intention to do so,[387] although it is of course equally easy to construe these parties into acceding to the contract.

Also, the analysis is influenced by the desired result. Often, courts and authors ultimately want to arrive at the conclusion that the consignee has obligations under the bill lading, and assuming him to have acceded to the contract of carriage is a fairly straightforward (and admittedly not entirely implausible) way of arriving at that conclusion. In other cases, they want to see the holder acceded to the contract of carriage in order to grant him standing to sue.[388] This is, nevertheless, putting the cart before the horses. A party does not accede to a contract simply because it is convenient for other parties that he should have done so.

123 The intention to accede is a fundamental requirement both for the multi-party contract approach and for the accession approach. If such intention is proven or assumed, however, both approaches have other obstacles to overcome.

124 The (mostly French) concept of a three-party contract from the beginning is difficult to construct from a legal point of view. In most cases, the consignee is not physically present (and may not even be known yet) when the contract of carriage is made. Nevertheless, his acceptance is required – a party cannot be forced into a contract against its will. One solution is to have the consignee represented by the shipper, who is present when the contract of carriage is made. That, however, is a rather theoretical solution, which is hardly compatible with practice,

---

386 See below, n° 156 p. 140.
387 On intermediate holders: R. Japikse, "Boekbeschouwing: Mr. G.J. van der Ziel, Het cognossement, naar een functionele benadering", *RM Themis* 2000/5, at p. 194; M. Spanjaart, *Vorderingsrechten uit cognossement*, Zutphen, Uitgeverij Paris, 2012, fn. 280 at p. 91; R. Zwitser, "De cognossementhouder als derde uit derdenbeding", *T.V.R.* 2002, at p. 163; R. Zwitser, *De rol van het cognossement als waardepapier in het handelsverkeer*, Zutphen, Uitgeverij Paris, 2012, at p. 108.

On the non-contracting shipper: M. Spanjaart, "The Konnossementsbegebungsvertrag – a suggestion for further reformation", *TransportR* 2011, at p. 335; M. Spanjaart, *Vorderingsrechten uit cognossement*, Zutphen, Uitgeverij Paris, 2012, at p. 148.
388 V.-E. Bokalli, "Crise et avenir du connaissement", *D.M.F.* 1998, at p. 123. The author refers to *Ramona* (CA Poitiers 30 June 1993, *unreported*, confirmed by Cass. com. 19 December 1995, *D.M.F.* 1996, 389), where the first holder had negotiated the bill of lading to a second holder, who had taken delivery of the goods. There turned out to be an important shortage, but due to the terms of the sales contract, the loss was suffered by the first holder rather than the ultimate holder. The first holder's claim against the carrier, however, was dismissed for lack of standing to sue. In order to solve such problems, the author would have the holder accede to the contract of carriage.

certainly if the bill of lading is transferred several times during the voyage and the shipper had no idea who the ultimate holder would be when he made the contract of carriage with the carrier. An alternative solution is to see the consignee as a party from the beginning, but to require his later acceptance of this 'position' of contract party.[389] It is, however, a contradiction in terms to consider someone a party to a contract, when he is entirely free to accept or not the position of party and does not have obligations and only potential rights as long as he has not accepted. There is, furthermore, very little difference between accepting the position of contract party and acceding to a contract, except perhaps the moment of acquiring the capacity of party to the contract. It could be said that if a party 'accepts the position', it must be considered to have been a party to the contract from the beginning, whereas a party that accedes to the contract only becomes a party from the moment of its accession. There are, however, no binding reasons why the consignee should be a party from the very beginning or only from the moment of his accession. In the end, therefore, it is simply a *choice* whether one *wants* the consignee to have rights and/or be bound from the date of the contract, or only from the date the consignee has acceded to the contract. It should be noted that the former position could have strange consequences, as it would mean that a party that only acquires the bill of lading some days before the arrival of the ship is nevertheless considered to have been a party to the contract – and thus liable under the contract – during the entire carriage, at times when he may not even have been aware of the ship or the cargo.

125 If the holder is not seen as an initial party to the contract of carriage, but as an acceding party, the next bifurcation is between accession to the contract as made between the shipper and the carrier and accession to the contract as incorporated in the bill of lading.

One of the reasons to have the holder accede to the contract as made between the shipper and the carrier is that, in practice, there is only one carriage. The carrier does not perform certain services for the shipper and other services for the consignee. The legal analysis, it is said, should take into account this single reality and not dissect it into separate legal relationships.[390] Different relationships, however, are inevitable when the terms of the contract of carriage between the shipper and the carrier are not identical to the terms of the bill of lading. This is very clear when the contract between the shipper and the carrier is a charter party. Even in that case, there is only one physical carriage, but (at least) two different legal relationships.[391] There are also different relationships when the

---

389 A. Kpoahoun Amoussou, *Les clauses attributives de compétence dans le transport maritime de marchandises*, Presses Universitaires d'Aix-Marseille, 2002, n° 652 at p. 415. The same author however also repeatedly writes that the consignee accedes to the contract ("... *du destinataire qui adhère à ce contrat* ...") – see for instance n° 419 at p. 269 and n° 421 at p. 271.
390 A. Kpoahoun Amoussou, *Les clauses attributives de compétence dans le transport maritime de marchandises*, Presses Universitaires d'Aix-Marseille, 2002, n° 645–646 at pp. 410–411.
391 A. Kpoahoun Amoussou, *Les clauses attributives de compétence dans le transport maritime de marchandises*, Presses Universitaires d'Aix-Marseille, 2002, n° 648 at p. 413.

'carrier' under the bill of lading is not the party that entered into a contract with the shipper, but a party that is, by operation of law, deemed to be the carrier (e.g. the shipowner).

126 If the holder is seen as acceding to the contract of carriage as made between the shipper and the carrier, the consequence should be that the holder is bound by (and can himself invoke) all clauses of that contract.[392] Acceding indeed necessarily implies consent to be bound, and a party that decides to accede to a contract can be expected to have first checked what that contract entails. Therefore, unless the existing parties have actively hidden certain content from the acceding party or have defrauded the acceding party, the latter must accept all clauses of the contract, even if he was not actually aware of them.[393] It is true, of course, that the existing parties can decide what the rights and obligations of acceding parties will be and that these do not have to be identical to the rights and obligations of the existing parties. An obvious example is a corporation, where different classes of stockholders can be created. A party that buys actions of class A (and thereby accedes to the corporate contract) may have different rights and obligations than a class B stockholder. Such differences, however, will be detailed in the corporation's bylaws. Contracts of carriage on the other hand do not usually distinguish between the rights and obligations of the original parties and those of later acceding parties. In principle, therefore, the acceding holder should have the same rights and obligations as the original parties. That result, however, is nonsensical in some situations and not accepted in most other situations.

The result is nonsensical when the contract between the shipper and the carrier is not a contract of carriage (in the largest sense of the term), but for example a time charter party or a volume contract. It is possible of course, in theory, to say that the holder of the bill of lading accedes to the time charter party or to the volume contract, but what would be his rights or obligations under those contracts? Hardly any clause of these contracts would make sense if applied to the holder of the bill of lading.[394] And what is the point of saying that the holder accedes to the contract, if one must then admit that (almost) none of the rights and obligations of the contract apply?

If the contract between the shipper and the carrier is a 'contract of carriage' (in the larger sense, e.g. including a voyage charter party), it is easier to apply the rights and obligations of the contract to the acceding holder. The acceding holder may be covered explicitly, by a Merchant Clause type of provision, or could be considered part of the 'cargo side' of the contract. A clear majority

---

392 Compare M. Rèmond-Gouilloud, "Des clauses de connaissements maritimes attribuant compétence à une juridiction étrangère: essai de démystification", *D.M.F.* 1995, at p. 348.
    See also I. Arroyo, "Relation entre Charte Partie et Connaissement: La Clause d'Incorporation", *E.T.L.* 1980, at p. 741 and p. 751, who is of the opinion that the holder does not become a party to the contract of carriage, precisely because the holder cannot enforce rights under that contract.
393 HR 15 April 1977, *N.J.* 1978, 163 (*Staalcom '66 BV / Neher Nederland BV*).
394 Compare M. Davies and A. Dickey, *Shipping Law*, Lawbook Co., 2004 (3th Ed.), at p. 255.

of the authors however does not accept that the holder is bound by all of the provisions of the contract he accedes to. Some have argued that the holder only accedes to those provisions that are 'germane' to a contract of carriage, or those that are still 'relevant' to the holder at destination, or only those that are part of the 'economy', the giving and taking of the contract (*l'économie du contrat*). The problem, however, is that these distinctions or categories are hardly objective, and thus introduce an element of uncertainty and unpredictability.[395]

127 It has also been argued that the holder of the bill of lading is only bound by what appears from the bill of lading itself, and not by undisclosed extras in the contract between the shipper and the carrier, because the bill of lading is (also) a negotiable instrument, and the holder of a negotiable instrument is only bound by the contents of the instrument itself.[396] Invoking the negotiable instrument character of the bill of lading, however, deducts from the strength of the accession argument. The holder of a negotiable instrument is not generally considered to accede to the underlying contract between the drawer and the drawee.

128 Spanjaart argues that the negotiable instrument argument is not even needed, since the holder of the bill of lading, as a third party in good faith, is protected and may assume that the initial contract parties have provided him all the relevant information (in the bill of lading).[397] Information, agreements, etc. that have not been incorporated in the bill of lading cannot be invoked against the holder of the bill of lading. That position, however, is difficult in two respects. First, the holder of the bill of lading is only a 'third party' in the sense that he was not one of the initial contracting parties. He does become a *contracting party* afterwards, though, by acceding to the contract. Second, it is highly debatable whether an acceding party can indeed remain passive and rely on the initial parties to feed him all the information he needs. On the contrary, the Dutch Supreme Court in a 1977 decision held that an acceding party must be proactive and must enquire itself as to the contents of the contract it accedes to.[398]

---

395 V.-E. Bokalli, "Crise et avenir du connaissement", *D.M.F.* 1998, at pp. 126–127; C. Paulin, *Droits des transports*, Paris, Litec, 2005, n° 449 at p. 233.

M. Rèmond-Gouilloud, "CA Caen 20 March 1997 (Navire Westfield)", *D.M.F.* 1997, 716 (note), at p. 722 has suggested to put together a typology of 'exorbitant' clauses, based on the risks that these clauses present to the holder.

See also Ph. Delebecque, "Cass. com. 16 January 1996 (Navire Monte Cervantes)", *D.M.F.* 1996, 629 (note), at p. 632. The author defends the '*économie du contrat*' concept, but sees a jurisdiction clause as outside the economy of the contract, whereas the French Supreme Court in 1986 held that a jurisdiction clause is indeed part of the economy (Cass. civ. 25 November 1986, *Rev. crit. DIP* 1987, 396).

396 M. Spanjaart, *Vorderingsrechten uit cognossement*, Zutphen, Uitgeverij Paris, 2012, at p. 109.

397 M. Spanjaart, *Vorderingsrechten uit cognossement*, Zutphen, Uitgeverij Paris, 2012, at pp. 109–110.

Compare C. Smeesters and G. Winkelmolen, *Droit maritime et Droit fluvial*, Vol. I, Brussels, Larcier, 1929 (2nd Ed.), n° 444 at p. 604.

398 HR 15 April 1977, *N.J.* 1978, 163 (*Staalcom '66 BV / Neher Nederland BV*).

Compare R. Japikse, *Verkeersmiddelen en Vervoer. Deel I. Algemene bepalingen en rederij*, Asser Serie, Deventer, Kluwer, 2004, n° 216 at p. 122.

129 It has also been said that the holder, although acceding to the contract between the shipper and the carrier, is entitled to assume that this contract does not contain other clauses or provisions than those of the bill of lading. Why, however, would the holder be entitled to make such assumption? It is clear that, as a *practical matter*, the holder would often have a hard time trying to find out the exact terms of the contract between the shipper and the carrier: he may not have leverage on those parties, he will be under time pressure, etc. On a theoretical level, however, that is not a sufficient answer. The question is, again, what can be expected of an acceding party: must an acceding party be proactive, or can it be passive? If it is accepted that the acceding holder can indeed remain passive, this will often lead to the carrier having a different set of rights and obligations to the holder than to the shipper. As between the shipper and the carrier, indeed, the contract may be limited to the terms of the bill of lading, but that is not always the case. In theory, there is a difference between saying that the holder accedes to the contract of carriage, by definition restricted to the terms of the bill of lading, and saying that the holder accedes to the bill of lading as such, but in practice that difference is very small.

130 Finally, a number of countries in their national law on the carriage of goods have included rules on the extent to which the holder of a bill of lading is bound by terms or provisions not apparent from the bill of lading. In the Netherlands, Article 8:441.2 of the Civil Code provides that if the holder is the original shipper, the carrier can invoke the terms of the contract of carriage and personal defences. Against a third-party holder, the carrier is bound by the terms and conditions of the bill of lading, and can invoke those terms and conditions. Claims for payment of money against the holder are only possible if these claims are 'readily knowable' from the bill of lading.[399] In Germany, § 522.(1) HGB

Compare also *United States of America vs. Ashcraft-Wilkinson Company*, 1927 A.M.C. 872 (N.D. Georgia, April 28, 1927), at p. 876: "*The rule must be held to be that one who accepts a cargo intended for him and as to which he knows bills of lading and charter party are outstanding, without obtaining those papers or enquiring of the master touching their contents, simply takes the risk of what their provisions may turn out to be.*"

399 Article 8:441.2: "*Jegens de houder van het cognossement, die niet de afzender was, is de vervoerder onder cognossement gehouden aan en kan hij een beroep doen op de bedingen van dit cognossement. Jegens iedere houder van het cognossement kan hij de uit het cognossement duidelijk kenbare rechten tot betaling geldend maken. Jegens de houder van het cognossement, die ook de afzender was, kan de vervoerder zich bovendien op de bedingen van de vervoerovereenkomst en op zijn persoonlijke verhouding tot de afzender beroepen.*" (Against the holder of the bill of lading, who was not the shipper, the carrier under the bill of lading is bound by and can invoke the terms of the bill of lading. Against any holder of the bill of lading he can enforce the rights to payment that are readily knowable from the bill of lading. Against the holder of the bill of lading, who also was the shipper, the carrier can additionally invoke the terms of the contract of carriage and his personal relationship with the shipper.)

See also S. Geense, "De 'merchant-clausule'", *NTHR* 2011-5, at p. 203.

In addition, Article 8:415.(1) provides that if the bill of lading refers to external content, such content only becomes part of the bill of lading if it is 'readily knowable' (*duidelijk kenbaar*) for the holder.

provides that the carrier can only invoke against the holder those defences that concern the validity of the statements in the bill of lading, that follow from the contents of the bill of lading, or that directly arise from the relation between the carrier and the holder.[400] The Norwegian Maritime Code in section 310 provides that jurisdiction or arbitration clauses in a charter party, that are not explicitly declared applicable in the bill of lading, do not bind the holder. Similarly, Article 251 of the Spanish Act 14/2014 on Maritime Navigation provides that the holder succeeds to all rights and actions of the shipper, with the exception however of jurisdiction and arbitration agreements, which have to be specifically accepted.

It is clear from these provisions that at least some legislators feel that the acceding holder should not be bound by terms that are not apparent or knowable from the bill of lading itself. To take these provisions as proof that the holder accedes to the contract of carriage, 'reduced' to what appears of it from the bill of lading, however, is a bridge too far. These provisions do not explicitly say that the holder accedes to a contract, and neither is such accession a necessary prerequisite for these provisions to exist or to apply. The fact that such provisions exist can also be interpreted as proof that the contractual approach does not lead to the desired results, and that therefore the legislator has stepped in to create a statutory position for the third-party holder.[401]

131 If the holder accedes to the contract of carriage between the shipper and the carrier, the normal contract law consequence would be that the acceding holder can invoke and is bound by all provisions of the contract.[402] That consequence, however, is hardly ever accepted with regard to bills of lading. Different theories have been developed to explain why the acceding holder is bound by certain provisions but not by others. This problem, and the imperfect solutions that have been proposed to solve it, are a weak point in the accession and multi-party theory.[403] It does require quite a bit of 'creative construction' to have the holder accede to the contract of carriage, only to then have to engage in a second round of creative construction to explain why he is not bound by the provisions of the contract he has just acceded to.

132 If, on the other hand, the holder is seen as acceding to the contract as incorporated in the bill of lading, he doesn't need to be protected against

---

400 § 522.(1) HGB: "*Dem aus dem Konnossement Berechtigten kann der Verfrachter nur solche Einwendungen entgegensetzen, die Gültigkeit der Erklärungen im Konnossement betreffen oder sich aus dem Inhalt des Konnossements ergeben oder dem Verfrachter unmittelbar gegenüber dem aus dem Konnossement Berechtigten zustehen.*" (Against the person entitled under the bill of lading the carrier can only invoke such defences that relate to the validity of the statements in the bill of lading or that appear from the contents of the bill of lading or that the carrier has directly against the person entitled under the bill of lading.)
401 See also below, para 4.3.
402 Unless the shipper and the carrier have taken care to detail the position of the acceding party, which in theory is perfectly possible and valid, but never happens in practice.
403 Compare G.J. van der Ziel, *Het cognossement, naar een functionele benadering*, Deventer, Kluwer, 1999, at p. 7.

unknown clauses in the contract between the shipper and the carrier. In that case, however, a single physical carriage will be subject to two (sometimes very) different legal regimes. The carrier's rights and obligations to the holder will be different than his rights and obligations to the shipper. Also, there is a 'technical' problem to this approach, in that the bill of lading is not always a contract. If the shipper and the carrier have entered into a separate contract (charter party, volume contract, etc.), the bill of lading does not have a contractual function between them. In such case, the bill of lading only *becomes* a contract by the 'accession' of the holder. Accession however requires a pre-existing contract that can be acceded to, whereas here the 'accession' *creates* a new contract that did not exist before. Having the holder accede to the contract laid down in the bill of lading is thus very close to construing the bill of lading as an offer to contract, which is accepted by the holder, a theory which has its own set of issues.[404]

133 In addition to the major issues already discussed, there are several other ones. Spanjaart distinguishes between the right to claim delivery, which for him is incorporated in the bill of lading as a negotiable instrument and is linked to the holdership of that instrument, and the 'other rights' under the contract of carriage, among which he counts the right to claim damages and for which the holder of the bill of lading must accede to the contract of carriage.[405] This 'separation' of the right to claim delivery on the one hand and the alternative right to claim damages if the goods are lost or damaged is hard to defend, however. Both rights are, in fact, two sides of the same coin. The holder of the bill of lading is entitled to claim delivery of the goods, and if they are not delivered or not delivered in the expected condition, he can claim monetary compensation. There is, quite obviously, no need to have the holder accede to the contract between the shipper and the carrier to grant him this right of action. Suppose, for instance, that A is the holder of a financial instrument, which promises payment of a certain amount in a certain currency. At the maturity date of the instrument, payment in that currency has become unlawful or impossible. Would it be argued then that A cannot sue the issuer of the instrument for payment of a corresponding amount in a different currency, unless he first accedes to the underlying contract entered into by the issuer? The real reason, however, why Spanjaart wants to see the right to claim delivery and the right to claim damages as two separate rights, the former deriving from the bill of lading taken as a negotiable instrument and the latter deriving from the contract of carriage, is because he does not see the right to claim damages as a right that *exclusively* belongs to the holder, whereas the right to claim delivery clearly is and must be exclusive.[406] If the right to claim damages is a contractual right under the contract of carriage, then the shipper also has a right of action, and there might even be other parties that also

---

404 See below, para 3.2.3.1.
405 M. Spanjaart, *Vorderingsrechten uit cognossement*, Zutphen, Uitgeverij Paris, 2012, at p. 105 and p. 209.
406 M. Spanjaart, *Vorderingsrechten uit cognossement*, Zutphen, Uitgeverij Paris, 2012, at pp. 124–125.

accede to the contract of carriage and thus also acquire a right of action.[407] There is indeed an argument to be made for extending the right of action beyond the sole holder of the bill of lading, to which it is currently limited in Belgium and the Netherlands,[408] but it is doubtful whether such extension can or should be based on an artificial separation between the right to claim delivery and the right to claim damages.

134 If the holder is or becomes a party to the contract of carriage, he then has the possibility to take contractual actions regarding this contract. He could, for example, try to have the contract of carriage as such annulled if that suited his purposes under the circumstances.[409] Although this is a logical consequence of the holder becoming one of the parties to the contract, it nevertheless goes beyond what is usually perceived as the powers of the holder.

3.2.3 A direct contractual relationship between the carrier and the holder

135 For those who do not see a third-party beneficiary clause in a contract of carriage and do not believe that the holder accedes to the contract of carriage, but nevertheless want to construe the relationship between the carrier and the holder as a contractual one, there is a third option. Why not see the relationship between the carrier and the holder not as a derivative of the initial relationship between the shipper and the carrier, but as a new and separate relationship that they form directly between themselves?

3.2.3.1 The bill of lading as an offer to contract

136 It has been argued that, between the carrier and the holder, the bill of lading is an offer to contract which, if accepted, gives rise to a new and separate contract between the carrier and the holder. By issuing a bill of lading and allowing it to be transferred to a third party, the carrier puts out an open offer to whomever will turn out to be the lawful holder of the bill of lading at destination to contract under the terms of the bill of lading. By presenting the bill of lading and claiming delivery of the goods, the holder at destination accepts the carrier's offer and thus concludes a contract with the carrier.[410] It would, of course, destroy the certainty and usability of the bill of lading as a commercial instrument if the carrier were

---

407 M. Spanjaart, *Vorderingsrechten uit cognossement*, Zutphen, Uitgeverij Paris, 2012, at p. 125.
408 In France, on the other hand, virtually every party that has suffered damage as a result of the carriage has title to sue the carrier under the bill of lading. See in this respect F. Stevens, "Consignees' rights in European legal systems", in B. Soyer and A. Tettenborn (Eds), *International trade and Carriage of Goods*, Oxon, Informa Law, 2017, at pp. 108–111.
409 P. Seck, *Reisbevrachting en cognossementsvervoer*, Zutphen, Uitgeverij Paris, 2011, at p. 193.
410 J. Loeff, *Vervoer ter zee*, Deel I, Zwolle, Tjeenk Willink, 1981, n° 55 at p. 39 and n° 64 at p. 44; J.-P. Tosi, "L'adhésion du destinataire au contrat de transport", in X., *Mélanges Christian Mouly*, Paris, Litec, 1998, at p. 189.
See also H. Boonk, "Cognossement en cognossementhouder", *NTBR* 2007-9, at p. 374.

allowed, at destination, to claim that his offer had already expired, or that he was no longer willing to contract on the terms of the bill of lading, but only on other terms. The carrier's offer, as laid down in the bill of lading, must therefore be an irrevocable offer.[411]

137 The inverse theory is also possible. In that case, it is the holder who, by presenting the bill of lading and claiming delivery, makes an offer to the carrier to contract on the terms of the bill of lading, and the carrier who accepts the offer by delivering the goods.[412]

138 In this view, the relationship between the carrier and the holder comes into being when the holder accepts the carrier's offer, i.e. when the holder presents the bill of lading in the port of destination.

139 If the relationship between the holder and the carrier only comes into being by an offer and acceptance consisting of presenting the bill of lading and delivering the cargo, there is no place for intermediate holders and non-contracting shippers. They have not accepted the carrier's offer, and thus do not enter into a contractual relationship with the carrier.

3.2.3.2 *Implied*, Brandt v Liverpool *type contracts*

140 Under English common law, the position of the consignee was a difficult one. The consignee had not been involved in the making of the contract of carriage and thus, because of the privity rule, could not have rights or obligations under that contract. Furthermore, it was generally accepted that a transfer of the bill of lading, even though such transfer initially transferred title to the goods

---

See also *Hispanica de Petroleos S.A. and Compania Iberica Refinadera S.A. v Vencedora Oceanica Navegacion S.A. (The Kapetan Markos N.L. (No. 2))* [1987] 2 Lloyd's Rep 321 (Court of Appeal, 28–30 April and 1 and 5 May 1987), at p. 332. During the hearing, an argument was made that "... *a contract later came into existence because the bill of lading contained an open offer by the owners directed towards any person who might have or thereafter acquired a proprietary interest in the goods, to make a contract in the terms of the contract of carriage, such offer being accepted (as I understood the argument) when any such person became a holder of the bill of lading.*" The Court, Mustill LJ writing, considered this argument fraught with practical as well as theoretical difficulty.

Compare CA Rouen, 1 December 1977, *D.M.F.* 590: "*Mais attendu qu'en se prévalant des connaisse-ments pour retirer leur marchandise, ce qu'ils ont fait sans formuler aucune réserve, les réclamateurs en ont nécessairement accepté les clauses*" (But considering that by using the bill of lading to take delivery of their goods, which they have done without any reservation, the claimants have necessarily accepted the clauses of the bill of lading).

411 J. Loeff, *Vervoer ter zee*, Deel I, Zwolle, Tjeenk Willink, 1981, n° 65 at p. 44.

412 *Brandt v Liverpool, Brazil and River Plate Steam Navigation Co. Ltd* [1924] 1 K.B. 575 (Court of Appeal, 19 November 1923), at p. 589: "*By those authorities* [Stindt v Roberts, 5 D.&L. 460; Young v Moeller, 5 El.&Bl. 755; Allen v Coltart & Co., 11 QBD 782] *it has been clearly established that where the holder of a bill of lading presents it and offers to accept delivery, if that offer is accepted by the shipowner, the holder of the bill of lading comes under an obligation to pay the freight and to pay the demurrage (...)*" (per Bankes LJ).

See also W. Bennett, *The History and Present Position of the Bill of Lading as a Document of Title to Goods*, Cambridge, University Press, 1914, at p. 57.

130 Contractual theories

described in the bill of lading, did not transfer contractual rights against the carrier.[413] In principle, therefore, the consignee was not in a (contractual) relationship with, and did not have rights against the carrier.

There are, however, from very early on, a number of cases holding that a *new* contract can come into being between the consignee and the holder, upon the consignee's offer or promise to take delivery under the terms of the bill of lading, or at least certain terms (in particular payment of freight or demurrage), if that offer or promise is accepted by the carrier.[414] This was not seen as a case of novation; the existing contract between the shipper and the carrier was not dissolved and replaced by the contract between the carrier and the holder. The new contract between the carrier and the holder came in addition to the contract of carriage between the shipper and the carrier. The existence of such separate contract between the carrier and the consignee has never become an inference *of law*, but has always remained an inference *of fact*: a contract between the carrier and the consignee could only be inferred if the facts of the case supported such inference.[415] A further difficulty was the consideration, which under English law must be given for a contract to be legally binding. On the consignee's side, consideration could be found in the engagement to pay the freight and/or demurrage, or even simply in the engagement to accept the terms of the bill of lading.[416] On the carrier's side, consideration was seen in the carrier delivering the goods to the consignee (although the obligation to deliver already existed under the

---

413 *Brandt v Liverpool, Brazil and River Plate Steam Navigation Co. Ltd* [1924] 1 K.B. 575 (Court of Appeal, 19 November 1923), at p. 594: "*Before the Bills of Lading Act, 1855, was passed, by the custom of merchants the indorsement of the bill of lading passed the property in the goods contained therein, but it did not assign the contract contained therein, and therefore the person who by indorsement became the owner of the goods did not by the same indorsement acquire a right to sue the shipowner upon his contract, which was evidenced in the bill of lading*" (per Scrutton LJ).
414 *Cock v Taylor* 13 East 399, 104 ER 424 (King's Bench, 2 May 1811); *Chappel v Comfort*, 10 CB(NS) 802, 142 ER 669 (Court of Common Pleas, 29 May 1861), at pp. 808–809; *Allen v Coltart & Co.* 11 QBD 782 (Queen's Bench Division, 12 June 1883), at p. 785; *Brandt v Liverpool, Brazil and River Plate Steam Navigation Co. Ltd* [1924] 1 K.B. 575 (Court of Appeal, 19 November 1923), at p. 589.
  See also W. Bennett, *The History and Present Position of the Bill of Lading as a Document of Title to Goods*, Cambridge, University Press, 1914, at p. 57.
415 *Young v Moeller* 5 El. & Bl. 755, 119 ER 662 (Exchequer Chamber, 29 November 1855), at p. 760: "*No doubt, where a cargo is received under a bill of lading, that, though not necessarily raising a contract in law, is evidence from which a jury may infer a contract to pay freight*".
  Borealis AB v Stargas Ltd and others and Bergesen D.Y. A/S (The Berge Sisar) [2001] UKHL 17, [2001] 2 All ER 193 (House of Lords, 22 March 2001), point 20: "*The inferred contract is not a fiction. It is a contract which the court concludes has come into existence because that is the proper finding of fact to make on the evidence in the case. (. . .) if the facts do not justify it, the court will decline to find that there was a contract.*"
416 *Stindt v Roberts* 5 Dowl. & L. 460, 79 R.R. 869 (Queen's Bench, 1848).
  See also M. Bools, *The Bill of Lading. A Document of Title to Goods. An Anglo-American Comparison*, London, LLP, 1997, at pp. 109–110.

contract of carriage) or in the carrier parting with his lien on the goods.[417] Once an implied contract was found, there was little hesitation that it would be on the terms of the bill of lading.[418]

141 With the passing of the Bills of Lading Act 1855, the need for an implied contract between the carrier and the consignee largely disappeared, as the consignee, under certain conditions, now had a statutory position and right of action against the carrier.[419] For those consignees, however, that did not meet the Act's requirement of the property in the goods passing to them by reason of the consignment or endorsement, the problem continued. In *Brandt v Liverpool*,[420] the Court of Appeal confirmed the continuing validity of the implied contract cases in such circumstances.[421] A consignee, which does not come within the scope of the Bills of Lading Act 1855 or COGSA 1992, can still sue the carrier on the bill of lading if an implied contract can be inferred from the facts of the case. As before, the existence of such contract is a question of fact. The court will only infer a new contract between the carrier and the consignee if the dealings between those parties allow it to do so.[422] There is, however, no clear line in the case law as

---

417 *Young v Moeller* 5 El. & Bl. 755, 119 ER 662 (Exchequer Chamber, 29 November 1855), at p. 760; *Chappel v Comfort*, 10 CB(NS) 802, 142 ER 669 (Court of Common Pleas, 29 May 1861), at p. 809.
418 *Dobbin v Thornton* 6 Esp. 16, 170 ER 816 (Nisi Prius, 3 March 1806): "*The defendant has here taken to the goods and has received them; he is bound by all the conditions of the bill of lading and is liable to all the terms of it, one of which is the payment of demurrage to which he is clearly liable.*"; *Jesson v Solly* 4 Taunt. 52, 128 ER 247 (29 June 1811); *Stindt v Roberts* 5 Dowl. & L. 460, 79 R.R. 869 (Queen's Bench, 1848), at p. 473; *Wegener v Smith* 15 C.B. 285, 139 ER 432 (6 November 1854); *Young v Moeller* 5 El. & Bl. 755, 119 ER 662 (Exchequer Chamber, 29 November 1855), at p. 762.
See also *Glyn Mills Currie & Co. v The East and West India Dock Company* (1882) 7 App Cas 591 (House of Lords, 1 August 1882), at p. 596: "*Every one claiming as assignee under a bill of lading must be bound by its terms*" (per Lord Selborne L.C.).
See also *Cock v Taylor* 2 Camp. 587, 170 ER 1261 (Nisi Prius, 26 February 1811), per Lord Ellenborough ("*The defendants, by becoming assignees of the bill of lading and receiving the goods, adopt the contract. They were aware on what terms the goods were to be delivered, and by accepting them they accede to those terms.*"), although Lord Ellenborough seems to be thinking more along the lines of an accession to the contract than in terms of a new, implied contract.
Compare S. Baughen, "Case Comment. The Gudermes. What future for Brandt v Liverpool?", *J.B.L.* 1994, at p. 62.
419 See below, para 4.3.1.1.
420 *Brandt v Liverpool, Brazil and River Plate Steam Navigation Co. Ltd* [1924] 1 K.B. 575 (Court of Appeal, 19 November 1923).
421 J. Chua, "Carriage of Goods by Sea Act 1992 – bills of lading – intermediate holders of bill of lading – transfer of liabilities", *Stud. L. Rev.* 1999, at p. 52; S. Girvin, *Carriage of Goods by Sea*, Oxford University Press, 2011 (2nd Ed.), n° 9.11 at p. 119.
422 R. Aikens, R. Lord and M. Bools, *Bills of Lading*, London, Informa, 2006, n° 8.22 at p. 159; P. Bugden and S. Lamont-Black, *Goods in Transit and Freight Forwarding*, London, Sweet & Maxwell, 2010 (2nd Ed.), n° 8-07 at p. 141; J. Cooke et al., *Voyage Charters*, London, Informa, 2007 (3rd Ed.), n° 18.108–18.113 at pp. 491–493; M. Davies and A. Dickey, *Shipping Law*, Lawbook Co., 2004 (3rd Ed.), at p. 250; R. De Wit, *Multimodal*

132   Contractual theories

to which circumstances are sufficient to imply a contract and which are not, thus making the *Brandt v Liverpool* solution a rather unpredictable one.[423] Since *The Aramis*, it seems clear that simply taking delivery of the cargo is in itself not sufficient to imply a contract.[424] In *The Captain Gregos (No. 2)*, the Court of Appeal implied a contract between the carrier and the consignee since there had been active and extensive co-operation between them with regard to the discharge of the vessel.[425] In *The Gudermes*, however, the Court of Appeal held that substantial cooperation between the carrier and the consignee, which went beyond what was required of them under the existing contracts, nevertheless does not allow to imply a contract, if that cooperation was forced by the circumstances and merely an effort to find a solution to a problem.[426]

142 In this view, the relationship between the carrier and the consignee comes into being at the time and place the consignee's offer is accepted by the carrier.

143 The implied contract concept could, at least in theory, also be applied to intermediate holders and non-contracting shippers. As the implied contract is a new contract, between parties that before were not contracting partners, there is no limit to the number of implied contracts that may exist. As regards intermediate holders, they usually will not have sufficient dealings with the carrier (if at all) to imply a contract, but there could be exceptions, e.g. in case of a salvage or general average incident in the course of the voyage, which leads to interaction between the carrier and the then holder, which afterwards transfers the bill of lading to a subsequent holder.

144 It would be easier to imply a contract between the carrier and the non-contracting shipper, as these parties do necessarily interact.[427] In *Pyrene v Scindia*, Devlin J mentioned an implied contract as an alternative to his preferred approach

---

   Transport: Carrier Liability and Documentation, London, Lloyd's of London Press, 1995, n° 5.27 at p. 262.
   See also *Ilyssia Compania Naviera S.A. v Ahmed Abdul-Qawi Bamaodah (The Elli 2)* [1985] 1 Lloyd's Rep 107 (Court of Appeal, 22–24 October 1984).
423 G. Humphreys and A. Higgs, "Waybills: a case of common law laissez faire in European commerce", *J.B.L.* 1992, at p. 464.
424 In *Peter Cremer v General Carriers S.A.* [1974] 1 WLR 341, [1973] 2 Lloyd's Rep 366 (Queen's Bench Division, 5 July 1973), the Court accepted the existence of a Brandt v Liverpool contract between the shipowner and the buyer of the cargo, who held delivery orders and had paid the freight. In *New Zealand Shipping Co Ltd v AM Satterthwaite & Co Ltd (The Eurymedon)* [1975] A.C. 154, [1974] 1 Lloyd's Rep 534 (Privy Council (New Zealand), 25 February 1974), the Privy Council accepted the existence of a Brandt v Liverpool contract based on the consignee's acceptance of the bill of lading and his request for delivery of the goods thereunder. In *The Aramis*, [1989] 1 Lloyd's Rep 213 (Court of Appeal, 17 November 1988), however, the Court of Appeal held that merely presenting the bill of lading is not sufficient, as the Bills of Lading Act 1855 would not have been necessary if simply presenting the bill of lading automatically created an implied contract.
425 *Compania Portorafti Commerciale v Ultramar Panama Inc. (The Captain Gregos, No. 2)* [1990] 2 Lloyd's Rep 395 (Court of Appeal, 21–25 March 1990).
426 *Mitsui & Co Ltd v Novorossiysk Shipping Co (The Gudermes)* [1993] 1 Lloyd's Rep 311 (Court of Appeal, 16–27 November 1992).
427 S. Baughen, *Shipping Law*, London, Routledge-Cavendish, 2009 (4th Ed.), at pp. 27–30.

of an agency contract between the FOB buyer and seller.[428] As with a consignee, however, the facts of the case would need to be such as to support an inference of a new and separate contract between the carrier and the non-contracting shipper. Simply presenting the goods for shipment will not be sufficient, as simply taking delivery is not sufficient for the consignee either.[429] In *Cho Yang Shipping v Coral (UK)*, however, the shipper (Coral) had contracted with Nortrop, which in turn had contracted with Interport, and the latter again with Cho Yang Shipping (through its local agent EOS). The bill of lading was issued on Cho Yang's form and named Coral as the shipper. Although the Court expressly found that all parties involved had acted as principals rather than as agents, and that the contracts made (Coral – Nortrop, Nortrop – Interport, Interport – Cho Yang) were all contracts of carriage, it had no hesitation in seeing Coral as contracting party to the (Cho Yang) bill of lading contract,[430] even without any specific facts or circumstances.

145 German law implies not one, but two contracts between the non-contracting shipper and the carrier. Unless the right to a bill of lading has been excluded in the contract of carriage, the non-contracting shipper has a statutory right to obtain a bill of lading (§ 513.(1) HGB). If he exercises this right, he then enters into a '*Begebungsvertrag*' (literally: a contract to issue) with the carrier.[431] This (implied) contract is not a contract of carriage, but only concerns the issuing of the bill of lading. It is presumed to be made between the carrier, who issues the bill of lading, and the party to which the bill of lading is first handed over.[432] Once a bill of lading has been issued pursuant to the '*Begebungsvertrag*', the non-contracting shipper then becomes a party to the bill of lading contract.[433] The carrier's obligations under the bill of lading are, under German law, strictly separate from his obligations under the contract of carriage.[434] The

---

428 *Pyrene Co. LD. v Scindia Navigation Co. LD.* [1954] 2 WLR 1005, [1954] 2 QB 402 (Queen's Bench Division, 14 April 1954).
429 S. Baughen, "Case Comment. The Gudermes. What future for Brandt v Liverpool?", *J.B.L.* 1994, at p. 65.
430 *Cho Yang Shipping Co. Ltd v Coral (U.K.) Ltd* [1997] 2 Lloyd's Rep 641 (Court of Appeal, 14–15 April & 15 May 1997). The end result, of course, is that Coral had in fact entered into *two* contracts for the same cargo and the same carriage: one with Nortrop, and one with Cho Yang.
431 C. Stumm, *Der Ablader im Seehandelsrecht. Eine rechtsvergleichende Darstellung des deutschen und des amerikanischen Rechts*, Berlin, LIT Verlag, 2010, at pp. 45–46.
432 Which depending on the case may be the contracting shipper, the non-contracting shipper, a transport intermediary, etc.
433 C. Stumm, *Der Ablader im Seehandelsrecht. Eine rechtsvergleichende Darstellung des deutschen und des amerikanischen Rechts*, Berlin, LIT Verlag, 2010, at p. 67.
434 O. Hartenstein and F. Reuschle, *Handbuch des Fachanwalts: Transport- und Speditionsrecht*, Cologne, Luchterhand, 2010, n° 74 at p. 178; R. Herber, *Seehandelsrecht. Systematische Darstellung*, Berlin, De Gruyter, 2016 (2nd Ed.), at p. 247 and p. 307; G. Schaps and H. Abraham, *Das Seerecht in der Bundesrepublik Deutschland, Seehandelsrecht*, Berlin, Walter de Gruyter, 1978 (4th Ed.), Vol. 2, N° 2 at p. 814; C. Stumm, *Der Ablader im Seehandelsrecht: Eine rechtsvergleichende Darstellung des deutschen und des amerikanischen Rechts*, Berlin, LIT Verlag, 2010, at p. 45, 68 and 74.

134   Contractual theories

fact that the non-contracting shipper enters into a 'Begebungsvertrag' and a bill of lading relationship with the carrier, however, does not necessarily mean that he thereby undertakes obligations towards the carrier, particularly with regard to the payment of freight. The German courts have repeatedly held that the non-contracting shipper's request to be named as 'Shipper' on the bill of lading is not indicative of an intention to become bound towards the carrier.[435] Neither is the fact that the non-contracting shipper has negotiated the bill of lading or used it to obtain payment under a documentary credit.[436]

3.2.3.3 A sui generis *contractual relationship*

146 Some authors start from the assumption that the holder's position must be contractual in nature, because they see that as the *communis opinio*,[437] or because they interpret Article 1.b of the Hague-Visby Rules and similar statutory provisions as imposing a contractual nature.[438] If, however, the relationship between the carrier and the holder must by definition be contractual, and if neither the third-party beneficiary construction nor the multiparty contract or contract accession construction are accepted as (fully) satisfactory, there are not many other options left than to see the relation between the carrier and the holder as a *sui generis* relation, a particularity of maritime law.[439] The particularity primarily lies in the fact that a bill of lading issued pursuant to a charter party initially is a mere receipt, but later transforms into a contract of carriage when it is negotiated to a third-party holder.[440]

3.2.3.4 *Appraisal*

147 There is a certain obvious appeal to seeing the bill of lading as an offer to contract. The bill of lading describes a service, the terms under which the service will be performed, and can easily be passed around among those potentially

---

435   OLG Düsseldorf 26 October 1995, Case 18 U 46/95, *NJW-RR* 1996, 1380, *TranspR* 1996, 165; OLG München 3 November 1988, Case 24 U 814/87, NJW-RR 1989, 803, VersR 1990, 998, RIW 1989, 650; OLG Rostock 27 November 1996, Case 6 U 113/96, *TranspR* 1997, 113: LG Bremen 10 October 2007, Case 11 O 381/05, *BeckRS* 2010, 25028.
See also above, n° 120 p. 118.
436   OLG Rostock 27 November 1996, Case 6 U 113/96, *TranspR* 1997, 113.
437   P. Seck, *Reisbevrachting en cognossementsvervoer*, Zutphen, Uitgeverij Paris, 2011, at p. 206: "*Er is wel een* communis opinio *omtrent de contractuele aard van de rechtsverhouding tussen de vervoerder onder cognossement en de derde-cognossementhouder.*" (There is however a common opinion concerning the contractual nature of the legal relation between the carrier under a bill of lading and the third-party holder of the bill of lading).
438   P. Seck, *Reisbevrachting en cognossementsvervoer*, Zutphen, Uitgeverij Paris, 2011, at p. 213.
439   P. Seck, *Reisbevrachting en cognossementsvervoer*, Zutphen, Uitgeverij Paris, 2011, at p. 206; G.J. van der Ziel, *Het cognossement, naar een functionele benadering*, Deventer, Kluwer, 1999, at p. 7.
440   P. Seck, *Reisbevrachting en cognossementsvervoer*, Zutphen, Uitgeverij Paris, 2011, at p. 207.

interested. Ultimately, someone will come forward to claim the results of the service.

If, however, the bill of lading were really an offer to contract, there would be fundamental consequences. For starters, the obligations of the carrier under the contract of carriage with the shipper would change. Under a contract of carriage, the carrier's obligation is not only to carry the goods, but also to *deliver* them to whomever will turn out to be entitled to delivery. Delivery is an essential obligation of the carrier; he is never entitled to keep the goods himself. If, however, the bill of lading is an offer to contract, the carrier's obligation changes: he is no longer bound to deliver the goods, he is only bound to offer a contract. Of course, that obligation can be construed to mean an irrevocable offer, the terms of which cannot be changed by the carrier once the offer (the bill of lading) has been negotiated to a third party. It is nevertheless only an offer to contract, and there may be circumstances that the holder of the bill of lading is unable or not allowed by law to accept that offer. In that case, the holder cannot claim delivery of the goods, since he has not accepted the carrier's offer, but the carrier has complied with his obligations under the contract of carriage with the shipper, who therefore cannot (re)claim the goods either. Admittedly, that problem could be solved through appropriate clauses or provisions in the contract of carriage, but such clauses or provisions are generally absent from today's contracts of carriage.

Furthermore, if the holder of the bill of lading does accept the carrier's offer, what kind of contract would they have entered into? In this view, the holder of the bill of lading does not accede to a pre-existing contract; a *new* contract springs up between the carrier and the holder upon the latter's acceptance of the carrier's offer. That new contract is made at the time and place of the acceptance, i.e. generally in the port of destination when the goods have been discharged from the ship and are ready for delivery. That means, for instance, that the law of the port of destination may govern the question whether the contract between the carrier and the holder was validly made.[441] If the contract is validly made, what is its nature? It can hardly be said to be a contract of carriage, as the carriage has already been performed and the goods are already at destination when the contract is made. Not being a contract of carriage, it would not be subject to the mandatory carriage laws or conventions either. This clearly would be an unexpected (and undesirable) result, and shows that the bill of lading cannot be an offer by the carrier to enter into a new contract.

---

441 The majority of bills of lading contain a choice of law provision. In the EU, Article 10.1 of Regulation 593/2008 ("Rome I") provides that the existence and validity of the contract shall be determined by the law which would govern if the choice of law provision was valid, which will often take the matter away from the law of destination. Article 10.2, however, provides that a party may rely upon the law of the country of his habitual residence if it appears from the circumstances that applying the standard rule (Article 10.1) would not be reasonable. This could bring the matter back to the port of destination, if the holder is established in that country.

148 The implied contract approach suffers from the same problem. Here also, a new contract is entered into at the port of destination, after the carriage has been completed. In addition, an implied contract is a legal fiction. Parties that never really contracted with each other are nevertheless assumed to be contractually obliged towards each other. Legal fictions are not *per se* bad, though, and can indeed serve useful purposes. In the *Brandt v Liverpool* context, the fiction of an implied contract has been used to grant certain holders of a bill of lading an easier right of action against the carrier than they would otherwise have had, a right of action also that is in line with that of other holders. That purpose is certainly acceptable. The question is, however, whether implying a *contract* is the only or the best solution to achieve that purpose. A contract, indeed, is an engagement that is freely and consciously undertaken. Furthermore, it has never been easy to exactly draw the boundaries of the *Brandt v Liverpool* contract, thus making this a rather unpredictable solution.[442]

149 The *sui generis* answer is never very popular in law. It is easily seen as a capitulation before a difficult problem, a failure to look hard enough for the real answer.[443] In addition, it introduces new elements into the system, thus making it more complex. Such criticism, however, is not necessarily fair. It presupposes indeed that the law is an exhaustive, coherent system that contains the answers to every possible question, which often is not true. Commercial law, which changes and adapts to keep up with the underlying economic realities, can hardly be seen as a closed system. Furthermore, the phenomena to be explained are maritime law phenomena, while the concepts used to try to explain them are civil law concepts. That is not to say, of course, that maritime law is an entirely independent area of law, completely disconnected from the civil law, but it is a fact that the bill of lading was not devised by scholars or legislators using civil law constructs, but created by merchants and seamen through their usages and practices. In such context, an obstinate desire to force new developments and mechanisms into the familiar concepts of old can be a hindrance rather than a benefit.

150 That being said, simply classifying a relationship as *sui generis* is of course not very helpful, as such classification (by definition) has no predictive force: it does not provide any answers to questions yet unsolved. When a relationship is seen as *sui generis*, an effort should be made to ascertain and describe the characteristics of that relationship.

3.3 Contractual theories: conclusions

151 A contract of carriage, in essence and in origin, is a contract between two parties, the shipper and the carrier. In theory, it could be kept a pure two-party contract, with only the shipper entitled to claim against the carrier in case of loss

---

442 J. Bassindale, "Title to sue under bills of lading: the Carriage of Goods by Sea Act 1992", *Journal of International Banking Law* 1992, at p. 415.
443 M. Spanjaart, *Vorderingsrechten uit cognossement*, Zutphen, Uitgeverij Paris, 2012, at p. 102 and fn. 324.

of or damage to the cargo. It is obvious, however, that in practice this approach would have serious disadvantages. In many cases, the loss will not have been suffered by the shipper, which would require legal constructions to 'transfer' the loss to the shipper so as to provide him with title to sue. The competent court as between the shipper and the carrier might be geographically remote from the place where the loss or damage was ascertained, making the gathering of evidence more difficult, etc. The alternative would be for the consignee to sue the carrier on another basis than the bill of lading or the contract of carriage. Tort is the most obvious alternative basis, but then the burden of proof on the consignee is quite different than under carriage law, and also the liability of the carrier, if the claim is successful, is different than under carriage law.[444] It is clearly desirable and efficient, therefore, for the holder of the bill of lading to have a proper and direct right (of action) against the carrier with regard to the carried goods.[445]

From this position, however, a surprising number of authors immediately jump to the statement that such proper and direct right of the holder must necessarily be a *contractual* right.[446] Apparently, this is self-evident and does not require

---

[444] Compare S. Baughen, "Case Comment. The Gudermes. What future for Brandt v Liverpool?", *J.B.L.* 1994, at p. 62.

See also M. Davies and A. Dickey, *Shipping Law*, Lawbook Co., 2004 (3th Ed.), at p. 250, who writing on *Brandt v Liverpool* contracts say that such contracts will be implied *"if it is necessary to do so in order to give business reality to a transaction and to create enforceable obligations between parties who are dealing with one another in circumstances in which one would expect that business reality, and those enforceable obligations, to exist"*. If one is (very sensibly) prepared to take into account business reality and business necessities, however, why take the long way around of implying a contract rather than simply accepting that business reality requires the holder of a bill of lading to have standing to sue under the bill of lading?

[445] P. Todd, *Modern Bills of Lading*, Oxford, Blackwell Scientific Publications, 1990 (2nd Ed.), at p. 166. Compare A. Mesritz, *De Vrachtbrief*, Amsterdam, J.H. de Bussy, 1904, at p. 70.

Similar evolutions have also occurred in other areas of transport law. Mesritz for instance describes how in France, where in the 19th century contracts for the carriage of goods by land were often made through a forwarder, a custom developed that allowed the shipper to directly act against the carrier, even though he had no direct contractual relationship with the carrier (at pp. 42–43.)

[446] L. Li, "Binding Effect of Arbitration Clauses on Holders of Bills of Lading as Nonoriginal Parties and a Potential Uniform Approach Through Comparative Analysis", 37 *Tul. Mar. LJ* 2012–2013, at p. 122. The author simply states that the holder has a contractual status and is a party to the bill of lading, without any supportive analysis.

M. Tilche, A. Chao and P. Berthod, "Contrat de transport. Adhésion du destinataire?", 471 *BT* N° 2484, 20 July 1992, at p. 472: *"Sans être totalement assimilable à un titre cambiaire, le connaissement confère à son détenteur (qui est le plus souvent le destinataire) un droit propre et direct à l'encontre des transporteurs. Ce droit ne peut être que contractuel."* (Without being completely identical to a bill of exchange, the bill of lading grants its holder (most often the consignee) his own and direct right against the carriers. That right can only be contractual.) The authors even consider a non-contractual approach a 'catastrophic scenario' (*"qu'on songe au scénario catastrophique si le destinataire se retrouvait un jour hors contrat!"*).

See also *Higgins v Anglo-Algerian S.S. Co.* 248 F. 386 (2nd Circuit Court of Appeals, 13 February 1918).

any explaining or reasoning. It is true, of course, that at the origin of a carriage of goods lies a contract of carriage, but that contractual starting point does not mean that all subsequent rights must invariably be contractual in nature, certainly not when those subsequent rights belong to parties which were not a party to the initial contract.

152 The (relatively few) authors that do bother to explain their position that the rights of the bill of lading holder against the carrier must be contractual, have advanced a number of arguments.

153 It is uniformly accepted that a bill of lading has different functions: it is not only a receipt for the goods and a title to claim delivery, but also at least evidence of, and often the actual contract of carriage between the shipper and the carrier.[447] This has led some authors to argue that this contractual function of the bill of lading must extend to the third-party holder: since the bill of lading is (evidence of) a contract, it must be a contract vis-à-vis the holder.[448] This, however, is a *non sequitur*. The bill of lading is indeed evidence of, or the actual contract in one relation (between the shipper and the carrier), but that does not mean that the bill of lading must also be a contract or have a contractual function in another relation (between the carrier and the third-party holder). If a service contract requires the service provider to carry liability insurance and to provide the policy as proof thereof, that policy clearly is a contract between the service provider and its insurer, and has a function in the relation between the customer and the service provider, but it does not thereby become a contract between those latter parties.

154 It has also been argued that a bill of lading is, by law, a *contract* of carriage and thus must create a contractual relationship between the parties involved with the bill of lading, i.e. the carrier and the holder of the bill of lading.[449] Article 1.b of the Hague-Visby Rules indeed provides that the term 'contract of carriage' refers to *'contracts of carriage covered by a bill of lading or any similar document of title'*. The Hague-Visby Rules, however, primarily deal with the obligations of the carrier under a specific type of contract of carriage, i.e. contracts of carriage covered by a bill of lading or similar document (as opposed to charter parties and contracts of carriage for which no bill of lading is issued). There are only a few provisions on the obligations of the shipper, and the holder of the bill of lading

---

447 See above, para 2.2.
 Article 1.a of the Hague-Visby Rules defines that carrier as the owner or charterer who enters into a *contract of carriage* with a shipper. The relation between the carrier and the shipper thus is undeniably contractual in nature.
448 M. Spanjaart, *Vorderingsrechten uit cognossement*, Zutphen, Uitgeverij Paris, 2012, at p. 243.
449 P. Seck, *Reisbevrachting en cognossementsvervoer*, Zutphen, Uitgeverij Paris, 2011, at p. 163; J.-P. Tosi, "L'adhésion du destinataire au contrat de transport", in X., *Mélanges Christian Mouly*, Paris, Litec, 1998, at p. 187.
 The same approach is found in *Excel Shipping Corp. v Seatrain International S.A.* 584 F.Supp. 734 (E.D. New York, 13 April 1984), at p. 746: "*According to* [46 USC] *§ 1301(b), a bill of lading is a contract of carriage.*"

is hardly mentioned at all. It is a rather farfetched argument, therefore, to claim that the Hague-Visby Rules purposefully intended to provide that the relation between the carrier and the holder of the bill of lading would be of a contractual nature, or that the duties imposed on the carrier only apply within the boundaries of his contract with the shipper. There is, in any case, nothing in the *Travaux Préparatoires* of the Hague-Visby Rules to support such intention.

The Hamburg Rules in Article 1.6 and the Rotterdam Rules in Article 1.1 define a 'contract of carriage' more generally as any contract whereby the carrier undertakes against payment of freight to carry goods from one place to another. The bill of lading is defined in Article 1.7 Hamburg Rules as a document which evidences a contract of carriage by sea and the taking over or loading of the goods by the carrier, and by which the carrier undertakes to deliver the goods against surrender of the document. The Rotterdam Rules no longer talk about bills of lading, but use the term 'transport document' instead, which is defined in Article 1.14 as a document issued by a carrier that (a) evidences the carrier's or a performing party's receipt of goods under a contract of carriage; and (b) evidences or contains a contract of carriage.

Again, though, these definitions only confirm that a carriage of goods by sea ordinarily starts out with a contract of carriage between the shipper and the carrier, and that the relation between the shipper and the carrier is contractual in nature. These points are beyond discussion. These definitions do not explicitly or implicitly say, however, that also the relation between the carrier and a third-party holder of the bill of lading is, or should be, of a contractual nature.

155 In a similar vein, Dutch authors[450] have argued that the relationship between the carrier and holder must be contractual, because Article 8:441 of the Dutch Civil Code provides that the carrier is bound '*in accordance with the obligations that rest on the carrier*'.[451] It is true, of course, that the holder's rights are not strictly limited to only claiming delivery and that the holder may on occasion be obliged against the carrier, but again, that does not prove that the relationship between the carrier and the holder must necessarily be contractual. The carrier's obligations that Article 8:441 refers to may as well be *statutory* obligations. The fact that the legislator has deemed it necessary to expressly provide that the carrier's obligations also bind him as against the holder of the bill of lading is rather a counterargument to a contractual position. If indeed the relationship between the carrier and the holder were contractual, there would be no need for a confirmation that the carrier is bound by the obligations he has assumed.

---

450 H. Boonk, "Cognossement en cognossementhouder", *NTBR* 2007-9, at p. 373.

451 Article 8:441, par. 1 of the Dutch Civil Code provides: "*Indien een cognossement is afgegeven, heeft uitsluitend de regelmatige houder daarvan, tenzij hij niet op regelmatige wijze houder is geworden, jegens de vervoerder onder het cognossement het recht aflevering van de zaken* overeenkomstig de op de vervoerder rustende verplichtingen *te vorderen.*" (When a bill of lading has been issued, only the proper holder thereof, unless he did not become holder in a lawful way, has the right to claim delivery of the goods from the carrier under the bill of lading *in accordance with the obligations that rest on the carrier.*)

156 It has further been argued that the relationship between the carrier and the holder must be contractual, because the carrier's essential obligation – to deliver the goods at destination – is an obligation that the carrier has contractually undertaken vis-à-vis the shipper.[452] Also the carrier's obligations to properly and carefully load, stow and carry the goods are obligations deriving from his contract with the shipper.[453] Since these obligations are *contractual* obligations, the holder of the bill of lading must acquire, or be put in, a contractual position to enforce them.[454]

Is the claim for delivery (and the claim to have the goods properly cared for during the voyage) really a contractual claim, though? It certainly is if there is only the contract of carriage, without a bill of lading being issued. Once there is a bill of lading, however, the situation changes. The carrier's obligation to deliver the goods *vis-à-vis the B/L holder* is based on the B/L itself, not on the contract of carriage, and the obligation to the holder under the bill of lading is not identical to the carrier's obligation to the shipper under the contract of carriage. The consignee, if he does not hold at least one original of the bill of lading, cannot *oblige* the carrier to deliver the goods to him, even if he can clearly prove that he is the intended holder of the bill of lading and/or that this document should in due course come into his hands.[455] The shipper on the other hand *can* force the carrier

---

[452] See, for example, *Sze Hai Tong Bank v Rambler Cycle Co* [1959] A.C. 576, [1959] (Privy Council (Singapore), 22 June 1959) at p. 586: "*The contract is to deliver, on production of the bill of lading, to the person entitled under the bill of lading.*" (per Lord Denning). See also *Kuwait Petroleum Corp v I&D Oil Carriers Ltd (The Houda)* [1994] CLC 1037, (Court of Appeal, 21 July 1994) at p. 1051: "*Under a bill of lading contract a shipowner is obliged to deliver goods upon production of the original bill of lading. Delivery without production of the bill of lading constitutes a breach of contract . . .*" (per Leggatt LJ).

English law, however, sees the relation between the carrier and the holder as unquestionably contractual, as COGSA makes it so, and it is not always clear, when courts or authors say that 'the contract' obliges the carrier to deliver against the bill of lading, whether they are referring to the initial contract of carriage between the shipper and the carrier, or to the bill of lading contract between the carrier and the holder.

See also Ph. Delebecque, *Droit maritime*, Paris, Dalloz, 2014 (13th Ed.), n° 731 at p. 512: "*le contrat de transport fait naître une créance contre le transporteur, et il s'agit de savoir qui est créancier de l'obligation de livraison dont le transporteur est le débiteur*". (The contract of carriage brings into being a claim against the carrier, and the question is to know who is the creditor of the claim for delivery of which the carrier is the debtor.)

[453] M. Spanjaart, *Vorderingsrechten uit cognossement*, Zutphen, Uitgeverij Paris, 2012, at p. 248.

[454] C. Cashmore, *Parties to a Contract of Carriage, or Who Can Sue on a Contract of Carriage of Goods?* London, Lloyd's of London Press, 1990, at p. 108.

Compare *Higgins v Anglo-Algerian S.S. Co. Limited* 248 F. 386 (Court of Appeals 2nd Circ., 13 February 1918) at p. 387: "*The libelants, as holders of the bill of lading, are in contractual relation with the carrier and entitled to enforce the contract.*"

[455] In practice, the carrier may accept to deliver the goods to such consignee in exchange for an LOI, but that requires the carrier's consent. The latter cannot be forced to such course of action. See *Carlberg v Wemyss Coal Co. Ltd* 1915 S.C. 616 (Court of Session, Inner House, First Division, 11 March 1915), at p. 624. Compare *Motis Exports Ltd v Dampskibsselskabet AF 1912, Aktieselskab & Anor* [1999] CLC 914 (QBD (Commercial Court), 1 March 1999), at p. 920: "*There is, it seems to me, no support there, at any rate without the intervention of the court, for the concept that a shipowner can be obliged to deliver not against a bill of lading but against a reasonable explanation of its loss.*"

to comply with his delivery obligation under the contract of carriage. If the goods remain unclaimed at the port of destination, the carrier cannot, as against the shipper, refuse to deliver the goods and keep them to himself. Even though the shipper does not hold the bill of lading, he should, as a party to the contract of carriage, still be able to enforce the delivery obligation under the contract of carriage.[456]

Another illustration of the fact that the carrier's obligations under the contract of carriage are not the same as his obligations under the bill of lading is the situation where the bill of lading is stolen. Suppose indeed that a contract of carriage is made between shipper A and carrier B. A bill of lading is issued to order of C. The bill of lading, however, is stolen from C and sold by the thief to D, who is unaware of the theft and acquires the bill of lading in good faith. If also the carrier is unaware of the theft and the bill of lading is presented by D, the goods will be delivered to D. What happens, however, if the carrier is informed of the theft by shipper A and intended consignee C, which both confirm and instruct the carrier that the goods should be delivered to C? If the claim for delivery is indeed a contractual claim under the contract of carriage, A and C's claim to deliver to them should trump D's claim. It is submitted, however, that in many legal systems, priority would actually be given to D's claim as holder of the bill of lading.

Similarly, in *Padus*,[457] an inland shipping case, the shipper had not requested the carrier to issue a bill of lading. Afterwards, however, at the request of the shipper's bank, a bill of lading was nevertheless issued. During the voyage, the shipper instructed the carrier to change the place of delivery and authorized him to deliver without presentation of the bill of lading. The carrier was then sued by the holder of the bill of lading. The Dutch Supreme Court held that, once a bill of lading is issued (even though the parties had not intended to do so), the rules and principles regarding bills of lading apply and the instructions of the shipper cannot override the rights of the holder of the bill of lading.

It is quite clear, therefore, that once a bill of lading has been issued and negotiated to a third party, the carrier has obligations under the bill of lading to the holder of that document, which may not entirely coincide with his obligations under the contract of carriage to the shipper. It may be impossible for the carrier to simultaneously comply with both sets of obligations, which may result in liability towards the shipper or the holder, but that risk in itself is not exceptional. The books are full of cases where a party (inadvertently or knowingly) allowed a gap to exist between related contracts and had to bear the consequences. The fact that the coexistence of two separate sets of obligations may result in liability is not an argument to say that there could not be two different sets of obligations.

157 It has also been said that the relationship must be contractual, because the holder of a bill of lading has rights against the carrier (the right to give instructions, the right to compel the carrier to perform the carriage, the right to claim

---

456 In such case, the shipper might need to hold the carrier harmless against the possibility that, at a later stage, there is a claim under the bill of lading after all.
457 HR 23 June 1989, S&S 1989, 120 (*ms Padus*).

delivery, etc.), and such rights apparently can only be contractual.[458] It is quite obviously true that the holder of a bill of lading has rights against the carrier – the document would not be of much use if that weren't the case –, but it does not follow that these rights must necessarily be contractual. The law itself may recognize rights of action, even in the absence of any contractual relationship. Maritime law actually has several examples of such rights: the right to claim contribution in general average, the right to claim a salvage award, etc. In those cases, parties have rights and obligations towards each other, because the opinion developed and became generally accepted that they should have such rights. In the same vein, it is perfectly possible for the law to accept that the holder of a bill of lading should have rights against the issuer of that document, without the need for a contract to exist between them. In addition, or alternatively, modern legal theory has come to accept the concept of a voluntary obligation, i.e. a legally binding obligation, unilaterally created by one party. From that angle, the bill of lading can be seen as a binding obligation, created by the carrier, which can be called upon by anyone who satisfies the conditions, i.e. by anyone who is the proper and lawful holder of the bill of lading. Again, there is no need for a contract between the carrier and the holder to allow the latter to have enforceable rights against the carrier.

158 Another argument is that the carrier has indeed undertaken to carry and deliver the goods, but only subject to certain conditions, *viz.* the terms of his bill of lading. It would be unfair to the carrier if he was held up to his promise to carry and deliver the goods, but without being able to invoke the limits that he had set to his promise.[459] The point was clearly made by Atkin LJ in *Brandt v Liverpool*:[460]

---

[458] In *The President of India v Metcalfe Shipping Co Ltd (The Dunelmia)* [1969] 3 WLR 1120, [1970] 1 QB 289 (Court of Appeal, 8 October 1969), the arbitrator in point 18 of his intial decision had held: "*once A.N.I.C. had in their possession a bill of lading signed by the master and calling upon the ship to deliver the cargo to their order at Madras, they were in a position to compel the ship to do so, and that power of compulsion can only be founded on a contract between themselves (as principals) and the owners.*"

See also H.-J. Puttfarken, *Seehandelsrecht*, Heidelberg, Verlag Recht und Wirtschaft, 1997, n° 107 at p. 39. The author argues that, in the old days, the consignee had to be able to take action against the carrier on his own, as the limitations of the communication systems of those days simply did not allow to involve the shipper, who had made the contract of carriage. The author then continues that in order to take action against the carrier, the consignee must be a party to the contract of carriage. ("*Dies muss der Empfänger allein bewältigen; anderes lassen die Entfernung und die Verbindungen der Segelschiffszeit nicht zu. Dafür muss er Partei des Vertrages sein, der Vertrag insgesamt auf ihn übergehen.*")

[459] M. Tilche, A. Chao and P. Berthod, "Contrat de transport. Adhésion du destinataire?", *BT* N° 2484, 20 July 1992, at p. 472: "*Si les dispositions contractuelles passées entre expéditeur et transporteur (ou commissionaire) deviennent inopposable au destinataire, c'est tout l'équilibre économique du contrat de transport qui se trouve rompu*" (If the contractual provisions agreed between the shipper and the carrier (or forwarder) are no longer binding on the consignee, the entire economic balance of the contract of carriage is disturbed.)

See also C. Cashmore, *Parties to a Contract of Carriage, or Who Can Sue on a Contract of Carriage of Goods?* London, Lloyd's of London Press, 1990, at p. 108; P. Todd, *Modern Bills of Lading*, Oxford, Blackwell Scientific Publications, 1990 (2nd Ed.), at p. 166.

[460] *Brandt v Liverpool, Brazil and River Plate Steam Navigation Co. Ltd* [1924] 1 K.B. 575 (Court of Appeal, 19 November 1923), at p. 599.

> *Shipowners would be surprised to hear it suggested that having undertaken to carry goods upon terms in their bill of lading qualifying and limiting their liability they are nevertheless under an absolute obligation to deliver the goods and not an obligation qualified by the exceptions in the bill of lading.*

In the early days of the bill of lading, before the carriage laws and conventions, this was indeed a valid point. In the absence of a statutory framework of rights, obligations and defences, the carrier only had the terms of its bill of lading to define and qualify its rights and obligations.[461] Since then, however, national laws and international conventions have come into being that create a (mandatory) framework of obligations and defences. In addition to such substantive provisions, several legal systems have enacted rules directly dealing with the position of the holder of the bill of lading. As a result, the carrier's position could today be based entirely on the law, without regard to the terms and conditions of the bill of lading. That, of course, does not mean that the bill of lading would become superfluous. Even in an entirely statutory approach, the carrier still has choices and options within that legal position. If the freight is payable at destination, for example, the *amount* of the freight will have to be communicated to the holders of the bill of lading. If the cargo is in carrier provided containers, the carrier will have to communicate how many 'free days' the holder gets before container demurrage is charged. Since, even in an entirely statutory approach, the bill of lading will still function as a document of title, it is also the most obvious choice to communicate such information to the holder.

159 A very similar argument is that the liability of the carrier towards the holder of the bill of lading depends on the terms of the contract of carriage and the law that governs that contract. If the contract or the governing law exonerates the carrier for loss of or damage to the goods, he cannot be held liable by the holder of the bill of lading. Therefore, the holder's position could not be disconnected from the contract of carriage.[462] That position, however, is not correct. It is true, of course, that in certain circumstances, the carrier is not liable for loss or damage. That is not, however, because the contract of carriage or the law governing that contract provides so, but because the (mandatory) law that governs the position *of the holder* (in many countries the Hague or Hague-Visby Rules) provides such defences to the carrier. Suppose, for instance, that the contract of carriage or the national law that governs this contract contains an exemption that is not in the Hague-Visby list of exemptions. It is clear that, in a Hague-Visby

---

461 Compare *Glyn Mills Currie & Co. v The East and West India Dock Company* (1882) 7 App Cas 591 (House of Lords, 1 August 1882), at p. 614: "*The nature and extent of the obligation, undertaken by the shipowner, to deliver the goods at the end of the voyage, must depend upon the terms of the bills of lading, which contain his contract with the shipper: and every assignee of a bill of lading has notice of, and must be bound by, those stipulations, which have been introduced into the contract,* for his own protection, *by the shipowner.*" (per Lord Watson).
462 M. Spanjaart, *Vorderingsrechten uit cognossement*, Zutphen, Uitgeverij Paris, 2012, at p. 103.

country, the carrier will not be able to invoke that additional exemption against the holder of the bill of lading. Conversely, the holder will be able to exercise such rights as the Hague-Visby Rules grant him (e.g. the right to demand that the carrier give all reasonable facilities for inspecting and tallying the goods[463]), even if such rights are not stated or confirmed in the contract of carriage or the governing national law. This again shows that the position of the holder of a bill of lading, certainly in the present day and age, is a statutory position much more than a contractual position.

160 It has been argued that the consignee is obviously a party to the contract of carriage, because this contract is made precisely because there is a consignee.[464] That position is untenable, however, in a double way. First, a contract of carriage can perfectly be a two-party affair, with the shipper also collecting the goods at another location. Second, even if in many contracts of carriage there is a third-party consignee, that in itself does not imply that the consignee must necessarily be a party to the contract of carriage. Businesses carry liability insurance because they may cause damage to third parties, but that does not mean that an injured party becomes a party to the insurance contract between the business and the insurer.

161 A similar argument is that the holder must become a party to the contract of carriage, because that contract protects him against carriage losses in those case where, *under the contract of sale*, he as the buyer bears the risk rather than the seller/shipper.[465] In the international sale of goods, the transport risk is indeed regularly borne by the buyer, who often will be the consignee or ultimate holder of the bill of lading. If the latter did not have rights against the carrier, he would be left without recourse if the goods are damaged or lost during the carriage. The argument does not explain, however, why the holder's rights against the carrier must be contractual. It is generally accepted that the holder of a bill of lading should indeed have rights against the carrier, but there is no reason why those rights should necessarily be contractual in nature. The position of the buyer, who bears the transport risk under the sales contract, is equally well protected, or maybe even better protected, if he is given a statutory right of action against the carrier, defined and modeled primarily by the substantive carriage conventions and laws and subsidiarily by the terms and conditions of the bill of lading itself.

162 Another possible argument is that, when the freight is payable at destination, the position of the holder must be contractual because not only is the obligation to pay freight a contractual obligation, but also the amount of the freight due is determined by the contract of carriage. The argument is not convincing,

---

463 Article 3.6 Hague-Visby Rules.
464 M. Remond-Gouilloud, *Le contrat de transport*, Paris, Dalloz, 1993, at p. 31: "*Qu'il soit partie au contrat ne devrait pas faire de doute: son existence est la raison d'être du contrat de transport.*" (That he is a party to the contract should not be in doubt: his existence is the reason that the contract of carriage exists).
465 R. Thomas, "A comparative analysis of the transfer of contractual rights under the English Carriage of Goods by Sea Act 1992 and the Rotterdam Rules", *J.I.M.L.* 2011, at p. 438.

though. For the holder of the bill of lading, the obligation to pay freight results from the bill of lading, not from the underlying contract of carriage. Suppose, indeed, that shipper and carrier agree that the freight is to be collected at destination, but because of a clerical error, a clause to that effect is not inserted in the bill of lading. In most legal systems, it will not be possible to nevertheless force the holder to pay the freight.[466] On the other hand, unless there is a cesser clause, the shipper remains liable under the contract of carriage. The holder's obligation to pay freight is a different obligation than the shipper's obligation, therefore. Clearly, if the holder is liable to pay the freight, the amount of the freight has to be determined and communicated to the holder. That amount may come from different sources – the contract of carriage, through a referral in the bill of lading, a general tariff, even the *usual* freight if there is no explicit freight provision[467] – but even if the amount of the freight has been determined in the contract of carriage, that fact in itself does not mean that the holder must have become a party to the contract of carriage.

163 It has also been said that the issuing, negotiating and presenting of the bill of lading are all 'juridical acts' (*rechtshandelingen*), i.e. actions that are meant by the actor to create legal effects. Since in this view the holder of the bill of lading by presenting it to the carrier intends that action to have legal consequences, that must mean that he intends to enter into a contract with the carrier.[468] That intention, however, is purely presumed. It is, in essence, the same legal fiction that has the holder accede to or enter into a contract of carriage with the carrier. As pointed out above, a legal fiction is not *per se* bad. It is a technique to arrive at a certain result (here, a contractual relationship between the carrier and the holder). The defence of a legal fiction, however, requires first and foremost an analysis of why the desired result is necessary. Unless it is first shown why the relationship between the carrier and the holder must be contractual, presumed intentions to enter into a (presumed) contract are not very convincing.

164 There is also a systemic argument in favour of the contractual approach. Trade, commerce, society itself is constantly evolving, which obliges the law to also evolve. If every time a new phenomenon has to be given legal status, new concepts are introduced, the legal system ultimately becomes very complex. In that sense, there is an advantage to fitting new phenomena within the existing concepts of a legal system. There is, however, a limit to the validity of this argument. From a certain point, the disadvantages of forcing a new evolution into existing concepts that do not exactly fit the situation outweigh the advantages of limiting the system to the known and trusted concepts of old.

165 Finally, some authors purposefully want to arrive at the conclusion that the relationship between the carrier and the holder is contractual, because that

---

466 Unless it can be proven that the holder was not in good faith, in that he knew that the bill of lading should have been freight collect.
467 R. Herber, *Seehandelsrecht. Systematische Darstellung*, Berlin, De Gruyter, 2016 (2nd Ed.), at p. 255.
468 P. Seck, *Reisbevrachting en cognossementsvervoer*, Zutphen, Uitgeverij Paris, 2011, at p. 206.

then will allow them to defend a desired result, for instance that the holder is bound by the jurisdiction clause in the bill of lading,[469] or that title to sue is not exclusive to the holder of the bill of lading,[470] etc. It goes without saying that this is not an objective analysis.

166 In light of the foregoing, it is important to take a step back and to consider how the holder of the bill of lading enters into relation with the carrier. The holder of the bill of lading, bar the odd exception, is not present when the contract of carriage is made and is not an initial party to that contract. In reality, legal fiction aside, he does not afterwards want to become a party to that contract either. The holder obviously wants to collect the goods described in the bill of lading, but to his mind, he has already made the contract(s) required to that end. He has bought the goods from someone, he has been instructed by a principal to receive the goods and store or forward them, etc. Why then would he need or want to enter into a further contract with a carrier? In a well-known analogy, the bill of lading has been likened to the 'key to the warehouse'. Suppose, however, that a party buys a collection of goods. The contract of sale is made, the price is paid, and the seller hands him the actual key, or a digital code to enter the warehouse where the goods are stored. In the buyer's mind, the only thing left to do is to drive over to the warehouse and pick up the goods. Imagine his surprise if he were told that, before he can pick up the goods he bought, he must first enter into a contract with the warehouse company, or that if he turns the key into the lock or enters the digital entrance code, he is now bound by a contract with the warehouse company. The fact that the warehouse company, like a carrier, will often have terms and conditions (e.g. that the warehouse is only accessible between 9.00 AM and 5.00 PM, that vehicles cannot drive faster than 10 km per hour, etc.) does not take away from the conclusion. Clearly, the warehouse company can enforce such terms and conditions without the need for a contractual relationship with the person coming to pick up goods.

167 If the holder of the bill of lading does not really intend to enter into a contract with the carrier – it is particularly clear that he doesn't do so when in the contract of sale he has agreed that the seller would take care of the carriage –, and does not even realize that by presenting the bill of lading and collecting the goods he might be entering into a contract (of carriage), the question is whether the law should make their relationship into a *contract*. Holder and carrier are undeniably in a legal relationship, with mutual rights and obligations, but is that relationship of a contractual nature? That in turn raises the question of what exactly is a 'contract'? The European Court of Justice has repeatedly held that

---

469 V.-E. Bokalli, "Crise et avenir du connaissement", *D.M.F.* 1998, at pp. 125–126. The author is so anxious to have the holder of the bill of lading bound by the jurisdiction clause that, on a single page, he proposes three different theories (the shipper is the agent of the consignee, the consignee accedes to the contract, and there is also a *porte-fort* agreement somewhere) which he seems to consider equally valid.

470 M. Spanjaart, *Vorderingsrechten uit cognossement*, Zutphen, Uitgeverij Paris, 2012, at p. 209.

there is no contract when the parties have not *voluntarily* assumed obligations towards each other.[471] Admittedly, those decisions deal with the meaning of 'contract' in the context of the Brussels I Regulation. To say that a contract requires a voluntary action of the parties, however, is not really surprising or extraordinary. Freedom of contract may not be as absolute as before, with the law intervening in several ways (in some areas (much) more than in others), but the starting point is still that contractual obligations are voluntarily assumed by the parties.[472] If contracts are implied whenever parties have rights or obligations against each other, or if contracts can be created by statute, the concept of a 'contract' becomes so encompassing and covers such divergent situations that it loses its distinctive force. Moreover, it would be rather strange that something that is not a contract for jurisdictional purposes is a contract in other respects, or vice versa. Where the holder of the bill of lading does not (really) intend to enter into a contract, and furthermore is not at liberty *not* to enter into a relationship with the carrier,[473] it is arguable that the relation between the holder and the carrier is not of a *contractual* nature.[474] The argument is even stronger when the carrier under the bill of

---

471 ECJ 17 June 1992, Case C-26/91, *Jakob Handte & Co. v Traitements Mécano-chimiques des Surfaces*, point 15; ECJ 27 October 1998, Case C-51/97, *Réunion Européenne v Spliethoff's Bevrachtingskantoor*, point 17; ECJ 17 September 2002, Case C-334/00, *Fonderie Officine Meccaniche Tacconi SpA v Heinrich Wagner Sinto Maschinenfabrik*, point 23; ECJ 5 February 2004, Case C-265/02, *Frahuil v Assitalia*, point 24; ECJ 20 January 2005, Case C-27/02, *Petra Engler v Janus Versand*, point 50–51; ECJ 14 March 2013, Case C-419/11, *Česká spořitelna v Gerald Feichter*, point 47.
472 *Chitty on Contracts*, Vol. 1, *General Principles*, London, Sweet & Maxwell, 1989 (26th Ed.), n° 1 at p. 2; W. Keener, "Quasi-contract, its nature and scope", 7 *Harv. L. Rev.*, No. 2, 25 May 1893, at p. 58; G. Treitel, *The Law of Contract*, London, Sweet & Maxwell, 1991 (8th Ed.), at p. 1.
   See also J.-P. Tosi, "L'adhésion du destinataire au contrat de transport", in X., *Mélanges Christian Mouly*, Paris, Litec, 1998, at p. 187: "*Le destinataire ne saurait se voir conférer cette qualité [de partie au contrat] automatiquement, ès qualités. Comme tout contractant, il doit manifester son acceptation du contrat.*" (This capacity [of party to the contract] could not be bestowed upon the consignee automatically, simply because of his capacity as consignee. Like any other contracting party, he must manifest his acceptance of the contract.)
   But see C. Paulin, *Droits des transports*, Paris, Litec, 2005, fn. 27 at p. 226, who confirms that the consent of the contracting parties is required for there to be a contract, but seems to imply that such consent could be given or created by the law.
473 Compare *Hispanica de Petroleos S.A. and Compania Iberica Refinadera S.A. v Vencedora Oceanica Navegacion S.A. (The Kapetan Markos N.L. (No. 2))* [1987] 2 Lloyd's Rep 321 (Court of Appeal, 28–30 April and 1 and 5 May 1987), at p. 332: "*. . . in many cases, it would be hard to regard the act of becoming endorsees as referable to an acceptance of the open offer* [allegedly contained in the bill of lading], *since it would be very often (although not in this particular case) be an act done because the contract of sale requires the endorsee to take up and pay for the documents when duly tendered.*"
474 Compare G. Treitel, *The Law of Contract*, London, Sweet & Maxwell, 1991 (8th Ed.), who at p. 3 lists a number of cases in which the law plays so large, and the agreement of parties so small, a part that it becomes doubtful whether the relationship can still be called contractual, and at p. 5 a number of cases in which a relationship created by legal compulsion is clearly not contractual.

lading is not the party that entered into a contract with the shipper, but another party, deemed to be the carrier by operation of law (e.g. the owner of the carrying ship). To consider the bill of lading in such case a contract between the third-party holder and the statutory carrier, neither of whom have actually negotiated or consciously entered into a contract of carriage, requires a contractual concept that is so broad as to risk becoming meaningless.

168 The relation between the holder and the carrier must not necessarily be contractual, either. Alternative, non-contractual approaches are possible. Negotiable instruments, for instance, are an example of this. The position of the holder of a negotiable instrument against the issuer of that document could have been construed as a contract; instead, the law of negotiable instruments developed as a separate branch of law, carving out a specific position for the holders of such instruments. With regard to bills of lading, just as the concept and the functions of this document developed in practice and by the custom of merchants, legal practice and custom could have developed to accept a proper right of action of the holder against the carrier, on the basis of the bill of lading itself, simply because this is an efficient and (commercially) desirable outcome.[475] In the present day and age, customs no longer develop easily. Nevertheless, a gradual development and acceptance of a new approach or conception is still possible. The development of the direct action against liability insurers is a prime example thereof. Once considered pure heresy, the possibility of a direct action was gradually introduced, in national law and international conventions, and has now almost become a standard feature of maritime law.[476] As with bills of lading, there is an initial contract between the liable party and its insurer, which a third party (the damaged party) is allowed to invoke, because that is considered proper and expedient. The initial contract (the insurance policy) will be relevant to determine the extent of the damaged party's rights against the insurer, but civil law system generally do not suggest that the damaged party, because it can now enforce rights against the insurer, has acceded to the contract between the liable party and the insurer, or that the damaged party has entered into a contract with the insurer.[477] In the same way, it would be possible for the thinking about bills

---

475 Compare A. Mesritz, *De Vrachtbrief*, Amsterdam, J.H. de Bussy, 1904, at p. 70.
476 The term 'direct action' can encompass two different situations. A first possibility is that the damaged party is given the right to exercise *the insured's action* against the insurer. This is basically a statutory assignment and means that the damaged party takes over the claim as it existed for the insured himself. The insurer can invoke all defences and exceptions that he could have invoked against the insured. The second possibility is that the damaged party is given a right of its own against the insurer, the limits and contents of which are not (necessarily) the same as the right of the insured himself. In this second case, the law that grants the direct action also defines which defences the insurer can invoke against the damaged party. Most of the maritime law direct actions are of the second type (see, for example, Article VII.8 CLC, Article 4*bis*.10 PAL 2002, Article 12.8 HNS, Article 7.10 Bunkers, Article 12.10 WRC).
477 The direct action is generally conceived to be of a statutory nature. See, for example, H. Cousy and C. Van Schoubroeck, "Compulsory liability insurance in Belgium", in A. Fenyves, C. Kissling, S. Perner and D. Rubin (Eds), *Compulsory Liability Insurance From a*

of lading to move away from the contractual conception towards an independent, statutory conception. To a certain extent, that evolution has already started. Non-contractual approaches of the bill of lading do indeed exist.[478]

169 It is, of course, not difficult to understand how or why the contractual approach of the bill of lading came into being. Carriage of goods by sea initially was a two-party affair, involving only the merchant and the carrier and using only charter parties as documents of carriage. The third-party consignee and the bill of lading as a negotiable document of title only developed afterwards. Also, in law, contract and tort have traditionally been the most important basis for claims. Tort based claims against the carrier, although not impossible, are not the most advantageous solution for either the carrier or the cargo claimant. To think of the holder's claim against the carrier as a contractual claim would have seemed the better solution.

Nevertheless, the question should be asked whether the contractual approach is, or still is, the best possible approach. As was shown above, there is no contractual theory that is a perfect fit. Within the group of theories that have the holder step into the shoes of the shipper, some are clearly more legal fiction and implication than actual reality (agency, novation). Assignment has a number of issues, but could work, certainly in a modern conception of assignment. The problem, however, is that the holder of the bill of lading then must take over all of the shipper's rights and obligations. It is quite generally accepted that that is not, or should not be the case. Within the group of theories that create a separate position for the holder, there is, again, a lot of fiction and implication. The basic assumption, indeed, is that the holder intends to enter into a contractual relationship with the carrier, which in reality he most often does not. Furthermore, if the holder does indeed become a party to the contract of carriage, the normal implication would be that he is then bound by the entire contract. Again, that is a consequence that is not generally accepted. Several theories have been proposed to distinguish between those parts of the initial contract that do bind the holder and those that don't, but they are all to a larger or lesser extent arbitrary and do not provide predictability or legal certainty. The only certain solution is to see the bill of lading as a distinct contract between the carrier and the holder, separate from the initial contract of carriage between the carrier and the shipper. In that case, the bill of lading itself will determine the terms and conditions

---

European Perspective, Berlin, Walter de Gruyter, 2016, n° 61–63 at pp. 67–68; G. Franck, *Der Direktanspruch gegen den Haftpflichtversicherer. Eine rechtsvergleichende Untersuchung zum deutschen und skandinavischen Recht*, Tübingen, Mohr Siebeck, 2014, at p. 32; Y. Lambert-Faivre and L. Leveneur, *Droit des assurances*, Paris, Dalloz, 2005 (12th Ed.), n° 684 at p. 528; T. Langheid and M. Wandt, *Münchener Kommentar zum Versicherungsvertragsgesetz*, Vol. 2, München, Verlag C.H. Beck, 2011, § 115, n° 1 at p. 631.

In the U.K., on the other hand, the direct action is conceived to be of a contractual nature. See, for example, *London Steamship Owners' Mutual Insurance Association Ltd v Spain & Anor (The Prestige)*, [2015] EWCA Civ 333, [2015] 1 CLC 596 (Court of Appeal, 1 April 2015).

478 See below, Part 4.

that are binding on the holder. The carrier, however, will then have two sets of (possibly divergent) obligations with regard to the same carriage. Moreover, the bill of lading as a separate contract that the holder makes with the carrier is possibly not a contract *of carriage* anymore and not subject to the carriage laws and conventions.

170 The contractual approach thus is not an easy approach. There are difficulties explaining why the relationship between the carrier and the holder has to be contractual in the first place, there are difficulties explaining how a contractual relationship between the carrier and the holder can come into being, and there are difficulties explaining why not all standard consequences of a contractual relationship apply in case of a bill of lading. All in all therefore, the contractual approach is not a very satisfactory solution.

4 Non-contractual theories

1 There is no denying that the commercial carriage of goods by sea, self-carriage excepted, is pursuant to a contract of carriage between the carrier and a shipper. This contractual origin, however, does not mean that the position of the consignee must necessarily also be contractual, certainly not when, in addition to the contract, a negotiable document is created that is meant to be transferred to third parties. A number of theories have tried to explain the position of the holder of the bill of lading independently, without deriving it from the position of the shipper or from the contract of carriage as such.[1]

4.1 The holder as the owner of the goods

4.1.1 *The concept*

2 In the early days, when the shipper endorsed (or 'assigned') the bill of lading to a third party, that endorsement in itself transferred title to the goods described in the bill of lading to the endorsee. The holder of the bill of lading was therefore also the owner of the goods and thus had ownership rights. The carrier on the other hand could clearly not claim to be the owner of the goods he carried, and could at most be a bailee of the goods. Obviously then, the owner of the goods (holder) should have rights against the person who is only holding the goods (carrier).[2] Conversely, the owner of the goods may be obliged against the person who has been holding and taking care of the goods. In this approach, the bill of lading could be seen as the terms the bailee has set for the bailment.

---

1 Compare R. De Smet, *Droit maritime et droit fluvial belges*, Vol. I, Brussels, Larcier, 1971, n° 374 at p. 464: "... *le connaissement n'est pas un contrat entre le transporteur et le destinataire*" (the bill of lading is not a contract between the carrier and the consignee), who does not explain or corroborate his position however.
2 See L. Josserand, *Les Transports*, Paris, Arthur Rousseau, 1910, n° 382 at p. 323, who considers this theory both insufficient and incorrect.
   Compare R. De Wit, *Multimodal Transport: Carrier Liability and Documentation*, London, Lloyd's of London Press, 1995, n° 5.7 at p. 247.

152 Non-contractual theories

3 In the 1960s, the Dutch author Cahen argued that ownership and title to the carried goods should be given a much more important place in the law of carriage. The carrier's undertaking to deliver the goods to the holder of the bill of lading is based on the contract of carriage between the carrier and the shipper, but is only valid and binding on the carrier if the (ultimate) holder indeed has title to the goods. If the – even lawful – holder of the bill of lading does not have a valid title to the goods, the carrier is not obliged, and not even allowed, to release the goods to him.[3] This then leads this author to see the rights and obligations of the holder as 'qualitative' rights and obligations, i.e. rights and obligations that are attached to and transferred with the ownership of the carried goods.[4] This position, however, has always remained an isolated one, attacked and rejected by other authors.[5]

4.1.2 When does the relationship come into being?

4 Since the position of the holder is based upon his becoming owner of the carried goods, the relationship comes into being at the moment the holder becomes the owner by having the bill of lading transferred to him, which very likely is before the goods arrive at destination and the bill of lading is presented to the carrier.

4.1.3 Intermediate holders

5 The rights of the holder come into being when the latter becomes owner by reason of having the bill of lading transferred to him. Logically, then, if the first holder transfers the bill of lading – and by that title to the goods – to a subsequent holder, his (ownership) rights against the carrier are at that moment also transferred to the subsequent holder. In principle, the holder/owner's obligations against the carrier also end at that time. At least theoretically, however, it is possible that the carrier can prove that, although the bill of lading was presented at destination by B, he has had to disburse costs to preserve the goods at a time when A was the holder of the bill of lading. In that case, the carrier could still have a claim against A for those costs.

4.1.4 The non-contracting shipper

6 The non-contracting shipper does not get title to the goods transferred to him by means of the bill of lading, but he may initially be the owner of the goods to be shipped. For as long as he remains owner of the goods, he should in this view have ownership rights and obligations against the carrier.

---

3 J. Cahen, *Het cognossement*, Arnhem, Gouda Quint, 1964, at p. 2.
4 J. Cahen, *Het cognossement*, Arnhem, Gouda Quint, 1964, at pp. 8–10.
5 See, for example, R. Cleveringa, "Book Review J.L.P. Cahen *Het Cognossement*", *R.M.T.* 1965, at pp. 137–143.

4.1.5 Appraisal

7 The origin of this theory is the idea that the transfer of the bill of lading in and of itself transfers title to the goods. Since the end of the 19th century, however, it has become accepted that transferring a bill of lading does not automatically or necessarily have that effect. The bill of lading only transfers (constructive) possession.[6] Also, in modern day practice, the holder of the bill of lading is very often *not* the owner of the goods, but a transport or logistics intermediary or a bank. The holder of the bill of lading, who is closest to the carriage, thus would not have title to sue. The carrier, on the other hand, can no longer assume that the holder is the owner of the goods either, and will have to try and find out who is the owner, which will often prove difficult, if not impossible.

8 Also, this theory reduces or even destroys the relevance and reliability of the bill of lading as a commercial and negotiable document. If it is accepted that the owner of the goods has rights against the carrier because of the fact that he is the owner, conflicts between the holder of the bill of lading and the owner of the goods may well be decided in favour of the latter. Holdership of the bill of lading thus no longer guarantees the right to obtain delivery of the goods.

9 It also means that the relationship between the carrier and the holder is no longer governed by carriage law, but instead will be regulated by general property law, bailment law, etc. These other branches of the law will also be able to provide solutions for issues between the carrier and the holder, but the specificity that is provided by the carriage law will be lost.

10 Not surprisingly, then, the view that the holder's position against the carrier is derived from and determined by his capacity of owner of the goods is today mostly rejected.[7]

4.2 The bill of lading as a quasi-contract

4.2.1 The concept

11 The law of obligations, both in civil law and in common law, recognizes a third type of obligation in addition to the two main categories of contract and tort, i.e. that of the quasi-contract (or 'Restitution' in the UK). A quasi-contract is a legal relationship between parties, that does not come into being in a contractual way, i.e. by the agreement of the parties involved, but that, once it has come into being, resembles a contractual relationship, with the parties having rights and obligations towards each other.[8] An archetypical example is the person who,

---

6 Obviously, if the parties so agreed, transferring possession may be the trigger to also transfer title. See also A. Lista, *International Commercial Sales: The Sale of Goods on Shipment Terms*, Oxon, Informa Law, 2017, at p. 104.
7 See, for example, Ph. Delebecque, *Droit maritime*, Paris, Dalloz, 2014 (13th Ed.), n° 73 at p. 512.
8 *Chitty on Contracts*, Vol. 1, *General Principles*, London, Sweet & Maxwell, 1989 (26th Ed.), n° 2031 at p. 1306; W. Keener, "Quasi-contract, its nature and scope", 7 *Harv. L. Rev.*, No. 2, (25 May 1893, at pp. 57–75.

seeing someone else in need, takes action to help that other person. If he does intervene, he is under a duty to do so with proper care (taking into account the circumstances, of course), and the assisted person is under a duty to reimburse the costs or losses that the helping person may have had as a result of his intervention. Although the relationship, once created, much resembles a contract, a quasi-contract is not a real *contract*, as it is not based on the intention and agreement of the parties involved.[9]

12 The quasi-contract is not unknown in maritime law. Compulsory pilotage and the right of a refused pilot to half-pilotage fees, for instance, have been seen in the USA as quasi-contractual relationships.[10] Non-contractual salvage is also commonly regarded as a quasi-contract.[11] The relationship between the salvor and the owner of the vessel in danger does not come into being by those parties making an agreement, but by the physical actions of the salvor. Once the salvor has intervened, however, both salvor and owner have rights and obligations, which currently are largely determined by the London Salvage Convention 1989.

4.2.2 The bill of lading creating a quasi-contractual relationship

13 If it is accepted that the consignee, when presenting the bill of lading to the carrier, has no intention to enter into a contract with the latter, the fact of presenting the bill of lading and claiming delivery could still be seen as an action that triggers a quasi-contractual relationship. The carrier and the consignee do not agree to enter into an agreement, but once the consignee has claimed delivery, they have mutual rights and obligations, imposed and defined by the law. This is, at present, only a possible point of view, though, rather than an established theory in the countries that are the subject of this research. It has been suggested, however, that the liability of a common carrier is, or should be seen as, quasi-contractual in nature,[12] so the quasi-contract concept is not entirely unknown to the law of carriage of goods.

14 If desired, the relationship between intermediate holders and the carrier could also be seen as a quasi-contract. There is an 'action' on the part of the intermediate holder by his acquiring the bill of lading. Very often, the carrier will not be aware of this acquisition, but such awareness is not required for a quasi-contract to come into being. If a salvor takes action with regard to a ship that was

---

9 W. Keener, "Quasi-contract, its nature and scope", 7 *Harv. L. Rev.*, No. 2, 25 May 1893, at p. 59 (citing H. Maine, *Ancient Law, Its Connection With the Early History of Society, and Its Relation to Modern Ideas*).
10 *Steamship Co. v Joliffe* 69 US 450, 1864 WL 6611, 17 L.Ed. 805, 2 Wall. 450 (US Supreme Court, 1 December 1864).
   See also A. Corbin, "Quasi-contractual obligations", 21 *Yale LJ* at p. 537; W. Keener, "Quasi-contract, its nature and scope", 7 *Harv. L. Rev.*, No. 2, 25 May 1893, at p. 68.
11 *Chitty on Contracts*, Vol. 1, *General Principles*, London, Sweet & Maxwell, 1989 (26th Ed.), n° 2149 at p. 1410.
12 W. Keener, "Quasi-contract, its nature and scope", 7 *Harv. L. Rev.*, No. 2, 25 May 1893, at p. 69.

abandoned by the crew, the shipowner is not immediately aware of this intervention either, but there will nevertheless be a salvage situation.

15 The relationship between a non-contracting shipper and the carrier can also, and quite easily, be seen as a quasi-contract, as these parties directly interact with each other. The non-contracting shipper and the carrier are, by definition, not in a contractual relationship, but once the non-contracting shipper delivers the goods to the carrier for shipment, they do have mutual rights and obligations. In a way, this concept is clearly present in German maritime law, which construes a separate contract between the carrier and the non-contracting shipper if the latter requests and obtains the bill of lading (the *Begebungsvertrag*, or 'contract to issue'). This *Begebungsvertrag*, however, is not based on any real intention of the parties involved to enter into a contract, but is purely a creation of the law. A 'contract' created by law is not a real contract, though, but a quasi-contractual or statutory position.

4.2.3 Appraisal

16 Qualifying the relationship between the carrier and a third-party holder (or intermediate holder or non-contracting shipper) as a quasi-contract is, in itself, not very useful. It does not provide any answers as to the rights or obligations of the holder, the position of intermediate holders or the non-contracting shipper, etc. Those (needed) answers will have to come from elsewhere. It does show, however, that the relationship between the carrier and a third-party holder does not inevitably have to be looked upon as a *contractual* relationship. In addition, the international conventions and national laws have already, at least in certain respects, worked out the position of the holder. Accepting that the position of the holder is quasi-contractual does not mean, therefore, that his position has to be entirely reconstructed.

4.3 The position of the holder as a statutory position

4.3.1 Explicit position: the UK Bills of Lading Act 1855 and COGSA 1992

4.3.1.1 The Acts

17 The English common law did not allow the assignment of contracts in general, and contracts of carriage in particular. In the first half of the 19th century, therefore, the transfer of a bill of lading transferred title to the goods described in the bill of lading, but did not transfer any contractual rights against the carrier. The consignee, owner of the goods, thus in principle did not have a remedy against the carrier.[13] Although there were some indications that the courts might be

---

13 W. Bennett, *The History and Present Position of the Bill of Lading as a Document of Title to Goods*, Cambridge, University Press, 1914, at p. 57.

prepared to accept an implied contract between the carrier and the consignee, on the terms of the bill of lading, a legislative intervention was considered necessary.

On 14 August 1855, an Act to amend the Law relating to Bills of Lading (commonly known as the Bills of Lading Act 1855) was passed. The preamble of the Act explicitly refers to the then accepted concept that the transfer of the bill of lading *ipso facto* transfers title to the goods:

> "*Whereas by the Custom of Merchants a Bill of Lading of Goods being transferable by Endorsement, the Property in the Goods may thereby pass to the Endorsee, but nevertheless all Rights in respect of the Contract contained in the Bill of Lading continue in the original Shipper or Owner, and it is expedient that such Rights should pass with the Property.*"

Not surprisingly, then, Section 1 of the Bills of Lading Act ties in the transfer of rights under the bill of lading with the transfer of property:

> "*Every Consignee of Goods named in a Bill of Lading, and every Endorsee of a Bill of Lading to whom the Property in the Goods therein mentioned shall pass, upon or by reason of such Consignment or Endorsement, shall have transferred to and vested in him all Rights of Suit, and be subject to the same Liabilities in respect of such Goods as if the Contract contained in the Bill of Lading had been made with himself.*"

The text of Section 1 would seem to suggest that the provision only applies to named consignees under straight bills of lading and endorsees of order bills of lading. It has always been accepted, though, that the rule equally applies to holders of bearer bills of lading.[14]

If, by becoming holder of the bill of lading, the holder also acquires title to the goods, the rights and liabilities contained in the bill of lading are transferred to him. He can sue the carrier under the bill of lading, and conversely can be sued by the carrier himself. Although the 1855 Act explicitly refers to the 'contract' contained in the bill of lading, there has been little hesitation in accepting that it also applies when the bill of lading does not contain a contract at all, as when the bill of lading is issued under a charter party.[15] Even if the bill of lading is or evidences a contract, it is not the contractual rights and liabilities as they were

---

14 S. Baughen, *Shipping Law*, London, Routledge-Cavendish, 2009 (4th Ed.), at p. 40.
15 S. Baughen, *Shipping Law*, London, Routledge-Cavendish, 2009 (4th Ed.), at p. 40; M. Davies and A. Dickey, *Shipping Law*, Lawbook Co., 2004 (3th Ed.), at p. 254; S. Peel, "The development of the bill of lading: its future in the maritime industry", 2002, thesis submitted to the University of Plymouth, Institute of Marine Studies, at pp. 168–169.

Tate & Lyle Ltd v Hain Steamship Co Ltd (1936) 55 Ll. L. Rep 159 (House of Lords, 11 June 1936), at p. 174: "*The consignee has not assigned to him the obligations under the charterparty, nor, in fact, any obligations of the contract under the bill of lading for ex hypothesi there is none. A new contract appears to spring up between the ship and the consignee on the terms of the bill of lading.*"

actually agreed between the original parties that are transferred, but the rights and liabilities as expressed in the bill of lading.[16]

18 Over the years, however, it became apparent that several categories of holders fell outside the scope of the Bills of Lading Act, and thus could not act against the carrier under the bill of lading.[17] A consignee to whom the property of the carried goods was passed independently of the endorsement of the bill of lading, did not satisfy the requirements of the 1855 Act and could not sue the carrier under the bill of lading.[18] Buyers of unascertained bulk cargo, for instance, cannot obtain ownership before the cargo is separated and ascertained on discharge.[19] If the bill of lading is endorsed to them before that time, that endorsement cannot pass the property, and thus cannot transfer the rights and liabilities under the bill of lading. Also, since *Sewell v Burdick*,[20] holders that only held the bill of lading as security (such as banks under a letter of credit) did not acquire the rights and liabilities under the bill of lading, as they only acquired 'special property' (i.e. a security interest) but not 'general property' (i.e. ownership) as required for the 1855 Act to apply.

19 In 1985, following a case in which the buyers of an undivided bulk cargo had to suffer the consequences of an attachment by the unpaid seller,[21] commodity trade associations requested the UK Law Commission to consider a law reform to better protect the buyers of undivided bulk cargos. In 1989, the UK and Scottish Law Commissions published papers on bulk goods, inviting comments

---

16 W. Bennett, *The History and Present Position of the Bill of Lading as a Document of Title to Goods*, Cambridge, University Press, 1914, at p. 61, who refers to *The Helene* 1865 B.&L. 415 (the shipper's knowledge of the defectiveness of the packing was not imputed to the holder) and *Leduc v Ward* 1888 20 QBD 476 (the shipper's knowledge of the intended deviation was not imputed to the holder).

M. Davies and A. Dickey, *Shipping Law*, Lawbook Co., 2004 (3th Ed.), at p. 254.

See also *Homburg Houtimport BV v Agrosin Private Ltd (The Starsin)* [2003] UKHL 12, [2004] 1 A.C. 715 (House of Lords, 13 March 2003), n° 129: "The second observation is that the claimants are subsequent holders of the bills of lading by endorsement. Their contractual rights must be ascertained *by reference to the bill of lading document itself*. Look at the bill of lading, front and back, and arrive at a conclusion."

17 Such holders may have had alternative actions on a tort or bailment basis, or under an implied contract, but such alternative actions are not the most desirable solution, neither for the holder nor for the carrier.

18 S. Baughen, *Shipping Law*, London, Routledge-Cavendish, 2009 (4th Ed.), at p. 41; W. Bennett, *The History and Present Position of the Bill of Lading as a Document of Title to Goods*, Cambridge, University Press, 1914, at pp. 61–62.

19 Section 16 Sale of Goods Act 1979. Since the 1995 amendments, however, property in an undivided share in the bulk can be transferred to the buyer (Sect. 20A.(2).(a)).

20 *Sewell v Burdick (The Zoe)* 10 App Cas 74 (House of Lords, 5 December 1884). In this case, the bill of lading had been endorsed in blank by the consignee and deposited with his bankers, as security for a loan. The consignee later disappeared and never claimed delivery of the goods. After a while, the goods were sold by the authorities at the port of destination, bringing only enough to cover the storage costs and government dues. The shipowner then sued the bankers, which still held the bills of lading, in payment of the freight.

21 Court of Rotterdam 20 February 1985, *S&S* 1985, 91 (*The Gosforth*). The case was decided in the Netherlands, but on the basis of English law.

158 Non-contractual theories

from interested parties.[22] Following this consultation, it became apparent that the problem was more general than bulk cargos and that a reform of the Bills of Lading Act and the rights of suit under bills of lading was widely perceived as required and overdue. In 1991, the Law Commissions produced a report on rights of suit in respect of carriage of goods by sea, with a draft Bill attached.[23] That draft Bill was enacted, without amendment, as COGSA 1992.

20 COGSA 1992 repeals the Bills of Lading Act 1855 and introduces a new regime for the holder of a bill of lading, that is more detailed than under the Bills of Lading Act and divorced from the passing of property. Pursuant to Section 2 (1), the rights of suit are vested in the lawful holder of the bill of lading:

Subject to the following provisions of this section, a person who becomes

(a) the lawful holder of a bill of lading;

(...)

shall (by virtue of becoming the holder of the bill (...) have transferred to and vested in him all rights of suit under the contract of carriage as if he had been a party to that contract.

Who is the 'lawful holder' of a bill of lading is defined in Section 5.(2) of COGSA:

References in this Act to the holder of a bill of lading are references to any of the following persons, that is to say

(a) a person with possession of the bill who, by virtue of being the person identified in the bill, is the consignee of the goods to which the bill relates;

(b) a person with possession of the bill as a result of the completion, by delivery of the bill, of any indorsement of the bill or, in the case of a bearer bill, of any other transfer of the bill;

(c) a person with possession of the bill as a result of any transaction by virtue of which he would have become a holder falling within paragraph (a) or (b) above had not the transaction been effected at a time when possession of the bill no longer gave a right (as against the carrier) to possession of the goods to which the bill relates;

and a person shall be regarded for the purposes of this Act as having become the lawful holder of a bill of lading wherever he has become the holder of the bill in good faith.

---

22 The Law Commission, Working Paper No. 112, *Rights to Goods in Bulk*, and The Scottish Law Commission, Discussion Paper No. 83, *Bulk goods: section 16 of the sale of goods act 1979 and section 1 of the bills of lading act 1855.*
23 The Law Commission and The Scottish Law Commission, *Rights of Suit in Respect of Carriage of Goods by Sea*, 19 March 1991, (LAW COM No 196 and SCOT LAW COM No 130).

The transfer of the rights of suit to a lawful holder extinguishes the rights of the shipper and of previous holders, per Section 2.(5) of COGSA:[24]

> *Where rights are transferred by virtue of the operation of subsection (1) above in relation to any document, the transfer for which that subsection provides shall extinguish any entitlement to those rights which derives*
>
> > *(a) where that document is a bill of lading, from a person's having been an original party to the contract of carriage; or*
> > *(b) in the case of any document to which this Act applies, from the previous operation of that subsection in relation to that document;*
>
> *but the operation of that subsection shall be without prejudice to any rights which derive from a person's having been an original party to the contract contained in, or evidenced by, a sea waybill and, in relation to a ship's delivery order, shall be without prejudice to any rights deriving otherwise than from the previous operation of that subsection in relation to that order.*

When the holder of the bill of lading makes a claim in respect of the carried goods against the carrier, he becomes subject to the liabilities under the contract of carriage per Section 3.(1) of COGSA:

> *Where subsection (1) of section 2 of this Act operates in relation to any document to which this Act applies and the person in whom rights are vested by virtue of that subsection*
>
> > *(a) takes or demands delivery from the carrier of any of the goods to which the document relates;*
> > *(b) makes a claim under the contract of carriage against the carrier in respect of any of those goods; or*
> > *(c) is a person who, at a time before those rights were vested in him, took or demanded delivery from the carrier of any of those goods,*
>
> *that person shall (by virtue of taking or demanding delivery or making the claim or, in a case falling within paragraph (c) above, of having the rights vested in him) become subject to the same liabilities under that contract as if he had been a party to that contract.*

21 The lawful holder of the bill of lading acquires the rights and becomes subject to the liabilities as contained in the bill of lading. This was very clear under the Bills of Lading Act 1855, which explicitly refers to 'the contract *contained in the bill of lading*'. If, therefore, the actual contract between the shipper and

---

24 See also M. Spanjaart, *Vorderingsrechten uit cognossement*, Zutphen, Uitgeverij Paris, 2012, at pp. 315–316.

the carrier included rights or liabilities that were not expressed in the bill of lading, such rights and liabilities were not transferred to the holder. COGSA 1992 changed the terminology, however, and now refers to the rights of suit and liabilities *under the contract of carriage*. This could be interpreted to mean that the holder now has to look at the actual contract made by the shipper and the carrier. The majority position, though, is that there was no intention to change the existing law and that the position of the holder is still only governed by what appears from the bill of lading itself.[25] *Carver* does see a difference between the Bills of Lading Act and COGSA, however, in situations where the actual contract of carriage between the shipper and the carrier is void or voidable.[26] The Bills of Lading Act 1855 seemed to dictate that there is (always) a contract in the bill of lading, and that the rights and liabilities under that contract are transferred to the holder if property also passes, whereas COGSA 1992 provides that the holder obtains the rights under the contract of carriage as if he had been a party to that contract. Therefore, if the contract of carriage is void or voided, the holder can no longer become a party to that contract, and thus cannot obtain rights. It is submitted, however, that that conclusion is not unavoidable. The 'contract of carriage' in section 2.(1), to which the holder is deemed to become a party to, is indeed defined in section 5.(1) as the contract contained in or evidenced by the bill of lading. Furthermore, at least with regard to its terms, the contract is *exclusively* and *exhaustively* contained in or evidenced by the bill of lading.[27] It is arguable, therefore, that the COGSA 'contract of carriage' exists and that the holder can become a party to it if a bill of lading has been issued, even if the contract of carriage between the shipper and the carrier is void or voidable. Such position would not be exceptional, either. It is generally accepted under German law, for

---

25 R. Aikens, R. Lord and M. Bools, *Bills of Lading*, London, Informa, 2006, n° 8.58 at p. 168; S. Baughen, *Shipping Law*, London, Routledge-Cavendish, 2009 (4th Ed.), at p. 42; J. Cooke et al., *Voyage Charters*, London, Informa, 2007 (3rd Ed.), n° 18.82 at p. 483; C. Debattista, *Bills of Lading in Export Trade*, Haywards Heath, Tottel Publishing, 2009 (3rd Ed.), n° 7.4 at p. 151; N. Gaskell, R. Asariotis and Y. Baatz, *Bills of Lading: Law and Contracts*, London, LLP, 2000, n° 2.24 at pp. 45–46; P. Bugden and S. Lamont-Black, *Goods in Transit and Freight Forwarding*, London, Sweet & Maxwell, 2010 (2nd Ed.), n° 13–15 at p. 236; G. Treitel and F. Reynolds, *Carver on Bills of Lading*, London, Sweet & Maxwell, 2011 (3rd Ed.), n° 3–009 at pp. 106–108, n° 5–028 at pp. 234–235 and n° 5–033 at p. 238.
   See also *Homburg Houtimport BV and Others v Agrosin Private Ltd and Another (The Starsin)*, [2003] UKHL 12, [2004] 1 A.C. 715 (House of Lords, 13 March 2003), n° 129: "The second observation is that the claimants are subsequent holders of the bills of lading by endorsement. Their contractual rights must be ascertained by reference to the bill of lading document itself. Look at the bill of lading, front and back, and arrive at a conclusion."
26 G. Treitel and F. Reynolds, *Carver on Bills of Lading*, London, Sweet & Maxwell, 2011 (3rd Ed.), n° 5–033 at p. 237.
27 *Carver* explicitly invokes Sect. 5.(1) COGSA to support the position that elements extrinsic to the bill of lading cannot change or influence the holder's position: "*The fact that, where a valid contract exists, the holder may not be bound by terms which restrict the shipper's rights under that contract follows, not from the fiction in s2(1), but from the definition of contract of carriage in s5(1).*" (G. Treitel and F. Reynolds, *Carver on Bills of Lading*, London, Sweet & Maxwell, 2011 (3rd Ed.), n° 5–033 at p. 238.)

instance, that the bill of lading remains valid and enforceable, even if the underlying contract of carriage is void or voidable.[28] Similarly, in the Netherlands, an insurance certificate issued pursuant to a void policy was held to remain enforceable in the hands of a third-party holder in good faith.[29]

4.3.1.2 When does the relationship come into being?

22 Historically, the Bills of Lading Act 1855 did not explicitly define when the relationship between the holder and the carrier comes into being, but since the creation of that relationship is dependent upon the passing of the property of the carried goods to the holder, it may be assumed that the relationship comes into being concurrently with the passing of the property. In many cases, therefore, the relationship would have come into being *before* the bill is lading is presented to the carrier in the port of destination.

23 Currently, COGSA 1992 does not explicitly define the relevant moment either, and moreover divorces the transfer of rights from the transfer of liabilities. With regard to the rights under the bill of lading, the wording of section 2.(1) hardly leaves room for doubt. The lawful holder of a bill of lading has the rights of suit transferred to and vested in him *by virtue of becoming the holder*. The rights are transferred because, and therefore also at the moment, the bill of lading is transferred to the holder. As under the Bills of Lading Act 1855, this will often be before the presentation of the bill of lading in the port of destination. With regard to the liabilities, however, the situation is (much) more complex. The Law Commissions indeed decided to divorce rights from liabilities, and not to automatically impose liabilities on every holder of the bill of lading.[30] The liabilities under the bill of lading only attach when the holder takes or demands delivery or makes a claim against the carrier (section 3.(1)). What exactly is 'taking delivery', 'claiming delivery', or 'making a claim under the contract of

---

28 W. Bayer, *Der Vertrag zugunsten Dritter*, Tübingen, J.C.B. Mohr (Paul Siebeck), 1995, at p. 178; C.-W. Canaris, W. Schilling and P. Ulmer (Eds), *Handelsgesetzbuch Großkommentar, begründet von Hermann Staub*, Berlin, De Gruyter, 2001 (4th Ed.), § 363, n° 64 at p. 67 and n° 66 at p. 69; H. Gramm, *Das neue Deutsche Seefrachtrecht nach den Haager Regeln*, Berlin, E.S. Mittler & Sohn, 1938, at p. 152; D. Rabe, *Seehandelsrecht*, München, Verlag C.H. Beck, 2000 (4th Ed.), n° 2 at p. 749; G. Schaps and H. Abraham, *Das Seerecht in der Bundesrepublik Deutschland, Seehandelsrecht*, Vol. 1, Berlin, Walter de Gruyter, 1978 (4th Ed.), n° 14 at p. 750.
BGH 10 October 1957, *BGHZ* 25, 300, *NJW* 1957, 1917 (Case II ZR 278/56): "*Die Verpflichtung des auf Grund des Konnossements Empfangenden zur Frachtzahlung besteht (...) selbständig und unabhängig davon, ob ein Frachtvertrag wirksam zustande gekommen ist.*" (The obligation of the person that takes delivery under the bill of lading to pay the freight exists on its own and independently of the question whether a contract of carriage was validly made.)
29 HR 19 April 2002, *RvdW* 2002, 73, *S&S* 2002, 126, *NJ* 2002, 456 (*Zürich / Lebosch*).
30 The Law Commission and The Scottish Law Commission, *Rights of Suit in Respect of Carriage of Goods by Sea*, 19 March 1991 (LAW COM No 196 and SCOT LAW COM No 130), n° 3.15 at p. 32.

carriage', though? This question explicitly came up in the House of Lords' decision in *The Berge Sisar*.[31]

24 Before addressing this question, however, Lord Hobhouse starts by pointing out that section 3.(1) on liabilities only works against parties that have acquired the *rights* under the bill of lading pursuant to section 2.(1).[32] That would mean, however, that if a party takes delivery of the goods without having become the lawful holder of the bill of lading, that party would not be subject to any liabilities. Such a scenario is perhaps not an everyday occurrence, but it is not impossible either. It is not unheard of for order bills of lading to be transferred to a subsequent holder without a (proper) endorsement. That subsequent holder is then not a lawful holder in the sense of section 5.(2), and thus cannot have the rights of suit vested in him pursuant to section 2.(1). The issue of endorsement, and delivery of the document to complete the endorsement, also came up in *The Aegean Sea*.[33] In that case, Louis Dreyfus had sold crude oil to ROIL, the trading company of Repsol, a Spanish oil company. ROIL in turn sold the oil to its parent company Repsol on an 'Ex Ship' basis. When Louis Dreyfus sent its invoice, the bills of lading and the other shipping documents to ROIL, however, it inadvertently endorsed the bills of lading to Repsol rather than to ROIL. ROIL then forwarded the bills of lading to Repsol. The latter, upon noticing the incorrect endorsement, returned the bills of lading to Louis Dreyfus, which voided the first endorsement and re-endorsed the bills of lading to ROIL. Louis Dreyfus then again sent the re-endorsed bills of lading to ROIL. The question then was whether Repsol under those circumstances had become the 'holder' of the bills of lading.[34] The shipowner argued that it did, as it intended to hold Repsol liable under the bill of lading for having nominated an unsafe port (a duty allegedly incorporated into the bill of lading from the charter party), which would have caused the ship to run aground and explode, resulting in the loss of the vessel and most of the cargo. Thomas J however held that erroneously endorsing the bill of lading to a party and physically delivering the bill of lading to that party does not

---

31 *Borealis AB v Stargas Ltd and others and Bergesen D.Y. A/S (The Berge Sisar)* [2001] UKHL 17, [2001] 2 All ER 193 (House of Lords, 22 March 2001).
   See also P. Bugden and S. Lamont-Black, *Goods in Transit and Freight Forwarding*, London, Sweet & Maxwell, 2010 (2nd Ed.), n° 13–13 at p. 235.

32 *Borealis AB v Stargas Ltd and others and Bergesen D.Y. A/S (The Berge Sisar)* [2001] UKHL 17, [2001] 2 All ER 193 (House of Lords, 22 March 2001), point 32.
   See also *Primetrade AG v Ythan Ltd (The Ithan)*, 2005 EWHC 2399 (Comm), [2005] 2 CLC 911 (Queen's Bench Division (Commercial Court), 1 November 2005), point 91. The parties in that case agreed "*that it is clear from the terms of s 3.(1) of COGSA that a person can only become subject to liabilities under a bill of lading by virtue of that section if rights of suit are vested in him by virtue of s 2.(1)*".
   See also A. Lista, *International Commercial Sales: The Sale of Goods on Shipment Terms*, Oxon, Informa Law, 2017, at pp. 108–116.

33 *Aegean Sea Traders Corp. v Repsol Petroleo SA & Anor (The Aegean Sea)* [1998] CLC 1090, [1998] 2 Lloyd's Rep 39 (Queen's Bench Division (Admiralty Court), 7 April 1998).

34 There was no real debate that, if Repsol had indeed become 'holder', it had done so in good faith, i.e. through honest conduct ([1998] CLC at p. 1117).

make it the 'holder' of the bill of lading in the sense of section 5.(2) COGSA. In order to become the holder of the bill of lading, a party must accept the endorsement and delivery of the document, which Repsol never did. There were commercial reasons to have the purchasing done by the trading company ROIL, Repsol itself did not need the bills of lading, and when it noticed the error, it immediately pointed it out and returned the bills of lading to Louis Dreyfus for correction. Under those circumstances, it is clear that Repsol had never accepted to become endorsee of the bill of lading.

In addition, however, Thomas J also pointed out that Louis Dreyfus had never delivered the bill of lading to the endorsee. It had (incorrectly) endorsed the bill of lading to Repsol, but had then sent the documents to ROIL. ROIL in turn had forwarded the bill of lading to Repsol, but as principal, not as an agent for Louis Dreyfus. If that position is correct, however, the party actually taking delivery of the cargo could be a party that is not the 'holder' of the bill of lading under section 5.(2) COGSA. Suppose, indeed, that ROIL and Repsol had been unrelated companies, with Repsol needing the bill of lading to obtain delivery at destination. The same sequence of events could have played out, with Louis Dreyfus mistakenly endorsing the bill of lading to Repsol and forwarding it to ROIL, and ROIL after payment forwarding the (already endorsed) bill of lading to Repsol, the latter presenting the bill of lading to the carrier and taking delivery of the cargo. Since endorsement and delivery do not concur, this would mean under *The Aegean Sea* that Repsol is not the 'holder' of the bill of lading, which in turn under *The Berge Sisar* would mean that Repsol cannot become subject to liabilities under the contract of carriage, even though it did benefit from the bill of lading. It seems rather unlikely that this was the intention of the draftsmen of COGSA.

In *The Ythan*,[35] the bill of lading was held by the bank pursuant to a documentary credit when the ship and cargo were lost. The bill of lading was eventually transferred by the bank to the cargo underwriters (through the broker, acting as an agent of Primetrade), following a settlement between Primetrade, the buyer of the cargo, and the underwriters. Primetrade was later sued by the owner of the lost ship, which argued that Primetrader had become the lawful holder of the bill of lading and had, as such, made a claim against the shipowner by demanding security under threat of arrest.[36] Aikens J however held that the bill of lading, when it was transferred to Primetrade's agent, was a spent bill of lading, that it was transferred pursuant to an agreement entered into when the bill of lading had already become spent, and that therefore no rights of suit were vested in Primetrade as a result. That in turn meant that, although Primetrade had taken action against the shipowner regarding the cargo loss, it could not have become subject to liabilities.[37]

---

35 *Primetrade AG v Ythan Ltd (The Ithan)*, 2005 EWHC 2399 (Comm), [2005] 2 CLC 911 (Queen's Bench Division (Commercial Court), 1 November 2005).
36 On the 'making a claim' aspect of the case, see below, n° 25 p. 164.
37 *Primetrade AG v Ythan Ltd (The Ithan)*, 2005 EWHC 2399 (Comm), [2005] 2 CLC 911 (Queen's Bench Division (Commercial Court), 1 November 2005), point 91.

25 With regard to the concepts of 'taking delivery', 'demanding delivery' and 'making a claim', Lord Hobhouse in *The Berge Sisar* remarked that 'taking delivery' is a clear enough concept, involving a full and voluntary transfer of possession from one person to another.[38] The requirement of a voluntary act by the holder (or prospective holder under section 3.(1).(c)) had already been pointed out by Thomas J in *The Aegean Sea*. After the grounding and explosion, a small part of the oil was pumped out of the wreck and, under orders of the government body coordinating the salvage, put into storage in tanks at Repsol's refinery. After some months, this small parcel of oil was sold to Repsol at a discounted price, and then processed and used by Repsol. The shipowner argued that by doing so, Repsol had taken delivery of part of the cargo while being, or later becoming, the lawful holder of the bill of lading. Thomas J however held that such forced reception, under compulsion from the civil government, did not amount to taking delivery of the goods from the carrier.[39] Similarly, simply cooperating in the discharge of the cargo from the vessel does not, in itself, constitute 'taking delivery'.[40]

'Demanding delivery' is not as clear a concept, as a 'demand' can take multiple forms. In *The Berge Sisar*, Lord Hobhouse felt that the construction of this term should take into account the consequences of that act under COGSA, i.e. the imposition of liability under the bill of lading. One should therefore not decide too easily that the holder has 'demanded delivery'; this is only the case if he has made a formal demand to the carrier asserting the right as holder of the bill of lading to have the carrier deliver the goods to him.[41] In *The Berge Sisar*, Borealis, the then holder of the bill of lading, had allowed the vessel to dock at its jetty and had taken samples of the cargo of liquid propane. Upon finding these samples contaminated, Borealis had immediately refused the cargo. Under those circumstances, it was held that Borealis had never demanded delivery. The issue was also before the court in *The Aegean Sea*. As the bill of lading was not expected to arrive before discharge, the charter party called for discharge and delivery against a Letter of Indemnity. As the shipowner was not prepared to accept a Letter of Indemnity by ROIL (an offshore company with little assets), it was issued by Repsol itself.[42] After the incident, in its attempt to hold Repsol liable, the shipowner argued that by providing the Letter of Indemnity, Repsol had 'demanded delivery' within the meaning of s 3.(1) of the COGSA. The argument was rejected by Thomas J, who held that the Letter of Indemnity on its terms was not a demand for delivery (the Letter only provided that *if* the oil

---

38 *Borealis AB v Stargas Ltd and others and Bergesen D.Y. A/S (The Berge Sisar)* [2001] UKHL 17, [2001] 2 All ER 193 (House of Lords, 22 March 2001), point 32.
39 *Aegean Sea Traders Corp. v Repsol Petroleo SA & Anor (The Aegean Sea)* [1998] CLC 1090 (Queen's Bench Division (Admiralty Court), 7 April 1998), at p. 1120.
40 *Borealis AB v Stargas Ltd and others and Bergesen D.Y. A/S (The Berge Sisar)* [2001] UKHL 17, [2001] 2 All ER 193 (House of Lords, 22 March 2001), point 36.
41 *The Berge Sisar*, point 33.
   See also R. Thomas, "Bills of Lading – The position of holders and intermediate holders under the English Carriage of Goods by Sea Act 1992", *Int.M.L.* 2001, at pp. 169–170.
42 The LOI was issued on 26 November 1992, i.e. about a week before the vessel arrived at La Coruna on 3 December 1992.

was delivered to Repsol without presentation of the bill of lading, Repsol would hold the shipowner harmless from claims by another holder of the bill of lading), and furthermore did not change or abolish the shipowner's obligation to deliver to the holder of the bill of lading. If, for example, Louis Dreyfus would have presented the bill of lading in La Coruna, the shipowner would have been obliged to deliver to Louis Dreyfus, regardless of the Letter of Indemnity issued by Repsol.[43]

The third concept, 'making a claim', is the broadest and least clear of the three. The Law Commissions report refers in this respect to the holder enforcing '*any rights conferred on him under the contract of carriage*'.[44] This would mean that if the holder for example orders a change of destination, he has made a claim under the contract of carriage and has thereby become subject to the liabilities under the contract of carriage. In *The Berge Sisar*, however, Lord Hobhouse advocates a strict construction of the concept of 'making a claim', because of the potentially detrimental consequences of that act for the holder.[45] Also, since making a claim imposes liability, this act should not be such that it remains possible for a later endorsee to exercise the rights under the bill of lading.[46] He proposes to limit the concept to formal claims against the carrier asserting a legal liability of the carrier under the contract of carriage to the holder of the bill of lading.[47] If that is the correct construction, ordering a change of destination would not count as 'making a claim' and thus would not make the holder liable. In *The Ythan*, Aikens J added that a claim can only be made, with the effect of making the holder subject to the liabilities, *after* the holder has become vested with the rights of suit pursuant to s 2.(1).[48] He further held that, although actually arresting a vessel would clearly be 'making a claim',[49] an (even successful) demand for security did not constitute 'making a claim' within the meaning of s 3.(1) COGSA, primarily because, on the facts of the case, the claims adjuster that had requested and negotiated the security had never made it clear on whose behalf exactly it was acting, and the security had ultimately been provided in favour of a group of potential claimants.

4.3.1.3 Intermediate holders

26 Historically, the Bills of Lading Act 1855 did not explicitly address the issue of intermediate holders. It only provided, in general, that the rights under the

---

43 *The Aegean Sea* [1998] CLC at p. 1119.
44 The Law Commission and The Scottish Law Commission, *Rights of suit in respect of carriage of goods by sea*, 19 March 1991 (LAW COM No 196 and SCOT LAW COM No 130), n° 3.15 at p. 32.
45 *The Berge Sisar*, point 33.
46 *The Berge Sisar*, point 41.
47 *The Berge Sisar*, point 33.
48 *Primetrade AG v Ythan Ltd (The Ithan)*, 2005 EWHC 2399 (Comm), [2005] 2 CLC 911 (Queen's Bench Division (Commercial Court), 1 November 2005), point 100.
49 *Primetrade AG v Ythan Ltd (The Ithan)*, 2005 EWHC 2399 (Comm), [2005] 2 CLC 911 (Queen's Bench Division (Commercial Court), 1 November 2005), point 98: "*So, in my view, an arrest plainly constitutes a choice by the holder of the bill of lading to enforce its contractual rights against the carrier and has the character of an election.*"

contract of carriage are transferred to the holder if the property to the carried goods passes to the holder upon or by reason of the transfer of the bill of lading. This provision equally applied when the bill of lading is transferred by a first holder to a subsequent holder, on condition always that the property also passed. As the primary right under a bill of lading (delivery) is an exclusive right, and given the use of the term 'transfer', it stands to reason that when the bill of lading and the rights under it are transferred to a subsequent holder, the rights of the previous holder are extinguished. With regard to liabilities, however, the situation is less clear. The 1855 Act provided that when a bill of lading is endorsed and property to the goods passes as a result of that endorsement, the holder 'shall be subject' to the liabilities contained in the bill of lading. It is, however, unclear what 'being subject' to these liabilities exactly meant. Did it mean that the holder can now be sued for any liability that has already accrued under the bill of lading, even if the holder was not in any way involved in the events that created the liability, or can the holder only be held liable if he is personally in breach of the obligations under the bill of lading? If indeed the holder becomes accountable for pre-existing liabilities, the consequences could be far-reaching. Suppose, for instance, that the shipper had shipped dangerous goods without declaring their nature to the carrier, or had caused demurrage in the port of loading. The resulting liabilities could be very extensive, but do not appear from the bill of lading document itself. Most of the authors were (strongly) opposed to the holder becoming subject to pre-existing liabilities,[50] but the issue has never been decided authoritatively.[51] It was clear, on the other hand, that the liability of the holder came in addition to the liability of the original shipper, which was not extinguished by the transfer of the bill of lading.[52] It was indeed considered unacceptable that, if the shipper had become liable (e.g. with regard to the undeclared

---

50 See J. Bassindale, "Title to sue under bills of lading: the Carriage of Goods by Sea Act 1992", *Journal of International Banking Law* 1992, at p. 416; R. Colinvaux, *Carver's Carriage of Goods by Sea*, London, Stevens & Sons Ltd, 1957 (10th Ed.), at p. 49.
  But see *Alexander M'Gonnell v Craig & Rose* (1879) 6 R. 1269 (Court of Session, 1st Division, 15 July 1879), where a cargo of oil had been shipped in leaky casks. The court held that the fault of the shipper in providing leaky casks was the sole cause of the damage. The shipper would have been liable to the carrier, and thus the consignee, who becomes subject to the same liabilities as the shipper, was also liable to the carrier and could not sue the carrier for the oil lost en route.
51 The Law Commission and The Scottish Law Commission, *Rights of Suit in Respect of Carriage of Goods by Sea*, 19 March 1991 (LAW COM No 196 and SCOT LAW COM No 130), n° 3.2 at p. 29.
  Compare R. De Wit, *Multimodal Transport: Carrier Liability and Documentation*, London, Lloyd's of London Press, 1995, fn. 169 at p. 263; S. Lamont-Black, "Transferee liability under the Rotterdam Rules: a dance between flexibility and foreseeability", *J.I.M.L.* 2013, at pp. 409–411.
52 *Fox v Nott* (1861) 158 ER 260, 6 Hurl.&N. 630 (Court of Exchequer, 25 April 1861): "*The statute creates a new liability, but it does not exonerate the person who has entered into an express contract.*" (at p. 636, per Pollock C.B.). *Effort Shipping Co. Ltd v Linden Management S.A. (The Giannis N.K.)* [1998] A.C. 605, [1998] 2 WLR 206, [1998] CLC 374 (House of Lords, 22 January 1998), at pp. 617–618.

shipping of dangerous goods), he could escape that liability simply by transferring the bill of lading to another party.

There is a further question with regard to liabilities. Once the holder has become subject to the liabilities under the bill of lading, does he then permanently remain liable, even after he has transferred the bill of lading to another party? There was no 'transfer' language with regard to the liabilities in section 1 of the Bills of Lading Act 1855, and liabilities need not be exclusive: plurality of debtors is perfectly possible. It would not be impossible, therefore, to argue that a holder of the bill of lading remains subject to the liabilities, even when he is no longer the holder. The English courts, however, have always been very reluctant to impose liabilities on a holder of the bill of lading, simply on account of his being the holder.[53] In *Sewell v Burdick*, the Earl of Selborne LC pointed out that it is not unreasonable to impose a burden on the holder if he gets a benefit from the bill of lading, but that it would be very unreasonable to impose a burden if the holder had never claimed or obtained such benefit.[54] In the earlier case of *Smurthwaite v Wilkins*, Erle C.J held that construing the Act in such way that it would leave the consignee always liable, although he has parted with all interest and property in the goods, would result in 'monstrous' and manifestly unjust consequences.[55]

27 When the Law Commissions were asked to examine the Bills of Lading Act and to make recommendations for reform, they found it difficult to decide to what extent the holder of a bill of lading should be liable under the bill of lading.[56] In the end, they decided to separate the rights from the liabilities, and COGSA 1992 now has two different regimes. The rights under the bill of lading are transferred to the holder upon his becoming the lawful holder, but COGSA

W. Bennett, *The History and Present Position of the Bill of Lading as a Document of Title to Goods*, Cambridge, University Press, 1914, at p. 62; R. Thomas, "Bills of Lading – the position of holders and intermediate holders under the English Carriage of Goods by Sea Act 1992", *Int.M.L.* 2001, at p. 167.

53 N. Campbell, "Defining the frontiers of the bill of lading holder's liability – the Berge Sisar and the Aegean Sea", *J.B.L.* 200, at p. 201; S. Lamont-Black, "Third party rights and transport documents under the DCFR – potential for an appropriate and effective EU unification and an improvement for the UK?", 21 *J.I.M.L.* 2015, at p. 297.

54 *Sewell v Burdick (The Zoe)* 10 App CasApp Cas 74 (House of Lords, 5 December 1884), at pp. 85–86: "*It is to be observed that the statute contemplates beneficium cum onere and not onus sine beneficio. It may be reasonable if the indorsee has the benefit (. . .) that he should take it with its corresponding burden, quoad the shipowner. But it would be the reverse of reasonable to impose upon him such a burden, when he has neither entered into any contract of which it might be the natural result, nor (having taken a mere security) has obtained any benefit from it.*" At p. 83, the Lord Chancellor had already remarked that it would be strange if the Bills of Lading Act had made a person, who has never acted upon the bill of lading, liable to an action by the shipowner.

55 *Smurthwaite v Wilkins* 142 ER 1026, (1862) 11 CB(ns) 842 (Court of Common Pleas, 11 February 1862), at p. 848.

56 The Law Commission and The Scottish Law Commission, *Rights of Suit in Respect of Carriage of Goods by Sea*, 19 March 1991 (LAW COM No 196 and SCOT LAW COM No 130), n° 3.1–3.14 at p. 29–32.

now also explicitly provides that these rights are extinguished again upon transfer of the bill of lading to a subsequent holder (section2.(5)). An intermediate holder thus has rights against the carrier during the time that he holds the bill of lading, but loses those rights again when he transfers the bill of lading to a subsequent holder. The liabilities, on the other hand, are not automatically transferred to the lawful holder of the bill of lading. The Law Commissions, in line with the decisions under the Bills of Lading Act 1855, considered it (commercially) unacceptable that a party that has merely taken the bill as security would become liable to pay such charges as freight and demurrage.[57] Such liability should only exist if they actually seek to enforce their security.[58] COGSA therefore provides that the liabilities under the bill of lading only attach when the holder takes or demands delivery or makes a claim against the carrier (section3.(1)). Although COGSA thus has made matters clearer than they were under the Bills of Lading Act 1855, two important questions that were unresolved under the Bills of Lading Act still remain unresolved. First, what exactly is 'becoming subject to the same liabilities under the contract of carriage' and does it cover pre-existing liabilities? Second, once liability has attached, is the holder again released from that liability if he transfers the bill of lading to a subsequent holder??

28 As explained above, it was not clear under the Bills of Lading Act 1855 whether 'becoming subject to the liabilities' meant that the holder could be sued for any liability that the original shipper or the previous holders had caused to exist, or whether a personal act or omission of the current holder was required. Suggestions were made to the Law Commissions to distinguish between pre- and post-shipment liabilities, or to include a provision specifically dealing with liability for dangerous goods. These suggestions were not taken up, however, and COGSA 1992 does not explicitly address the issue. From the Law Commissions' Report, however, it is clear that they did not consider it unacceptable for a subsequent holder to be sued on account of liabilities previously incurred by the original shipper or by a previous holder, such as demurrage caused in the load port by strikes, congested ports, etc. or liability in respect of the shipment of dangerous goods.[59] On the other hand, COGSA does explicitly confirm, as had

---

57 The Law Commission and The Scottish Law Commission, *Rights of Suit in Respect of Carriage of Goods by Sea*, 19 March 1991 (LAW COM No 196 and SCOT LAW COM No 130), n° 2.17 at pp. 13.

58 The Law Commission and The Scottish Law Commission, *Rights of Suit in Respect of Carriage of Goods by Sea*, 19 March 1991 (LAW COM No 196 and SCOT LAW COM No 130), n° 2.31 at p. 18.

59 The Law Commission and The Scottish Law Commission, *Rights of Suit in Respect of Carriage of Goods by Sea*, 19 March 1991 (LAW COM No 196 and SCOT LAW COM No 130), No. 3.21 at p. 33: "*For instance, demurrage can accrue by reason of delays caused by strikes, congested ports, bad weather, etc. It seems odd to say that fairness dictates that the holder should be liable for demurrage when these matters occur at the port of discharge but not at the port of loading.*", and No. 3.22 at p. 33: "*We do not think that liability in respect of dangerous goods is necessarily more unfair than liability in respect of a range of other matters over which the holder of the bill of lading has no control and for which he is not responsible, as for instance liability for loadport demurrage and dead freight.*"

been decided under the Bills of Lading Act 1855, that the liability of the holder does not extinguish the liability of the original shipper (section 3.(3)).[60]

29 With regard to the release from liability upon a subsequent transfer, COGSA 1992 explicitly provides that the rights of the holder are extinguished if he transfers the bill of lading to a subsequent holder (section 2.5), but there is no similar provision as regards liabilities.[61] In *The Aegean Sea*, Thomas J did not find it necessary to reach a conclusion on this issue, but did say that in his preliminary view, the liabilities, once imposed by section 3, remain with that holder.[62] In *The Berge Sisar*, however, Lord Hobhouse held that, save for particular circumstances, a party that no longer holds the rights under the bill of lading should no longer be subject to the liabilities either. First, he pointed out, that decision is in line with the decision in *Smurthwaite v Wilkins*,[63] which was explicitly referred to in the Law Commissions' Report and approved rather than criticized. Furthermore, COGSA is based on a principle of mutuality: benefits and burdens are tied in with each other.[64] If a party elects to claim the benefits of a bill of lading, it must also accept the burdens, but if that party can no longer obtain benefits from the bill of lading, it should not suffer the burdens either.[65]

See also *Borealis AB v Stargas Ltd and others and Bergesen D.Y. A/S (The Berge Sisar)* [2001] UKHL 17, [2001] 2 All ER 193 (House of Lords, 22 March 2001). Lord Hobhouse advocates a strict interpretation of the concept of 'making a claim', because of the consequences of that action, i.e. the imposition of liabilities. He then continues: "*The liabilities, particularly when alleged dangerous goods are involved, may be disproportionate to the value of the goods; the liabilities may not be covered by insurance; the endorsee may not be fully aware of what the liabilities are.*" It is quite clear, therefore, that to him, the 'liabilities' include pre-existing liabilities.

See also J. Bassindale, "Title to sue under bills of lading: the Carriage of Goods by Sea Act 1992", *Journal of International Banking Law* 1992, at p. 416; N. Campbell, "Defining the frontiers of the bill of lading holder's liability – the Berge Sisar and the Aegean Sea", *J.B.L.* 200, at p. 202; R. Thomas, "A comparative analysis of the transfer of contractual rights under the English Carriage of Goods by Sea Act 1992 and the Rotterdam Rules", *J.I.M.L.* 2011, at p. 444.

60 The same is true under Article 58.2 of the Rotterdam Rules. See S. Lamont-Black, "Transferee liability under the Rotterdam Rules: a dance between flexibility and foreseeability", *J.I.M.L.* 2013, at pp. 416–417.
61 Compare L. Li, "The legal status of intermediate holders of bills of lading under contracts of carriage by sea – a comparative study of US and English law", *J.I.M.L.* 2011, at p. 116.
62 *Aegean Sea Traders Corp. v Repsol Petroleo SA & Anor (The Aegean Sea)* [1998] CLC 1090, [1998] 2 Lloyd's Rep 39 (Queen's Bench Division (Admiralty Court), 7 April 1998), at p. 1121.
63 *Smurthwaite v Wilkins* 142 ER 1026, (1862) 11 CB(ns) 842 (Court of Common Pleas, 11 February 1862).
64 Compare S. Lamont-Black, "Transferee liability under the Rotterdam Rules: a dance between flexibility and foreseeability", *J.I.M.L.* 2013, at p. 394; R. Thomas, "Bills of Lading – The position of holders and intermediate holders under the English Carriage of Goods by Sea Act 1992", *Int.M.L.* 2001, at p. 170.
65 A similar principle has been codified in Article 58.1 and 58.2 of the Rotterdam Rules. Article 58.1 provides that "*a holder that is not the shipper and that does not exercise any right under the contract of carriage does not assume any liability under the contract of carriage solely by reason*

170 Non-contractual theories

The consequence, however, is that if an intermediate holder causes liability – e.g. by giving instructions to the carrier regarding the goods, that result in damage to the goods or extra costs for the carrier – and then transfers the bill of lading to a new holder, the party that is actually to blame will *not* be liable, since by transferring the bill of lading he has been released of the liabilities under it,[66] but the subsequent holder *will* be, since the liabilities under COGSA most likely include pre-existing liabilities. Lord Hobhouse in *The Berge Sisar* stressed the importance of the actual facts of the case, though, so it is possible that in such a case the intermediate holder would remain liable for the consequences of his own actions, even after he has transferred the bill of lading to a subsequent holder. It seems likely, however, that the subsequent holder will also be liable, even if his predecessor remains liable. At any rate, the absence of case law would seem to indicate that such scenarios are very rare in practice, although not entirely impossible.

Another consequence is that liability caused by an intermediate holder could become unenforceable. Suppose, in the example above, that the subsequent holder never takes or demands delivery, e.g. because he has learned that the goods are not of contractual quality. The holder which by his instructions has caused the damage or costs cannot be sued since he has transferred the bill of lading, and the subsequent holder cannot be sued either because he never takes the action that under section 3.(1) is required to become subject to the liabilities.[67] Again, it is possible that if a situation like that ever arose, an exception to the *Berge Sisar* principle would be accepted based on the specific facts of the case.

4.3.1.4 *The non-contracting shipper*

30 The Bills of Lading Act 1855 could not accommodate the non-contracting shipper. The latter may be named in the bill of lading and the bill of lading may be handed over to him by the carrier, but the property in the goods does not pass to him upon or by reason of the consignment or endorsement. Even when the non-contracting shipper was holding the bill of lading, therefore, he did not have rights or liabilities under it.

31 In this respect, COGSA 1992 has not improved matters. The lawful holder of the bill of lading has the rights transferred to him by virtue of becoming the holder, but the definition of 'holder' in section 5.(2) generally does not allow

---

of being a holder". If the holder does exercise a right, however, he assumes any liabilities that are incorporated in or ascertainable from the negotiable transport document (Article 58.2). See on these provisions S. Lamont-Black, "Transferee liability under the Rotterdam Rules: a dance between flexibility and foreseeability", *J.I.M.L.* 2013, at pp. 397–418; R. Thomas, "A comparative analysis of the transfer of contractual rights under the English Carriage of Goods by Sea Act 1992 and the Rotterdam Rules", *J.I.M.L.* 2011, at pp. 446–450.

66 If the concept of 'making a claim' is interpreted strictly, giving instructions to the carrier might not even qualify to make the holder liable at all under Sect. 3.(1) COGSA.

67 N. Campbell, "Defining the frontiers of the bill of lading holder's liability – the *Berge Sisar* and the *Aegean Sea*", *J.B.L.* 2000, at p. 199.

the non-contracting shipper to become the holder (in the legal sense) of the bill of lading. The 'holder' is indeed, under a straight bill of lading, the named consignee and under an order bill of lading the person to whom the bill has been endorsed. A non-contracting shipper will not be the named consignee, and will not have the bill of lading endorsed to it either. Only if the bill of lading is to bearer and if the release of the bill by the carrier to the non-contracting shipper is considered a 'transfer' of the bill within the meaning of section 5 COGSA could the non-contracting shipper become the legal holder, and thus entitled to enforce the rights under the bill of lading.

4.3.1.5 Appraisal

32 The Bills of Lading Act 1855 clearly assumed that a bill of lading contains a contract,[68] and is generally taken to operate a 'statutory assignment' of that contract to the holder.[69] The holder is put in a position *as if* he had made the bill of lading contract with the carrier. Similarly, under COGSA 1992 the lawful holder has vested in him the rights of suit under the contract of carriage as if he had been a party to that contract. It is quite clear that English authors, at least implicitly, assume that the rights that these Acts create for the holder are *contractual* rights.[70] Nevertheless, the Bills of Lading Act 1855 and the subsequent COGSA 1992 are here discussed in the section on *non*-contractual approaches, since the position that the holder acquires pursuant to these Acts is not a truly contractual position. It is, indeed, precisely because the holder could not acquire a contractual position (under the English law as it then was) that an Act of Parliament was

---

68 See, for example, *Leduc v Ward* 20 QBD 475 (Court of Appeal, 13 February 1888), at p. 483: "*Here is a plain declaration of the legislature that there is a contract contained in the bill of lading . . .*" (per Fry LJ).

69 S. Baughen, *Shipping Law*, London, Routledge-Cavendish, 2009 (4th Ed.), at p. 40; The Law Commission and The Scottish Law Commission, *Rights of Suit in Respect of Carriage of Goods by Sea*, 19 March 1991 (LAW COM No 196 and SCOT LAW COM No 130), n° 2.34.(iv) at p. 19; R. Thomas, "A comparative analysis of the transfer of contractual rights under the English Carriage of Goods by Sea Act 1992 and the Rotterdam Rules", *J.I.M.L.* 2011, at p. 438 and p. 439.

See also *Effort Shipping Co. Ltd v Linden Management S.A. (The Giannis N.K.)* [1998] A.C. 605, [1998] 2 WLR 206, [1998] CLC 374 (House of Lords, 22 January 1998), at p. 616; *East West Corporation v DKBS AF 1912 A/S* [2003] EWCA Civ 83, [2003] QB 1509, [2003] 3 WLR 916 (Court of Appeal, 12 February 2003), at para 45 and 47.

Occasionally, the effect of the 1855 Act has also been described as a 'statutory novation'. See M. Bridge, L. Gullifer, G. McMeel and S. Worthington, *The Law of Personal Property*, London, Sweet & Maxwell, 2013, n° 30-019 at p. 823.

70 See, for example, R. Thomas, "Bills of Lading – the position of holders and intermediate holders under the English Carriage of Goods by Sea Act 1992", *Int.M.L.* 2001, at p. 166.

See also M. Bools, *The Bill of Lading. A Document of Title to Goods. An Anglo-American Comparison*, London, LLP, 1997, at p. 89, who explicitly refers to a *statutory* right of action and a *statutory* cause of action created by the Bills of Lading Act, but nevertheless considers the bill of lading a *contract* between the carrier and the holder.

deemed necessary.[71] Also, a bill of lading is not necessarily a contract. A bill of lading issued pursuant to a charter party is, between the owner and the charterer, a mere receipt and not a contract. In such cases, there simply is no contract that could be assigned by statute. Even where the bill of lading is indeed a contract between the carrier and the shipper, that contract is not assigned by the parties' intention or agreement, but by the Act. Furthermore, it is not the actual contract between the parties that is assigned, but only the contract as incorporated in the bill of lading document.[72] Undeniably, the Bills of Lading Act 1855 and COGSA create a legal relationship between the carrier and the holder, defined (and limited) by a document that may or may not be a contract between other parties, but such relationship is, it is submitted, statutory rather than contractual. A 'contract' created by law, and imposed by law on the parties, is indeed not a contract in the true sense of the term.[73]

33 The Bills of Lading Act and COGSA have the merit of explicitly addressing (and at least partially solving) the legal position of the holder of the bill of lading. Also, the options taken by the Law Commissions – the acquisition of rights on becoming the lawful holder of the bill of lading, without ownership requirements, the separation of rights and liabilities, the imposition of liability only when the holder takes action on the bill of lading – are sensible and in line with the requirements and sentiments of bill of lading practice.

It is probably not surprising that in 1855, when the Bills of Lading Act was enacted, the rights and obligations of the holder were put in a contractual key. In those days, the legislature was hardly in the habit of creating statutory rights of

---

71 See also F. Reynolds, "The Carriage of Goods by Sea Act 1992 put to the test. The Berge Sisar", *LMCLQ* 1999, at p. 161, who writes that COGSA creates something like a 'statutory contract', "*. . . freed, because of its statutory provenance, of difficulties of consideration which could affect the use of the common law device, and of other problems such as that of contractual intent.*" If, however, a 'contract' has to be created by statute in order to satisfy (or avoid) basic contractual requirements, is that still a contract in the real sense of the word?
72 See above, n° 21 p. 159.
73 Compare G. Treitel, *The Law of Contract*, London, Sweet & Maxwell, 1991 (8th Ed.), at p. 3 and p. 5.
   Compare A. Higgs and G. Humphreys, "An overview of the implications of the Carriage of Goods by Sea Act 1992", *J.B.L.* 1993, at p. 62, who write that the cargo receiver is given "*. . . a general statutory right of action*".
   See also *Primetrade AG v Ythan Ltd (The Ithan)*, 2005 EWHC 2399 (Comm), [2005] 2 CLC 911 (Queen's Bench Division (Commercial Court), 1 November 2005), point 8: "*Primetrade would not actually become a party to the contracts of carriage with the Owners, contained in or evidenced by the bills of lading. But,* [if the COGSA requirements are met], *then both parties would be relying on the bill of lading contracts 'as if they had been a party' to those contracts.*"
   See also the US Federal Bill of Lading Act 1994 (49 USC §§80101–80116), which has a comparable provision, but without the explicit reference to a contract or a contractual relationship. § 80105.(a).(2) provides that when a bill of lading is negotiated, "*. . . the common carrier issuing the bill becomes obligated directly to the person to whom the bill is negotiated to hold possession of the goods under the terms of the bill the same as if the carrier had issued the bill to that person.*"

suit for specific groups of people. Even in those early days, however, the contractual logic of the Bills of Lading Act was not entirely consistent. A bill of lading issued under a charter party was generally accepted to be a mere receipt, and not a contract, between the shipper and the carrier, but if that bill of lading was endorsed to a third-party holder, the Act was deemed to create a 'contract', on the terms of the bill of lading, between the carrier and the third-party holder.[74] Furthermore, such 'receipt-become-contract' allowed the holder to sue for breaches of contract that occurred when the bill of lading was not a contract yet.[75] COGSA has moved away from the 'contract contained in the bill of lading' and now uses more general 'contract of carriage' terminology, but the rights and obligations of the holder are still determined, and exclusively determined, by what appears from the bill of lading document itself. The holder does not become a party to the underlying contract of carriage, as it was actually made by the shipper and the carrier. It would have been perfectly possible, therefore, to remove the references in COGSA to the contract of carriage or the contractual character of the bill of lading as between the shipper and the carrier, and still arrive at the same end result as regards the holder of the bill of lading: a person who becomes the lawful holder of a bill of lading shall, by virtue of becoming the holder, have transferred to and vested in him all rights of suit under the bill of lading, and shall, when

---

74 Compare M. Davies and A. Dickey, *Shipping Law*, Lawbook Co., 2004 (3th Ed.), at p. 254, who considers this result '*conceptually inelegant and only questionably justified by the words of the legislation*'. See also S. Peel, "The development of the bill of lading: its future in the maritime industry", 2002, thesis submitted to the University of Plymouth, Institute of Marine Studies, at p. 171, who terms this result "... *surprising in view of the consensual nature of contract*".

75 S. Peel, "The development of the bill of lading: its future in the maritime industry", 2002, thesis submitted to the University of Plymouth, Institute of Marine Studies, at pp. 171–172, who refers to *Monarch Steamship Co., Ltd v Karlshamns Oljefabriker (A/B)* [1949] A.C. 196 (House of Lords, 9 December 1948). In that case, a vessel carrying soy beans to Sweden was delayed because of unseaworthiness (the vessel's boilers were in bad condition, which only allowed the vessel to sail at a speed of about 5 knots rather than the normal 9.5 knots, and made it necessary for the vessel to stop three times en route for repairs). During that delay, the Second World War broke out and the vessel was prohibited by the British Admiralty to proceed. The cargo was discharged in Glasgow and had to be transshipped to a neutral vessel. The holder of the bill of lading, who only became holder after the discharge in Glasgow, later sued the carrier in reimbursement of the extra costs of the transshipment. The debate mainly turned on whether the unseaworthiness or the Admiralty's Order was the effective cause of the loss, and on whether the war and the prohibition to proceed were foreseeable when the charter party was made. The shipowner, however, also argued that once the vessel had been ordered to discharge at Glasgow, the voyage terminated there and the charterer (which at that time still held the bills of lading) could not have sued for damages. Since the charterer could not sue, the argument went, he could not transfer this non-existent right to a third-party holder, or create such right by endorsing the bill of lading. To this, Lord Porter said that although the endorser of a bill of lading cannot give his endorsee more rights than he himself possesses, he was prepared to some extent to accept that under the Bills of Lading Act 1855, the holder is put in a position as if the contract contained in the bill of lading had been made with himself *at the time of shipment*, rather than at the time of endorsement of the bill of lading (at p. 218).

he takes or demands delivery or makes a claim under the bill of lading, become subject to the liabilities under the bill of lading. Such provisions would essentially put the holder in the same position he has today, based on the bill of lading itself and the substantive carriage laws (Hague-Visby Rules, COGSA 1971, etc.). The Rotterdam Rules, which also explicitly deal with the transfer of rights, simply refer to the rights incorporated in the negotiable transport document, without explicitly characterizing these rights as contractual in nature.[76]

34 A point of criticism with regard to COGSA 1992 is the issue of pre-existing liabilities, i.e. liabilities that arose before the current holder of the bill of lading became holder. Can the holder be held liable for, for example, the fact that the shipper did not properly declare dangerous cargo?? Admittedly, this does not seem to be an issue often in practice, but the potential consequences for the holder are important enough to merit attention. The Law Commissions in their report did discuss the problem, but elected not to include rules in this regard in the Act. It would not be impossible, however, to lay down rules in this respect. There is, first of all, a difference between assuming an obligation to pay money and becoming subject to liabilities. It is one thing to accept a bill of lading that explicitly states freight, demurrage, etc. to be payable at destination. The (prospective) holder knows that he will have to pay before he can collect the goods, he can check with the carrier or with his seller what those amounts will (approximately) be, and he can have protective clauses in the sales contract in case the costs turn out higher than anticipated. It is something else entirely if the holder, by accepting the bill of lading, now finds himself subject to very extensive liabilities, based on acts or omissions of the shipper or of a previous holder of which he knew nothing and could not have prevented or influenced. If such liabilities are to be imposed on the holder, it would certainly be preferable to have this clearly and explicitly stated in the Act,[77] and to have the policy reasons for such imposition made clear.

35 Finally, there is a gap in the Bills of Lading Act 1855 and COGSA 1992 as regards the non-contracting shipper, who will generally not be the 'holder' (in the legal sense) of the bill of lading and thus not entitled to act upon it. That does not necessarily mean that the non-contracting shipper is entirely without recourse against the carrier (he may be able to sue the carrier in bailment or in tort), but a position within COGSA would be preferable. It would make the statutory regime more comprehensive, and it would avoid the carrier being held liable in other ways than under the bill of lading and the carriage laws.

---

76 See Article 57.(1) of the Rotterdam Rules.
77 By way of comparison, Article 8:488 of the Dutch Civil Code provides that if the carrier has to take measures with regard to the cargo during the voyage, the shipper, the consignee and the holder of the bill of lading are jointly and severally liable to reimburse to the carrier the costs of those measures. Article 267 of the Norwegian Maritime Code has a similar provision.

4.3.3 Implicit position

4.3.3.1 Belgium: Art. 91 of the Maritime Act

36 The Belgian courts and authors have traditionally remained (very) vague as to the exact position of the third-party holder of the bill of lading and the basis in law for that position. There is no doubt that the holder of the bill of lading has rights against the carrier (primarily the right to demand delivery and the right to claim damages) and may be obliged to the carrier, and there is quasi unanimity that a third-party holder does not succeed to the rights and obligations of the shipper, but how the holder acquires those rights and to what extent he is bound to the carrier is not often explicitly dealt with. To some, the holder accedes to the contract of carriage as expressed in the bill of lading,[78] but that is not the dominant view and probably not even a majority view. As an alternative, there is a quite strong (though very implicit) view that the position of the holder is, in fact, a statutory position.[79] The bill of lading serves to identify the holder as the person entitled to exercise the rights under the bill of lading (and the debtor of possible obligations under the bill of lading),[80] and to describe the nature and condition of the carried goods, the voyage, etc., but the actual rights and obligations of the

---

78 See above, n° 154.
79 This view is already presented in Smeesters & Winkelmolen, one of the seminal works on Belgian maritime law. The authors write: "*Le connaissement constate principalement à charge du capitaine, au profit du titulaire, une obligation de donner, dont l'objet est déterminé par l'ensemble des clauses et mentions descriptives de la chose embarquée. Cette règle découle nécessairement du principe posé à l'article 89. Cet article confère au porteur du connaissement, et à lui seul, le droit de se faire délivrer la cargaison. Il puise donc son droit dans la loi elle-même, et n'a pas à se préoccuper des relations ni des contestations qui peuvent exister entre le chargeur et le capitaine. La situation juridique créée par l'article 89 de la loi est analogue à celle qui est faite, en matière de lettre de change, au tiers porteur de la traite. Il résulte également de l'article 26 de la loi du 20 mai 1872 que le tiré ne peut opposer au cessionnaire les exceptions qui lui compétaient contre le tireur.*" (The bill of lading primarily attests, as a burden for the Master to the benefit of the holder, an obligation to give, the object of which is determined by the combination of clauses and descriptions of the goods loaded. This rule necessarily follows from the principle laid down in article 89. This article provides the holder of the bill of lading, and him alone, with the right to have the goods delivered to him. He therefore obtains his right from the statute itself, and doesn't have to occupy himself with the relations or disputes that might exist between the shipper and the Master. The legal situation created by article 89 of the statute is similar to that of the third party holder of a bill of exchange. Article 26 of the statute of 20 May 1872 equally provides that the drawee cannot invoke against the acquirer the defences he had against the drawer.) (C. Smeesters and G. Winkelmolen, *Droit maritime et Droit fluvial*, Vol. I, Brussels, Larcier, 1929 (2nd Ed.), n° 443 at p. 598).
See also I. De Weerdt, *Het verhandelbaar cognossement*, Antwerpen, ETL, 1991, n° 136 at p. 106.
80 See CA Antwerp 10 October 1990, 115 *R.H.A.* 1993, at p. 118: "*dat in het cognossement appellante niet alleen eigen rechten put, zoals deze voortvloeien uit artikel 89 van de Zeewet, doch ook eigen verplichtingen*" (that the appellant not only obtains proper rights from the bill of lading, as they derive from Article 89 of the Maritime Act, but also proper obligations).

176 *Non-contractual theories*

holder are primarily determined by Article 91 of the Belgian Maritime Act, which is the word-for-word incorporation in Belgian law of the Hague-Visby Rules.[81] The actual terms of the bill of lading are largely or even entirely disregarded, unless perhaps they fit squarely within the Hague-Visby scheme (such as a 'Before and After' clause, which is explicitly allowed by Art. 7 of the Hague-Visby Rules). A third-party holder of the bill of lading is said to have its own set of rights and obligations, which it derives directly 'from the bill of lading', i.e. from the possession of that document of title that provides its holder with constructive possession of the carried goods.

4.3.3.2 Germany – The Netherlands

37 German maritime law and the German Commercial Code (HGB) know the concept of the '*Ablader*', i.e. the party that hands over the goods to be carried to the sea carrier. The *Ablader* might be the shipper, but may also be a *non-*contracting shipper. In all cases, however, § 513.(1) of the German Commercial Code explicitly recognizes the *Ablader*'s right to obtain the bill of lading from the carrier. If the *Ablader* is the shipper, that right is easily explained as deriving from the contract of carriage, but that way is not open if the *Ablader* is a non-contracting shipper. Most often, a special contract – the '*Begebungsvertrag*', or 'contract to issue' (the bill of lading) – is implied between the carrier and the non-contracting *Ablader*, so that these parties are put into a contractual relation after all, but occasionally, a statutory position is hinted at.[82]

---

81 P. Verguts en O. Gossieaux, "Deklading: vrijbrief of guillotine?", *E.T.L.* 1998, n° 8 at p. 198: "... *omdat de verhouding derde cognossementshouder – zeevervoerder enkel door de bepalingen van artikel 91 ZW wordt beheerst*" (... because the relation third-party holder of the bill of lading – carier is governed solely by the provisions of Article 91 of the Maritime Act).
  See CA Antwerp, 26 February 1986, 216 *E.T.L.* 1986, at p. 218: "*Overwegende dat tweede geïntimeerde (...) als derde-houder (...) houder is van een zelfstandige titel, die zij van de inlader verkregen heeft en die recht geeft op de aflevering van de in het cognossement omschreven goederen onder de voorwaarden en bescherming van de Haagse Regels zoals bepaald in het Brussels Zeevaartverdrag van 25 augustus 1924, gewijzigd bij protocol van 23 februari 1968; dat tweede geïntimeerde aldus drager is van een titel met autonome rechten en verplichtingen voor de houder, onafhankelijk van de overeenkomst van zeevervoer die door de inlader afgesloten werd*" (Considering that the second defendant (...) as third-party holder (...) is the holder of an autonomous title, which it received from the shipper and which entitles it to delivery of the goods described in the bill of lading under the conditions and protection of the Hague Rules as provided in the Brussels Maritime Convention of 25 August 1924, as modified by the protocol of 23 February 1968; that the second defendant thus holds a title with autonomous rights and obligations for the holder, independent of the contract of sea carriage made by the shipper). An almost identical paragraph can be found in CA Antwerp, 9 April 1986, *E.T.L.* 1986, (397), at p. 400, CA Antwerp 16 April 1986, *R.H.A.* 1986, (133), at p. 138, and in CA Antwerp, 16 September 1987, *E.T.L.* 1987, (695), at p. 698.
82 BGH 10 October 1957, *BGHZ* 25, 300, *NJW* 1957, 1917 (Case II ZR 278/56): the carrier's claim in payment of freight is "... *einen durch die Annahme des Gutes entstehenden gesetzlichen Anspruch*" (a statutory claim that comes into being by taking delivery of the goods), independently of the contract of carriage and even if there was no valid contract of carriage.

38 In the Netherlands, the majority position is that the holder, as third-party beneficiary, accedes to and becomes a party to the contract of carriage. As in Germany, however, there are, on occasion, echoes of a more statutory position. In *Damco/Meister*, for example, bills of lading had been issued for containers that had never actually been shipped. The holder of the bills of lading, who had in good faith relied on them, sued the carrier. The Dutch Supreme Court confirmed the lower courts' decision that held the carrier liable, as such result is in line with the statutory system that protects third-party holders in good faith, such protection being required by equity and commerce.[83]

4.3.3.3 The position of the holder as an 'institution'

39 A legal 'institution' is a situation, a specific combination of facts or circumstances, that is governed by a rule or set of rules that is generally known and commonly observed by the relevant public.[84] Institutions are, for example, contract, ownership, testation, marriage, etc.[85] Over time, of course, some or most of the (practical) aspects of the institution may become detailed in specific rules of law, but the institution as such both predates and is larger than those specific rules. To some Belgian and French authors, the position of the third-party holder of a bill of lading is an 'institution' in this sense. By acquiring a bill of lading, the holder

---

See also H.-J. Puttfarken, *Seehandelsrecht*, Heidelberg, Verlag Recht und Wirtschaft, 1997, n° 106 at p. 39.

83 HR 4 April 2003, *RvdW* 2003, 71, *S&S* 2003, 122, *NJ* 2003, 592 (Damco Maritime International / Meister Werkzeuge Werkzeugfabrik), point 3.5: "*dat het toerekenen van de (gevolgen van de) gepleegde fraude aan Damco past in het wettelijk systeem (zie met name de art. 8: 414 lid 1, 441 lid 2, 461 en 462 lid 1, tweede volzin) dat aan de bescherming van derden die te goeder trouw rechten ten aanzien van een cognossement hebben verworven, uit een oogpunt van billijkheid en met het oog op de eisen van het handelsverkeer een aanzienlijk gewicht toekent*" (that holding Damco liable for the (consequences of the) fraud is consistent with the statutory system (see in particular Article 8:414 par. 1, 441 par. 2, 461 and 462 par. 1, second sentence) that places considerable importance in the protection of third parties that in good faith have acquired rights with regard to the bill of lading, for reasons of equity and because of the demands of commerce).

84 R. Roland, "La clause de juridiction du connaissement en droit belge", in X, *Liber Amicorum Lionel Tricot*, Antwerpen, Kluwer, 1988, at p. 450: "*On reconnait la présence d'une institution chaque fois qu'une règle s'impose à des tiers par le fait de leur adhésion à une pratique ou de leur entrée dans une sphère déterminée, sans que l'obligation qui en découle résulte pour eux d'une convention*" (One recognizes the presence of an institution when third parties become bound by a rule because of their adherence to a practice or because of their entering a specific sphere, without their obligation being based on a contract).

See also H.-J. Puttfarken, *Seehandelsrecht*, Heidelberg, Verlag Recht und Wirtschaft, 1997, n° 985 at p. 408: "*Das Seehandelsrecht kristallisiert sich seit jeher in Institutionen: quellen- und länderübergreifenden Regelungskomplexen*" (Maritime law, since always, has cristallized in 'institutions': complexes of rules that transcend sources and countries.) The author concludes by qualifying maritime law as '*Institutionenrecht*', a law of institutions (n° 993-995 at pp. 412-413).

85 N. MacCormick and O. Weinberger, *An Institutional Theory of Law: New Approaches to Legal Positivism*, Dordrecht, D. Reidel Publishing Company, 1986, at p. 51.

'accedes' to this institution, rather than to the contract of carriage between the shipper and the carrier.[86]

4.3.3.4 When does the relationship come into being?

40 Under the Belgian statutory approach, the position of the third-party holder is tied to his being the (lawful) holder of the bill of lading. The question has apparently never been answered explicitly, but the logical consequence would be that the relationship between the carrier and the holder comes into being the moment the holder acquires the bill of lading, even if at that time the carrier is unaware of this acquisition and of the identity of the holder.[87]

41 If the holder is seen as acceding to an institution, the logical consequence is that the relationship comes into being at the time of that accession, or at the time that accession becomes publicly apparent, e.g. by interaction of the holder with the carrier.[88]

4.3.3.5 Intermediate holders

42 If the position of the holder depends on his holdership of the bill of lading, a previous holder who since has transferred the bill of lading to a subsequent holder no longer has a legal position as regards the bill of lading or the carrier. In principle, therefore, an intermediate holdership of the bill of lading would not leave residual liabilities. That could be different if the intermediate holder had actively interacted with the carrier during his holdership.

43 If the position of the holder of a bill of lading is seen as an institution that has to be acceded to, then it is possible, depending on the form such accession is required to take, that intermediate holders do not accede to the institution, and thus do not have a legal position as against the carrier. If intermediate holders

---

86 P. Bonassies, *Cass. com. 29 November 1994 (Navires Harmony et Nagasaki)*, 209 D.M.F. 1995 (note), at p. 217: "*En adhérant au contrat de transport, le destinataire entend d'abord adhérer au "statut" de destinataire*" (By acceding to the contract of carriage, the consignee primarily intends to accede to the "capacity" of consignee); R. Roland, "La clause de juridiction du connaissement en droit belge", in X, *Liber Amicorum Lionel Tricot*, Antwerpen, Kluwer, 1988, at p. 450. See also R. De Wit, *Multimodal Transport. Carrier Liability and Documentation*, London, Lloyd's of London Press, 1995, n° 5.42 at p. 274; J. Van Ryn and J. Heenen, *Principes de Droit Commercial*, Vol. IV, Brussels, Bruylant, 1988 (2nd Ed.), n° 765 at p. 629.
87 In that sense: L. Delwaide, *CA Antwerp 10 October 1990*, R.H.A. 1993, 121 (note), at p. 122.
  Contra: L. Delwaide and J. Blockx, "Kroniek van het zeerecht. Overzicht van rechtsleer en rechtspraak 1976–1988", Part 2, *T.B.H.* 1990, at p. 591. The authors state that the holder's rights do not come into being when the bill of lading is handed over to him, but only when he presents the bill of lading to the carrier.
88 Compare J. Van Ryn and J. Heenen, *Principes de Droit Commercial*, Vol. IV, Brussels, Bruylant, 1988 (2nd Ed.), n° 765 at p. 629.

4.3.3.6 The non-contracting shipper

44 It does not happen very often in practice that a non-contracting shipper must exercise the rights under the bill of lading. In any case, there is no reported case law on this issue in Belgium. There is no fundamental objection, however, to seeing the non-contracting shipper, as long as he physically possesses the bill of lading, as the lawful holder.

45 If the bill of lading and the position of the holder is seen as an institution, it is somewhat more difficult to accommodate the non-contracting shipper. The party exercising rights under the bill of lading is most often the consignee. The non-contracting shipper is clearly the exception and thus not immediately considered when the institution is analysed or described. Nevertheless, there is, as with the implicit approach, no fundamental objection to expanding the institution to also include the non-contracting shipper in possession of the bill of lading.

4.3.3.7 Appraisal

46 An implicit approach is, of course, never an optimal solution. By definition, some aspects of the problem are left un- or underanalysed, the solutions proposed are not fully detailed or motivated, and the predictive power of such approach is weak. Also, the institution concept cannot be a full answer. It might explain (to a certain extent) what the position of the holder is once that institution has come into being, but it does not explain *how*, by which mechanism, that institution comes into being in the first place. On the other hand, both the Belgian statutory approach and the institution approach at least show that a contractual analysis is not the only possible one and that a statutory approach to the position of the holder is feasible.

4.4 The bill of lading as a negotiable instrument

(*titre négociable, Wertpapier, waardepapier*)

4.4.1 The concept

47 A negotiable instrument is a document that incorporates a claim, in such way that the claim can be transferred by transferring the document and that possession of the document is required to enforce the claim.

48 Negotiable instruments are, like bills of lading themselves, the product of commercial needs and the customs of merchants in reaction to those needs. Negotiable instruments probably originated in the Middle Ages, in the form of

180 *Non-contractual theories*

promissory notes,[89] bills of exchange and similar. The bill of exchange, often regarded as the archetypical negotiable instrument, was an instrument devised by merchants to avoid the cumbersome (and dangerous) process of transporting physical money from one place to another. Suppose, for example, that merchant A of Venice had bought goods from the travelling merchant B of Paris. Rather than pay B in Venetian coins, which B would then have to carry with him and exchange them at some place for Parisian money, A could draw a bill of exchange on a money exchanger in Paris,[90] instructing him to pay the sales price, in local Parisian currency, to merchant B. The latter could then travel back to Paris, only carrying the bill of exchange, issued to him (or possibly his order), and obtain the actual money in Paris in his own currency. Bills of exchange may at some point also have been used to circumvent the prohibition against charging interest,[91] although such use was considered unlawful even at the time. In those days, given the limited means of communication, the document itself served to describe and define both the contents and the beneficiary of the obligation. Initially, the beneficiary of the obligation was a specific person; later, through the development of order and bearer clauses, it became accepted (and easy) to change the beneficiary. In that way, bills of exchange and similar instruments also provided a solution for the impossibility under early common law to assign claims or contracts to another party. An intangible could not be assigned, but if that intangible was incorporated into a physical object (a piece of paper), that physical object could then be sold as any other object, thus transferring the incorporated claim to the buyer of the object.[92]

49 Since those early beginnings, negotiable instruments have become firmly established as a legal concept, even if the exact boundaries of the concept and the rules that apply to it are, to this very day, not entirely settled.[93] An essential feature of a negotiable instrument is that it is a document that incorporates a

---

89 A promissory note is a written undertaking to pay a certain sum of money to another person.
90 If A had a direct relation with that money exchanger. Alternatively, A could go to a local money exchanger in Venice, who had a correspondent in Paris. See E. McKendrick (Ed.), *Goode on Commercial Law*, London, Penguin Books, 2016 (5th Ed.), n° 18.12 at p. 520.
91 W. Holdsworth, "Origins & Early History of Negotiable Instruments", 31 *L.Q.Rev*. 1915, at pp. 25-26; M. Spanjaart, *Vorderingsrechten uit cognossement*, Zutphen, Uitgeverij Paris, 2012, at p. 182.
92 W. Holdsworth, "Origins & Early History of Negotiable Instruments", 31 *L.Q.Rev*. 1915, at pp. 13-14.
93 Many legal systems do not have a general legal or statutory framework on negotiable instruments, but only specific rules dealing with certain types of negotiable instruments. Swiss law is one of the exceptions to this rule, in that it has a general definition in Article 965 of its Code of Obligations: "*Sont papiers-valeurs tous les titres auxquels un droit est incorporé d'une manière telle qu'il soit impossible de le faire valoir ou de le transférer indépendamment du titre.*" (Negotiable instruments are all titles in which a right is incorporated in such way that it is impossible to exercise or to transfer the right independently of the title.)
   Compare K.-H. Gursky, *Wertpapierrecht*, Heidelberg, C.F Müller Verlag, 2007 (3d Ed.), at p. 1; J. Van Ryn and J. Heenen, *Principes de Droit Commercial*, Vol. III, Brussels, Bruylant, 1981 (2nd Ed.), n° 81 at p. 82.

claim (for payment of money, for delivery of goods, for performance of services, etc.) in such way that possession of the document is a necessary prerequisite to be entitled to enforce the claim.[94] Every claimant of course has to prove his claim, and in order to do so, written documents are often very important, but they are nevertheless only means of proof. If they are lacking, there will often be alternative ways to prove one's right. With negotiable documents on the other hand, possession of the document is required to have a right at all. Furthermore, negotiable instruments are transferrable – the current holder of the document can be replaced by another holder.[95] Since possession of the document is required to exercise the rights, such transfer must necessarily involve the document as such (physical delivery, endorsement and delivery, assignment and delivery). There are different views as to whether the concept of negotiable instruments only refers to documents that are easily transferrable (documents to order or to bearer), or also includes documents that are less easily transferred (named documents, that need to be assigned).[96] A third characteristic is that negotiable instruments are separated from the underlying (contractual) relation. The party creating a negotiable instrument has a reason to do so, of course, and that reason may well be contractual obligations of the creator against a contract partner. Once the negotiable instrument has been created and released into the world, however, it is disconnected from that underlying (contractual) origin and becomes an independent source of rights and obligations. This means, for instance, that defences and exceptions from the underlying contract can in general not be invoked against the holder of the negotiable instrument.[97] It also means that the rights (and obligations) of the holder only derive from the document itself, which is generally

---

[94] R. De Wit, *Multimodal Transport. Carrier Liability and Documentation*, London, Lloyd's of London Press, 1995, n° 5.15 at p. 245; E. Dirix, R. Steennot and H. Vanhees, *Handels- en economisch recht in hoofdlijnen*, Antwerpen, Intersentia, 2014 (10th Ed.), n° 199 at p. 167 and n° 200 at p. 168; T. Eckardt, *The Bolero Bill of Lading Under German and English Law*, München, Sellier European Law Publishers, 2004, at p. 64; K.-H. Gursky, *Wertpapierrecht*, Heidelberg, C.F Müller Verlag, 2007 (3d Ed.), at p. 2; W. Van Gerven, *Handels- en Economisch Recht*, Vol. 1, *Ondernemingsrecht*, in X, *Beginselen van Belgisch Privaatrecht*, Antwerpen, Standaard, 1975, at p. 482; J. Van Ryn and J. Heenen, *Principes de Droit Commercial*, Vol. III, Brussels, Bruylant, 1981 (2nd Ed.), n° 79 at p. 81.

Compare *Chitty on Contracts*, Vol. 2, *Specific Contracts*, London, Sweet & Maxwell, 1989 (26th Ed.), n° 2752 at p. 181.

[95] E. Dirix, R. Steennot and H. Vanhees, *Handels- en economisch recht in hoofdlijnen*, Antwerpen, Intersentia, 2014 (10th Ed.), n° 201 at pp. 168–169.

[96] M. Spanjaart, *Vorderingsrechten uit cognossement*, Zutphen, Uitgeverij Paris, 2012, at pp. 191–194.

[97] Ph. Delebecque and M. Germain, *Traité de droit commercial*, Vol. 2, Paris, L.G.D.J., 2004 (17th Ed.), n° 1913 at p. 2; K.-H. Gursky, *Wertpapierrecht*, Heidelberg, C.F Müller Verlag, 2007 (3d Ed.), at pp. 8–9; G. Treitel, *The Law of Contract*, London, Sweet & Maxwell, 1991 (8th Ed.), at p. 595; W. Van Gerven, *Handels- en Economisch Recht*, Vol. 1, *Ondernemingsrecht*, in X, *Beginselen van Belgisch Privaatrecht*, Antwerpen, Standaard, 1975, at p. 483; J. Van Ryn and J. Heenen, *Principes de Droit Commercial*, Vol. III, Brussels, Bruylant, 1981 (2nd Ed.), n° 79 at p. 81.

182 Non-contractual theories

considered to be of strict construction (*rigor cambialis*).[98] In addition, a subsequent holder in good faith of a negotiable instrument can obtain a better title than his predecessor had. Ordinarily, the *Nemo plus* or *Nemo dat* rules[99] would prevent a party from transferring more rights to another than the party itself possessed. The transfer of a negotiable instrument, however, can provide the transferee with more rights than the transferor had. Finally, it should be noted that negotiable instruments are generally not a closed system. It is, at least in theory, possible for (commercial) parties to create new types of negotiable instruments.[100]

50 Under English law, the term (negotiable) 'instrument' is generally reserved for documents incorporating a claim for payment of money.[101] Documents incorporating a claim for goods are called 'documents of title', and the general term for both documents of title and negotiable instruments is 'documentary intangibles'.

The 'abstraction', or separation of the negotiable instrument from the underlying contract, is almost never absolute, though (see E. McKendrick (Ed.), *Goode on Commercial Law*, London, Penguin Books, 2016 (5th Ed.), n° 18.20 at p. 522.

[98] W. Van Gerven, *Handels- en Economisch Recht*, Vol. 1, *Ondernemingsrecht*, in X, *Beginselen van Belgisch Privaatrecht*, Antwerpen, Standaard, 1975, at p. 482.

[99] In civil law systems, the rule is known as '*Nemo plus iuris transfere (ad alium) potest quam ipse habet*' (nobody can transfer more rights (to another) than he himself has), in common law countries it is known as '*Nemo dat quod non habet*' (nobody gives what he doesn't have).

[100] In *Zürich / Lebosch*, the Dutch Supreme Court held that, in principle, any claim can be made into a negotiable instrument, and that an insurance certificate is indeed such negotiable instrument (HR 19 April 2002, *RvdW* 2002, 73, *S&S* 2002, 126, *NJ* 2002, 456 (*Zürich / Lebosch*), point 3.4.2.).

P. Seck, *Reisbevrachting en cognossementsvervoer*, Zutphen, Uitgeverij Paris, 2011, at p. 166; M. Spanjaart, *Vorderingsrechten uit cognossement*, Zutphen, Uitgeverij Paris, 2012, at p. 197; G. Treitel, *The Law of Contract*, London, Sweet & Maxwell, 1991 (8th Ed.), at p. 595; J. Van Ryn and J. Heenen, *Principes de Droit Commercial*, Vol. III, Brussels, Bruylant, 1981 (2nd Ed.), n° 80 at p. 82. Compare *Chitty on Contracts*, Vol. 2, *Specific Contracts*, London, Sweet & Maxwell, 1989, n° 2754 at p. 183.

In practice, however, it will probably be difficult for a new type of document to gain the widespread acceptance that is required to really function as a negotiable instrument.

German law is an exception; parties cannot create additional, non-statutory negotiable instruments. See K.-H. Gursky, *Wertpapierrecht*, Heidelberg, C.F Müller Verlag, 2007 (3d Ed.), at p. 14.

[101] R. De Wit, *Multimodal Transport. Carrier liability and documentation*, London, Lloyd's of London Press, 1995, n° 5.15 at p. 253; E. McKendrick (Ed.), *Goode on Commercial Law*, London, Penguin Books, 2016 (5th Ed.), n° 18.02 at p. 517.

Some authors, however, do rank bills of lading with the negotiable instruments. See for example M. Lobban, "Negotiable instruments", in J. Baker (Ed.), *The Oxford History of the Laws of England: Volume XII: 1820–1914 Private Law*, Oxford, Oxford University Press, 2010, at p. 758. See also W. Bennett, *The History and Present Position of the Bill of Lading as a Document of Title to Goods*, Cambridge, University Press, 1914, at p. 19.

See also, in the USA, *Pollard v Reardon* 65 F. 848 (1st Circuit, 18 January 1895), at p. 852: "*In the developments of commerce and commercial credits the bill of lading has come to represent the property, but with greater facility of negotiation, transfer, and delivery than the property itself. It is a negotiable instrument, even though not in the same sense as promissory notes or bills of exchange.*"

Nevertheless, the term 'negotiable instruments' is preferred here, because that is more in line with the terminology in other countries, because the concept of 'document of title' is vaguer and less precise,[102] and because the differences between documents of title (to goods) and negotiable instruments (money) are less important than they are sometimes made out to be.[103]

51 The negotiable instruments approach is here discussed as a non-contractual approach. That is not self-evident, though. It is not impossible to argue that a negotiable instrument simply incorporates obligations arising from the underlying contract,[104] or that it is a contract between the issuer and the holder of the instrument, or that a contractual relationship springs up when the holder of the instrument presents it to the issuer and claims performance. English law for instance sees negotiable instruments as contractual[105] and discusses them as part of the law of contract.[106] The Bills of Exchange Act 1882 explicitly refers to the contract on the bill (s. 21) and requires the parties to a bill of exchange to have capacity to contract (s 22.(1)).[107] German law hesitates between the contractual approach (*Vertragstheorie*) and the non-contractual approach (*Kreationstheorie*).[108] Belgian, Dutch and French[109] law tend to see the relation between the issuer and the holder of a negotiable instrument as non-contractual. In *Anthea Yachting*, for instance, the Dutch Supreme Court described the relationship between the beneficiary of a performance bond and the bank that had issued that bond as 'a

---

102 There is no doubt that order and bearer bills of lading, and since the *Rafaela S* also straight bills of lading, are indeed 'documents of title', but the authors all agree that the concept of a 'document of title' is not well defined. See, for example, C. Debattista, *Bills of Lading in Export Trade*, Haywards Heath, Tottel Publishing, 2009 (3rd Ed.), at p. 26.
103 See below, n° 60–61 p. 189–192.
104 That is known as the 'declaratory' conception of negotiable instruments, as opposed to the 'constitutive' conception. In the former, the negotiable instrument simply incorporates obligations that were created by, and thus already existed under the underlying contract. In the latter, the issuing of the negotiable instrument creates new obligations, independent of the underlying contract. See in general I. Arroyo, "Relation entre Charte Partie et Connaissement: La Clause d'Incorporation", E.T.L. 1980, at pp. 736–738; K.-H. Gursky, *Wertpapierrecht*, Heidelberg, C.F Müller Verlag, 2007 (3d Ed.), at pp. 12–13.
105 E. McKendrick (Ed.), *Goode on Commercial Law*, London, Penguin Books, 2016 (5th Ed.), n° 18.17 at p. 521.
106 *Chitty on Contracts*, Vol. 2, *Specific Contracts*, London, Sweet & Maxwell, 1989, at p. 180 et seq.; G. Treitel, *The Law of Contract*, London, Sweet & Maxwell, 1991 (8th Ed.), at pp. 595–596.
107 The Bills of Exchange Act dates back to 1882. At that time, there were only two possible sources of obligations, contract and tort. A bill of exchange clearly wasn't a tort, so if it was to be legally binding, it had to be a contract. It is admitted, though, that it is a contract of a different kind than ordinary contracts, with different rules on privity and consideration (see *Chitty on Contracts*, Vol. 2, *Specific Contracts*, London, Sweet & Maxwell, 1989, n° 2751 at p. 180).
108 K.-H. Gursky, *Wertpapierrecht*, Heidelberg, C.F Müller Verlag, 2007 (3d Ed.), at pp. 15–19.
109 Ph. Delebecque and M. Germain, *Traité de droit commercial*, Vol. 2, Paris, L.G.D.J., 2004 (17th Ed.), n° 1913 at p. 2; J. Van Ryn and J. Heenen, *Principes de Droit Commercial*, Vol. III, Brussels, Bruylant, 1981 (2nd Ed.), n° 115 at p. 109.

184 Non-contractual theories

legal relationship based on a legal transaction'.[110] It goes without saying that the Supreme Court would not have used this rather cumbersome description if it was referring to a contractual relationship.

4.4.2 The bill of lading as a negotiable instrument

52 There is little doubt that a bill of lading has several characteristics of a negotiable instrument and is, at least in certain respects or to a certain extent, such an instrument.[111] Some authors see the negotiable instrument character of the bill of lading and the law of negotiable instruments as sufficient to explain the functions of the bill of lading and the position of the holder, without any need to fall back on underlying contracts.[112] Many authors, on the other hand, explicitly refuse

---

110 Dutch Supreme Court (Hoge Raad) 26 March 2004, Case N° C02/266HR, (*Anthea Yachting / ABN Amro Bank*), point 3.6: "... *op een rechtshandeling berustende rechtsverhouding*".
111 Belgium: E. Dirix, "Bewarend beslag op zeeschepen en op scheepsdocumenten. Actuele ontwikkeling", in X., *De bank & de zee*, Brussels, Bruylant, 1998, at p. 58; C. Smeesters and G. Winkelmolen, *Droit maritime et Droit fluvial*, Vol. I, Brussels, Larcier, 1929 (2nd Ed.), n° 422 at p. 568; W. Van Gerven, *Handels- en Economisch Recht*, Vol. 1, *Ondernemingsrecht*, in X, *Beginselen van Belgisch Privaatrecht*, Antwerpen, Standaard, 1975, n° 55 at p. 481; J. Van Ryn and J. Heenen, *Principes de Droit Commercial*, Vol. III, Brussels, Bruylant, 1981 (2nd Ed.), n° 81 at p. 83.
   France: J.P. Beurier, *Droits maritimes (Dalloz Action)*, Dalloz, 2009–2010, n° 345.65 at p. 402; R. Rodière, *Traité général de droit maritime*, Tome II, *Les contrats de transport de marchandises*, Paris, Librairie Dalloz, 1968, n° 480 at p. 109.
   Germany: W. Bayer, *Der Vertrag zugunsten Dritter*, Tübingen, J.C.B. Mohr (Paul Siebeck), 1995, at p. 179; T. Eckardt, *The Bolero Bill of Lading Under German and English Law*, München, Sellier European Law Publishers, 2004, at p. 65; O. Hartenstein and F. Reuschle, *Handbuch des Fachanwalts. Transport- und Speditionsrecht*, Cologne, Luchterhand, 2010, n° 91 at p. 181; R. Herber, *Seehandelsrecht. Systematische Darstellung*, Berlin, De Gruyter, 2016 (2nd Ed.), at p. 307; H.-J. Puttfarken, *Seehandelsrecht*, Heidelberg, Verlag Recht und Wirtschaft, 1997, n° 92 at p. 35; D. Rabe, *Seehandelsrecht*, München, Verlag C.H. Beck, 2000 (4th Ed.), n° 4 at p. 692; C. Stumm, *Der Ablader im Seehandelsrecht: Eine rechtsvergleichende Darstellung des deutschen und des amerikanischen Rechts*, Berlin, LIT Verlag, 2010, at p. 42.
   The Netherlands: H. Boonk, "Cognossement en cognossementhouder", *NTBR* 2007-9, at p. 379; A. Korthals Altes and J.J. Wiarda, *Vervoerrecht*, Serie Recht en Praktijk, Deventer, Kluwer, 1980, at p. 51 and p. 234; J. Loeff, *Vervoer ter zee*, Deel I, Zwolle, Tjeenk Willink, 1981, n° 52 at p. 34; P. Seck, *Reisbevrachting en cognossementsvervoer*, Zutphen, Uitgeverij Paris, 2011, at p. 169; M. Spanjaart, *Vorderingsrechten uit cognossement*, Zutphen, Uitgeverij Paris, 2012, at p. 179; H. Völlmar, *Het zeerecht*, Haarlem, Tjeenk Willink, 1937, at pp. 169–170; R. Zwitser, *De rol van het cognossement als waardepapier in het handelsverkeer*, Zutphen, Uitgeverij Paris, 2012, 333 p.
   United Kingdom: A. Guest, *The Law of Assignment*, London, Sweet & Maxwell, 2012, n° 1–59 at p. 39.
   Compare I. Arroyo, "Relation entre Charte Partie et Connaissement: La Clause d'Incorporation", *E.T.L.* 1980, at p. 736; R. De Wit, *Multimodal Transport: Carrier Liability and Documentation*, London, Lloyd's of London Press, 1995, n° 5.34 at p. 267.
112 E. du Pontavice, "Sur la clause attributive de juridiction d'un connaissement venu de Chine", *D.M.F.* 1994, at p. 740.

to see the bill of lading as a true negotiable instrument or to accept that the bill of lading can be explained solely by means of the law of negotiable instruments.

53 A bill of lading incorporates a claim for delivery of the carried goods, possession of the document itself is required to be able to exercise that right, and the document and the incorporated claim can be transferred to a new holder. Those are all characteristic features of negotiable instruments. Given the obvious similarities, courts have on occasion found it useful to refer to the law on negotiable instruments to solve issues not addressed by the law on bills of lading, such as for instance the concept of endorsement.[113]

54 The position that a bill of lading is a true negotiable instrument, and that the functions of the bill of lading and the position of the holder can be fully explained by the negotiable instrument character alone has mainly been defended in Germany and in the Netherlands in the nineteenth century.[114] In Germany, this view of the bill of lading has been explicitly confirmed in the Commercial Code since the *Allgemeines Deutsches Handelsgesetzbuch* 1861. Currently, § 363. (2) HGB lists the bill of lading as one of the '*kaufmännische Orderpapiere*' (commercial negotiable instruments). The provisions of the HGB on indorsement of negotiable instruments (§§ 364–365) thus also apply to bills of lading. In addition, several provisions of the *Wechselgesetz* (Bills of Exchange Act) also apply to the commercial negotiable instruments of the HGB (§ 365.(1) HGB). To this date, German maritime law authors primarily analyse and discuss the bill of lading as a negotiable instrument. In the Netherlands, authors such as Kist, Polak, Reepmaker and Diephuys were of the opinion that the bill of lading is a fully independent source of rights and obligations, created by a unilateral action of the carrier and entirely disconnected from the underlying contract of carriage.[115] The

---

Generally in favour of the negotiable instruments approach: E. van Beukering-Rosmuller, "De ontvangstexpediteur als cognossementshouder", *T.V.R.* 2000, at p. 64; P. van Huizen, "Het incasso (endossement) in het vervoer", *T.V.R.* 1999, at p. 74.

113 HR (Dutch Supreme Court) 18 January 1856, *W.* 1856, N° 1717, p. 1: Since the Commercial Code allows bills of lading to be endorsed, but does not give rules regarding such endorsement, the provisions on the endorsement of bills of exchange must be deemed to apply.
   See also M. Spanjaart, *Vorderingsrechten uit cognossement*, Zutphen, Uitgeverij Paris, 2012, at pp. 182–183.
114 F. Frets, *De kracht van een cognossement, en het regt van den houder*, Rotterdam, F. W. Krieger, 1818, calls the bill of lading 'the bill of exchange of the sea' (at p. 30 and p. 36).
   For a more recent author, see I. Arroyo, "Relation entre Charte Partie et Connaissement: La Clause d'Incorporation", *E.T.L.* 1980, at p. 742 and p. 747. As against third-party holders, the author considers the bill of lading "*un véritable titre négociable*" (a true negotiable instrument).
115 In chronological order: J.G. Kist, *Het Handelspapier, Part 2. Het cognossement*, Amsterdam, J.H. Gebhard & Comp., 1861, at pp. 16–24; A. Polak, *Historisch-juridisch onderzoek naar den aard van het cognossement*, Amsterdam, Gebroeders Binger, 1865, at p. 256; W. Reepmaker, *Over de verbindbaarheid der chertepartij voor den cognoscementhouder*, Rotterdam, Kramers, 1873, at pp. 80–88; G. Diephuis, *Handboek voor het Nederlandsch Handelsregt*, Vol. 2, Groningen, J.B. Wolters, 1874, n° 8 at p. 185.

underlying contract is, at the most, the *de facto* reason or motive for the carrier to issue the bill of lading, but it is not legally relevant with regard to the bill of lading.[116] These authors base their position on such elements as the fact that the carrier must deliver to a third-party holder the number of goods indicated in the bill of lading, even if such quantity was never actually loaded (or could not even have fitted into the vessel),[117] the fact that the shipper can only terminate the contract of carriage if he undertakes to hold the carrier harmless against possible claims by the holder of the bill of lading,[118] etc. A consequence of this position is that the holder of the bill of lading has rights of his own, which are not derived from the rights of the shipper, but are directly created and defined by the bill of lading itself.[119] These authors, however, saw the bill of exchange and the bill of lading as totally 'abstract', i.e. disconnected from the underlying contract, *even* with regard to the parties to that contract themselves. If, for example, the buyer accepted a bill of exchange to pay for the goods, but the goods were in fact never delivered, the buyer could not raise that fact as a defence in the seller's claim under the bill of exchange. The abstraction, as applied to the parties to the underlying contract, was challenged from the late 19th century on, and eventually abandoned. This development led to a decline of the negotiable instruments approach, a decline that was probably reinforced by the growing importance of carriage under bills of lading. Before, carriage was under charter parties, and the bill of lading was issued pursuant to the charter party. The charter party could then be seen, in an obvious parallelism with a sales contract and a bill of exchange, as the underlying contract, which leads to the creation of a negotiable instrument. When there is no charter party, however, and the bill of lading itself is the contract of carriage, or at least evidence of that contract, the parallelism is less clear and it requires a bigger effort to see the bill of lading as a contractual document in one relation (shipper – carrier), but a negotiable instrument in another relation (carrier – third-party holder).

55 It is generally accepted to this day, though, that the bill of lading is like a negotiable instrument in that the holder may rely on what is stated in the document itself, even if those statements are not correct or not in line with the

---

See also M. Spanjaart, *Vorderingsrechten uit cognossement*, Zutphen, Uitgeverij Paris, 2012, at pp. 185–186.
116 J.G. Kist, *Het Handelspapier, Part 2. Het cognossement*, Amsterdam, J.H. Gebhard & Comp., 1861, at p. 17 and p. 24. See also J. Cahen, *Het cognossement*, Arnhem, Gouda Quint, 1964, at p. 14.
117 J.G. Kist, *Het Handelspapier, Part 2. Het cognossement*, Amsterdam, J.H. Gebhard & Comp., 1861, at p. 16; A. Polak, *Historisch-juridisch onderzoek naar den aard van het cognossement*, Amsterdam, Gebroeders Binger, 1865, at p. 257.
118 J.G. Kist, *Het Handelspapier, Part 2. Het cognossement*, Amsterdam, J.H. Gebhard & Comp., 1861, at p. 15; A. Polak, *Historisch-juridisch onderzoek naar den aard van het cognossement*, Amsterdam, Gebroeders Binger, 1865, at p. 256.
119 J.G. Kist, *Het Handelspapier, Part 2. Het cognossement*, Amsterdam, J.H. Gebhard & Comp., 1861, at p. 14; A. Polak, Historisch-juridisch onderzoek naar den aard van het cognossement, Amsterdam, Gebroeders Binger, 1865, at p. 264 and p. 269.

underlying contract of carriage.[120] The most obvious example of this is the rule that proof against a bill of lading is not admissible as against a third party in good faith.[121] The purpose, of course, is to enforce the reliability of the bill of lading, and thereby its strength as a negotiable commercial instrument.[122]

56 Many authors, however, are adamant that a bill of lading is not a (true) negotiable instrument, for several reasons.[123] First and foremost is the argument that the obligations under the bill of lading can never be entirely disconnected from the underlying contract of carriage between the shipper and the carrier. This argument has two aspects: (1) the obligations that the carrier undertakes in the bill of lading to carry the goods to destination and to deliver them there to the holder are initially and essentially contractual obligations of the carrier to the shipper under the contract of carriage,[124] and (2) defences arising from the underlying contract of carriage can, at least to a certain extent, be invoked against the holder of the bill of lading.

57 Neither of these objections is really convincing, though. It is, first of all, not correct that the carrier's obligations under the bill of lading are necessarily contractual obligations. It is indeed possible for a bill of lading to exist *without* an underlying contract of carriage. Suppose, for instance, that a carrier has shipped goods to a port in country A. The goods are never collected and the applicable law allows the carrier to appropriate the goods to cover his charges. Since the goods are worth more in country B, the carrier decides to ship them to country B. The customs authorities however require a bill of lading to process the export and import of the goods, so the carrier issues a bill of lading. There is no underlying contract of carriage, and at this point, the bill of lading is in fact simply an administrative document. If, however, the carrier finds a buyer while the vessel is still at sea and delivers the goods by endorsing the bill of lading to the buyer, the bill of lading will from that time on function as any other bill of lading, allowing the buyer for example to further endorse the bill of lading to a subsequent buyer. Admittedly, this is not an everyday scenario, but it is not impossible either, and it does show that a bill of lading does not require an underlying contract of carriage. Another possible, if not very frequent, scenario is that the underlying contract is later annulled or voided. The German courts and authors are unanimous that in such case, the carrier's obligations under the bill of lading remain intact.[125]

---

120 French authors refer to this characteristic as "*le charactère littéral*", the literal nature of the bill of lading. See, for example, R. Rodière, *Traité général de droit maritime*, Tome II, *Les contrats de transport de marchandises*, Paris, Librairie Dalloz, 1968, n° 480 at p. 109.
121 Article 3, par. 4 Hague-Visby Rules.
122 Compare R. Cleveringa, *Zeerecht*, Zwolle, Tjeenk Willink, 1961 (4th Ed.), at p. 634.
123 See, in general, R. Cleveringa, *Zeerecht*, Zwolle, Tjeenk Willink, 1961 (4th Ed.), fn. 1 at p. 638.
124 T. Eckardt, *The Bolero Bill of Lading Under German and English Law*, München, Sellier European Law Publishers, 2004, at p. 56.
125 W. Bayer, *Der Vertrag zugunsten Dritter*, Tübingen, J.C.B. Mohr (Paul Siebeck), 1995, at p. 178; C.-W. Canaris, W. Schilling and P. Ulmer (Eds), *Handelsgesetzbuch Großkommentar, begründet von Hermann Staub*, Berlin, De Gruyter, 2001 (4th Ed.), § 363, n° 64 at p. 67 and n° 66 at p. 69; H. Gramm, *Das neue Deutsche Seefrachtrecht nach den Haager*

The issue has not received much attention in other legal systems, but many would probably give priority to the rights of the holder of the bill of lading and consider the carrier still bound to deliver the goods at destination. A further, more likely, scenario is that shipper A enters into a contract of carriage with carrier B, which then has the bill of lading issued by a company C with which B has some form of cooperation (slot charter, slot sharing, consortium agreement, etc.). In that case, there is a contract of carriage, but the party issuing the bill of lading (C) is not a party to or bound by that contract.

58 It is, furthermore, not self-evident that the carrier's main obligations under the bill of lading coincide with his obligations under the contract of carriage. Under the contract of carriage, the carrier undertakes to carry the goods from one place to another and to deliver them at destination to the holder of the bill of lading. Under the bill of lading, the carrier clearly undertakes to deliver the goods to the holder, but does he also undertake to *carry* the goods? In practice, in most cases, the question is moot, since the goods cannot be delivered at destination if they are not first carried to that place. Exceptions are, however, imaginable. Suppose that a US manufacturer sells a consignment of car parts to a European buyer, the parts to be shipped from the USA to the port of Antwerp. A bill of lading is issued accordingly. Due to an error of the stevedore, the parts are not shipped. In order to avoid claims, the manufacturer, in agreement with the carrier, puts together an identical consignment from his warehouse in the UK, and has those goods shipped to Antwerp by other means. When the holder of the bill of lading comes to collect the goods, the carrier offers him the replacement consignment, with parts that perfectly correspond to the description of the goods in the bill of lading, but were not in fact carried from the USA to Antwerp. If the holder of the bill of lading knew about this substitution, would he legally be entitled to refuse the goods? Is, in other words, the carriage described in the bill of lading an essential element? From a purely legal point of view, the answer

---

Regeln, Berlin, E.S. Mittler & Sohn, 1938, at p. 152; D. Rabe, *Seehandelsrecht*, München, Verlag C.H. Beck, 2000 (4th Ed.), n° 2 at p. 749; G. Schaps and H. Abraham, *Das Seerecht in der Bundesrepublik Deutschland, Seehandelsrecht*, Vol. 1, Berlin, Walter de Gruyter, 1978 (4th Ed.), n° 14 at p. 750.

BGH 10 October 1957, *BGHZ* 25, 300, *NJW* 1957, 1917 (Case II ZR 278/56): "*Die Verpflichtung des auf Grund des Konnossements Empfangenden zur Frachtzahlung besteht (. . .) selbständig und unabhängig davon, ob ein Frachtvertrag wirksam zustande gekommen ist.*" (The obligation of the person that takes delivery under the bill of lading to pay the freight exists on its own and independently of the question whether a contract of carriage was validly made.)

Even if the *Begebungsvertrag* itself, which under German law creates the obligations under the bill of lading, is invalid, a holder in good faith of the bill of lading would still have rights against the carrier, because it would hardly be acceptable if he did *not* acquire rights against the carrier. See C.-W. Canaris, W. Schilling and P. Ulmer (Eds), *Handelsgesetzbuch Großkommentar, begründet von Hermann Staub*, Berlin, De Gruyter, 2001 (4th Ed.), § 363, n° 61 at pp. 65–66.

See also M. Spanjaart, *Vorderingsrechten uit cognossement*, Zutphen, Uitgeverij Paris, 2012, at p. 241.

would seem to be negative. If that is indeed correct, this is another illustration that the carrier's obligations under the bill of lading are not identical to, and not dependent on his obligations under the contract of carriage.

59 Finally, even when the carrier's obligations under the bill of lading are indeed identical to his contractual obligations to the shipper, this does not mean that the obligations under the bill of lading must be contractual in nature.[126] The undertaking is, indeed, not to the same person. The carrier's undertaking under the contract of carriage is to the shipper, with whom he has negotiated and made a contract; the undertaking under the bill of lading is to a third party, which is often unknown at the time the bill of lading is issued and with whom the carrier has no contact at that time. From a legal point of view, it is perfectly possible to separate the carrier's contractual obligations to the shipper from his obligations under the bill of lading to third-party holders, even if the factual content of those two sets of obligations is largely identical.[127] Also, the fact that a single document is used in both relations does not imply that it must necessarily have the same functions. The bill of lading does not become a contract between the carrier and a third-party holder simply because it is evidence of, or the actual contract of carriage between the carrier and the shipper.

60 It is further argued that a bill of lading, unlike a bill of exchange where the payment obligation can be fully disconnected from incidents in the underlying (sales) contract, can never be entirely disconnected from the performance of the underlying contract of carriage and the difficulties encountered therewith.[128] An example cited here is the fact that the holder may be liable to pay the freight, which is essentially an obligation of the shipper under the contract of carriage, and that the carrier may in certain circumstances refuse to deliver the goods until the freight has been paid.[129] That argument, however, does not carry much weight, as the carrier is only able to enforce a freight claim against a third-party holder of the bill of lading if such (possible) liability is apparent from the bill of lading itself. From a factual point of view, there is of course a link between the freight collectable from the holder under the terms of the bill of lading and the

---

126 Compare J. Van Ryn and J. Heenen, *Principes de Droit Commercial*, Vol. III, Brussels, Bruylant, 1981 (2nd Ed.), n° 115 at pp. 109–110.
127 Compare C. Cauffman, *De verbindende eenzijdige belofte*, Antwerpen, Intersentia, 2005, n° 651 at p. 417, who points out that the obligations of the bank under an irrevocable documentary credit are based on the bank's unilateral engagement, even though the underlying contracts between the parties are the reason for the bank's engagement.
  See also J. Cahen, *Het cognossement*, Arnhem, Gouda Quint, 1964, at p. 14: with regard to third-party holders, the bill of lading creates "... *een geheel opzichzelfstaande rechtsbetrekking*" (an entirely independent legal relationship).
128 R. De Wit, *Multimodal Transport. Carrier liability and documentation*, London, Lloyd's of London Press, 1995, n° 5.34 at p. 268; R. Rodière, *Traité général de droit maritime*, Tome II, *Les contrats de transport de marchandises*, Paris, Librairie Dalloz, 1968, n° 480 at p. 109 and n° 485 at p. 116; M. Spanjaart, *Vorderingsrechten uit cognossement*, Zutphen, Uitgeverij Paris, 2012, at p. 103.
129 Compare R. De Wit, *Multimodal Transport: Carrier Liability and Documentation*, London, Lloyd's of London Press, 1995, n° 5.34 at p. 267.

freight due under the contract of carriage, but from a legal point of view, that link does not exist. The creator of a negotiable instrument shapes the obligation incorporated in the instrument as he sees fit (be it within the boundaries of the applicable law), and thus can require the holder to satisfy certain conditions before being able to claim 'payment', in the largest sense of the term, under the instrument. The possible liability of the holder of the bill of lading to pay freight and/or other costs exclusively derives from the bill of lading itself, not from the underlying contract of carriage. An interesting illustration of this point is to be found in the *Agatha*, an inland shipping case of the Dutch Supreme Court.[130] The importer of a consignment of chemicals had entered into a contract with Atlas for the carriage of this consignment by inland barge from Rotterdam to Mannheim. Atlas had subcontracted to Stasse, and Stasse to NPRC, and NPRC had then issued a bill of lading naming Milchsack as consignee. Milchsack did not discharge the consignment within the allotted time, and demurrage was incurred. The demurrage was paid by Milchsack to Stasse, which then went bankrupt before it could pay NPRC, the carrier under the bill of lading. NPRC then sued Milchsack under the bill of lading for a (second) payment of the demurrage. The Advocate-General in his opinion explicitly pointed out that a bill of lading creates a separate obligation that is independent from the contracts of carriage, and the Supreme Court did indeed hold Milchsack liable to pay demurrage under the bill of lading, even though it had already paid that same demurrage under an underlying contract of carriage.

It is further true, of course, that the party liable under a negotiable instrument usually has less defences available to him than the carrier under a bill of lading,[131] who can invoke a more or less long list of defences related to the performance of the carriage and the practical difficulties that may arise during that performance. It is, in fact, to this circumstance that several authors refer when they claim the bill of lading is caused, or semi-caused (*halbkausal*), or a '*titre concret*'.[132] The difference however is not essential – it is quantitative rather than qualitative. One of the reasons for the difference is that the paying of money is simply easier and less likely to be influenced by extraneous elements than the carriage of goods. Also, money is generic, whereas cargo consists of specific goods. Nevertheless, the

---

130 HR 15 February 1980, S&S 1980, 63 (*ms. Agatha*).
131 R. De Wit, *Multimodal Transport: Carrier Liability and Documentation*, London, Lloyd's of London Press, 1995, n° 5.17 at p. 255 and n° 5.34 at p. 267.
132 C.-W. Canaris, W. Schilling and P. Ulmer (Eds), *Handelsgesetzbuch Großkommentar, begründet von Hermann Staub*, Berlin, De Gruyter, 2001 (4th Ed.), § 363, n° 66 at p. 68; O. Hartenstein and F. Reuschle, *Handbuch des Fachanwalts. Transport- und Speditionsrecht*, Cologne, Luchterhand, 2010, n° 125 at p. 187; R. Herber, *Seehandelsrecht: Systematische Darstellung*, Berlin, De Gruyter, 2016 (2nd Ed.), at p. 308; P. Seck, *Reisbevrachting en cognossementsvervoer*, Zutphen, Uitgeverij Paris, 2011, at pp. 172–173; M. Spanjaart, *Vorderingsrechten uit cognossement*, Zutphen, Uitgeverij Paris, 2012, at p. 241.
 Contra: J. Cahen, *Het cognossement*, Arnhem, Gouda Quint, 1964, at p. 14: the underlying contract of carriage is at most the motive for issuing the bill of lading, but never the legal cause of the bill of lading.

party liable under a negotiable instrument which usually has (very) few defences available could see those defences extended or increased, while the carrier could see his list of defences reduced. The sanctions regime against Iran, which made it unlawful for financial institutions to finance certain transactions, is a clear example of the former. With regard to carriage, the Montreal Convention on air carriage and the Hamburg and Rotterdam Rules on sea carriage show that the long list of exceptions in the Hague-Visby Rules is not essential and could indeed be reduced. The fact that the liable party under a negotiable instrument generally has less defences than the carrier under a bill of lading can therefore not be seen as an essential difference between negotiable instruments and bills of lading.

It is also said in this respect that the bill of lading needs to remain tied in with the underlying contract of carriage, because that underlying contract is the source of the carrier's defences, and it would be unfair and unjust to rob the carrier of those defences and make him, in fact, an insurer of the carried goods. It is, indeed, generally accepted that a carrier should not be liable for certain types of damage occurring during the carriage. The resulting defences however often do not derive from the underlying contract, but from the (usually mandatory) law on the carriage of goods by sea (the Hague Rules, the Hague-Visby Rules, the Hamburg Rules, the national laws that give effect to those conventions, etc.). The carrier will be able to invoke the statutory defences, even if they were not included in the underlying contract of carriage or if there is no underlying contract at all,[133] while a defence that *is* included in the underlying contract but not permitted by the law of carriage, will not be available to the carrier. This argument, of course, is only valid in states that do have (mandatory) provisions on the carriage of goods by sea. The Hague and Hague Visby Rules, however, have more than 80 Member States, the Hamburg Rules more than 30. Compared with the 195 states in the world, that means that a clear majority of them does indeed have carriage laws, certainly when considering that not all of those 195 states are equally important in the field of ocean carriage, and that some states are not party to the conventions but do have domestic legislation that is strongly inspired by them. The fact that the carrier should have certain defences is not an argument, therefore, to say that the bill of lading must remain connected to, or influenced by, the underlying contract of carriage.

61 The second argument that is advanced to say that a bill of lading cannot be a real negotiable instrument is that the transferee of a negotiable instrument gets a *better* title than the transferor, which is not the case with the holder of a bill of lading. That statement needs to be qualified, though.[134] First, it is generally accepted, indeed, that with regard to the obligations of the carrier, the holder of a bill of lading can, and often does, have a better position than the shipper.[135] Proof

---

133 An admittedly exceptional situation, but not entirely impossible: see above, n° 57 p. 187.
134 Compare C. Debattista, *Bills of Lading in Export Trade*, Haywards Heath, Tottel Publishing, 2009 (3rd Ed.), n° 3.19 at p. 77 and n° 3.25 at p. 79.
135 Compare H.-J. Puttfarken, *Seehandelsrecht*, Heidelberg, Verlag Recht und Wirtschaft, 1997, n° 92 at p. 35.

192 *Non-contractual theories*

against the bill of lading is possible as regards the shipper, but is not admissible as regards a third-party holder in good faith, for instance. Unpaid freight and costs are recoverable from the shipper even if the bill of lading bears a 'freight prepaid' mark, but not from a third-party holder in good faith. Furthermore, the statement that the holder of a bill of lading does not get a better title primarily concerns title to the carried goods, and came into being when the bill of lading was still thought to transfer *title*. A third-party holder, even in good faith, did not in principle acquire a valid title to the goods if the transferor of the bill of lading did not have a good title himself.[136] Since then, however, it has become accepted that a bill of lading, in itself, does not confer title, but only (constructive) possession. The question whether a bill of lading can provide its holder with a better *title*, in the strict sense of the word, is thus no longer relevant. On the other hand, since the bill of lading provides (constructive) possession of the carried goods, and since the holder must be acting in good faith, he does become a possessor in good faith and may as such, depending on the applicable law, enjoy protection, even against the real owner of the goods. The conclusion would seem to be that the statement that the holder of a bill of lading cannot get a better title has become somewhat of a slogan, and that the actual impact or importance of this rule is rather limited.

62 A third argument that is advanced against seeing the bill of lading as a negotiable instrument is that it leads to an overly restrictive right of action against the carrier. If the bill of lading is a negotiable instrument, then only the holder of the instrument can enforce the obligations under it, and only the holder has title to sue under the bill of lading. For those who advocate a broader right of action, that is a disadvantage of the negotiable instrument approach.[137] It is clear, though, that this is a biased analysis. The starting point is not an analysis of the

---

136 There were exceptions to this principle, however, such as when the seller could be considered a 'factor' (commercial agent) of the real owner, or under the (in the UK now abolished) 'market overt' rule. See, for example, M. Lobban, "Negotiable instruments", in J. Baker (Ed.), *The Oxford History of the Laws of England: Volume XII: 1820–1914 Private Law*, Oxford, Oxford University Press, 2010, at p. 761.

137 The argument has primarily been made in France, where initially the courts strictly limited the right of action to the holder of the bill of lading. In the *Mercandia Transporter II* case, that traditional position led the Commercial Section of the French Supreme Court to dismiss the claim of the shipper, who had suffered the loss. The outcry that followed the decision and the refusal of the Court of Appeal of Montpellier, to which the case had been remanded to follow the Supreme Court's decision (CA Montpellier 1 December 1987, *D.M.F.* 1988, 250) led to a second decision of the joint Civil and Commercial Sections of the Supreme Court, which allowed the shipper's claim (Cass. 22 December 1989, *Bull.* 1989 A.P. N° 4 p. 9, *D.M.F.* 1990, 29). Since then, the French courts have allowed a very broad group of cargo interests to sue under the bill of lading.

This change of course was hailed as a victory of the contractual approach over "*la théorie cambiaire*", the negotiable instruments approach. See P. Bonassies, *Cass. com. 29 November 1994 (Navires Harmony et Nagasaki)*, *D.M.F.* 1995, 209 (note), at p. 215; P. Bonassies, *Cass. com. 19 December 2000 (Navire Norberg)*, *D.M.F.* 2001, 222 (note), at p. 231. See

nature of the bill of lading, to then determine what that nature implies for the right of action against the carrier, the starting point is the desire to grant a right of action to the cargo interests, which then leads to a rejection of the negotiable instruments approach, because that approach does not (easily) lead to the pre-set goal. Furthermore, seeing the bill of lading as a negotiable instrument does not necessarily imply that only the holder of the bill of lading has title to sue the carrier. The right to claim delivery of the goods must, of course, be exclusive to the holder of the bill of lading, but once the goods have been delivered with loss or damage, or cannot be delivered at all, it is no longer absolutely essential to restrict the right of action to the holder of the bill of lading. If it was the shipper that actually suffered the damage, the shipper can be allowed to sue the carrier under the contract of carriage. Such approach would result in a dual right of action, of the holder under the bill of lading and of the shipper under the contract of carriage, depending on which of them has actually suffered the loss, without conflicting with the negotiable instruments approach of the bill of lading.[138] A further extension of the right of action, beyond the holder and the shipper, would be hard to construe, though.[139]

63 A final, somewhat far-fetched argument is that if the vessel has actually loaded *more* cargo than is stated in the bill of lading, the holder of the bill of lading would only be entitled to receive the numbers stated in the bill of lading. The holder of a negotiable instrument is indeed only entitled to what appears from the instrument itself, which moreover is of (very) strict interpretation. That conclusion, in itself, is not really shocking. A party acquiring a bill of lading does indeed go forth on what is stated in the document itself, and will not be surprised or disadvantaged if it 'only' receives the goods described in the bill of lading. If there is an underlying contract (e.g. a sales contract) and the number stated in the bill of lading is less than what the holder of the bill of lading is entitled to under that contract, the holder will have a claim against his contract partner. The real criticism is that this would result in the carrier getting to keep the surplus for himself. That conclusion, however, is clearly not correct. A carrier does not become the owner of the goods that are entrusted to him for carriage: he is only a bailee. If more goods have been entrusted to him than he has to deliver at destination under the bill of lading, he still remains bound to account for those goods to the bailor, i.e. the (non-contracting) shipper.

---

also J.-P. Tosi, "L'adhésion du destinataire au contrat de transport", in X., *Mélanges Christian Mouly*, Paris, Litec, 1998, at p. 177.
138 The Belgian Supreme Court has however rejected such a dual right. In its decision of 23 January 2017 (Case N° C.16.0247.N), the Supreme Court held that once a Bill of Lading has been issued, claims for loss of or damage to the cargo can only be filed on the basis of the Bill of Lading, by the holder of that document, and no longer by the shipper on the basis of the contract of carriage.
139 Cargo interests, not being the holder or the shipper, can in some legal systems sue the carrier on a tort basis, but that is not an optimal solution, neither for the carrier nor for the cargo interests themselves.

4.4.3 When does the relationship come into being?

64 The relation between the holder of a negotiable instrument and the creator of that document depends on the former's capacity of holder: the holder has rights (and possibly obligations) because he holds the instrument. In principle, therefore, the relationship between the holder of the bill of lading and the carrier comes into being the moment the holder acquires the bill of lading, with the proviso however that the relationship is initially unidirectional. The holder can exercise rights against the carrier from the moment he becomes holder, but the carrier generally cannot act against the holder on the mere basis that he is the holder. The carrier can only act against the holder once the latter has exercised rights or obtained benefits under the negotiable instrument.[140] In practice, of course, the carrier will often not be aware of the fact that the bill of lading has been transferred or of the identity of the new holder, and it may well be very difficult (or even impossible) for the carrier to find out that information should he want to do so. In that sense, the relationship is, in a way, 'imperfect'. The holder, on the other hand, can step forward at any desired moment to enforce rights under the bill of lading. At that time, his identity becomes known to the carrier, which will allow the latter, the case being, to enforce rights against the holder.

4.4.4 Intermediate holders

65 The rights and obligations of the holder are tied to his holdership of the bill of lading. Once a holder has transferred the bill of lading to a subsequent holder, it is beyond doubt that the previous holder can no longer enforce rights under the bill of lading. With regard to liabilities, however, the situation is less clear. When liabilities arise because of an act or intervention of an intermediate holder of the bill of lading – e.g. the holder instructs the carrier to proceed to a different port of destination, or to steam at a higher speed – the carrier would be well advised to take steps to fix and preserve the liability of that holder independently from the bill of lading. The liability of the subsequent holder will indeed depend on the terms of the bill of lading, and those terms may not encompass the costs or other liabilities caused by the previous holder's acts or interventions. In some situations, the carrier will need to collect the existing bill of lading and issue a new, amended bill of lading (e.g. in case of a change of port of destination). In those cases, however, since there is an active intervention of the intermediate holder, the carrier will be aware of the identity of that holder. The situation becomes even more complex when liabilities arise without an intervention of the holder. Suppose, for example, that there is a general average expenditure or salvage services performed while the bill of lading is held by an intermediate holder. At the time of the incident itself, the carrier is probably unaware of the identity of the holder and not able to discover that identity either. At the end of the voyage, when the

---

140 Compare G. Schaps & H. Abraham, *Das Seerecht in der Bundesrepublik Deutschland, Seehandelsrecht*, Vol. 1, Berlin, Walter de Gruyter, 1978 (4th Ed.), n° 13–14 at p. 687.

goods are delivered, the carrier will learn who is the holder of the bill of lading *at that time*, but it will often be very difficult, if not impossible, to find out who held the bill of lading at the time of the incident. In practice, therefore, an intermediate holder will often be shielded from liability, if only because his identity remains unknown. What if his identity *is* known, however? Can an intermediate holder be held liable for a general average contribution or a salvage award, simply because he held the bill of lading at the time of the incident, even if he has never exercised any rights under it, and will not do so in the future either? Such a 'clinging' liability is not inconceivable. Under a bill of exchange, for example, every indorser guarantees payment to the ultimate holder. In the bill of lading context, however, it would likely be rejected.[141] German law, for example, which primarily conceives the bill of lading as a negotiable instrument,[142] explicitly provides in § 494 HGB that the holder of the bill of lading only becomes liable to the carrier for freight and demurrage once he has claimed delivery of the goods. That provision in fact stands for the more general principle that the holder of a bill of lading cannot be subjected to burdens if he has not also enjoyed (or at least claimed) the benefits of the bill of lading.[143]

4.4.5 *The non-contracting shipper*

66 The non-contracting shipper often receives the bill of lading from the carrier, even though he is not the party that entered into the contract of carriage with the carrier. The non-contracting shipper does indeed need the bill of lading, both as a receipt, to be able to prove that he has surrendered the goods to the carrier, and as a document of title. The bill of lading as a document of title enables the non-contracting shipper to deliver the goods to the consignee while they are afloat and physically in the hands of the carrier, and allows him to reclaim the goods from the carrier should the underlying deal fall through. The problem, however, is whether a non-contracting shipper can be seen as the 'holder' of the bill of lading, and thus entitled to enforce the rights incorporated in the bill of lading. The analysis of the holdership of a bill of lading usually focuses on the

---

141 In the USA, 49 USC § 80107.(d) explicitly provides that "*Indorsement of a bill of lading does not make the indorser liable for failure of the common carrier or a previous indorser to fulfill its obligations.*"

142 § 363.(2) HGB defines the bill of lading as a '*kaufmännisches Orderpapier*", a commercial negotiable instrument. The indorsement of such *Orderpapier* is governed by §§ 364–365 HGB, and by a number of provisions of the *Wechselgesetz* (Bills of Exchange Act).

143 Compare S. Lamont-Black, "Transferee liability under the Rotterdam Rules: a dance between flexibility and foreseeability", *J.I.M.L.* 2013, at pp. 395–396; D. Rabe, *Seehandelsrecht*, München, Verlag C.H. Beck, 2000 (4th Ed.), n° 2 at p. 626 and n° 2 at p. 749.
　It is also clear under German law that the indorsement of a bill of lading does not make the indorser into a guarantor. See K.-H. Gursky, *Wertpapierrecht*, Heidelberg, C.F Müller Verlag, 2007 (3d Ed.), at p. 121; G. Schaps and H. Abraham, *Das Seerecht in der Bundesrepublik Deutschland, Seehandelsrecht*, Vol. 1, Berlin, Walter de Gruyter, 1978 (4th Ed.), n° 19 at p. 751 ("*Dagegen fehlt dem Indossament des Orderkonnossements die beim Wechsel und Scheck vorhandene Garantiewirkung.*").

receiver of the bill of lading: the named consignee in a straight bill of lading, the last endorsee in an order bill of lading, or the physical holder in a bearer bill of lading. The shipper, when he still holds the bill of lading, is not often mentioned. In case of a bearer bill of lading, the non-contracting shipper simply is the bearer as long as he holds the bill of lading. In case of a straight or order bill of lading, however, the non-contracting shipper will not be the named consignee and the bill of lading will not be endorsed to him. If the non-contracting shipper is named as the 'shipper' in the bill of lading,[144] however, it is submitted that that identification is sufficient to be considered the lawful holder of the instrument and thus entitled to act upon it against the carrier, as long of course as the non-contracting shipper remains in possession of the bill of lading. In this respect, the law of negotiable instruments, influenced as it is by commercial practice, provides more leeway than the UK COGSA, which explicitly defines the lawful holder in such way that a non-contracting shipper can generally not be the lawful holder of a bill of lading. If the non-contracting shipper is not identified in the bill of lading at all, however, it does become difficult to construe him as a 'holder' of the bill of lading. He will still have a *de facto* position, of course, since he holds the original bill of lading and can hold on to the document, thus preventing other parties from becoming the lawful holder of the bill of lading. He could also make arrangements with the carrier and surrender the bill of lading back to the carrier, thus ensuring that the carrier will not later be held liable under the bill of lading. Formally exercising rights under the bill of lading, as holder of that document, will probably not be possible, though.

4.4.6 *Appraisal*

67 There are obvious parallels between the bill of lading and the archetypical negotiable instrument that is the bill of exchange. Both are commercial documents, meant to make obligations easily transferable to third parties, and protecting those third parties against circumstances or defences that are not apparent from the document itself. There are indeed some differences, primarily with regard to the (number of) defences available, but those differences are not nearly as important or as substantial as they are sometimes made out to be. Essentially, the law of negotiable instruments is able to explain all of the functions of the bill of lading as between the carrier and third-party holders. It does not explain the relation between the carrier and the shipper, but it is not called upon to do so either. The relation between the carrier and the shipper is undeniably a contractual one, primarily governed by the contract of carriage, even when the shipper also holds the bill of lading.

68 It is further undeniable that a bill of lading, once it has been created and certainly once it is in the hands of third-party holders, becomes a separate legal reality, with its own impact and consequences. A clear illustration of this effect is

---

[144] The Rotterdam Rules have created the term 'documentary shipper' for such situation.

found in the *Condorcamp/Bosman* decision of the Dutch Supreme Court.[145] Condorcamp had bought a consignment of shoes from distributor Pemaco, which had contracted with forwarder Bosman to arrange the shipment of the shoes from the Far East to Rotterdam. Bosman issued negotiable bills of lading, which were negotiated to Condorcamp. The actual sea carriage was carried out under a non-negotiable carrier's bill of lading, which was held and presented by Bosman to obtain delivery of the shoes in Rotterdam. When Condorcamp then presented the negotiable bill of lading to Bosman, the latter refused delivery, invoking a lien on the shoes based on a clause in its contract with its principal (Pemaco). The Dutch Supreme Court however refused Bosman the right to invoke this lien against Condorcamp, as holder of a negotiable bill of lading. The Court held that when the owner of goods allows a negotiable bill of lading covering those goods to be brought in circulation, he thereby, and as regards those persons that are or ought to be aware of the existence of that bill of lading, surrenders the right to create liens or other rights on those goods, unless the existence, or at least the possible existence of such liens appears from the bill of lading itself.

69 Another illustration of the independence of the bill of lading is the fact that it is perfectly possible for the bill of lading to be subject to a different law than the contract of carriage. Also, the Dutch Civil Code in Article 8:375 and the Spanish Navigation Act in Article 276.(2) provide that when the carrying vessel is sold, the new owner of the vessel is bound to perform the bills of lading with regard to the cargo on board (the party that initially issued these bills of lading obviously also remains liable). Such effects are entirely in line with the law of negotiable instruments.

70 It is remarkable, however, that a bill of lading, once issued, also has effects between the shipper and the carrier, i.e. between the parties to the contract of carriage. For example, the shipper, even though the contract partner of the carrier, can no longer change his instructions to the carrier, unless he possesses all originals of the bill of lading and returns them to the carrier.[146] If, for some reason, the shipper needs to claim delivery of the goods at destination himself, he can only do so if he possesses at least one original of the bill of lading.[147] Also, as the *Condorcamp/Bosman* case[148] demonstrates, the shipper might be limited in or deprived of his power to create liens or other rights over the goods, once a bill of lading has been released into the world. Clearly, therefore, the bill of lading influences the shipper's position under the contract of carriage, which would seem to suggest that bill of lading and contract of carriage can, indeed, not be separated. The argument can also be reversed, however. The fact that even the shipper and the carrier, in their internal (contractual) relation, may lose or be

---

145 HR 26 November 1993, *S&S* 1994, 25 (*Condorcamp / Bosman*).
146 § 520.(1) of the German Commercial Code (HGB) explicitly confirms this principle.
147 H.-J. Puttfarken, *Seehandelsrecht*, Heidelberg, Verlag Recht und Wirtschaft, 1997, n° 108 at pp. 39–40.
148 HR 26 November 1993, *S&S* 1994, 25 (*Condorcamp / Bosman*).

limited in their rights once they allow a bill of lading to be issued, or certainly to be released into the world, shows how powerful and independent an instrument the bill of lading is.

71 It is sometimes questioned whether the ultimate holder of the bill of lading can claim for loss or damage that occurred before he became holder. If the bill of lading is a contract, and the holder's claim thus a claim for breach of contract, how can the holder claim for a breach, or how can there be a breach at all, if at that time there was no contract yet between the carrier and the ultimate holder?[149] It is clear, though, that the holder should be entitled to claim for all transport loss or damage to the goods, even if these occurred before he acquired the bill of lading. The security and the commercial utility of the bill of lading would be much impaired if the ultimate holder could only claim for such loss or damage that he can prove to have occurred while he held the bill of lading. The negotiable instruments approach on the other hand has no problem explaining why the ultimate holder can claim for all loss or damage. A negotiable instrument indeed is a title for the goods described in the instrument, and those goods, as described, must be delivered to the holder of the instrument. If they are not so delivered, the issuer of the instrument (the carrier) is liable, regardless of when and where the loss or damage occurred – unless of course the carrier is exempted by the applicable law.

72 Finally, it is generally accepted that negotiable instruments are of strict interpretation. The rights (and possibly obligations) of the holder are entirely determined by the document itself; the (future) holder must indeed be able to appreciate his position simply by looking at the document. That, of course, is a protection for the holder, who in a carriage context will often be unaware of the underlying contract(s) of carriage, charter part(y)(ies), etc. In a contractual setting, on the other hand, a strict interpretation is not impossible, but generally not the rule. The intentions of the contract parties are taken into account, external elements may sometimes be taken into account, etc. Some authors have tried to answer those concerns by arguing that a third-party holder may rely on the appearance created by the document, or that the interpretation of a bill of lading, when a third-party holder is concerned, must be objective rather than subjective, but such attempts are in fact as many steps away from a true contractual approach towards a more negotiable instruments approach.

---

149 See, for example, CA Antwerp 5 October 2009 (interim) and 9 May 2011 (final), *T.B.H.* 2011, 731. Due to engine problems, the ms. Moa had run aground and had to be refloated by tugs. Cargo paid part of the salvage award directly to the salvors, and then filed a recovery action against the carrier, arguing that unseaworthiness of the vessel was the initial and actual cause of the problems. The Court of Appeal held that such claim is a claim under the bill of lading, and can only be filed by the party that held the bill of lading *at the time of the incident.* The Court, however, did not elaborate on why that is the rule, and did not indicate whether they saw the position of the holder as contractual or as statutory.

4.5 The bill of lading as a voluntary engagement

(*eenzijdige wilsuiting, engagement unilatéral, einseitiges Leistungsversprechen*)

4.5.1 The concept

73 A voluntary engagement is a legally binding undertaking, made unilaterally by a single party.[150]

74 Traditionally, the primary, or even only sources of legal obligations were torts and contracts.[151] In order to distinguish legal, binding obligations from purely social or moral obligations, several requirements must be satisfied for there to be a contract. There must be a 'meeting of the minds', i.e. an offer and an acceptance of that offer, there must be a *causa* and/or consideration, etc. Over time, however, the question arose whether a party can create a legally binding obligation for itself, simply by unilaterally expressing the will to be so bound, and without any requirement of acceptance. A prime example of such unilateral or voluntary engagements are scientific and technological challenges.[152] At the time of writing, for example, the Royal Aeronautical Society has the 'Kremer Competitions', in which prizes of 50,000 GBP and 100,000 GBP can be earned by the participant that successfully designs and builds a human powered aircraft. NASA also regularly has challenges, to design a Mars Ascent Vehicle, a 3-D Printed Habitat, etc. Are the organizations that create such challenges *legally* bound by their engagement to pay the promised sum of money if someone builds an engine that complies with the specifications that were set? Belgian and French law generally accept the possibility for a party to create legally binding obligations by a voluntary, unilateral engagement.[153] The obligation is created by the engagement as such, not by the later acceptance of that engagement ('offer') by a third party. There must be a valid reason for the engagement taken,[154] the creator of the engagement must be legally capable, and must not have been induced by fraud or error to make the engagement. Dutch law is more restrictive and tends to only recognize specific types of voluntary engagements. The German Civil Code explicitly recognizes the possibility of a voluntary engagement, be it only in those cases where 'the law' permits it,[155] and that provision is interpreted very strictly

---

150 See, in general, M. Hogg, "Promise: the neglected obligation in European private law", *I.C.L.Q.* 2010, 461–479.
151 In early English law, torts and contracts were the only sources of legal obligations. Civil law had a somewhat wider range of sources, in that it also knew quasi-torts and quasi-contracts.
152 M. Hogg, "Promise: the neglected obligation in European private law", *I.C.L.Q.* 2010, at pp. 470–472.
153 C. Cauffman, *De verbindende eenzijdige belofte*, Antwerpen, Intersentia, 2005, n° 402 at p. 244.
   Under Belgian law, the obligation of the bank to the beneficiary of a letter of credit is, for example, generally seen as based on a unilateral, voluntary engagement of the bank. See C. Dehouck, *Documentair krediet*, Brugge, die Keure, 2007, n° 634 at p. 315.
154 That reason could be an underlying contract that binds the party making the engagement.
155 § 311 (1) BGB: "*Zur Begründung eines Schuldverhältnisses durch Rechtsgeschäft sowie zur Änderung des Inhalts eines Schuldverhältnisses ist ein Vertrag zwischen den Beteiligten erforderlich, soweit nicht das Gesetz ein anderes vorschreibt*" (To create an obligation by legal

in practice. The UK has the strictest position and only sees the 'engagement' as an offer, which has to be accepted in order to become binding. The party making the engagement/offer may in certain circumstances be estopped from withdrawing the engagement/offer, but the engagement as such does not, as a matter of principle, create a binding obligation.

4.5.2 The bill of lading as a voluntary engagement

75 The bill of lading can quite easily be seen as a voluntary engagement of the carrier.[156] The carrier undertakes to the person identified by or in the bill of lading to deliver the goods, if that person satisfies the (possible) conditions set by the bill of lading, such as payment of freight or other costs. There is, of course, a reason why the carrier assumes this engagement, and that reason may well be a contract of carriage between the carrier and the shipper, but that is not relevant from a legal point of view. The carrier's obligation results from its unilateral engagement, detailed in the bill of lading. In the non-contractual conception of negotiable instruments, this approach dovetails perfectly with the negotiable instruments approach: the carrier's unilateral engagement creates the negotiable instrument.[157] If the bill of lading is not accepted as a (true) negotiable instrument, the voluntary agreement concept serves as an independent theory to explain the position of the holder.

76 It is also argued sometimes that it is in fact the holder of the bill of lading that assumes a voluntary, unilateral engagement by accepting the bill of lading and claiming under it.[158] That, however, is hardly more than word play. It means, in essence, that the bill of lading is seen as an offer to contract, or possibly as an institution, which is then accepted by the holder when and because he presents the bill of lading to the carrier and claims delivery. Acceptance of an offer, however, is always unilateral and voluntary, as is the offer itself. The

---

    act and to modify the content of an obligation an agreement between the parties involved is required, unless the law provides otherwise). The question is whether 'the law' (*das Gesetz*) only refers to a formal Act, or refers to legal norms in general.

156 J. Van Den Dries, *Nederlands Zeerecht*, Zwolle, Tjeenk Willink, 1926, n° 473 at p. 399: "*Het cognossement is dus wettelijk geworden een eenzijdige verklaring afkomstig van den vervoerder en door deze opgemaakt*" (The bill of lading thus has become, by statute, a unilateral declaration issued by the carrier).

    Compare R. De Wit, *Multimodal Transport: Carrier Liability and Documentation*, London, Lloyd's of London Press, 1995, n° 5.41 at p. 273.

    See also Hans. OLG Bremen 25 April 2014, *TranspR* 2015, (452), at p. 456: "*Die Beklagte hat (…) eine eigene Erklärung abgegeben, indem Sie dem Inhaber der Bill of Lading einen Auslieferungsanspruch verschaffte*" (The defendant has issued a declaration of its own, in which it procured the holder of the Bill of Lading a right to claim delivery).

157 I. Arroyo, "Relation entre Charte Partie et Connaissement: La Clause d'Incorporation", *E.T.L.* 1980, fn. 68 at p. 750: "*l'obligation cambiaire trouve son fondement dans la déclaration de volonté de l'émetteur*" (the obligation under the negotiable instrument is based upon the declaration of will of the isssuer).

158 J. Loyens, "Noot: Castelletti t./ Trumpy: geen wijziging van de rechtspositie van de derde-houder van het cognossement", *E.T.L.* 1999, at p. 667.

combination of those two unilateral acts then produces a contract. It is clear that this 'voluntary engagement' of the holder is simply the acceptance of the (presumed) offer by the carrier, and fundamentally different from the voluntary engagement of the carrier, which is the separate and independent source of the carrier's obligation.

4.5.3 When does the relationship come into being?

77 In the voluntary engagement concept, the obligation of the carrier comes into being the moment the carrier makes his engagement public, by issuing the bill of lading. The party holding the bill of lading thus immediately has rights against the carrier. Of course, a party cannot be forced into a position against its will, so the holder cannot be forced to actually present the bill of lading and claim delivery. That also means that the holder cannot be forced to satisfy the conditions to which the carrier has subjected his engagement. In that sense, the relationship between the carrier and the holder remains 'in suspense' until the holder decides to claim the benefit that the carrier has promised, which then in turn obliges the holder to satisfy the conditions that the carrier may have set.

4.5.4 Intermediate holders

78 Intermediate holders, while they are in possession of the bill of lading, have the right to take up the carrier on his voluntary engagement, but if they do not actually do so and transfer the bill of lading 'unused' to a subsequent holder, no relationship exists anymore between the carrier and the previous holder(s). The latter do not have rights against the carrier anymore, but cannot be held liable by the carrier either.

4.5.5 The non-contracting shipper

79 As the author of the voluntary engagement freely defines and construes that engagement (within the boundaries of the law, of course), there is no problem with including the non-contracting shipper as a potential lawful holder of the bill of lading.

4.5.6 Appraisal

80 The voluntary agreement approach helps to show that the carrier's obligations and the holder's position can be construed in a non-contractual way, but is very similar to the negotiable instruments approach. In fact, where the bill of lading can be construed as a negotiable instrument, that theory is preferable. The law of negotiable instruments is better developed than the concept of voluntary engagements, and probably offers a better protection for the holder of the bill of lading. A voluntary engagement requires a valid (expression of) will of the party creating the engagement. If that party was legally incapable of assuming obligations, or was induced by fraud to create the engagement, the engagement is void or voidable.[159] With negotiable instruments, the will of the party creating the engagement is incorporated in, *and reduced to*, the instrument, which further limits the defences available to the party that takes on the engagement.

4.6 Conclusions

81 Carrier and third-party holder, by definition, do not negotiate a contract of carriage with each other. It is undeniable, however, that at least from the time the third-party holder requests delivery of the carried goods, there is a legal relationship with the carrier, and the rules that govern that relationship have to be determined. In doing so, the contract of carriage – even though not made with the third-party holder of the bill of lading – immediately and obviously comes to mind. Why make matters difficult by searching for another solution when there is a contract of carriage, specifically dealing with the transport of the goods involved, that defines the rights and obligations of at least some of the parties concerned? Why not simply 'extend' the reach of this existing contract to the third-party holder?

82 One of the most fundamental objections to 'extending' the reach of the contract of carriage and the contractual approach in general is that the holder does not *intend* to enter into a contract with the carrier; he simply wants to recover from the carrier what he believes to be already his. It is true, of course, that once the holder has claimed delivery, he is in a legal relationship with the carrier, with reciprocal rights and obligations. The source of those rights and obligations does not have to be a contract, though. It is, indeed, possible for parties to become obliged against each other without having entered into a contract (and without having committed a tort). Some legal systems, for example, allow the right of retention to be invoked against non-contracting parties. In such case, there is no contract between the retentor and the other party, but they may have rights or obligations towards each other.[160] From a legal point of view, this reality is best expressed by seeing the relationship between the carrier and the third-party holder as a statutory relationship, with the rights and obligations of the parties determined by law rather than by contract.[161]

---

159 R. De Wit, *Multimodal Transport: Carrier Liability and Documentation*, London, Lloyd's of London Press, 1995, n° 5.41 at p. 273.
160 Suppose a manufacturer who instructs a freight forwarder to arrange the carriage of his products to the customers. The forwarder enters into a storage agreement with a warehouse company, and the products are stored in the warehouse. Afterwards, because the forwarder does not pay the bills or goes bankrupt, the warehouse invokes the right of retention and refuses to release the products to their owner, the manufacturer. There is no contract between the manufacturer and the warehouse company, but the manufacturer will have to pay the warehouse company if it wants its products released. Conversely, the warehouse company will be liable to the manufacturer for the proper storage and care of the products.
161 Compare C. Cauffman, *De verbindende eenzijdige belofte*, Antwerpen, Intersentia, 2005, n° 482 at p. 306. When a reward is offered for the performance of a service, the person

83 A non-contractual position generally also implies stronger protection than a contractual position, in that the (subjective) intentions of the party drafting or issuing the relevant document are subordinated to the objective meaning or interpretation of that document. In the contractual world, freedom of contract is the norm. It are the parties themselves that have to define their rights and obligations. In the construction of the resulting contract, therefore, the intentions of the parties, information exchanged during negotiations etc. may be taken into account. If the relation between the parties is non-contractual (statutory), on the other hand, there have been no negotiations and there were no common intentions. In that case, the construction of the parties' positions can only be based on the document itself, which must be given a more or less objective meaning.[162] The bill of lading quite clearly falls within this latter category. In general, the position of a third-party holder is determined exclusively by the contents of the bill of lading itself. External content or contracts can only be taken into account if there is an explicit incorporation clause, and even then, recent maritime laws and codes seem increasingly doubtful about incorporation clauses. As regards interpretation of the bill of lading, Lord Hoffmann in *The Starsin* held that a bill of lading is destined to come into the hands of different parties (merchants, bankers, lawyers) and that it must be interpreted in light of the knowledge reasonably available to all of those parties. It is, indeed, hardly acceptable that a bill of lading would mean one thing to some parties, but another thing to other parties.[163] In practice, of course, that amounts to an almost objective standard of interpretation.

---

performing the service does so to claim the reward, not to enter into a contract with the promisor.

162 In the Netherlands, for example, the Dutch Supreme Court has held that the interpretation of a collective bargaining agreement (which, once made, becomes binding on all employers and employees, most of which did not personally take part in the negotiations) must be based on the wording of the agreement, and that 'private' knowledge of an employer, who actually took part in the negotiations, cannot be invoked against employees (HR 17 september 1993, *NJ* 1994, 173 (*Gerritse/HAS*)).

Similarly, in *Zürich / Lebosch* the Dutch Supreme Court held that a negotiable instrument (an insurance certificate) must be interpreted based on objective standards (HR 19 April 2002, *RvdW* 2002, 73, *S&S* 2002, 126, *NJ* 2002, 456 (*Zürich / Lebosch*)): "*Voor de beoordeling van de rechtsgevolgen van een toonderstuk tegenover derde-houders te goeder trouw, is niet beslissend wat de uitgever met de uitgifte beoogde, maar welke rechtsgevolgen daaraan naar objectief recht dienen te worden verbonden*" (To appreciate the legal consequences of a bearer bill vis-à-vis third-party holders in good faith, it is not decisive what the issuer intended when he issued the bill, but which consequences such bill should have by objective law).

163 *Homburg Houtimport BV v Agrosin Private Ltd (The Starsin)* [2003] UKHL 12, [2004] 1 A.C. 715 (House of Lords, 13 March 2003), at § 73-76: "*The interpretation of a legal document involves ascertaining what meaning it would convey to a reasonable person having all the background knowledge which is reasonably available to the person or class of persons to whom the document is addressed.* (. . .) *To whom is a bill of lading addressed? It evidences a contract of carriage but it is also a document of title, drafted with a view to being transferred to third parties either absolutely or by way of security for advances to finance the underlying*

204 *Non-contractual theories*

84 There is, however, an immediate objection to seeing the holder's position as a statutory position. How can the position be statutory, indeed, if the bill of lading has been in existence and functioning for more than a century, without an (explicit, comprehensive) statutory regime in place? The UK is an exception in this respect, in that it has had statutory provisions dealing with certain aspects of the position of the holder since the Bills of Lading Act 1855. On the continent, however, the older maritime Acts and Codes such as the Belgian Maritime Act of 1879[164] or the French Act n° 66–420 of 1966[165] hardly have any provisions at all that deal directly, or even indirectly, with the position of the holder. More modern maritime Acts and Codes such as the Dutch or German Codes explicitly deal with some aspects of the position of the holder, but still do not provide a comprehensive framework. The international conventions follow the same pattern: the older ones (Hague/Hague-Visby Rules) hardly have any provisions concerning the holder at all, while more recent conventions (Hamburg Rules, Rotterdam Rules) show an increasing attention to this issue. This evolution, however, is also the answer to the objection. It has been pointed out before that the bill of lading was never invented or created as a full-fledged concept. It gradually developed, driven by the needs and desires of the merchants and mariners. They knew, at least in general, what they needed or wanted the bill of lading to do. Inevitably, however, there were at times disputes and court cases, which obliged lawyers and judges to fit the economic realities of the bill of lading into legal concepts and rules. In the early days of the bill of lading, a contractual construction of the holder's position would have seemed obvious, and may indeed have been the only possible construction. The carriage is performed because of the contract of carriage between the shipper and the carrier, there were, at the time, hardly any statutory rules on the bill of lading, let alone on the position of the holder, rights or obligations directly created by statute were few and far between, etc. It is submitted, however, that even though the lawyers and judges of those days were putting a contractual label to the holder's position, they in

---

transaction. (. . .) The reasonable reader of the bill of lading will therefore know that it is addressed not only to the shipper and consignee named on the bill but to a potentially wide class of third parties including banks which have issued letters of credit. (. . .) As it is common general knowledge that a bill of lading is addressed to merchants and bankers as well as lawyers, the meaning which it would be given by such persons will usually also determine the meaning it would be given by any other reasonable person, including the court. The reasonable reader would not think that the bill of lading could have been intended to mean one thing to the merchant or banker and something different to the lawyer or judge."

164 Wet 21 augustus 1879 houdende Boek II van het Wetboek van Koophandel (Act of 21 August 1879 establishing Book II of the Commercial Code). This Act has been amended from time to time, but important parts of the original 1879 Act are still in force at the time of writing.

165 Loi n° 66-420 du 18 juin 1966 sur les contrats d'affrètement et de transport maritimes (Act n° 66-420 of 18 June 1966 on contracts of affreightment and maritime transports). Almost all of the provisions of this Act have now been moved to the *Code des Transports*.

fact created a position that was not entirely contractual, but at least partially law-made, e.g. by allowing exceptions to ordinary contractual rules to conform to what trade and commerce required the bill of lading to do. To date, indeed, no contractual theory has been proposed that can perfectly explain all of the aspects and functions of the bill of lading. Rather to the contrary, the attention of the national and international legislators for the position of third parties connected to the carriage – the third-party holder, but also the non-contracting shipper[166] – has only continued to grow over the years, as is clear from the growing number of explicit statutory provisions in this respect. The objection does not seem conclusive, therefore.

85 Furthermore, one of that growing number of statutory provisions deserves to be mentioned in particular. Introduced in the carriage of goods by sea by the Visby Protocol,[167] this provision is now found in all carriage conventions[168] and stipulates that the defences and limits of liability of the convention apply in any cargo claim against the carrier, whether that claim be founded in contract, in tort, or otherwise. It is irrelevant, therefore, how the cargo interests want to characterize their claim against the carrier (and, by extension, their legal relationship with the carrier): the substantive rules of the convention apply anyhow. This clearly indicates a move towards an independent, statutory conception of the carriage relations.

86 It is clear, however, that a statutory approach places more of a burden on legislators and/or courts. The rights and obligations of the parties are no longer worked out by the parties themselves, but must be determined by the law. That in turn means that the freedom of the parties, and primarily of the carrier, is reduced. The applicable law may leave some options to the carrier (such as the possibility under the Hague-Visby Rules to exclude liability before loading and after discharge), but the essential rights and obligations of the parties would be set by the law. With regard to the carriage of goods, however, that would not be new or surprising. Since the Harter Act, carriage under bills of lading has been subject to mandatory law, as have the other transport modes.[169] Also, making the rights and obligations of the carrier and holder part of the statutory package

---

166 The German Commercial Code (HGB), for example, has a number of provisions explicitly dealing with the position of the *Ablader* (non-contracting shipper): the *Ablader* is, for instance, entitled to demand a bill of lading (§513.(1) HGB), but is also strictly liable for loss or damage caused by inaccurate statements regarding marks, number, quantity or weight of the goods in the bill of lading or by the failure to inform the carrier about the dangerous nature of the goods (§ 488.(3) HGB).
167 Article 3 of the Visby Protocol, which inserted Article 4*bis*.1 into the Hague Rules.
168 Article 7.1 Hamburg Rules, Article 4.1 Rotterdam Rules.
  The conventions for the other modes of transport have quasi-identical provisions: Article 22 CMNI, Article 28.1 CMR, Article 41 § 1 COTIF-CIM, Article 29 Montreal.
169 Each transport mode today has its mandatory Convention: CMR, CMNI, COTIF-CIM, Montreal Convention.

would facilitate international uniformity in this respect. The existing sea carriage conventions do not explicitly define the position of the holder of the bill of lading. The interpretation that is adopted of this position and whether it is considered contractual or statutory may, however, influence the way the substantial provisions of the conventions are construed and applied.

87 Seeing the position of the holder as a statutory position is, to a certain extent, stepping away from the underlying contract of carriage. Such underlying contract is not absolutely essential – a bill of lading can exist and function *without* an underlying contract of carriage[170] – but in practice, there almost always is an initial contract of carriage. The statutory approach, however, does not mean that this contract must be entirely disregarded. It is indeed disregarded as far as third-party holders are concerned. Between carrier and third-party holders, rights and obligations are determined by the factual information stated in the bill of lading, the applicable law and the terms of the bill of lading to the extent permitted by that law. The source of the carrier's obligation is the engagement he has publicly taken by issuing and releasing the bill of lading, not the underlying contract of carriage. Since third-party holders are (by definition) not a party to the contract of carriage, which to them is a *res inter alios acta*, that result should not be surprising or shocking. If, however, the holder of the bill of lading is the shipper, i.e. the contract partner of the carrier, the contract of carriage between them does remain relevant and the carrier will be able to invoke the defences from the contract of carriage when faced with a claim by the shipper under the bill of lading. A statutory approach does not deny the contractual reality, but limits it to its true scope.

88 On the other hand, a statutory approach does make matters more complicated in 'non-standard' situations, particularly when the bill of lading is never presented to the carrier. In the *Star Ikebana*,[171] a cargo of fertilizer had caught fire, still in the port of loading, as a result of welding work on the ship. The damaged fertilizer was discharged again and disposed of, and the bills of lading obviously were not presented anymore. In the ensuing cargo claims, the claimants right of action was challenged. The Antwerp Court of Appeal, explicitly pointing out the exceptional circumstances, tried to reconstruct who would have been the holder of the different bills of lading in the port of destination. In the very similar case of the *Eendracht*,[172] brewery equipment was damaged shortly after the vessel left the port of loading. The shipper, carrier and consignee all agreed to have the vessel return to port and the equipment discharged and returned to the manufacturer for repairs. The bill of lading was not invoked or presented in this process. Afterwards, when the carrier was sued by the (insurers of the) consignee, he argued that the consignee did not have title to sue as it had never

---

170 See above, n° 57 p. 187.
171 CA Antwerp 3 December 2007, *R.H.A.* 2009, 361 (*ms. Star Ikebana*).
172 HR 22 September 2000, *NJ* 2001, 44, *S&S* 2001, 37 (*Eendracht*).

presented the bill of lading. The Dutch Supreme Court held that the third-party beneficiary clause in the contract of carriage could also be accepted in other ways than by presenting the bill of lading.[173] In such cases, it is admittedly easier in a contractual approach to create a link between the expected/intended holder of the bill of lading and the carrier than in a statutory approach.

---

173 That decision later came back to bite the Supreme Court in the *Ladoga 15* case (HR 29 November 2002, *NJ* 2003, 374, *S&S* 2003, 62), where the bill of lading had been presented by an agent, who had initially been instructed by one principal and had obtained an original of the bill in that capacity, but later changed principals and presented that original on behalf of the second principal (who never paid for the goods). Not only had the bill of lading been presented, the carrier also argued that the second principal and its agent had in any case accepted the third-party beneficiary clause under the *Eendracht* decision (HR 22 September 2000, *NJ* 2001, 44, *S&S* 2001, 37). Rather than holding that the agent, once it had changed principals, was no longer a lawful holder of the bill of lading, the Supreme Court felt obliged to hold, rather vaguely and unhelpfully, that the third-party beneficiary clause cannot be accepted 'at any time and in any way whatsoever'.

5 Bill of lading clauses

1 Bills of lading do not only contain 'factual' information – the description of the goods, the load and discharge ports, the identity of the shipper and consignee, etc. –, but also terms and conditions. Some of these terms and conditions are outside the scope of the carriage conventions (container demurrage clauses, for example), some are considered to be within the realm of the carrier's freedom of contract (transshipment clauses, for example), and some are explicitly allowed by the carriage conventions ('before and after' or 'period of responsibility' clauses, for example). The carrier, who has inserted these terms and conditions, wants to see them applied, while (third-party) holders are usually less enthusiastic about these terms and conditions. To what extent are they binding on the holder of the bill of lading under the different theories? This issue will be looked into with a bird's eye perspective for each of the three groups of theories.

2 A special type of clauses are the jurisdiction (or arbitration) clauses, often accompanied by choice of law clauses. Such clauses are special, first because of the impact they have and secondly because they have been the subject, at least in the EU, of specific legislation. Jurisdiction clauses in the bill of lading may mean that the claimant is forced to file suit in a foreign country, which is at the very least a strategic disadvantage and may even make lawsuits prohibitively expensive. Furthermore, within the EU, the 1968 Brussels Convention[1] and later the Brussels I and Brussels I Recast Regulations[2] have provided that jurisdiction clauses are only valid if they have been the subject of a real consensus of the contracting parties, which consensus must be clearly and precisely demonstrated.[3]

---

1 Convention on jurisdiction and the enforcement of judgments in civil and commercial matters, signed at Brussels on 27 September 1968.
2 Council Regulation (EC) No 44/2001 of 22 December 2000 on jurisdiction and the recognition and enforcement of judgments in civil and commercial matters, now Regulation (EU) No 1215/2012 of the European Parliament and of the Council of 12 December 2012 on jurisdiction and the recognition and enforcement of judgments in civil and commercial matters.
3 ECJ 14 December 1976, Case 24/76, *Estasis Salotti*, point 7; ECJ 14 December 1976, Case 25/76, *Segoura*, point 6; ECJ 19 June 1984, Case 71/83, *Partenreederei ms. Tilly Russ and Ernest Russ v NV Haven- & Vervoerbedrijf Nova and NV Goeminne Hout*, point 14 and 17; ECJ 11 July 1985, Case 221/84, *Berghoefer*, point 13; ECJ 20 February 1997, Case

That being said, jurisdiction clauses are of course very common, also in maritime law contracts. A charter party without a jurisdiction clause would be a rare find indeed. As long as jurisdiction clauses are invoked between the original parties to the contract (shipowner and charterer, shipper and carrier), they are, in general, not the subject of much contestation. With bills of lading, however, where jurisdiction clauses are often invoked against third-party holders, these clauses have always been, and continue to be a source of disputes.[4]

5.1 Contractual – the holder steps into the shoes of the shipper

3 The first group of theories has the holder of the bill of lading succeed to all rights and liabilities of the shipper. If that is the case, the validity and binding force of the bill of lading terms have to be appreciated with regard to the shipper, under the law that applies to the contract of carriage made between the carrier and the shipper. The result of that analysis might be that the bill of lading does not contain all of the terms of the contract or that its terms were amended later, that the choice of law and/or jurisdiction clauses are not valid under the applicable law, that the incorporation clause only incorporated certain parts of the charter party, etc. Once the position with regard to the shipper is established, that position is then automatically and entirely transferred to the holder, regardless of what the holder personally knew or agreed to. If the incorporation clause validly incorporated the charter party's arbitration clause as against the shipper, then the holder is also bound by that arbitration clause, even if he personally was entirely unaware of the charter party and the arbitration clause. This is the easiest and most straightforward solution; it is also the most dangerous one for the holder.

4 The same rules apply to jurisdiction clauses. In *Tilly Russ*,[5] the European Court of Justice has held that *if*, pursuant to the applicable national law, the holder succeeds to all rights and obligations of the shipper, the only question is whether the jurisdiction clause was validly agreed between the shipper and the carrier. That is not necessarily the case – the bill of lading may only have been issued after the contract of carriage was entered into, or even after the goods have already been shipped, and is in any case not always an agreement 'in writing'

C-106/95, *MSG*, point 15; ECJ 3 July 1997, Case C-269/95, *Benincasa*, point 29; ECJ 9 November 2000, Case C-387/98, *Coreck Maritime v Handelsveem*, point 13; ECJ 20 April 2016, Case C-366/13, *Profit Investment Sim SpA v Stefano Ossi et al.*, point 27.

4 In addition to numerous cases, notes and articles, there are even a number of books dedicated to this issue. See, for example, M. Davies (Ed.), *Jurisdiction and Forum Selection in International Maritime Law: Essays in Honor of Robert Force*, La Haye, Kluwer Law International, 2005, 344 p.; A. Kpoahoun Amoussou, *Les clauses attributives de compétence dans le transport maritime de marchandises*, Presses Universitaires d'Aix-Marseille, 2002, 507 p.; F. Sparka, *Jurisdiction and Arbitration Clauses in Maritime Transport Documents*, Berlin, Springer Verlag, 2010, 279 p.

5 ECJ 19 June 1984, Case 71/83, *Partenreederei ms. Tilly Russ and Ernest Russ v NV Haven- & Vervoerbedrijf Nova and NV Goeminne Hout*.

within the meaning of the Brussels I Regulation –, but if it is established that the jurisdiction clause was valid as between the shipper and the carrier, it automatically also binds the later holder, since the latter succeeds to all rights and obligations of the shipper. It is irrelevant in this case whether the later holder agreed to the jurisdiction clause or was even aware of the jurisdiction clause.[6]

5.2 Contractual – the holder has a right of his own

5 The second group of theories accepts that the holder and the carrier are in a contractual relationship, but with distinct rights and liabilities of the holder. This means that the validity of the terms of the bill of lading must be appreciated in the direct relationship between the carrier and the holder, in light of the law that applies to that relationship. It is possible that the applicable law is mandatory and does not allow choice of law provisions,[7] that it does not accept jurisdiction clauses in preprinted forms, that it does not allow incorporation by simple reference, etc. In order to determine which law applies, it will often be relevant when and where the relationship between the carrier and the holder came into being. If that relationship is thought to arise when and where the holder presents the bill of lading to the carrier and claims delivery, the carrier will be able to predict the applicable law. If, on the other hand, the relationship is thought to arise when and where the holder acquires the bill of lading, it is totally impossible for the carrier to predict which law will turn out to govern his relationship with the holder. Also, the applicable law may be the law of a landlocked country, that does not have any maritime or carriage law to speak of. The bill of lading will often have a choice of law clause, of course, but whether that clause will be effective depends on the applicable law.

6 If the holder enters into a contractual relationship with the carrier, that automatically implies that the holder has *accepted* the terms of that relationship. It is a contradiction in terms to say that the holder has entered into a contract with the carrier, but nevertheless did not accept the terms of that contract. There might be a difference of opinion about whether this is limited to the terms as they appear from the bill of lading or also includes other terms that the holder could have

---

6 ECJ 9 November 2000, Case C-387/98, *Coreck Maritime v Handelsveem*, point 25: "*If he did* [succeed to the rights and obligations of one of the original parties] *there is no need to ascertain whether he accepted the jurisdiction clause in the original contract.*"
    ECJ 20 April 2016, Case C-366/13, *Profit Investment Sim SpA v Stefano Ossi et al.*, point 33: "*If there is, under national law, such a relationship* [the holder succeeding to the shipper's rights and obligations], *there is no need for the court hearing the case to ascertain whether that third party accepted that jurisdiction clause.*"
    See also the Opinion of Advocate General Léger in Case C-159/97, *Castelletti*, point 82 and point 137–139.
7 In Belgium, the Supreme Court has held that 'Article 91 of the Maritime Act' (the incorporation of the Hague-Visby Rules) mandatorily applies to carriage to or from a Belgian port, notwithstanding a possible choice of law clause in the bill of lading. (Cass. 7 January 2011, *R.H.A.* 2010, 230 (Case C.09.0275.N)).

found out, but it is hard to deny that at least the terms of the bill of lading itself must be assumed *accepted* by the holder.

7 Here also, as with the first group of theories, the same rules apply to jurisdiction clauses. If one accepts that a third-party holder of the bill of lading accedes to or enters into a contract of carriage with the carrier, then that necessarily implies that the holder has accepted the jurisdiction clause in that contract. Acceding to or entering into a contract indeed presupposes consent, and (unless certain provisions would have been hidden from the acceding party) that consent also extends to the clauses of the contract.

8 In such case, the bill of lading simply becomes a 'written agreement' between the carrier and the holder within the meaning of the Brussels I Regulation. It has been tried to deny this conclusion by pointing out that the European Court of Justice in *Tilly Russ* held that a bill of lading was not a written agreement.[8] The Court, however, was referring to the bill of lading in the relation between the shipper and the carrier. In that relationship, the bill of lading is only issued after the contract of carriage is concluded, sometimes even after the goods have been loaded and the ship has sailed. Given those circumstances, it is indeed clear that a bill of lading is not, or not necessarily, a written agreement between the shipper and the carrier. The situation is different for the holder, though. The holder is, from the very first, aware of the bill of lading and its terms and conditions, and is – in the second group of theories – deemed to accede to the contract incorporated in or evidenced by the bill of lading. As regards the holder, therefore, the bill of lading is indeed a written agreement: it is a document in writing with terms and conditions that is proposed by the carrier and later accepted by the holder.

9 It has also been argued that neither the presentation of the bill of lading nor the possible signature of the holder on the bill of lading proves acceptance of the bill's clauses, such signature only being a proof of delivery.[9] It is indeed true that the holder is often required, sometimes even by law, to sign off on the bill of lading, and that such signature, in itself, does not prove agreement with the clauses of the bill of lading. The argument overlooks the fact, however, that such proof of agreement is not needed at all. If one accepts that the holder accedes to the contract, then the agreement of the holder is a given and no longer needs to be proven separately. It is indeed impossible to say that one has *acceded* to a contract, but has nevertheless not *agreed* to the clauses of that contract. Accession necessarily implies and includes agreement.

10 Also, even if the bill of lading is not considered a written agreement between the carrier and the acceding holder, it could be considered a usage in international trade and commerce to communicate jurisdiction clauses to contracting parties through the medium of the bill of lading.[10]

---

8 J. Eckoldt, *De forumkeuze in het zeevervoer*, Zutphen, Uitgeverij Paris, 2014, at p. 165.
9 J. Eckoldt, *De forumkeuze in het zeevervoer*, Zutphen, Uitgeverij Paris, 2014, at p. 164.
10 See P. Kuypers, *Forumkeuze in het Nederlandse internationaal privaatrecht*, Deventer, Kluwer, 2008, at pp. 379–380.

11 This position is less dangerous for the holder, as there are more possibilities to protect him against terms or conditions that he did not know or could not have known. Nevertheless, the holder is still assumed to have accepted a collection of clauses, whereas in most cases that was never his real intention.

5.3 Non-contractual

12 The third group sees the relationship between the carrier and a third-party holder as non-contractual. That means that, in principle, the carrier freely determines the contents of his undertaking. In practice, of course, that freedom is limited by mandatory carriage law and, *de facto*, by what the carrier has agreed with the shipper.[11] The holder must take the right as it has been created by the carrier, with the limitations that were imposed on it by the carrier. In principle, therefore, all terms and conditions of the bill of lading are binding on the holder who decides to take up the document and exercise the right incorporated in it.[12] This does not mean, however, that the carrier is free to include any term whatsoever in the bill of lading. There is indeed a distinction to be made. Some terms and conditions can be imposed unilaterally. If a shopkeeper decides that he will be closed from 12.00 to 14.00, there is no-one that can force him to open at 13.00. If a carrier supplies containers and provides that they must be returned empty within one day from delivery, nobody can claim that they are entitled to two free days. Other terms, however, can only be *agreed* by the parties concerned by them.

13 This is particularly true for jurisdiction clauses. Within the EU, it is clear that a jurisdiction clause is an agreement, which requires a real meeting of the minds of the parties involved.[13] The same is undoubtedly true for arbitration clauses and choice of law clauses.

In order to ensure real consensus of the contracting parties, the 1968 Brussels Convention and the Brussels I (Recast) Regulation impose formal requirements, which provide the only possible ways to prove the required consensus. Over the years, these formal requirements have been relaxed, to now also allow for practices which the parties have established between themselves and usages in international trade or commerce, but the European Court of Justice has repeatedly stressed,

---

11 Agreements between the carrier and the shipper are not binding on the third-party holder, but the carrier will be careful that what he puts in the bill of lading does not breach those agreements.
12 Compare E. du Pontavice, "Sur la clause attributive de juridiction d'un connaissement venu de Chine", *D.M.F.* 1994, at p. 748: "*les clauses du connaissement formant un titre sont opposables au destinataire et aux assureurs subrogés: le principe n'est même pas discutable (Paris, 27 janvier 1988, DMF 1988 IR, 53)*" (the clauses of the bill of lading, which is a document of title, are binding on the consignee and on the subrogated insurers: the principle cannot be contested (CA Paris, 27 January 1988, *DMF* 1988 IR, 53)).
13 Compare S. Lamont-Black, "Third party rights and transport documents under the DCFR – potential for an appropriate and effective EU unification and an improvement for the UK?", *J.I.M.L.* 2015, Vol. 21, at pp. 293–294.

in very clear words, that a real agreement still remains required.[14] A party cannot unilaterally impose a jurisdiction clause on other parties it does business with, and a party does not become bound by a jurisdiction clause simply because that party knows that such clause exists.

14 If the bill of lading is a non-contractual, unilateral document created by the carrier, then the bill of lading *as such* cannot prove the required agreement between the carrier and a third-party holder. Importantly, however, the usage in international trade or commerce cannot be invoked in this case either. Such usage, indeed, is only a way in which *contracting* parties can communicate a jurisdiction clause to each other. Both the Brussels I (Recast) Regulation and the European Court of Justice explicitly refer to *contracting parties* when dealing with usage in international trade or commerce.[15] If one buys a piece of art at an auction, for example, there could be a usage in that trade that the auction catalogue contains a jurisdiction clause. If that usage is proven, the contracting parties (buyer – seller) are bound by that clause. If, on the other hand, parties are *not* in a contractual relation – as in this group of theories the carrier and the third-party holder of the bill of lading –, the simple fact that one of the parties knows that bills of lading often contain jurisdiction clauses does not make that clause binding.[16] Suppose, indeed, that all road carriers would have general terms and conditions, containing an exclusive jurisdiction clause in favour of the place where the carrier is established, and that this is a well-known fact. No-one would argue, presumably, that if a traffic accident happens, the owner of the other car must be bound by that jurisdiction clause, since it is a well-known usage for road carriers to have such

---

14 ECJ 14 December 1976, Case n° 24/76, *Estasis Salotti*, point 7; ECJ 14 December 1976, Case n° 25/76, *Segoura*, point 6; ECJ 19 June 1984, Case n° 71/83, *Tilly Russ*, points 14 and 17; ECJ 11 July 1985, Case n° 221/84, *Berghoefer*, point 13; ECJ 20 February 1997, Case n° C-106/95, *MSG*, point 15; ECJ 3 July 1997, Case n° C-269/95, *Benincasa*, point 29; ECJ 9 November 2000, Case n° C-387/98, *Coreck Maritime*, point 13; ECJ 7 February 2013, Case n° C-543/10, *Refcomp / AXA*, point 26–28; ECJ 20 April 2016, Case C-366/13, *Profit Investment Sim SpA v Stefano Ossi et al.*, point 27.

15 Article 25.1.(c) of Brussels I Recast (Regulation 1215/2012) refers to a form "... *which in such trade or commerce is widely known to, and regularly observed by, parties to contracts of the type involved in the particular trade or commerce concerned*".

See also ECJ 20 February 1997, Case C-106/95, *MSG*, point 19 ("... *consensus on the part of the contracting parties*..."); ECJ 3 July 1997, Case C-269/95, *Benincasa*, point 28 ("... *the intentions of the parties to the contract*..."); ECJ 16 March 1999, Se C-159/97, *Castelletti*, point 21 ("... *the contracting parties' consent to the jurisdiction clause is presumed to exist where their conduct is consistent with a usage*..."); ECJ 20 April 2016, Case C-366/13, *Profit Investment Sim SpA v Stefano Ossi et al.*, point 43 (... *in relation to the branch of trade or commerce in which the parties to the contract operate*").

16 A proven usage in international trade or commerce creates a (rebuttable) presumption of acceptance of the jurisdiction clause, but only between contracting parties and precisely *because* those parties have entered into a contract with each other. Between parties that are *not* in a contractual relation, mere knowledge of the existence of a jurisdiction clause cannot suffice. To say that mere knowledge would suffice is entirely irreconcilable with the requirement of a real consensus, as repeatedly and very explicitly stressed by the European Court of Justice.

jurisdiction clauses. The carrier and the driver of the other car are not contract partners, and the carrier cannot impose a jurisdiction clause on the other road users simply by making sure that those other users are aware of the existence of that clause. Such tortious situation is, of course, not (international) trade or commerce, but the same applies when parties do have a (commercial) relation, which does not involve or extend to the issue that gives rise to a claim. Suppose, for example, that all shipowners would have general terms and conditions containing a jurisdiction clause, again a usage that is well-known to all in the maritime world. Ships and shipowners do have some form of (commercial) relation with the ports they call at, but if a ship damages port infrastructure, it would again not be argued, presumably, that the port must be bound by the jurisdiction clause since it has commercial dealings with the shipowner and is well aware of the fact that the latter's terms and conditions contain a jurisdiction clause. A comparable situation actually played out in the *Assens Havn v Navigators* case,[17] where port infrastructure was damaged by a ship. As the shipowner had gone into liquidation, the port authority brought a direct action against the liability insurer of the shipowner before the Danish courts. The insurer contested the jurisdiction of the Danish court, invoking the jurisdiction clause in its insurance policy. Jurisdiction clauses are of course to be found in most, if not all, marine insurance policies, and that fact is, or at least should have been known to a port authority. The European Court of Justice, however, did not hold that the port authority must be presumed to have accepted the jurisdiction since such clauses are a usage in marine insurance; on the contrary, the Court held that the port authority is removed from the *contractual relationship* that contains the jurisdiction clause (the insurance policy) and that the jurisdiction clause cannot be invoked against a third-party victim such as the port. Admittedly, the *Assens Havn* decision is not automatically transposable to bills of lading, as it is a decision in insurance matters, for which the Brussels I (Recast) Regulation establishes an autonomous system, designed to give the weaker party the benefit of specific rules of jurisdiction more favourable to his interests that the general rules.[18] There is no such autonomous system in the Regulation for the carriage of goods or bills of lading. On the other hand, however, from the 1983 Harter Act to the present day conventions, the carriage laws and conventions have also been created to protect the weaker party. Also, if the position of the holder of the bill of lading is seen as non-contractual, the holder, like the third-party victim in liability insurance, is (far) removed from the contractual relationship containing the jurisdiction clause.

15 A proven usage in international trade or commerce is therefore never sufficient in itself. Such usage only becomes relevant if it is first shown that the parties between which the jurisdiction clause is invoked are in a contractual relationship with each other. The reason is simple and straightforward: if a party is bound by a

---

17 ECJ 13 July 2017, Case C-368/16, *Assens Havn v Navigators Management (UK) Ltd.*
18 ECJ 13 July 2017, Case C-368/16, *Assens Havn v Navigators Management (UK) Ltd*, points 29–30.

jurisdiction clause, it is because it has *accepted* that clause and not merely because it is aware of the *existence* of that clause.

16 If, therefore, the position of the third-party holder of the bill of lading is seen as non-contractual, the holder can only be bound by the jurisdiction clause in the bill of lading if it is proven that he has really agreed to that clause. Neither the bill of lading itself nor the fact that it is widely known that bills of lading generally contain jurisdiction clauses can be used to the required consent of the third-party holder.

17 This position is the most protective of the holder's interests. His rights, but also his liabilities, are in any case limited to what appears from the document itself, and he will only be bound by terms requiring an agreement of the parties if it can be proven that he actually agreed to such terms.[19]

---

19 Compare CA Antwerp 30 November 2009, 54 *R.H.A.* 2010, at p. 61. The Court held that the third-party holder of the bill of lading was not bound by the jurisdiction clause, since he had never accepted that clause.

Bibliography

Aikens, R., R. Lord and M. Bools, *Bills of Lading*, London, Informa, 2006, 431 p.
Angell, J., *A Treatise on the Law of Carriers of Goods and Passengers, by Land and by Water*, Boston, Little, Brown and Company, 1877 (5th Ed.), 704 p.
Arroyo, I., "Relation entre Charte Partie et Connaissement: La Clause d'Incorporation", *E.T.L.* 1980, 713.
Barels, J., *Advysen over den Koophandel en Zeevaert*, Vol. I, Amsterdam, Hendrik Gartman, 1780, 464 p.
Basedow, J., *Der Transportvertrag*, Tübingen, J.C.B. Mohr (Paul Siebeck), 1987, 602 p.
Basset, F., "Droit français du connaissement", in F. Basset, *Droit romain des avaries communes. Droit français du connaissement. Thèse pour le doctorat*, Paris, Arthur Rousseau, 1889, 84 p. (avaries communes) and 205 p. (connaissement).
Bassindale, J., "Title to sue under bills of lading: the Carriage of Goods by Sea Act 1992", *Journal of International Banking Law* 1992, 414–417.
Baughen, S., "Case Comment. The Gudermes. What future for Brandt v Liverpool?", *J.B.L.* 1994, 62–66.
Baughen, S., *Shipping Law*, London, Routledge-Cavendish, 2009 (4th Ed.), 436 p.
Bayer, W., *Der Vertrag zugunsten Dritter*, Tübingen, J.C.B. Mohr (Paul Siebeck), 1995, 436 p.
Beale, J., "The history of the carrier's liability", XI *Harv. L. Rev* 1897, 158–168, and reprinted in Committee of the Association of American Law Schools (Ed.), *Select Essays in Anglo-American Legal History*, Vol. III, Boston, Little, Brown and Company, 1909, 148–160.
Beltjens, G., *Encyclopédie du Droit Commercial Belge*, Vol. IV, *Le Code Maritime Belge*, Brussels, Bruylant, 1927 (2nd Ed.), 1349 p.
Bennett, W., *The History and Present Position of the Bill of Lading as a Document of Title to Goods*, Cambridge, University Press, 1914, 101 p.
Bensa, E., *The Early History of Bills of Lading*, Genoa, Stabilimento d'Arti Grafiche Caimo & C., 1925, 13 p.
Beurier, J.P., *Droits maritimes (Dalloz Action)*, Dalloz, 2009–2010.
Bokalli, V.-E., "Crise et avenir du connaissement", *D.M.F.* 1998, 115–132.
Bonassies, P., *Cass. com. 29 November 1994 (Navires Harmony et Nagasaki)*, *D.M.F.* 1995, 209 (note).
Bonassies, P., *Cass. com. 19 December 2000 (Navire Norberg)*, *D.M.F.* 2001, 222 (note).
Bonassies, P., and C. Scapel, *Droit maritime*, Paris, L.G.D.J., 2010 (2nd Ed.), 946 p.
Bools, M., *The Bill of Lading. A Document of Title to Goods. An Anglo-American Comparison*, London, LLP, 1997, 275 p.

Boonk, H., *Zeevervoer onder cognossement*, Arnhem, Gouda Quint, 1993, 298 p.
Boonk, H., "HR 29 November 2002 RvdW 2002, 197 (Ladoga 15): de grondslag van de rechtsverkrijging door de derde cognossementhouder", *T.V.R.* 2003, 132–138.
Boonk, H., "Cognossement en cognossementhouder", *NTBR* 2007-9, 372–379.
Boulay-Paty, P.-S., *Cours de droit commercial maritime*, Tôme I, Brussels, Société belge de Librairie, 1838, 358 p.
Bradgate, R., and F. White, "The Carriage of Goods by Sea Act 1992", (1993) 56 *Mod. L. Rev.* 188–207.
Bridge, M., *The Sale of Goods*, Oxford, Oxford University Press, 2009 (2nd Ed.), 887 p.
Bridge, M., L. Gullifer, G. McMeel and S. Worthington, *The Law of Personal Property*, London, Sweet & Maxwell, 2013, 1098 p.
Bugden, P., and S. Lamont-Black, *Goods in Transit and Freight Forwarding*, London, Sweet & Maxwell, 2010 (2nd Ed.), 902 p.
Cahen, J., *Het cognossement*, Arnhem, Gouda Quint, 1964, 257 p.
Cahen, J., *Algemeen deel van het verbintenissenrecht*, Deel 4 van Pitlo, *Het Nederlands burgerlijk recht*, Deventer, Kluwer, 2002 (9th Ed.), 383 p.
Campbell, N., "Defining the frontiers of the bill of lading holder's liability – the Berge Sisar and the Aegean Sea", *J.B.L.* 2000, 196–202.
Canaris, C.-W., W. Schilling and P. Ulmer (Eds.), *Handelsgesetzbuch Großkommentar, begründet von Hermann Staub*, Berlin, De Gruyter, 2001 (4th Ed.).
Carette, N., *Derdenbeding*, Antwerp, Intersentia, 2011, 892 p.
Carreau, C., "Cass. fr. 21 November 1978", *Recueil Dalloz Sirey* 1980, 309 (note).
Cashmore, C., *Parties to a Contract of Carriage, or Who Can Sue on a Contract of Carriage of Goods?* London, Lloyd's of London Press, 1990, 246 p.
Cashmore, C., "Case Comment. Title to sue in contract of carriage: land", *J.B.L.* 1991, July, 362–364.
Cauffman, C., *De verbindende eenzijdige belofte*, Antwerpen, Intersentia, 2005, 952 p.
Chitty on Contracts, Vol. 1, *General Principles*, London, Sweet & Maxwell, 1989 (26th Ed.), 1449 p., Vol. 2, *Specific Contracts*, London, Sweet & Maxwell, 1989, 1391 p.
Chua, J., "Carriage of Goods by Sea Act 1992 – bills of lading – intermediate holders of bill of lading – transfer of liabilities", *Student Law Review* 1999, 51–52.
Claringbould, M., *Parlementaire Geschiedenis Boek 8, Verkeersmiddelen en vervoer*, Deventer, Kluwer, 1992, 1289 p.
Claringbould, M., *Het schip en zijn cognossementen*, Deventer, Kluwer, 1996, 51 p.
Claringbould, M., "Het cognossement", in *Preadvies van de Vereeniging Handelsrecht en de Nederlandse Vereniging voor zee- en vervoerrecht. Vervoersrecht in Boek 8 BW*, Zwolle, Tjeenk Willink, 1997, 169 p.
Cleton, R., *Hoofdlijnen van het vervoerrecht*, Zwolle, Tjeenk Willink, 1994, 339 p.
Cleveringa, R., "Een stap achterwaarts", *W.P.N.R.* 1921, 541–543.
Cleveringa, R., *Zeerecht*, Zwolle, Tjeenk Willink, 1961 (4th Ed.), 1115 p.
Cleveringa, R., Book Review J.L.P. Cahen *Het Cognossement*, *R.M.T.* 1965, at pp. 137–143.
Cooke, J., T. Young, A. Taylor, J. Kimball, D. Martowski and L. Lambert, *Voyage Charters*, London, Informa, 2007 (3rd Ed.), 1254 p.
Corbin, A., "Quasi-contractual obligations", 21 *Yale L.J.* 533–554.
Cornelis, L., *Algemene theorie van de verbintenis*, Antwerpen, Intersentia, 2000, 997 p.
Cousy, H., and C. Van Schoubroeck, "Compulsory liability insurance in Belgium", in A. Fenyves, C. Kissling, S. Perner and D. Rubin (Eds.), *Compulsory Liability Insurance From a European Perspective*, Berlin, Walter de Gruyter, 2016, 565 p.

Curwen, N., "The Bill of Lading as a document of title at Common Law", in P. Park and B. Andoh (Eds.), *Mountbatten Yearbook of Legal Studies*, Southampton Solent University, 2007, 139–162.

Davies, M., and A. Dickey, *Shipping Law*, Lawbook Co., 2004 (3th Ed.), 747 p.

Debattista, C., *Bills of Lading in Export Trade*, Haywards Heath, Tottel Publishing, 2009 (3rd Ed.), 335 p.

Dehouck, C., *Documentair krediet*, Brugge, die Keure, 2007, 1000 p.

Delebecque, Ph., "Cass. com. 16 January 1996 (Navire Monte Cervantes)", *D.M.F.* 1996, 629 (note).

Delebecque, Ph., "La clause attributive de compétence stipulée dans un connaissement et dûment convenue entre le chargeur et le transporteur est-elle de plein droit opposable au destinataire?", *D.M.F.* 2000, 12–15.

Delebecque, Ph., "La validité des clauses de compétence doit s'apprécier en application de la loi du contrat: une solution de droit commun qui froisse le particularisme du droit des transports maritimes", *D.M.F.* 2001, 995–1001.

Delebecque, Ph., "Nouvelles précisions et nouvelles interrogations sur le régime des clauses attributives de juridiction", *D.M.F.* 2003, 559–562.

Delebecque, Ph., *Droit maritime*, Paris, Dalloz, 2014 (13th Ed.), 896 p.

Delebecque, Ph., and M. Germain, *Traité de droit commercial*, Vol. 2, Paris, L.G.D.J., 2004 (17th Ed.), 1323 p.

Delwaide, L., *CA Antwerp 10 October 1990*, *R.H.A.* 1993, 121 (note).

Delwaide, L., and J. Blockx, "Kroniek van het zeerecht. Overzicht van rechtsleer en rechtspraak 1976–1988", Part 1, *T.B.H.* 1989, 1004–1045, Part 2, *T.B.H.* 1990, 564–598, Part 3, *T.B.H.* 1991, 123–168, Part 4, *T.B.H.* 1991, 943–1022.

De Pinto, A., *Handleiding tot het Wetboek van Koophandel*, Vol. 2, Part 2, The Hague, J. Belinfante, 1842, 295 p.

Desjardins, A., *Traité de droit commercial maritime*, Vol. IV, Paris, A. Durand and Pedone-Lauriel, 1885, 509 p.

De Smet, R., *Droit maritime et droit fluvial belges*, Vol. I, Brussels, Larcier, 1971, 608 p.

De Weerdt, I., *Het verhandelbaar cognossement*, Antwerpen, ETL, 1991, 142 p.

De Wit, R., *Multimodal Transport. Carrier Liability and Documentation*, London, Lloyd's of London Press, 1995, 583 p.

Diephuis, G., *Handboek voor het Nederlandsch Handelsregt*, Vol. 2, Groningen, J.B. Wolters, 1874, 295 p.

Dirix, E., "De Meerpartijenovereenkomst", *T.P.R.* 1983, 757–792.

Dirix, E., *Obligatoire verhoudingen tussen contractanten en derden*, Antwerpen, Kluwer, 1984, 318 p.

Dirix, E., "Bewarend beslag op zeeschepen en op scheepsdocumenten. Actuele ontwikkeling", in X., *De bank & de zee*, Brussels, Bruylant, 1998, 41–63.

Dirix, E., R. Steennot and H. Vanhees, *Handels- en economisch recht in hoofdlijnen*, Antwerpen, Intersentia, 2014 (10th Ed.), 537 p.

Dorhout Mees, T., and A. Van Empel, *Nederlands handels- en faillissementsrecht*, IV, *Vervoer*, Arnhem, Gouda Quint, 1980 (7th Ed.), 324 p.

du Perron, C., *HR 18 October 2002 (Butter/Besix)*, *N.J.* 2003, 503 (note).

du Pontavice, E., "Sur la clause attributive de juridiction d'un connaissement venu de Chine", *D.M.F.* 1994, 739–756.

du Toit, S.F., "The evolution of the Bill of Lading", 11-2 *Fundamina*, 2005, 12–25.

Eckardt, T., *The Bolero Bill of Lading Under German and English Law*, München, Sellier European Law Publishers, 2004, 256 p.

Eckoldt, J., *De forumkeuze in het zeevervoer*, Zutphen, Uitgeverij Paris, 2014, 306 p.
Emerigon, B., *Traité des assurances et des contrats a la grosse*, Tome I, Marseille, J. Mossy, 1783, 686 p.
Emerigon, B., *Traité des assurances et des contrats a la grosse*, Tome I, Rennes, Molliex, 1827 (2nd Ed.), 649 p.
Falkanger, T., H.J. Bull and L. Brautaset, *Introduction to Maritime Law. The Scandinavian Perspective*, Tano Aschehoug, 1998, 628 p.
Falkanger, T., H.J. Bull and L. Brautaset, *Scandinavian Maritime Law*, Oslo, Universitetsforlaget, 2004 (2nd Ed.), 609 p.
Franck, G., *Der Direktanspruch gegen den Haftpflichtversicherer Eine rechtsvergleichende Untersuchung zum deutschen und skandinavischen Recht*, Tübingen, Mohr Siebeck, 2014, 180 p.
Fredericq, L., *Handboek van Belgisch Handelsrecht*, Vol. III, Brussels, Bruylant, 1980 (2nd Ed.), 639 p.
Frets, F., *De kracht van een cognossement, en het regt van den houder*, Rotterdam, F. W. Krieger, 1818, 96 p.
Fridman, G., *The Law of Agency*, London, Butterworths, 1996 (7th Ed.), 434 p.
Gaskell, N., R. Asariotis and Y. Baatz, *Bills of Lading: Law and Contracts*, London, LLP, 2000, 853 p.
Gaudemet-Tallon, H., "Cass. fr. 10 January and 4 April 1995", *Rev. crit. dr. internat. privé* 1995, 610 (note).
Geense, S., "De 'merchant-clausule'", *NTHR* 2011-5, 190.
Ghestin, J., C. Jamin and M. Billiau, *Traité de droit civil. Les effets du contrat*, Paris, L.G.D.J. 1994 (2nd Ed.), 915 p.
Girvin, S., *Carriage of Goods by Sea*, Oxford, Oxford University Press, 2011 (2nd Ed.), 871 p.
Gramm, H., *Das neue Deutsche Seefrachtrecht nach den Haager Regeln*, Berlin, E.S. Mittler & Sohn, 1938, 202 p.
Grönfors, K., *Towards Sea Waybills and Electronic Documents*, Gothenburg, Akademiförlaget, 1991, 95 p.
Guest, A., *Anson's Law of Contract*, Oxford, Clarendon Press, 1984 (26th Ed.), 641 p.
Guest, A. (Ed.), *Benjamin's Sale of Goods*, London, Sweet & Maxwell, 1987 (3rd Ed.), 1688 p.
Guest, A., *The Law of Assignment*, London, Sweet & Maxwell, 2012, 380 p.
Gursky, K.-H., *Wertpapierrecht*, Heidelberg, C.F Müller Verlag, 2007 (3d Ed.), 139 p.
Haak, K., "HR 29 November 2002 (Ladoga 15)", *N.J.* 2003, 374 (note).
Hartenstein, O., and F. Reuschle, *Handbuch des Fachanwalts. Transport- und Speditionsrecht*, Cologne, Luchterhand, 2010, 1064 p.
Hartkamp, A., and C. Sieburgh, *Mr. C. Assers Handleiding tot de beoefening van het Nederlands Burgerlijk Recht. 6. Verbintenissenrecht. Deel III. Algemeen overeenkomstenrecht*, Deventer, Kluwer, 2014 (14th Ed.), 715 p.
Heenen, J., *Vente et commerce maritime*, Brussels, Bruylant, 1952, 439 p.
Herber, R. (Ed.), *Münchener Kommentar zum Handelsgesetzbuch*, Vol. 7, *Transportrecht*, München, Verlag C.H. Beck, 2014 (3rd Ed.), 2731 p.
Herber, R., *Seehandelsrecht. Systematische Darstellung*, Berlin, De Gruyter, 2016 (2nd Ed.), 477 p.
Higgs, A., and G. Humphreys, "An overview of the implications of the Carriage of Goods by Sea Act 1992", *J.B.L.* 1993, 61–66.

Hogg, M., "Promise: the neglected obligation in European private law", *I.C.L.Q.* 2010, 461-479.

Holdsworth, W., "Origins & Early History of Negotiable Instruments", 31 *L.Q.Rev.* 1915, 12-29 (Part I), 173-186 (Part II), 376-388 (Part III), 32 *L.Q.Rev.* 1916, 20-37 (Part IV).

Holdsworth, W., *A History of English Law*, Vol. VIII, London, Methuen & Co. Ltd., 1925, 500 p.

Holtius, A., *Voorlezingen over Handels- en Zeeregt*, Vol. 2, *Zeerecht*, Utrecht, Kemink en Zoon, 1861, 460 p.

Huizink, J., "De derde-cognossementshouder wordt geen partij", *T.V.R.* 1998, 15-16.

Humphreys, G., and A. Higgs, "Waybills: a case of common law laissez faire in European commerce", *J.B.L.* 1992, 453-480.

Hutchinson, R., *A Treatise on the Law of Carriers*, Chicago, Callaghan and Company, 1906 (3rd Ed.), 2350 p.

Insel, B., "Commentaar op recente transportrechtelijke uitspraken", *R.H.A.* 1996, 105-125.

Japikse, R., "Boekbeschouwing: Mr. G.J. van der Ziel, Het cognossement, naar een functionele benadering", *RM Themis* 2000/5, 193-195.

Japikse, R., *Verkeersmiddelen en Vervoer. Deel I. Algemene bepalingen en rederij*, Asser Serie, Deventer, Kluwer, 2004, 417 p.

Jean-Renard, M., "Charte-partie et connaissement", *D.M.F.* 1955, 3-9 and 67-75.

Jenks, E., "The early history of negotiable instruments", IX *L. Q. Rev*, 1893, 70-85, and reprinted in Committee of the Association of American Law Schools (Ed.), *Select Essays in Anglo-American Legal History*, Vol. III, Boston, Little, Brown and Company, 1909, 51-71.

Josserand, L., *Les Transports*, Paris, Arthur Rousseau, 1910, 947 p.

Josserand, L., *Cours de Droit Civil positif français*, Vol. II, *Théorie générale des obligations*, Paris, Sirey, 1939 (3rd Ed.)

Keener, W., "Quasi-contract, its nature and scope", 7 *Harvard Law Review*, No. 2, 25 May 1893, 57-75.

Kirberger, G., "De positie van den geadresseerde", *Rechtsgeleerd Magazijn* 1898, 41-63.

Kist, J.G., *Het Handelspapier, Part 2. Het cognossement*, Amsterdam, J.H. Gebhard & Comp., 1861, 74 p.

Knauth, A., *Ocean Bills of Lading*, Baltimore, American Maritime Cases, 1953 (4th Ed.), 538 p.

Korthals Altes, A., and J.J. Wiarda, *Vervoerrecht*, Serie Recht en Praktijk, Deventer, Kluwer, 1980, 343 p.

Kortmann, S., *Mr. C. Assers Handleiding tot de beoefening van het Nederlands Burgerlijk Recht. 2. Vertegenwoordiging en rechtspersoon. Deel I. De vertegenwoordiging*, Deventer, Kluwer, 2004 (8th Ed.), 212 p.

Kpoahoun Amoussou, A., *Les clauses attributives de compétence dans le transport maritime de marchandises*, Presses Universitaires d'Aix-Marseille, 2002, 507 p.

Krings, E., "Réflexions au sujet de la prorogation de compétence territoriale et du for contractuel", *Rev.Dr.Int.Comp.* 1978, 78-107.

Kuypers, P., *Forumkeuze in het Nederlandse internationaal privaatrecht*, Deventer, Kluwer, 2008, 733 p.

Lambert-Faivre, Y., and L. Leveneur, *Droit des assurances*, Paris, Dalloz, 2005 (12th Ed.), 918 p.

Lamont-Black, S., "Transferee liability under the Rotterdam Rules: a dance between flexibility and foreseeability", *J.I.M.L.* 2013, 387–418.

Lamont-Black, S., "Third party rights and transport documents under the DCFR – potential for an appropriate and effective EU unification and an improvement for the UK?", 21 *J.I.M.L.* 2015, 280–299.

Langheid, T., and M. Wandt, *Münchener Kommentar zum Versicherungsvertragsgesetz*, Vol. 2, München, Verlag C.H. Beck, 2011, 1914 p.

The Law Commission and The Scottish Law Commission, *Rights of Suit in Respect of Carriage of Goods by Sea*, 19 March 1991 (LAW COM No 196 and SCOT LAW COM No 130).

Lee, K., and A. See, "Rethinking unjust enrichment, bailment and necessity", *L.M.C.L.Q.* 2011, 178–184.

Li, L., "The legal status of intermediate holders of bills of lading under contracts of carriage by sea – a comparative study of US and English law", *J.I.M.L.* 2011, 106–120.

Li, L., "Binding effect of arbitration clauses on holders of Bills of Lading as nonoriginal parties and a potential uniform approach through comparative analysis", 37 *Tul. Mar. L.J.* 2012–2013, 107–126.

Lista, A., *International Commercial Sales: The Sale of Goods on Shipment Terms*, Oxon, Informa Law, 2017, 528 p.

Lobban, M., "Negotiable instruments", in J. Baker (Ed.), *The Oxford History of the Laws of England: Volume XII: 1820–1914 Private Law*, Oxford, Oxford University Press, 2010, 1190 p.

Loeff, J., *Vervoer ter zee*, Deel I, Zwolle, Tjeenk Willink, 1981, 289 p.

Logmans, H., *Zekerheid op lading*, Zutphen, Uitgeverij Paris, 2011, 468 p.

Loyens, J., "Noot: Castelletti t./ Trumpy: geen wijziging van de rechtspositie van de derde-houder van het cognossement", *E.T.L.* 1999, 666–674.

Lyon-Caen, Ch., and L. Renault, *Traité de droit maritime*, Vol. I, Paris, Librairie Cotillon, 1894, 596 p.

MacCormick, N., and O. Weinberger, *An Institutional Theory of Law. New Approaches to Legal Positivism*, Dordrecht, D. Reidel Publishing Company, 1986, 229 p.

Malaurie, Ph., L. Aynès and Ph. Stoffel-Munck, *Les obligations*, Paris, Defrénois, 2011 (5th Ed.), 856 p.

Mangone, G., *United States Admiralty Law*, The Hague, Kluwer Law International, 1997, 312 p.

McKendrick, E. (Ed.), *Goode on Commercial Law*, London, Penguin Books, 2016 (5th Ed.), 1388 p.

McLaughlin, C., "The evolution of the Ocean Bill of Lading", 35 *Yale L.J.* 1925–1926, 548–570.

Mesritz, A., *De Vrachtbrief*, Amsterdam, J.H. de Bussy, 1904, 210 p.

Miller, N., "Bills of lading and factors in nineteenth century English overseas trade", 24 *U. Chi. L. Rev.* 1956–1957, 256–291.

Molengraaff, W., *Leidraad bij de beoefening van het Nederlandsche Handelsrecht*, Haarlem, De Erven F. Bohn, 1912 (2nd Ed.), 885 p.

Molengraaf, W., *Kort begrip van het Nieuwe Nederlandsche Zeerecht*, Haarlem, De Erven F. Bohn, 1928, 339 p.

Murray, D., "History and development of the Bill of Lading", 37 *U. Miami L. Rev.* 1982–1983, 689–732.

Nicolas, P.-Y., "CA Paris 29 November 2000 (Navire Nuevo Leon)", *D.M.F.* 2001, 689–696 (note).

Oostwouder, W., *Hoofdzaken Boek 8 BW. Verkeersmiddelen en vervoer*, Deventer, Kluwer, 2001 (3th Ed.), 166 p.

Pappenheim, M., *Handbuch des Seerechts. Sachen des Seerechts. Schuldverhältnisse des Seerechts. I*, Leipzig, Verlag Duncker & Humblot, 1906, 620 p.

Pappenheim, M., *Handbuch des Seerechts. Schuldverhältnisse des Seerechts. II*, München, Verlag Dunckler & Humblot, 1918, 638 p.

Paulin, C., *Droits des transports*, Paris, Litec, 2005, 313 p.

Peel, S., "The development of the bill of lading: its future in the maritime industry", 2002, thesis submitted to the University of Plymouth, Institute of Marine Studies, 331 p.

Polak, A., *Historisch-juridisch onderzoek naar den aard van het cognossement*, Amsterdam, Gebroeders Binger, 1865, 314 p.

Pouget, L., *Principes de droit maritime suivant le Code de commerce français*, Vol. 2, A. Durand, 1858.

Purchase, H., *The Law Relating to Documents of Title to Goods*, London, Sweet & Maxwell, 1931, 215 p.

Puttfarken, H.-J., *Seehandelsrecht*, Heidelberg, Verlag Recht und Wirtschaft, 1997, 479 p.

Putzeys, J., and M.-A. Rosseels, *Droit des transports et Droit maritime*, Brussels, Bruylant, 1993 (3rd Ed.), 423 p.

Rabe, D., *Seehandelsrecht*, München, Verlag C.H. Beck, 2000 (4th Ed.), 1130 p.

Reepmaker, W., *Over de verbindbaarheid der chertepartij voor den cognoscementhouder*, Rotterdam, Kramers, 1873, 88 p.

Rèmond-Gouilloud, M., *Le contrat de transport*, Paris, Dalloz, 1993, 100 p.

Rèmond-Gouilloud, M., "Des clauses de connaissements maritimes attribuant compétence à une juridiction étrangère: essai de démystification", *D.M.F.* 1995, 339–352.

Rèmond-Gouilloud, M., "CA Caen 20 March 1997 (Navire Westfield)", *D.M.F.* 1997, 716 (note).

Reynolds, F., "The Carriage of Goods by Sea Act 1992 put to the test. The Berge Sisar", *LMCLQ* 1999, 161–164.

Ripert, G., *Droit Maritime*, Tôme II, Paris, Editions Rousseau et Cie., 1952 (4th Ed.), 963 p.

Rodière, P., "Cass. fr. 21 November 1978", *La Semaine Juridique, JCP* 1980, 643 (note).

Rodière, R., *Traité général de droit maritime*, Tome II, *Les contrats de transport de marchandises*, Paris, Librairie Dalloz, 1968, 472 p.

Rodière, R., *Droit des transports. Transports terrestres et aériens*, Paris, Sirey, 1977 (2nd Ed.), 941 p.

Roland, R., "La clause de juridiction du connaissement en droit belge", in X, *Liber Amicorum Lionel Tricot*, Antwerpen, Kluwer, 1988, 439–455.

Roosegaarde Bisschop, W., "Haagsche Conditiën, 1921", *W.P.N.R.* 1922, 151–152.

Sanders, H., *Het cognossement*, 's Gravenhage, Martinus Nijhoff, 1912, 356 p.

Schaps, G., and H. Abraham, *Das Seerecht in der Bundesrepublik Deutschland, Seehandelsrecht*, Berlin, Walter de Gruyter, 1978 (4th Ed.), 2 volumes, 1724 p.

Scheltema, F., *Het vervoercontract in het nieuwe zeerecht*, Rotterdam, S.E.T.A., 1925, 44 p.

Schmitthoff, C., "The development of the combined transport document", *Il Diritto Maritimo* 1972, 312–332 and C. Cheng (Ed.), *Clive M. Schmitthoff's Select Essays on International Trade Law*, BRILL, 1988, 369–383.

Schubert, C., *Münchener Kommentar zum BGB, Band 1: Allgemeiner Teil*, München, C.H. Beck, 2015 (7th Ed.), 2828 p.

Seck, P., *Reisbevrachting en cognossementsvervoer*, Zutphen, Uitgeverij Paris, 2011, 558 p.

Smeele, F., "The bill of lading contracts under European national laws (civil law approaches to explaining the legal position of the consignee under bills of lading)", in R. Thomas (Ed.), *The Evolving Law and Practice of Voyage Charterparties*, London, Informa, 2009, 432 p.

Smeesters, C., and G. Winkelmolen, *Droit maritime et Droit fluvial*, Vol. I, Brussels, Larcier, 1929 (2nd Ed.), 664 p.

Spanjaart, M., "The Konnossementsbegebungsvertrag – a suggestion for further reformation", *TransportR* 2011, 335–337.

Spanjaart, M., *Vorderingsrechten uit cognossement*, Zutphen, Uitgeverij Paris, 2012, 384 p.

Sparka, F., *Jurisdiction and Arbitration Clauses in Maritime Transport Documents*, Berlin, Springer, 2010, 279 p.

Starck, B., H. Roland and L. Boyer, *Obligations*, Vol. 2, *Contrat*, Paris, Litec, 1993 (4th Ed.), 873 p.

Stevens, F., *Vervoer onder cognossement*, Brussel, Larcier, 2001, 334 p.

Stevens, F., "Bevoegdheidsbedingen in cognossementen en de internationale handelsgewoonten", *T.B.H.* 2012, 743–750.

Stevens, F., "Treedt de cognossementhouder toe tot de vervoerovereenkomst?", (note, *Cass. 12 September 2013*), *R.A.B.G.* 2014, 598–601.

Stevens, F., "Consignees' rights in European legal systems", in B. Soyer and A. Tettenborn (Eds.), *International Trade and Carriage of Goods*, Oxon, Informa Law, 2017, 98–113.

Stumm, C., *Der Ablader im Seehandelsrecht. Eine rechtsvergleichende Darstellung des deutschen und des amerikanischen Rechts*, Berlin, LIT Verlag, 2010, 222 p.

Summers, D., "Third Party Beneficiaries and the Restatement (Second) of Contracts", *Cornell L. Rev.* 1982, 880–899.

Tassel, Y., *Cass. com. 29 November 1994 (Navire Stolt Osprey)*, *D.M.F.* 1995, 218 (note).

Terré, F., Ph. Simler and Y. Lequette, *Droit civil. Les obligations*, Paris, Dalloz, 2009 (10th Ed.), 1542 p.

Tetley, W., *Marine Cargo Claims*, Cowansville, Les Editions Yvon Blais, 2008 (4th Ed.), 3231 p.

Tettenborn, A., "Bills of Lading, multimodal transport documents and other things", in B. Soyer and A. Tettenborn (Eds.), *Carriage of Goods by Sea, Land and Air. Unimodal and Multimodal Transport in the 21st Century*, Oxon, Informa Law, 2014, 430 p.

Thomas, R., "Bills of Lading – the position of holders and intermediate holders under the English Carriage of Goods by Sea Act 1992", *Int.M.L.* 2001, 165–170.

Thomas, R., "A comparative analysis of the transfer of contractual rights under the English Carriage of Goods by Sea Act 1992 and the Rotterdam Rules", *J.I.M.L.* 2011, 437–451.

Thomas, R., "International sale contracts and multimodal transport documents: two issues of significance", in B. Soyer and A. Tettenborn (Eds.), *Carriage of Goods by Sea, Land and Air*, Milton Park, Informa Law, 2014, 145–160.

Tiberg, H., "Legal qualities of transport documents", 23 *Tul. Mar. L.J.* (1998), 1–44.

Tilche, M., A. Chao and P. Berthod, "Contrat de transport. Adhésion du destinataire?", *BT* N° 2484, 20 July 1992, 471.

Tilleman, B., *Lastgeving*, A.P.R., Gent, Story-Scientia, 1997, 396 p.

Tjong Tjin Tai, T., *Mr. C. Assers Handleiding tot de beoefening van het Nederlands Burgerlijk Recht. 7. Bijzondere overeenkomsten. Deel IV. Opdracht, incl. de geneeskundige behandelingsovereenkomst en de reisovereenkomst*, Deventer, Kluwer, 2014 (2nd Ed.), 455 p.

Todd, P., *Modern Bills of Lading*, Oxford, Blackwell Scientific Publications, 1990 (2nd Ed.), 332 p.

Todd, P., *Bills of Lading and Bankers' Documentary Credits*, London, LLP, 1993 (2nd Ed.), 299 p.

Tolhurst, G., *The Assignment of Contractual Rights*, Oxford, Hart Publishing, 2006, 478 p.

Tosi, J.-P., "L'adhésion du destinataire au contrat de transport", in X., *Mélanges Christian Mouly*, Paris, Litec, 1998, 175–192.

Trappe, J., "Zur Schiedsgerichtsklausel im Konnossement", in R. Lagoni and M. Paschke (Eds.), *Seehandelsrecht und Seerecht. Festschrift für Rolf Herber zum 70. Geburtstag*, Hamburg, LIT Verlag, 1999, 305–317.

Treitel, G., *The Law of Contract*, London, Sweet & Maxwell, 1991 (8th Ed.), 956 p.

Treitel, G., "Overseas sales in general", in *Benjamin's Sale of Goods*, London, Sweet & Maxwell, 2006 (7th Ed.), 2413 p.

Treitel, G., and F. Reynolds, *Carver on Bills of Lading*, London, Sweet & Maxwell, 2011 (3rd Ed.), 938 p.

van Beukering-Rosmuller, E., "De ontvangstexpediteur als cognossementshouder", *T.V.R.* 2000, 61–65.

van Bockel, B., "De positie van de geadresseerde in het wegvervoer, de binnenvaart en het gecombineerd vervoer", *T.V.R.* 2002/3, p. 79–87.

Van Bladel, G., *Le contrat de transport par bateaux d'intérieur et l'affrètement en séjour*, Vol. I, Antwerp, Lloyd Anversois, s.d., 496 p.

Van Delden, R., *Overzicht van de handelskoop*, Deventer, Kluwer, 1983, 448 p.

Van Delden, R., "Vervoersrecht in het algemeen", in J. Akveld et al. (Eds.), *Hoofdstukken Handelsrecht*, Deventer, Kluwer, 1989 (1st Ed.), 373–425.

Van Den Dries, J., *Nederlands Zeerecht*, Zwolle, Tjeenk Willink, 1926, 679 p.

van der Ziel, G.J., *Het cognossement, naar een functionele benadering*, Deventer, Kluwer, 1999, 34 p.

van Drooghenbroeck, J.-F., "La requalification judiciaire du contrat et des pretensions qui en découlent", in S. Stijns and P. Wéry (Eds.), *Le juge et le contrat. De rol van de rechter in het contract*, Brugge, die Keure, 2014, 1–73.

Van Gerven, W., *Handels- en Economisch Recht*, Vol. 1, *Ondernemingsrecht*, in X, *Beginselen van Belgisch Privaatrecht*, Antwerpen, Standaard, 1975, 584 p.

Van Gerven, W., and S. Covemaeker, *Verbintenissenrecht*, Leuven, Acco, 2006 (2nd Ed.), 719 p.

Van Hooydonk, E., "Towards a worldwide restatement of the general principles of maritime law", 20 *J.I.M.L.* 2014, 170–182.

van Huizen, P., "Het incasso (endossement) in het vervoer", *T.V.R.* 1999, 71–77.

Van Oven, A., *Handelsrecht*, Zwolle, Tjeenk Willink, 1981, 583 p.

Van Ryn, J., and J. Heenen, *Principes de Droit Commercial*, Vol. III, Brussels, Bruylant, 1981 (2nd Ed.), 709 p.

Van Ryn, J., and J. Heenen, *Principes de Droit Commercial*, Vol. IV, Brussels, Bruylant, 1988 (2nd Ed.), 885 p.

Verguts, P., and O. Gossieaux, "Deklading: vrijbrief of guillotine?", *E.T.L.* 1998, 193–241.

Verguts, P., "De overeenkomst van zeevervoer", in A. Poelmans (Ed.), "Overzicht van rechtspraak. Vervoersrecht 1976–2012", *T.P.R.* 2013, 2151–2319.

Völlmar, H., *Het zeerecht*, Haarlem, Tjeenk Willink, 1937, 419 p.

Wilson, J., *Carriage of Goods by Sea*, Harlow, Pearson Longman, 2008 (6th Ed.).

Zwitser, R., "Toetreden tot de vervoersovereenkomst; het Contship America", *T.V.R.* 2000, 33–44.

Zwitser, R., "De cognossementhouder als derde uit derdenbeding", *T.V.R.* 2002, 157–165.

Zwitser, R., "Het cognossement als zekerheidsinstrument", *NTHR* 2007-2, 83–94.

Zwitser, R., *De rol van het cognossement als waardepapier in het handelsverkeer*, Zutphen, Uitgeverij Paris, 2012, 333 p.

Index

Ablader: fn. 10 p. 3, fn. 6 p. 7, n° 15 p. 18, fn. 224 p. 85, fn. 240 p. 91, n° 37 p. 176, fn. 166 p. 205
Accession: n° 92 p. 93, n° 99 p. 96, para. 3.2.2, fn. 418 p. 131, n° 145 p. 134, n° 8 p. 211
Action oblique: para. 3.1.1
Agency: para 3.1.2, n° 71 p. 71, n° 144 p. 133, n° 168 p. 149
Assignment: para 3.1.3., n° 58 p. 65, n° 61 p. 67, n° 168 p. 149, n° 17 p. 155, n° 49 p. 181; - **statutory:** fn. 152 p. 66, fn. 476 p. 148, n° 32 p. 171

Bailment: n° 2 p. 151, n° 9 p. 153, fn. 17 p. 157, n° 35 p. 174
Bearer Bill of Lading: see Bill of Lading, Bearer
Begebungsvertrag: n° 15 p. 18, n° 74 p. 77, n° 107 p. 110, n° 144 p. 133, n° 15 p. 155, n° 37 p. 176, fn. 125 p. 187
Bill of Exchange: n° 20 p. 22, n° 20 p. 38, fn. 79 p. 175, n° 48 p. 180, n° 51 p. 183, n° 54 p. 186, n° 60 p. 189, n° 65 p. 195
Bill of Lading: - **bearer:** n° 5 p. 8, n° 76 p. 79, n° 82 p. 86, n° 85 p. 88, n° 115 p. 114, n° 17 p. 156, n° 31 p. 171, fn. 102 p. 183, n° 66 p. 196, fn. 162 p. 203; - **holder:** n° 5 p. 7; - **negotiation:** n° 45 p. 58; - **order:** n° 5 p. 8, n° 50 p. 61, n° 76 p. 79, n° 115 p. 114, n° 17 p. 156, n° 24 p. 162, n° 31 p. 171, n° 66 p. 196; - **presentation:** n° 17 p. 19; n° 18 p. 20, n° 50 p. 61, n° 77 p. 81, n° 78 p. 81, n° 85 p. 88, n° 113 p. 113, n° 115 p. 114, n° 116 p. 114, n° 23 p. 161, n° 9 p. 211; - **receipt:** para 2.3, n° 51 p. 63, n° 81 p. 85, n° 108 p. 111, n° 146 p. 134, n° 32 p. 172, n° 66 p. 195; - **straight:** n° 5 p. 8, n° 6 p. 8, n° 20 p. 38, n° 23 p. 41, n° 76 p. 78, n° 78 p. 83, n° 85 p. 87, n° 116 p. 114, n° 17 p. 156, n° 31 p. 171, fn. 102 p. 183, n° 66 p. 196; - **transferable:** n° 20 p. 22, n° 67 p. 196
BOLERO: n° 61 p. 66
Book of Lading: n° 8 p. 9, n° 9 p. 10, n° 18 p. 20
Booking Note: n° 60 p. 66
Bulk cargo: n° 18 p. 157, n° 19 p. 157

Cesser clause: n° 162 p. 145
Champerty: fn. 138 p. 63
Charter Party: fn. 1 p. 1, n° 14 p. 14, fn. 42 p. 15, fn. 45 p. 16, n° 15 p. 17, fn. 8 p. 32, n° 51 p. 62–63, n° 60 p. 66, n° 68 p. 71, n° 98 p. 95, n° 103 p. 99, n° 104 p. 101, n° 125 p. 122, n° 126 p. 123, n° 54 p. 186
Choses in action: n° 43 p. 56
CIF: n° 122 p. 120
Class certificate: n° 12 p. 14
Classification society: n° 12 p. 14
Consignee: n° 3 p. 2, n° 6 p. 8, n° 15 p. 18, n° 20 p. 23, para 3.1.2.2, para 3.1.2.3
Consols de la Mar: n° 8 p. 10
Consideration: n° 102 p. 98, n° 140 p. 130, fn. 107 p. 183, n° 74 p. 199
Contract; - **implied:** n° 108 p. 112, para 3.2.3.2, n° 148 p. 136, n° 17 p. 156; - **intuitu personae:** n° 40 p. 54, n° 41 p. 55, n° 43 p. 56, n° 44 p. 57; - **multi-party:** para 3.2.2; - **privity:** n° 23 p. 40, n° 32

p. 50, fn. 201 p. 79, n° 99 p. 96,
n° 140 p. 129, fn. 107 p. 183; - **of
sale**: n° 33 p. 51, n° 35 p. 52, n° 161
p. 144, n° 166 p. 146; - **special**:
n° 23 p. 41; - **three-party**: n° 26
p. 48, n° 36 p. 53, n° 99 p. 96,
n° 103 p. 99, n° 104 p. 99, n° 124
p. 121; - **volume**: see Volume contract

Damages: n° 27 p. 48, n° 104 p. 100,
fn. 326 p. 107, n° 133 p. 127, n° 36
p. 175
Dangerous cargo: n° 67 p. 69, n° 34
p. 174
Delegation: n° 42 p. 55
Demurrage: n° 4 p. 2, n° 23 p. 43,
n° 36 p. 53, fn. 220 p. 84, n° 89
p. 91, n° 140 p. 130, n° 158 p. 143,
n° 26 p. 166, n° 27 p. 168, n° 28
p. 168, n° 34 p. 174, n° 60 p. 190,
n° 65 p. 195
Direct action: n° 73 p. 74, n° 168
p. 148
Disclosed principal: see Principal,
disclosed
Document of title: para 2.5, n° 81
p. 85, n° 83 p. 86, n° 36 p. 176,
fn. 102 p. 183, n° 66 p. 195
Documentary credit: n° 7 p. 4, n° 120
p. 118, n° 145 p. 134, n° 24 p. 163,
fn. 127 p. 189
Documentary intangibles: n° 50
p. 182
Documentary shipper: fn. 10 p. 3,
fn. 145 p. 196

Economy of the contract (*l'économie
du contrat*): n° 104 p. 102, n° 126
p. 124
Endorsement: n° 20 p. 23, n° 23 p. 27,
n° 20 p. 38, n° 23 p. 40, n° 46 p. 58,
n° 2 p. 151, n° 24 p. 162, n° 53
p. 185
Equities, subject to: n° 43 p. 57, n° 46
p. 59
Estoppel: n° 11 p. 12

Factor: n° 9 p. 11, n° 21 p. 25, n° 19
p. 37, n° 22 p. 39, fn. 136 p. 192
FOB: n° 6 p. 3, n° 4 p. 7, n° 9 p. 33,
n° 21 p. 39, fn. 92 p. 53, n° 84 p. 86,
n° 144 p. 133
Freight: n° 3 p. 2, n° 5 p. 3, n° 16
p. 19, n° 23 p. 41, n° 24 p. 44, fn. 70
p. 47, fn. 73 p. 47, n° 36 p. 53, n° 46

p. 58, fn. 205 p. 80, n° 79 p. 84,
n° 89 p. 91, n° 108 p. 111, n° 121
p. 118, n° 140 p. 130, n° 145 p. 134,
n° 158 p. 143, n° 162 p. 144, n° 27
p. 168, n° 34 p. 174, n° 60 p. 189,
n° 61 p. 192, n° 65 p. 195, n° 75
p. 200
Fuero Real: n° 8 p. 10

General average: n° 142 p. 132, n° 157
p. 142, n° 65 p. 194
Guidon de la Mer: n° 18 p. 20, n° 20
p. 23

Holder: - **bill of lading**: n° 5 p. 7;
- **lawful**: n° 17 p. 19, n° 76 p. 79,
n° 78 p. 82, n° 82 p. 86, n° 85 p. 88,
n° 136 p. 128, n° 157 p. 142, n° 20
p. 158, n° 21 p. 159, n° 23 p. 161,
n° 24 p. 162, n° 27 p. 167, n° 31
p. 170, n° 32 p. 171, n° 33 p. 172,
n° 44 p. 179, n° 66 p. 196

Incorporation clause: n° 83 p. 203,
n° 3 p. 209
Institution (legal): para 4.3.3.3, n° 106
p. 108, n° 76 p. 200
Interpretation, strict: fn. 59 p. 168,
n° 63 p. 193, n° 72 p. 198
Intuitu personae: see Contract, intuitu
personae

Juridical act: n° 113 p. 114, n° 163
p. 145

Laytime: n° 25 p. 47
Letter of credit: n° 23 p. 43, fn. 375
p. 118, n° 118 p. 157, fn. 153 p. 199
Letter of indemnity: n° 51 p. 62, n° 25
p. 164
Lien: n° 54 p. 64, fn. 244 p. 92, n° 140
p. 131, n° 68 p. 197, n° 70 p. 197

Maintenance: fn. 138 p. 63
Mate's Receipt: n° 51 p. 62, n° 60
p. 66
Merchant Clause: n° 36 p. 53, n° 48
p. 60, n° 119 p. 117, n° 126 p. 123
Multi-party contract: see Contract,
multi-party

Negotiable instrument: n° 15 p. 18,
n° 25 p. 29, fn. 116 p. 58, fn. 234
p. 89, n° 88 p. 91, n° 99 p. 96,
n° 105 p. 105, n° 127 p. 124, n° 133

p. 127, n° 168 p. 148, para 4.4, n° 75 p. 200, n° 80 p. 201, fn. 162 p. 203
Negotiation, Bill of Lading: see Bill of Lading, Negotiation
Novation: n° 31 p. 31, n° 44. 57, para 3.1.4, n° 101 p. 98, n° 140 p. 130, n° 169 p. 149, fn. 69 p. 171

Offer: n° 87 p. 90, n° 89 p. 92, n° 102 p. 98, n° 132 p. 127, para 3.2.3.1, n° 140 p. 130, n° 142 p. 132, n° 147 p. 134, n° 74 p. 199, n° 76 p. 200
Order Bill of Lading: see Bill of Lading, Order
Ordinamenta et Consuetudo Maris: n° 8 p. 10
Ordonnance de Commerce: n° 20 p. 23
Ordonnance de la Marine: n° 10 p. 12, fn. 42 p. 15

Party in interest: n° 24 p. 48
Pilotage: n° 12 p. 154
Porte-fort: n° 104 p. 100, fn. 355 p. 112, fn. 469 p. 146
Presentation of the bill of lading: see Bill of Lading, presentation
Principal: - disclosed: fn. 9 p. 34, n° 15 p. 35, n° 16 p. 35, n° 36 p. 53; - undisclosed: n° 15 p. 35, n° 17 p. 36
Privity: see Contract, privity
Promissory note: n° 48 p. 180

Quasi-contract: para 4.2

Receipt, Bill of Lading as −: see Bill of lading, Receipt
Restitution: n° 11 p. 153
Retention, right of: n° 82 p. 202
Right of action (see also Title to sue): n° 132 p. 127, n° 141 p. 131, n° 148 p. 136, n° 161 p. 144, n° 168 p. 148, fn. 70 p. 171, fn. 73 p. 172, n° 62 p. 192, n° 88 p. 206
Roles d'Oleron: n° 8 p. 9

Sales contract: see Contract, of sale
Salvage: n° 5 p. 3, n° 143 p. 132, n° 157 p. 142, n° 12 p. 154, n° 14 p. 155, n° 65 p. 194, fn. 149 p. 198
Ship's Book: n° 8 p. 10, n° 9 p. 10, n° 14 p. 14

Ship's Clerk: n° 8 p. 10, n° 9 p. 10, n° 18 p. 20
Stoppage in transitu: n° 37 p. 53
Straight Bill of Lading: see Bill of Lading, straight
Strict interpretation: see Interpretation, strict
Subrogation: n° 2 p. 31
Sui generis: para 3.2.3.3

Things in action: n° 43 p. 56
Things in possession: n° 43 p. 56
Third party beneficiary clause: n° 41 p. 55, n° 69 p. 71, para 3.2.1, n° 105 p. 103, n° 107 p. 110, n° 38 p. 177, n° 88 p. 207
Three-party contract: see Contract, three-party
Time bar: n° 40 p. 55, n° 59 p. 66, n° 66 p. 68
Title: - better title: n° 49 p. 182, n° 61 p. 191; - to goods: n° 21 p. 24, n° 23 p. 32 p. 50, n° 50 p. 83, n° 140 p. 129, n° 2 p. 151, n° 3 p. 152, n° 5 p. 152, n° 6 p. 152, n° 7 p. 153, n° 17 p. 155, n° 26 p. 166, n° 61 p. 192; - to sue (see also Right of action): n° 23 p. 39, n° 24 p. 44, n° 32 p. 50, n° 53 p. 63, n° 78 p. 82, n° 106 p. 107, n° 117 p. 116, n° 122 p. 121, fn. 408 p. 128, n° 151 p. 137, n° 165 p. 146, n° 7 p. 153, n° 62 p. 192, n° 88 p. 206
Tort: n° 151 p. 137, n° 169 p. 149, fn. 17 p. 157, n° 35 p. 174, fn. 107 p. 183, fn. 139 p. 193, n° 74 p. 199, n° 85 p. 205
Transferable, Bill of Lading: see Bill of Lading, transferable

Undisclosed principal: see Principal, undisclosed

Vicarious performance: n° 44 p. 57
Visby, Laws of −: n° 8 p. 9
Volume contract: n° 15 p. 17, n° 51 p. 63, n° 88 p. 91, n° 126 p. 123, n° 132 p. 127
Voluntary engagement: para 4.5
Voluntary obligation: n° 157 p. 142